Praise for Deborah E. Lipstadt and
# HISTORY ON TRIAL

"A well-paced, expertly detailed, and fascinating account of the trial process. . . . Lipstadt's steadfastness, which can be seen throughout this book, stood her and historical truth well." —*Washington Post Book World*

"Deborah E. Lipstadt is writing for us. And for the ages."
—*Atlanta Journal-Constitution*

"A fascinating and meritorious work of legal—and moral—history."
—*Kirkus Reviews* (starred review)

"[A] powerful account. . . . No one who cares about historical truth, freedom of speech, or the Holocaust will avoid a sense of triumph."
—*Publishers Weekly* (starred review)

"Lipstadt gives a detailed account of the trial that never loses its suspense, readability, or momentum. Or humor." —*Salon.com*

"A compelling book, *History on Trial* is memoir and courtroom drama, a work of historical and legal import." —*Jewish Week*

"Fascinating. . . . Drawing on her journals, as well as on transcripts of the trial, [Lipstadt] takes us into the moment and produces a courtroom drama as enthralling as any fictional one. . . . Even if you know what happened, Lipstadt keeps you engaged with how it happened."
*San Jose Mercury News*

"Ms. Lipstadt's account of her journey from uncertainty and despair to triumph is immensely readable. . . . Fast-moving, shrewd, and often unexpectedly droll. . . . *History on Trial* restores one's faith in the power of good scholarship." —*Washington Times*

"Compelling. . . . [Lipstadt] clearly defines the differences between British and American courts. . . . But beneath the courtroom theatrics lies a deeper drama: the battle for the truth about a period of history receding into the past as those who experienced it dwindle in number."

—*Columbus Dispatch*

"[Irving-Lipstadt] was no ordinary libel case, but possibly the most important Holocaust-related trial since Adolf Eichmann was tried in Israel in 1961."

—*San Francisco Chronicle*

"Compelling. . . . Lipstadt's vigorous account is a window into a Jewish community still grappling with the loss of more than six million souls."

—*Newsweek International*

"Lipstadt proves to have the keen eye of a journalist . . . [and] she writes with a novelist's sense of plot. . . . Fascinating reading."

—*Los Angeles Jewish Journal*

"The forensic details will appeal to those who like a good detective story. . . . Irving's provocative testimony is often absurdly entertaining, and a reader can comfortably laugh at his claims because they were regularly rebutted by Lipstadt's attorneys."

—*Corporate Counsel*

"[A] sensational read. . . . Like her namesake from the book of Judges, Lipstadt can rightly be considered a latter-day Jewish heroine of truly biblical proportions. . . . By utterly destroying the credibility of Irving, the most prominent and well respected of Holocaust 'revisionists,' Lipstadt may not have crushed the Holocaust-denial movement, but she certainly dealt it a devastating blow."

—*The Australian Jewish News*

"Deborah Lipstadt's absorbing narrative of an event that has reverberated throughout the world will be read with interest and gratitude by future generations of students and teachers."

—Elie Wiesel

"In *History on Trial*, Deborah Lipstadt explores how David Irving's fraudulent use of texts coupled with his antisemitic zeal yielded historical views and narratives that falsified the history of the Holocaust in order to rehabilitate the perpetrators and blame the victims. In Lipstadt's vivid prose, we are brought into a British courtroom where the scene unfolds in a dramatic trial that demonstrates why it is essential for history's moral parameters to remain firm in the face of revisionists and deniers. This is an essential book." —Peter Balakian, author of *The Burning Tigris*

"Riveting. Shocking. Painful. Essential reading." —Maurice Sendak

"A London courtroom was the scene of a titanic struggle between the forces of historical distortion and those who upheld the truth about the Holocaust; this book, by the defender of that truth, is a powerful tribute to the vigilance, persistence, and integrity of its author and of all those who stood with her in the legal and humanistic battle." —Sir Martin Gilbert, author of *Churchill: A Life*

"Deborah Lipstadt's riveting and deeply moving memoir of her ordeal and triumph as a libel defendant in England is a joy to read. Lucidly written, Lipstadt's memorable book powerfully captures the drama of a fiercely fought trial about issues of enduring import." —Floyd Abrams

"This compelling human and edifying legal story exposes the subtle and less subtle mechanisms of prejudice and racism. A courageous fighter for the truth and a gifted storyteller, Lipstadt narrates a poignant autobiographical experience with modesty, judiciousness, and a wonderful simplicity. Deeply gratifying, *History on Trial* is about the victory of history, truth, and reality over the ruses of human deception and wishful thinking." —Shoshana Felman, Woodruff Professor of Comparative Literature and French, Emory University

# HISTORY
# ON
# TRIAL

Also by Deborah E. Lipstadt

*Denying the Holocaust: The Growing Assault on Truth and Memory*

*Beyond Belief: The American Press &*
*the Coming of the Holocaust 1933–1945*

# HISTORY
# ON
# TRIAL

*My Day in Court
with a Holocaust Denier*

DEBORAH E. LIPSTADT

AN **ecco** BOOK

HARPER PERENNIAL

NEW YORK • LONDON • TORONTO • SYDNEY

HARPER ● PERENNIAL

Photograph of the defense team members in the Auschwitz archives on page 1 © by Omer Arbel.

Photograph of Deborah Lipstadt and Anthony Forbes-Watson on page 75 © by the Associated Press.

Illustration of Judge Charles Gray reading his judgment on page 265 © by Priscilla Coleman.

A hardcover edition of this book was published in 2005 by Ecco, an imprint of HarperCollins Publishers.

P.S.™ is a trademark of HarperCollins Publishers.

First Harper Perennial edition published 2006.

*Designed by Joseph Rutt*

Library of Congress Cataloging-in-Publication Data
Lipstadt, Deborah E.
        History on trial : my day in court with a Holocaust denier / Deborah E.
Lipstadt.—1st Harper Perennial ed.
        p. cm.
"An Ecco book."
Includes index.
ISBN-10: 0-06-059377-6
ISBN-13: 978-0-06-059377-3
        1. Irving, David John Cawdell, 1938—Trials, litigation, etc. 2. Lipstadt, Deborah
E.—Trials, litigation, etc. 3. Penguin (Firm)—Trials, litigation, etc. 4. Trials (Libel)—
England—London. 5. Holocaust, Jewish (1939–1945) Historiography. 6. Holocaust
denial. I. Title.

KD379.5.I78L569 2006
940.53'1818—dc22                                                                        2005056395

06 07 08 09 10 ❖/RRD 10 9 8 7 6 5 4 3 2 1

Dedicated
to the victims of the *Shoah,*
and
To those who enabled me—in so many different ways—to
fight the attempt to ravage their history and memory

# CONTENTS

## THE AFTERMATH

But take utmost care, so that you do not forget the things that you saw with your own eyes and so that they do not fade from your mind as long as you live. And teach them to your children and your children's children.

—*Deuteronomy 4:9*

*Forsan et haec olim meminisse iuvabit.*
Someday, perhaps, it will bring pleasure to remember all this.

—*The Aeneid I: 203*

# INTRODUCTION

## By Anthony Lewis

————

I am a reader of British newspapers and magazines. Years ago I began notic-
ing articles by one David Irving. They were focused on Germany in the
Nazi period, and what I noticed is that they were sympathetic to Hitler.
Irving maintained that Hitler had never given an order to annihilate the Jews
of Europe. In his books, Irving questioned the existence of any organized
scheme of annihilation: the Holocaust. Jews who died in concentration
camps, he suggested, died of typhus or some other illness; there were no gas
chambers at Auschwitz.

What was striking was that the author of this outrageous nonsense was
treated respectfully. British editors continued to publish his articles. His
books were reviewed by serious historians, with praise for his diligent research and with occasional reservations about some of his conclusions.

Irving had a puzzling immunity from the kind of critical challenge his
work demanded. Deborah Lipstadt made that challenge. In her book Denying the Holocaust: The Growing Assault on Truth and Memory, she identified Irving as a denier, a dangerous one because his books on World War II were
widely respected. Her comments on Irving in the book were brief and, she
thought—because he had made his views so plain—uncontroversial. For instance, in 1988, testifying in a Canadian court in defense of a Holocaust denier, he said, "No documents whatever show that a Holocaust had ever
happened." Yet after publication of Denying the Holocaust, Irving sued Professor Lipstadt and her British publisher, Penguin UK, for libel.

For the next five years Deborah Lipstadt essentially devoted her life to that libel action. It was her work, her preoccupation, her nightmare. It required vast resources, of money—millions of dollars—and of moral stamina. It was a contest not just over some words in a book but over history. In the end it became the means to challenge not only the lies of David Irving but the whole effort to whitewash Hitler and his fellow monsters.

This book is, among other things, a powerful lesson on the importance of the First Amendment to Americans. As interpreted by the Supreme Court, the amendment's guarantees of freedom of speech and press leave little room for the David Irvings of this world to harass their critics. Britain has no such constitutional protections, and libel law is utterly different.

In American law the person who complains that something said or written about him or her was false and damaging must prove that it was false. In Britain, the defendant—author or publisher—must prove that it was true. That difference in the burden of proof can make all the difference. In addition, American law requires a plaintiff who is a public figure—that is, well known—to prove that the defendant published the offending statement with knowledge that it was false or in reckless disregard of its truth or falsity. In Britain, an editor or writer who makes every effort to check a statement for accuracy but makes an innocent mistake can be successfully sued for libel.

Defense of critical comments is so burdensome that British newspapers commonly give up when sued for libel. They settle for what are called "substantial sums" and make an apologetic statement in court. Even the threat of a libel action can be devastating. Weidenfeld & Nicolson, a distinguished British publishing house, first shelved plans to publish a book by the historian John Lukacs that described Irving as "an unrepentant admirer of Hitler" because it feared a libel suit. After Lipstadt won her case, Weidenfeld & Nicolson published the book but toned down the comments on Irving. The *Observer* complained that the section on Irving had been "bowdlerised." Unlike Weidenfeld & Nicolson, Penguin courageously stood by Deborah Lipstadt and joined her in financing the defense against Irving's legal assault.

It would be wrong in an introduction to give away the drama of Deborah Lipstadt's story. But I can mention one episode that hit me particularly hard. At a recess in the libel trial a woman came up to Irving and told him that her parents had been gassed at Auschwitz. A reporter who was standing there said Irving replied: "Madam, you may be pleased to know that they almost certainly died of typhus." Pleased to know.

The case was heard and decided by a judge alone, without a jury. His judgment was an extraordinary victory for Professor Lipstadt. But then came what was to me one of the most astonishing and disturbing events in the whole story of this case. Most commentary in Britain on the judgment in Deborah Lipstadt's favor was enthusiastic. But two professional historians dissented. Donald Cameron Watt wrote a column for the *Evening Standard* of London, published the afternoon of the judgment, that was headlined "History Needs David Irving." Watt said, "Show me one historian who has not broken into a cold sweat at the thought of undergoing similar treatment"— similar to the trial's exposure of Irving's lies. The next morning in the *Daily Telegraph* Sir John Keegan, an eminent military historian, said Judge Gray had "decided that an all consuming knowledge of a vast body of material does not excuse faults in interpreting it."

Watt and Keegan wrote as if Deborah Lipstadt had initiated this trial. But it was David Irving who sued her, who forced her either to swallow his lies or spend five years of her life proving him to be what he was, a racist faker. How can we explain the reaction of Watt and Keegan? Was it fostered by resentment of an outsider, someone who was not a member of the club, who was Jewish, a woman?

Whatever informed their perverse response, it was a chilling specter at the table of justice.

# NOTE TO THE READER

Long before I knew that David Irving's legal threats would evolve into a major lawsuit, I began to keep a detailed record of all my conversations with my lawyers and others involved in the case. Eventually, I decided to keep a journal in which I recorded conversations and my own thoughts. Virtually all the quotations in this book are drawn from those notes and journals. In a few rare instances I have re-created an exchange from memory. I have tried to be as faithful as possible—well aware that memory can be capricious—to my conversation partners. All quotes from the court transcripts appear as the transcriber recorded them. For the sake of consistency I have standardized the spelling of certain words, for example, antisemitism. I have periodically emphasized certain words because this is how I, according to my notes and memory, heard them. At any given trial, particularly a nonjury trial, a topic may be raised, put aside, and returned to at odd intervals. In order to make it easier for the reader to follow the discussion, I have occasionally collapsed a courtroom exchange that stretched out over two or more days. The endnotes indicate the source of the quotes.

# THE LETTER

It started on a perfect fall day. The 1995 academic year at Emory University had just begun. The summer heat had broken, the campus was resplendent, the foliage was turning autumnal colors, and the students were responding in kind. They poured out of the Italian Renaissance–style buildings surrounding the grassy quadrangle, the unofficial center of campus. This expanse of lawn was filled with people tossing frisbees, studying, playing ball, or just enjoying the last days before "winter," such as it is in Georgia, would drive them inside. I delighted in this scene as I crossed the quad to my office. I had come to Atlanta from Los Angeles a few years earlier to accept an endowed chair in Modern Jewish and Holocaust Studies and, though I missed my friends, I now considered Atlanta home.

I had just finished teaching a class on the history of the Holocaust. Relaxed and upbeat, I was scheduled to talk to a student about her graduate work and then spend the afternoon finishing a book proposal on my new research project—a study of how the Holocaust was represented in post–World War II America. As I came into my office, my secretary told me that an express letter had just arrived from Penguin, the British publisher of my book, *Denying the Holocaust: The Growing Assault on Truth and Memory,* a scholarly study of Holocaust denial. Intrigued, I asked the waiting student if she would mind if I quickly glanced at the letter. After reading but a few lines, I laughed aloud. The student, who was reviewing her notes, looked up as I said, still chuckling, "This is *really* nuts." I explained that David Irving, the world's most prominent Holocaust denier, was threatening to sue me for libel for calling him a denier.

In my book I had devoted a couple of hundred words to Irving, describing him as a "Hitler partisan wearing blinkers" who "distort[ed] evidence . . . manipulat[ed] documents, [and] skew[ed] . . . and misrepresent[ed] data in order to reach historically untenable conclusions." I wrote that "on some level Irving seems to conceive himself as carrying on Hitler's legacy." I considered him the most dangerous of Holocaust deniers because unlike other deniers, who were known only for being deniers, Irving was the author of numerous books about World War II and the Third Reich, some of which were well regarded. Virtually all aficionados of World War II history knew his name, even if they found his work a bit too sympathetic to the Third Reich. His books were reviewed in major periodicals and, consequently, his Holocaust-denial activities garnered far more attention than those of other deniers.

My words were admittedly harsh, but I considered them noncontroversial because Irving had so publicly expressed his Holocaust denial. In 1988, when the Canadian government charged a German émigré, Ernst Zündel, with promoting Holocaust denial, Irving testified on Zündel's behalf. He told the court that there was no "overall Reich policy to kill the Jews"; "no documents whatsoever show that a Holocaust had ever happened," and the gas chambers for mass killings were an impossibility.[1] Since then Irving had repeatedly denied the Holocaust. When asked by a reporter why all mention of the Holocaust had disappeared from a new edition of one of his books, he responded, "If something didn't happen, then you don't even dignify it with a footnote."[2] He denied the use of gas chambers to systematically kill Jews, argued that there was no officially sanctioned Third Reich plan to annihilate European Jewry, and contended that Hitler was "probably the biggest friend the Jews had in the 'Third Reich.' He was the one doing everything he could to prevent nasty things happening to them."[3] Irving considered survivors, who asserted that they had seen gas chambers, to be liars or charlatans. Given Irving's record, his threat seemed absurd. How, I wondered, could someone who had called the Holocaust a "legend" argue that he wasn't a denier?

Convinced that this was nothing more than sound and fury, I rather deliberately tossed the letter onto one of the perennial piles on my desk and turned my attention to the student. A few days later I dug the letter out—by this point it was nesting under other mail—gave it to my research assistant, and asked her to provide Penguin's lawyers with the sources on which I had built my critique of Irving. Given that virtually everything I said about him could be traced to a reliable source, I was certain that this would be the end of the matter. I cautioned my assistant not to expend too much time on it and to return as quickly as possible to collecting the material I needed for my new project.

Ironically, twenty-five years earlier, when I first learned of Holocaust denial, I had reacted in a similar fashion, brushing it off as insignificant. In the mid-1970s, Professor Yehuda Bauer, one of the leading scholars on the history of the Holocaust, told me that a California-based group, the Institute for Historical Review (IHR), was distributing a journal denying the Holocaust. I scoffed at the idea that someone would take them seriously. Now, sitting in my Emory office, I wondered who could possibly take David Irving's claims that he was not a denier seriously. Certainly this had to be just a ploy to intimidate me. Over coffee, I told some colleagues about the letter and predicted it would go nowhere.

As it turned out, I was wrong on all counts. Irving would take this very seriously as would the British courts. The fact that my sources were all documented did not protect me in the United Kingdom, as it would have in the United States. In fact, I was at a decided disadvantage. British law placed the burden of proof on me as the defendant. It was a mirror image of American law. In the United States Irving would have to prove I lied. In the United Kingdom I had to prove I told the truth.

As different people were galvanized into helping this campaign, I kept thinking how Irving, in his accusations against me, depicted me as part of a global conspiracy. According to Irving, I had "pursued a sustained malicious, vigorous, well-funded, and reckless worldwide campaign of personal defamation" against him.[4] Nothing could have been further from the truth. *Denying the Holocaust* was my individual project, carried out with the help of a modest research grant that enabled me to hire a research assistant, copy reams of material, and travel to a number of archives. Some Jewish organizations had collections of newspaper clippings on deniers and publications by deniers that they shared with me. Most of the time, I sat alone in my study trying to explicate for my readers the history of Holocaust denial. It was a solitary effort until Irving decided to pursue me. Then, and *only* then, did a group of people galvanize around me and help provide the funds that made it possible for me to stave off Irving's attacks. If my supporters constituted some sort of conspiracy—as Irving repeatedly charged was the case—it was one that was determined to ensure that history not be trampled for nefarious purposes.

On a number of occasions, I had been approached by people who wanted to bring legal action against deniers. I always cautioned them against doing so, because in the United States the First Amendment practically guaranteed their failure. Even in countries where it was legally possible to pass laws outlawing Holocaust denial, I opposed such efforts. Those laws would render denial "forbidden fruit," making it more—not less—alluring. In addition, I did not believe that courtrooms were the proper venue for historical inquiry. Deniers, I argued, should be stopped with reasoned inquiry, not with the blunt edge of the law. Courts, it seemed to me, dispensed justice by having parties present what they consider compelling evidence, such as physical proof and hard facts, to convince a jury or judge beyond a high standard of proof. Historians try to establish historical "truth" by objectively determining what happened. They consider the context and circumstance of an event or a document. They interpret evidence and offer their opinions, all the while aware that other historians may look at the same material and, without engaging in any deception, reach differing conclusions. Historians also know that as new sources and documents come to light, their "truths" may be set aside. Simply put, historical truths cannot be measured like smog that pollutes a town's air.[5]

For four years I prepared for this trial by immersing myself in the works of a man who exuded contempt for me and for much of what I believed. I lost many nights of sleep, worried that because of some legal fluke Irving might prevail. For ten weeks in the winter of 2000, I had to sit barely fifteen feet from him and silently listen as he openly expressed that contempt in front of a judge and the world media. My scholarly work was deconstructed and my attire, personality, and personal beliefs were dissected in the press. Much of what was reported about me—for example, my age, sources of support, and political beliefs—was simply wrong. But I had no way of challenging it. Through the course of the trial, at the insistence of my attorneys, I did not give interviews or testify in court. Though my words were at the heart of this struggle, I had to depend on others to speak for me. For someone who fiercely prized controlling her life—even when it was better not to—this was excruciatingly difficult.

A few years before filing the suit, Irving told a sympathetic audience that libel defendants are full of bluster upon learning they are to be sued. When they discover the onerous nature of fighting a libel suit in the United Kingdom, they "crack up and cop out."[6] Irving may well have anticipated that I would decide this battle was not worth pursuing and would agree to settle with him by issuing some sort of apology or retraction of my words. I was, after all, five thousand miles away and had to mount a defense in a foreign country whose laws heavily favored my opponent. Lawsuits can be exceedingly long and exceptionally expensive.

I was wrong to dismiss this as just a nuisance. But David Irving had erred even more greatly if he thought that I, as the defendant, would "crack up and cop out." I did neither. I fought this charge aggressively and never considered doing anything but that.

And so a bit naive about what lay ahead, annoyed that I would have to spend time on what seemed to be a completely frivolous matter, and yet somewhat eager, I set out on a journey intended to prove that what I had written was true. This book is the story of that journey.

# THE PRELUDE

Defense team members in the Auschwitz archives inspecting the architectural drawings of the crematoria.

# ONE

# A PERSONAL AND
# SCHOLARLY ODYSSEY

"**N**o, I am not a child of Holocaust survivors."
Ever since I began teaching about the Holocaust I have been asked about my background. Some questioners seemed surprised by my response. Why else would I be interested in the topic? Others, however, felt that my personal distance from the event allowed a more scholarly perspective.

My father left Germany before the Third Reich and my mother was born in Canada. Growing up on Manhattan's Upper West Side, I had known many "refugees." No one called them survivors. Some had emigrated in the 1930s, leaving behind a comfortable middle-class existence. Others came after the war. My father helped many of them when they arrived in New York. He attempted to bring his five sisters to the United States but could not do so. They survived in other countries and came to New York in the post-war period. As a young child, I remember sensing that these Central European Jewish homes, with their heavy, dark furniture and steaming cups of tea accompanied by delicate homemade strudel and other distinctly European pastries, were different from those of my American schoolmates.

My parents' Modern Orthodox home was shaped by a dedication to Jewish tradition together with an appreciation for the surrounding secular society. One was as likely to find on our living room table a book on Jewish lore as a book on Rembrandt. My brother, sister, and I all attended Jewish schools. When I was in first grade, my parents decided to move from Manhattan to the suburbs. They chose Far Rockaway, a beachside community in Queens, because they admired the local rabbi, Emanuel Rackman, and decided that this was the man they wanted as a spiritual leader and a role model for their children. A graduate of Columbia Law School, he combined knowledge of Judaism with the contemporary world. His well-crafted muscular sermons, delivered without notes, covered a wide range of topics—everything from the weekly *Torah* portion to Arnold Toynbee. Shortly after the fall of Stalin, during a period of Khrushchev-style *perestroika,* he traveled with a group of American rabbis to the Soviet Union. On the *Shabbat* of his return my father suggested that I stay in the synagogue during the sermon—a time that we children generally ran all over the expansive lawn in front of the building. "It will be memorable," he assured me. Though I was not quite sure what "memorable" meant, I knew the trip had been something important. I did not grasp all that Rabbi Rackman said, but I understood that he had made contact with a group of Jews who were not free to live as we did, and he said that we could not forget them.

A believer in intra- and interreligious dialogue, long before it was in vogue, Rackman reached out to people both within the Jewish community and outside of it. Right-wing religious Jews attacked him for his attempts to demonstrate how one could—and should—draw upon the best in both traditional Judaism and the secular world. I remember how my father would seethe at these attacks and stress how important it was for Rabbi Rackman's ideas not to be silenced. Long before I knew precisely what a role model was, I knew that I wanted to be like him.

Though synagogue attendance and observance of Jewish rituals set the rhythm of our home, we were very much part of the broader world. In addition to ensuring that my siblings and I received an intensive Jewish education, my parents exposed us to theater, museums, art, and politics. Even after we had moved to the suburbs my mother would often take us into Manhattan on Sundays to see exhibits, attend the special youth symphonies at New York's Ninety-second Street YMHA, watch parades, climb the rocks in Central Park, and even tour visiting aircraft carriers. My parents encouraged a degree of independence in us. When I was twelve and wanted to go into the city to see a movie at Radio City Music Hall or visit a museum, they encouraged it. The problem was finding a classmate whose parents did not think it a totally reckless excursion. I usually managed to find an intrepid soul. I soon learned to navigate my way through the city.

By middle school I had gained a reputation, particularly with my teachers at the Jewish day school I attended, as a feisty and combative student. When teachers did something that I did not consider fair, I would challenge them—often not very diplomatically. Invariably, my mother would appear in the principal's office to defend my actions and plead my case. I had the impression that, although she did not appreciate these school visits, she admired my gumption. I knew that I had been named Deborah because she loved the biblical character. When I was still quite young she had described how Deborah led her people in battle and dispensed justice. I liked the notion that I was named after such a person. When my mother admonished me for getting in trouble, I told her I was just emulating Deborah.

My mother was a free spirit. It was not unusual for her to announce: "There's a wonderful Van Gogh exhibit at the Guggenheim. Ditch school. Let's go." And I did. Despite—or possibly because—neither my father nor mother had been able to attend college, they became intense autodidacts, continually attending classes and lectures. I remember spirited discussions around our *Shabbat* table about Rachel Carson's *Silent Spring*, J. D. Salinger's *Franny and Zooey*, Philip Roth's *Goodbye, Columbus*, civil rights, the 1968 New York City teachers' strike, and the war in Vietnam, which we uniformly opposed. My mother and I marched in Harlem in solidarity with the Birmingham-Selma civil rights protestors. We took a vicarious pride in the fact that Andy Goodman, one of the civil rights workers murdered in Mississippi, had lived down the block from us and we always pointed out his building to visitors. The *New Republic, Saturday Review of Literature*, and *Commentary* were regular fixtures in our home.

I played basketball in high school and spent my summers at Jewish camps in Pennsylvania's Pocono Mountains teaching swimming. Somehow—I cannot pinpoint when—I learned about the Holocaust. Teachers in my Jewish day school made passing references to "Hitler, may his name be erased," but we were never formally taught about what took place then. Periodically Rabbi Rackman would refer to it in a sermon. At summer camp the Holocaust was woven into at least one program. At the Passover *Seder*, my father would recite a prayer commemorating the Holocaust and Warsaw Ghetto uprising. He would weep, as he spoke about those with whom he had grown up in Hamburg. I dreaded this moment. His tears frightened me. I was always glad when it was over. In our home there were books on this topic, including John Hersey's *The Wall,* Andre Schwarz-Bart's *The Last of the Just,* and Edward Wallant's *The Pawnbroker.* We watched portions of the Eichmann trial on television and read Leon Uris's *Exodus.* Yet the Holocaust did not occupy a dominant place in the construct of our Jewish identity. It was one thread—among many—in the tapestry of our Jewish lives.

## ENCOUNTERING THE HOLOCAUST: ISRAEL, 1967

At City College of New York, I studied twentieth-century American political history. I was intrigued by what scholars called the "paranoid style in American politics," an American susceptibility to all sorts of conspiracy theories, particularly those that fostered prejudice and antisemitism. It was the sixties and I participated in various student demonstrations. At one point, we managed to shut the school down for an extended period in a fight for "open admissions." We demanded that every high school graduate in New York city be guaranteed a place in the City University system. We won what proved to be a pyrrhic victory as the city colleges were filled by students who had been ill prepared by the public school system. Our victory effectively guaranteed the demise of high-quality education at these schools for many decades thereafter.

In 1966, anxious to experience travel abroad, I made a relatively impetuous decision to attend the Hebrew University in Jerusalem. Though my family were supporters of Israel, I was not driven by a Zionist commitment. I wanted to travel, improve my Hebrew, and experience a different culture. Going to Israel was not a purposeful choice but was to have a life-changing impact.

From 1948 to 1967, the sole border crossing between Israel and the rest of the Middle East was Jerusalem's Mandelbaum Gate. It was the equivalent of Berlin's Checkpoint Charlie. Israelis would stand and watch people crossing the hundred yards of no-man's-land between Israel and Jordan. They seemed to feel that if they stood there long enough, they would be able to see into the Old City. In order to make it difficult for tourists to visit Israel, Jordan permitted them to transit through the Mandelbaum Gate in only one direction, either into Israel or out of it. Once a year, at Christmas, the Jordanians made an exception, but only for Christians. They permitted them both to enter and depart through the Mandelbaum Gate, ostensibly so that Israeli Christians could celebrate the holiday in Bethlehem. In December 1966, a group of American students at the Hebrew University decided to take advantage of this. They told authorities that they were Christians and received their special travel permits. While I was tempted to accompany them and see the Old City of Jerusalem, I could not bring myself to declare that I was a Christian in order to do so.

Three months later, increasingly beset by a desire to visit these places, I decided to take a more circuitous route. In April 1967, during a long school break, I flew to Greece. Since Arab countries automatically denied entry to anyone with an Israeli entry or exit stamp in their passport, I headed for the American embassy to apply for a new passport. When I explained my situation to the American official, he shook his head knowingly. Obviously, I was not the first person to make this request. He looked at my existing passport and asked if I wanted to drop my middle name, Esther, from the new passport. "It's very ethnic you know." I had been named after an uncle's sister who was murdered in the Holocaust. Obliterating her name so that I could have this adventure seemed wrong. I told him to leave it in. He looked at me skeptically, but acceded to my request.

I then took a train to Istanbul and joined my sister who had arrived from London, where she was studying on a Fulbright fellowship. After a few days of sightseeing, I bid her goodbye and boarded a plane for Beirut, then still rightfully known as the "Paris of the Middle East." I planned to travel by taxi from Beirut to Damascus and then to Jordan. The night before I left for Beirut I combed my wallet and all the crevices of my luggage to make sure I wasn't carrying anything that would identify me as coming from Israel. I doubted that customs officials would pay close attention but I didn't want to take any chances.

I arrived in Beirut uneventfully, only to learn that Israel and Syria had engaged in a series of aerial dogfights and Israel had downed six Syrian MiGs in one afternoon. This did not seem to be an opportune time for a single American Jewish woman with a brand-new passport issued at a foreign embassy to be traveling through Lebanon, Syria, and Jordan and attempting to enter Israel through the Mandelbaum Gate. But there was no turning back.

I needed a visa for Jordan. Americans I had met at a student hostel in Greece assured me that obtaining one in Beirut was easy to do. Upon landing in Beirut, I headed for the Jordanian embassy. A male clerk gave me the visa application. It included a line for one's religion. I sat staring at it for a long time. I had come prepared to write "Protestant," and yet, when it came to actually writing it, I could not do so. If I wrote "Jewish," the Jordanians would automatically reject my application. I would then have to fly back to Istanbul and find a flight back to Israel. I knew that the couple of hundred dollars I had in traveler's checks—this was long before students had credit cards—would not cover the cost of a ticket. I would have to cable my parents—who assumed I was in Istanbul with my sister—to send funds to Beirut. Suddenly my little escapade did not seem like a lark. I decided to leave it blank, hoping no one would notice.

When I returned later in the day to pick up my passport and visa, the clerk who had taken my application asked me to wait. "The vice consul wants to talk to you." My heart was in my shoes. I would have fled but they had my passport. Soon I was ushered into the office of a Jordanian consular officer. A tall, olive-skinned man in a white shirt with dark hair, glasses, and a somber face was waiting. Holding my passport in his hand, he greeted me: "Hello, Devora." I was dumbstruck at his use of my Hebrew name, but I ignored it. "You have a very biblical name," he said. "My family loves the Bible," I said somewhat breathlessly. "Oh, and why," he wondered, "do you have a new passport?" I said that I was studying in London—I gave my sister's address—and had lost my passport while in Greece. In response to his question why I wanted to visit Jordan, I expressed my long-standing fascination with Petra. After a few minutes he stamped my passport. By then he had figured out, I assumed, that, whatever my background, I was no spy.

I crossed through Syria without an incident, and after a brief stop in Damascus, I arrived in Jordan. After a couple of days in Amman and in Jericho, I caught a taxi up to Jerusalem. I was directed to a student hostel right on the edge of the border with Israel. I realized I was only a hundred yards—and miles of barbed wire—from a street that I had often walked during the past ten months.

The next morning I headed for the Old City. In an attempt not to draw attention to myself, I did not ask directions to any Jewish site. Only on the next day, when I returned to the Old City, did I manage to find my way to the *Kotel,* the Western Wall, the sole remnant of the retaining wall of the Jewish Temple Mount. After the Temple was destroyed by the Romans in 70 C.E., the *Kotel* remains the holiest place in Jewish lore. Jews had been denied permission to visit since 1948, when the Jordanians took control of the Old

City. In contrast to the Christian sites, which were properly marked, there were no signs to this site. I wanted to touch the wall but I was concerned about attracting attention. Instead, I stood in front of it fiddling with my camera and thinking about the tens of thousands of people who dreamed of this opportunity. My reverie was interrupted by an Arab tour guide who arrived with a group from Britain. He told the group that "Jews used to come here to hatch plans on how to cheat people. But in 1948 they stopped coming. Now let's proceed to the Dome of the Rock." I cringed, but said nothing.

Bristling with anger, I left and walked up the Mount of Olives, from which there is a panoramic view of the Old City and West Jerusalem beyond it. I passed a massive Jewish cemetery, which had been used by Jews in Jerusalem for hundreds of years until 1948, when the Jordanians denied access to it. Since then, the place had been systematically vandalized. It was a mess. Gravestones had been toppled. Garbage was strewn about. Donkeys grazed among the graves. The path on which I walked was paved with gravestones. I could decipher the Hebrew characters. When I reached the top of the Mount of Olives, I looked over at West Jerusalem, saw familiar landmarks, and decided that Petra would have to wait. It was time to go "home." Never before had I thought of Israel with such emotion.

I hurriedly packed my bags and rushed to the Mandelbaum Gate. I knew the Jordanians could still deny me permission to cross. Two very bored-looking policemen waved me through. As I crossed into Israel and handed the border officials my passport, they asked the purpose of my visit. When I explained in fluent Hebrew that I was a student at the Hebrew University, I realized that for the first time in days, I could simply tell the truth and did not have to fear being identified as a Jew. As I left for the university, I heard one guard say, "She's got guts." His colleague shook his head. "But maybe not *sechel* [common sense]."

At the university word quickly spread about my escapade. All the Israelis who approached me—from the fervently religious to the devoutly secular— had the same question: "Were you able to visit the *Kotel?*" When I said yes, they looked wistful, obviously thinking that this was a place they would never see. No one realized that would change shortly. Approximately four weeks later the political situation in the Middle East markedly deteriorated. Egypt moved military forces into the Sinai Desert and closed the Strait of Tiran, the waterway at the foot of the Sinai Peninsula, to Israeli vessels. Jordan then joined the Syrian-Egyptian military alliance. Israelis feared an invasion by the surrounding Arab armies. Mass graves were prepared in anticipation of overwhelming casualties. Suddenly, Holocaust analogies were present in everyday conversation. Actually, it was not analogies one heard as much as contrasts to it. "This time we won't stand idly by. We are ready. We will fight," the Polish-born owner of the little grocery store I frequented told me. As he spoke, I noticed the number tattooed on his arm. The tension was palpable. I delivered mail and volunteered at a children's home whose staff had been drafted. My American classmates received calls from their parents urging them to return home. Most students ignored these pleas. My parents simply assumed that I planned to stay. And I did.

Israel's overwhelming victory in June 1967 marked, to some extent, the virtual closure of the Holocaust for the Jewish people. It was as if they now grasped that "Masada would really not fall again," the Jewish people would never again "allow themselves" to be destroyed. Talk about and study of the Holocaust became much more frequent. It was as if it was now safe to confront the issue.

When I returned to East Jerusalem after the war, instead of hearing antisemitic cracks, I watched Jews who were deeply moved to stand in front of the *Kotel*. At the cemetery on the Mount of Olives families were walking around with crude maps looking for their relatives' resting places. Some people were already collecting the garbage and trying to clear the gravestones. My year of study was ending. Convinced that to leave Israel now would be to miss seeing history unfold, I decided to remain in Jerusalem for another year.

By the time I returned to the United States in September 1968, I understood the deep imprint of both the Holocaust and Israel on the psyche of the Jewish people. No longer satisfied with the study of American political history, I began graduate work at Brandeis University in modern Jewish history. A number of my courses focused on modern antisemitism. Soon, I had an unexpected opportunity to see and, in some small measure, experience that phenomenon.

### USSR, 1972

In 1972, on the eve of the Jewish New Year—which happened to be a few days after the Palestinian massacre of Israeli athletes at the Munich

Olympics—I arrived in Moscow. I had come to make contact with Soviet Jews in general and particularly with refuseniks, those Jews who were refused permission to leave the Soviet Union for Israel or, for that matter, anywhere else. The Soviets considered the refuseniks' desire to emigrate a direct assault on the USSR's claim—one it had maintained for decades—that the country was the vanguard of a socialist paradise. The Soviets retaliated against them. Many were fired from their jobs. People who had once been professors became guards in empty office buildings, sitting at desks in poorly lit, unheated lobbies throughout the night. One physicist became a window washer, though, given the state of the windows around the city, I was never quite sure where he worked. Their children were harassed and their phones were tapped. Neighbors shunned them. The leaders of the refusenik movement were under KGB surveillance and were periodically arrested.

Israelis, delighted that these Jews wanted to emigrate, knew that they needed tremendous help to buck the Soviet system. The inability—some would say failure—of world Jewry to assist their fellow Jews during the Holocaust, loomed large in their memory. They were determined to demonstrate that now that there was a Jewish state, no Jews anywhere would be abandoned. But they faced a problem. The USSR had severed relations with Israel in May 1967. Israelis could not enter the country. Unable to reach the refuseniks directly, Israel turned to American Jews who spoke Hebrew and had spent an extended period of time in Israel, and quietly asked them to travel to the Soviet Union and make contact with refuseniks. One day, an Israeli I knew who was working in the United States called to ask if I wanted to spend Rosh Hashanah, Yom Kippur, and the festival of Sukkot in the USSR. I jumped at the opportunity. He suggested I travel with a mutual friend with whom we had studied in Jerusalem. In a slightly James Bond fashion, we were told to come to New York to the offices of a Jewish youth organization. We were greeted by a man of medium height with closely cropped hair and wearing a *kippah*. He introduced himself as "Aryeh from Kibbutz Sa'ad." There was nothing distinctive about him. He looked more like a bank clerk than a man running a clandestine operation. He told us about the refuseniks and how much these visits bolstered their spirits and helped them in their struggle against the communist regime. He never mentioned who was organizing the visits, and it was clear that we were not to ask. (Years later I learned that Aryeh worked with the Office of Communication in the Israeli government and reported directly to the prime minister.)

A few months later, on the night before we were to leave, we met with him again. He gave us the names and addresses of some refuseniks. We were to bring one family medication for their child. One refusenik, who had organized a Jewish history seminar, had sent a request via a previous group of travelers for Russian-language teaching materials. He gave us books on the Jewish holidays, tradition, and history, and souvenirs from Israel, including a number of small Jewish stars on a chain. He made sure to include a Russian-language edition of Leon Uris's *Exodus,* which was exceptionally popular among Russian Jews. Our primary goal was to let these Jews know that Israel and world Jewry were partners in their struggle. We also took a couple of pairs of jeans and some Marlboro cigarettes, commodities whose value for Soviet citizens was more precious than rubles. The refuseniks could sell them on the black market for a handsome profit.

Officially, the only reason a Soviet citizen was allowed to leave the country was for the purpose of family reunification. To have allowed people to leave for other reasons would have shattered the image of the USSR as a socialist paradise. Aryeh told us that some Soviet Jews might give us their names and addresses. Upon our return, we were to turn these over to him and he would arrange for someone in Israel with the same last name to invite their newfound Soviet "relatives" to reunite with the "family" in Israel.

Soviet law permitted tourists to visit Soviet citizens. However, officials were enraged when any Soviet citizens—particularly those anxious to leave—were in contact with Americans. They did whatever they could to make our lives, as well as the lives of those we visited, difficult. We were followed as we wended our way to people's homes. When we walked on the street, a car would slowly drive alongside. Our hotel room phone repeatedly rang in the middle of the night. It was unnerving, but the refuseniks assured us it was part of their daily routine. One took me over to the window of his apartment, pointed at a sedan parked in front, and waved at the man behind the wheel. "Wherever I go, he goes."

The refuseniks were pleased to meet someone who was studying for a Ph.D. in modern Jewish history. They asked many questions, particularly about the history of the Holocaust. The Soviet version of the Holocaust depicted the event as an assault by fascists on communists, not by Germans on Jews. To have identified the perpetrators as "Germans" would have implicated East Germany, a communist entity. To have identified the victims as Jews would have validated the notion of ethnicity, a concept contrary to

Marxist ideology. But it was not just Marxist ideology that prompted the Soviets to promote this revisionist view of the murder of European Jewry. The term "Jew" was virtually a dirty word in the Soviet Union. The USSR sanctioned expressions of antisemitism, not just against refuseniks. Soviet attacks on Israel were laced with traditional antisemitic stereotypes. Yevgeny Yevtushenko's poem "Babi Yar," about the site where the Germans massacred approximately thirty thousand Jews, protested not only this de-Judaization of the victims but contemporary Soviet antisemitism. It was a courageous rebuke of the Soviet system by one of its most prominent poets.

For the first ten days of our trip, we heard a great deal about the heavy hand of Soviet oppression. Then on Yom Kippur we had a personal encounter with it. We had come from Moscow to Czernowitz, a city in the area of the Ukraine known as Bukovina, which once had an immense Jewish population. The hundreds of people gathered in front of the synagogue peppered me with questions about Israel and American Jewry. Some people slipped me scraps of paper with their name and address. Around noon, people in the synagogue leaned out the windows and shouted to the crowds, "Yizkor!" Everyone grew silent as the memorial prayer began. People around me watched closely as I opened my prayer book and recited the prayer for my father, who had passed away a few months earlier. They seemed intrigued by a young, Westernized woman who was conversant with Jewish tradition. They had neither prayer books nor—even if I had loaned them my book—the ability to read the Hebrew text. Sensing their frustration, I offered to recite the memorial prayer on their behalf. At the appropriate place I paused so that they could insert the names of their dead. One elderly woman told me that she had many people for whom to say Yizkor. As if to explain why, she kept repeating "Hurban, Hurban," the Yiddish term for "Holocaust." When I finished, she kissed my hand. At that point I left for my hotel.

Later that afternoon I returned. A light rain was falling and the street was empty. I saw the old woman from the morning standing at the back of the sanctuary and squeezed myself in next to her. She held my arm in a gesture of familiarity. I handed her my small leather-bound prayer book. Unable to read it, she seemed proud just to hold it. When people walked by, she showed it to them. Suddenly, the relative calm of the moment was broken. The synagogue sexton who, it was commonly assumed, reported all unusual activities—including the presence of foreigners—to the KGB, burst in and accused me of being a provocateur, a serious charge by Soviet standards. When he saw that the old woman had my prayer book, his face grew bright red. Sputtering in a mix of Russian and Yiddish, he grabbed it and accused me of distributing religious items. People passionately argued with him. He brushed them off and disappeared down the street with my book in his hands.

The next day we were waiting in our hotel lobby to depart for Kishinev. Suddenly we found ourselves surrounded by men in trench coats who identified themselves as KGB. Had I not been so frightened, I would have laughed aloud at the predictability of their dress. I lost any inclination to laugh when I saw that they had my prayer book as well as a list of every home we had visited in Czernowitz. When they questioned us, they used traditional anti-semitic stereotypes, describing the Jews who wished to leave the Soviet Union as part of an international cabal and Jews in general as financial extortionists. They kept asking who sent us. We kept insisting we were just tourists. I suspected that the exercise was designed to frighten us. The Soviets probably knew precisely who had sent us. After a long day of strip searches and interrogation, my traveling companion and I—who were kept apart the entire time—were accused of spreading lies about the Soviet regime. We were "invited" to leave the country and, in the dark of the night, placed in an empty train car with an armed guard. Many hours later, after a long and circuitous route, we found ourselves in Romania.

After reporting on our travails to the American embassy, we headed to the synagogue. When we told the Jews we had come from Czernowitz in the USSR, they corrected us. "Czernowitz? That's occupied Romania." An elderly Jew standing nearby whispered under his breath, "USSR? Romania? Czernowitz is part of the Austro-Hungarian Empire." Had I not been so rattled by my recent experience, I would have been amused by this impromptu history lesson.

Throughout this experience, I never feared for my welfare. I believed— maybe naively so—that the Soviets were uninterested in two innocuous graduate students. They wanted to frighten future visitors and the Soviet citizens who invited us into their homes. But I feared we had subjected these people to danger. I was painfully aware that I was leaving behind Jews who were struggling to live the kind of Jewish life I took for granted. I kept thinking about German Jews during the 1930s. I knew that the refuseniks' situation was clearly not the same. But there was a parallel for me—the by-stander. Jews were being oppressed. How would their coreligionists in the free world respond? To all those who asked about my trip, I rather self-righteously proclaimed that, unlike our parents' generation, "this time" Jews were not going to sit silently by.

I returned to my graduate program at Brandeis in the fall of 1972, but I carried this experience with me. I found myself increasingly drawn to the study of the Holocaust, particularly to the question of how the bystanders—Jews and non-Jews—reacted.

In 1974, I accepted a position at the University of Washington's History Department, where I introduced a course on the history of the Holocaust. One day, while I was lecturing to my class on President Roosevelt's knowl-edge of the Final Solution, a student demanded, "But what could my par-ents—*not* the White House, Congress, or the State Department—have known?" Intrigued by his query, I decided to examine the American press coverage of the Holocaust. While the press may not determine what the public thinks, it certainly influences what it thinks *about*.

After working my way through thousands of articles, I concluded that, while news of the persecution of European Jewry appeared in many Ameri-can papers, it was presented in a way that made it eminently missable or dis-missible, i.e. in small articles in obscure places in the paper on the comics, weather, or, somewhat more appropriately, obituary page. Readers who no-ticed these articles would have been justified in assuming that the editors did not believe them. Otherwise, how might one explain a story on the murder of one million Jews placed on the bottom of page six next to an ad for Lava soap?[1]

During the 1970s, the American Jewish community began to show great interest in the Holocaust. The desire to learn more about this event was en-couraging, but I was disturbed by the tendency of Jewish communal leaders to invoke the Holocaust for a variety of causes. Young Jews were told that in order not to hand Hitler a posthumous victory, they should marry Jews, have children, and observe Jewish tradition. Fund-raisers cited the Holocaust to motivate Jews to contribute to a host of philanthropic causes. I found this a serious perversion of Jewish history and tradition. Jews have survived *despite* antisemitism not *because* of it. It was a terribly lachrymose message to trans-mit to younger generations of Jews. Why, I wondered, would the murder of

six million coreligionists strengthen one's Jewish identity? Though I, together with others, criticized this approach, I knew we were fighting a losing
battle.

By this time I had moved to Los Angeles to teach at UCLA. My depart-
mental home was the Department of Near Eastern Languages where my
colleagues were primarily older, male, European-trained philologists. Someone on campus described it as a place to study "dead languages taught by
nearly dead men." My colleagues dismissed my study of newspapers as a
form of "journalism" and, because I had large classes, considered me a "pop-
ularizer," an academic double kiss of death. Admittedly, it was a strange
place for someone whose research focused on the American response to the
Holocaust. I was not surprised when, despite the fact that three publishers
were vying for my manuscript on American press coverage of the Holocaust, UCLA denied me tenure.

## A TENTATIVE FORAY INTO THE WORLD OF
## HOLOCAUST DENIAL

Shortly thereafter, Professors Yehuda Bauer and Yisrael Gutman of the Center for the Study of Antisemitism of the Hebrew University in Jerusalem
asked me to conduct a research project on Holocaust denial. Convinced that
deniers were fringe extremists, I asked these two leading Holocaust scholars:
why study the historical equivalent of flat-earth theorists? Bauer and Gutman believed this a new, potentially dangerous form of antisemitism.
Though they thought it should be analyzed, I was not entirely convinced. I
doubted whether it warranted a book, and, if I did write one, whether there
would be substantial interest in it. Nonetheless, my deep respect for these
scholars convinced me to explore the project. I accepted a small research
subsidy in order to undertake what I anticipated would be a limited research
project. I signed the standard university contract, giving the university virtually all the royalties on any book that might result from my work. I anticipated a year's work and maybe a couple of articles on the topic. After that, I
assumed, I would move on to my project on America's postwar response to
the Holocaust.

As I did my research, my assessment of the deniers began to slowly
evolve. I was struck by the sophisticated camouflage tactics they had developed. The Institute for Historical Review (IHR), the California-based denial

group, depicted itself as a scholarly group driven by a "deep dedication to the cause of truth in history." Their conferences resembled academic confabs. Their journal had a scholarly veneer. Students at leading academic institutions who encountered it in their university libraries assumed it a product of genuine scholarship. Though the IHR claimed to be interested in the broad sweep of history, it focused all its energies on the Holocaust.[2] Their attacks had both an antisemitic and an anti-Israel bias. According to the IHR, the "corrupt, bankrupt government of Israel and its army of unpaid agents in the United States" had perpetrated a theft on the American people through the clever use of the "Greatest Lie in all of history—the lie of the 'Holocaust.' "[3]

The IHR also demonstrated racist sympathies. It contended that the Holocaust myth lowered the "self-image of White people." The IHR's founders were associated with the Liberty Lobby and Noontide Press. The New Republic considered Liberty Lobby to be so extreme that it was "estranged from even the fringes of the far right."[4] Noontide Press's catalog featured antisemitic works such as The Protocols of the Elders of Zion, as well as a series of books on the dangers of racial integration and the lower IQ of people of color. Deniers had made common cause with neo-Nazi groups in the United States, Germany, Austria, the United Kingdom, and other countries.[5] Denial was also finding a warm reception in the Muslim and Arab worlds. While I still did not consider deniers an imminent danger, I felt that given their camouflage tactics and their alliances, I could no longer dismiss them as a laughing matter.

I was also disturbed by the ambiguous response to them in certain quarters. During the 1990s, student newspapers on many American campuses accepted advertisements denying the Holocaust. They did so, despite the fact that these papers had a policy to reject ads that were hostile to an ethnic or religious group. When criticized by other students on their campuses, the editors of these papers—some of whom were Jews—protested that these ads were not antisemitic; they simply denied the Holocaust. I was more concerned by their inability to recognize Holocaust denial as a form of antisemitism than by the deniers themselves. These editorial boards argued that their papers were obliged to be forums for "diverse opinions" and to "tell all sides of the issue." I was struck by their elevation of denial to an "opinion" and wondered what "issue"?

The general media was equally blindsided by denial. Radio and television talk show hosts treated denial as an intriguing idea. When I received invitations to debate deniers, I consistently declined, explaining that while many things about the Holocaust are open to debate, the existence of the event is not. One producer, anxious to get me to reconsider, said, "Shouldn't our listeners hear the *other* side?" Their conception of denial as an "other" side convinced me that it was essential to expose the illusion of reasoned inquiry that concealed deniers' claims.[6]

My concern about deniers further escalated when I learned in 1988 that David Irving, the well-known author of an array of books dealing with various aspects of World War II and Nazi Germany, was now publicly denying the Holocaust. Born in 1938, Irving was the son of a book illustrator and a British naval officer, whose boat was torpedoed in 1942. According to Irving, his father survived but did not return home, leaving his wife and four children in what Irving claims was a state of "very reduced circumstances." Irving studied at London University but never completed his degree. He left the university and found employment in Germany's Ruhr Valley as a steelworker. While there he perfected his German. Upon his return to England in the early 1960s, he supported himself by writing articles about Germany. According to Irving, within a few months he was earning so much money that he abandoned his attempt to get a degree and devoted himself to a career of writing about history.

His first book, *The Destruction of Dresden*, appeared when he was only twenty-five. A scathing attack on the Allies for having bombed this German medieval city in the final months of the war, the book was a critical and commercial success. Irving wrote a number of other books in quick succession. In 1967, he published *Accident: The Death of General Sikorski*, in which he suggested that Sikorski, Poland's exiled leader, had been murdered on Winston Churchill's orders. The book aroused great controversy upon publication, particularly since there exists no documentary evidence of a Churchill assassination order. When another author attacked Irving's claims about Churchill and Sikorski, Irving unsuccessfully sued. He was compelled to pay the legal costs.

That same year, he published *The Destruction of Convoy PQ17*. It too provoked a legal battle. The convoy, composed of thirty-three American and British ships, carrying supplies for the Soviets, suffered devastating losses on its way to the Soviet Union. Irving charged that the negligent actions of the British commander of the twenty-ship escort, Captain Jack Broome, were at fault. Broome sued both Irving and his publisher, Cassell and Company, for libel. Irving lost and was forced to pay £40,000, then one of Great Britain's largest libel awards. Irving appealed and lost again. In 1968, Irving was sued for libel by Jillian Page, who had written a critical newspaper article about him. Irving had charged that the article was the result of her "fertile brain." In return for her withdrawing the action, Irving apologized and paid her expenses. As a result of these provocative books and legal entanglements, Irving gained, within a decade, a certain notoriety.

Though I was aware of Irving, I did not pay him close attention. He first appeared on my radar screen in 1977 when he published *Hitler's War*, in which he argued that Hitler did not know about the Final Solution and that when he learned of it, he tried to stop it. I believed that Irving's conclusions could only have been the result of willful distortions. My suspicions were confirmed when a number of scholars wrote extensive critiques documenting how Irving skewed the historical evidence.[7]

In 1983, Irving again found himself in the media spotlight. *Stern,* the German weekly, announced that it had purchased for $3.8 million, sixty-two previously unknown volumes of "Hitler's Diaries." For a brief moment it was the world's biggest news story. Irving, who had previously purchased documents—which turned out to be bogus—from the man who was selling the diaries, was sure they too were bogus. At a sensational press conference, *Stern* editors heralded the publication of the diaries, screened a film about them, and predicted that there would certainly be those who would challenge the diaries, including historians such as David Irving, who had "no reputation to lose." Unbeknownst to *Stern,* their rival, *Bild-Zeitung,* had snuck Irving into the press conference. A few minutes later, when it was time for questions from the horde of journalists, Irving rushed to the microphone clutching documents which, he said, proved that the diaries were fake. Dramatically raising them above his head, he demanded that the *Stern* executives, who had anticipated this as a triumphant moment, explain how Hitler could have written about the July bomb plot in his diary on the day it happened if, as the film they had just screened demonstrated, his right hand was badly injured. *Stern* quickly ended the press conference. Reporters and paparazzi made a beeline for Irving. NBC immediately put him on a live hookup with the *Today* show, which was then on the air. Irving found this "exhilarating" and marveled at the "trail of chaos" he left behind. After spending the rest of the day giving interviews, Irving rose at 3:30 A.M. to appear on ABC's *Nightline*. According to his diary he was paid 700 marks for the appearance. The German publication, *Der Spiegel,* paid him 20,000 marks for his story. Irving was pleased not only by the attention but by the fact that he earned about 15,000 marks in three days.

Within a few days, the diaries were becoming yesterday's news. Suddenly, Irving changed his mind and announced that he now believed the diaries were genuine. Robert Harris, author of *Selling Hitler,* a study of the diaries incident, believed Irving's reversal was motivated, in part, by the fact that the diaries "did not contain any evidence to suggest that Hitler was aware of the Holocaust," thereby supporting the thesis of *Hitler's War.* If Irving was hoping this move would win him publicity, he calculated correctly. The *London Times* immediately ran a story about it on its front page. But within a few days the highly respected *Bundesarchiv,* Germany's National Archives, concluded, based on careful forensic tests, that the diaries were a forgery and a bad one at that. When the results were announced, Irving quickly composed a press release, accepting the *Bundesarchiv*'s ruling but stressing that he had been the first person to declare the diaries fakes. "Yes," a reporter from the *Times* added when he heard the release, "and the last person to declare them authentic."

NBC dispatched a television crew to interview Irving, who was in Germany on a speaking tour sponsored by the *Deutsche Volksunion,* a right-wing group that advocates an ethnically pure Germany. As the cameras were rolling, the audience walked out of the room. Several people were wearing the uniform of the *Wiking-Jugend,* an extremist group of young neo-Nazis. "Fortunately," Irving wrote in his diary, "NBC did not observe them."[8]

## DAVID IRVING: FROM FELLOW TRAVELER TO HOLOCAUST DENIER

Well before becoming a denier, Irving had argued that Nazi wrongdoings were equaled, if not surpassed, by Allied evils. In 1984, he declared that Winston Churchill's underhanded warmongering policy caused the death of millions. In 1986, he told a South African audience, "We [British] went in and we bombed the Belgians, and the Poles, and the French, and the Dutch. We did appalling damage. We killed millions of people in Europe in the most bestial way, in defiance of all conventions." Eventually, he predicted, Britain's name would be "damned with infamy."[9] But Irving remained on the periphery of

Holocaust deniers, attending their gatherings and publishing in their journal, but not explicitly denying the Holocaust.

Then came the 1988 trial of Ernst Zündel, the Canadian Holocaust denier and author of *The Hitler We Loved and Why* (White Power Publications). Zündel commissioned Fred Leuchter, an American whose company marketed a lethal injection system which, it claimed, was more humane, to conduct a forensic analysis of the gas chambers in Auschwitz, Birkenau, and Maidanek.

Upon his return, Leuchter reported that, in his opinion, it was technically impossible for the gas chambers to have been used to kill humans. Irving, who had come to testify on Zündel's behalf, read the report the night he arrived in Toronto. By the next morning he declared himself much impressed with Leuchter's findings. Two days later he took the stand and announced, "My mind has now changed because I understand that the whole of the Holocaust mythology is, after all, open to doubt."[10] After the Zündel trial Irving told an interviewer, "[U]ntil quite recently, I believed the story, but I want to be the first one out there in front now saying I was tricked and it's time to stop this particular piece of propaganda." According to Irving, there were financial reasons for the creation and dissemination of the "myth" of the Holocaust.

> Nobody likes to be swindled, still less where considerable sums of money are involved. (Since 1949 the State of Israel has received over 90 billion *Deutschmark* in voluntary reparations from West Germany, essentially in atonement for the "gas chambers of Auschwitz.") . . . Too many hundreds of millions of honest, intelligent people have been duped by the well-financed and brilliantly successful post-war publicity campaign.[11]

In 1991, Irving reissued *Hitler's War.* I sat with the two editions before me, tracing Irving's migration to hard-core denial. In the 1991 edition, he eliminated any mention of the Holocaust, replacing "extermination of the Jews" with vague references to the "Jewish tragedy" and "Nazi maltreatment of the Jews." The 1977 edition referred to gas chambers. In the 1991 edition these had been replaced with "unsubstantiated, lurid rumors about 'factories of death.'" Both editions contained an account of a May 1944 speech by Hitler to a group of German generals in which he promised that Hungary's

Jewish "problem" would shortly be resolved. In the 1977 edition, Irving had written that, after Hitler's speech, "in Auschwitz, the defunct paraphernalia of death—idle since 1943—began to clank again as the first trainloads from Hungary arrived." In the 1991 edition that sentence was replaced with: "Four hundred thousand Jews were being rounded up in Hungary; the first trainloads arrived in Auschwitz as slave labor for the now completed I.G. Farben plant." In 1977, these Jews were going to their death. In 1991, they were to be slave laborers. Readers of the second edition would never have known that they ended up in the gas chambers.[12]

In 1992, Irving told the *Guardian* that "one year from now the Holocaust will have been discredited." He warned, "No one's going to like it when they find out that for 50 years they have been believing a legend based on baloney."[13] Irving also blamed Jews for Britain's wartime policies. Asked by an interviewer whether he believed Churchill was "paid by the Jews [and] that the Jews dragged Britain into the war," Irving replied that these were "facts which happen to be true, in my considered opinion as a historian."[14]

After the publication of *Hitler's War* in 1977, increasing numbers of historians conceded that Irving's ideology compromised his work. Some of them bifurcated between his work on the Holocaust and his other research. A. J. P. Taylor, one of the best-known British historians of the twentieth century and author of *The Origins of the Second World War*, believed Irving a master of "unrivaled industry" and "good scholarship" where it concerned research. Hugh Trevor-Roper, who received a life peerage from Queen Elizabeth for his contributions to the writing of history, believed that "no praise can be too high for his indefatigable scholarly industry." But he questioned Irving's use of sources: "How reliable is his historical method? How sound is his judgment? We ask these questions particularly of a man who, like Mr. Irving, makes a virtue—almost a profession—of using arcane sources to affront established opinions." World War II historian Paul Addison found Irving a "colossus of research" but castigated him for his notion that "Churchill was as wicked as Hitler." He believed Irving "a schoolboy in judgment."[15] Similarly, John Charmley, whose book *Churchill: The End of Glory* is a right-wing critique of Churchill's policies, observed that "Irving's sources, unlike the conclusions which he draws from them, are usually sound." Nonetheless, Charmley complained that Irving "has been unjustly ignored."[16] Rainer Zitelmann, a conservative German historian, praised Irving's research on Hitler. In 1989, after Irving declared the Holocaust a "legend," Zitelmann wrote in *Die Zeit* that Irving's argument that Hitler had not ordered the Final Solution and may not even have been aware of it, had "struck a nerve" among historians. Irving, Zitelmann argued, "must not be ignored. He has weaknesses, . . . [but he has] contributed much to research."[17] Sir John Keegan, the noted military historian, contended—long after Irving became a denier—that *Hitler's War* was one of the two best books on the Second World War.[18]

John Lukacs took a different tone. Troubled that these historians not only praised Irving, but relied on his research, Lukacs challenged them to check his sources. Had they done so, Lukacs wrote, they would have found that many of the "references and quotations are not verifiable. In his *Hitler's War* . . . unverifiable and unconvincing assertions abound."[19] Charles Sydnor carefully checked Irving's sources and, in a scathing critique, eviscerated Irving's research, accusing him of seriously misrepresenting and distorting the record of Hitler and the Third Reich and dismissing as "pretentious twaddle," Irving's claim to be a more careful and thorough historian than the others who have researched Hitler.[20]

## HOLOCAUST HISTORIOGRAPHY: DIFFERING VIEWS

My book was not arguing for historical orthodoxy. In fact, highly respected Holocaust historians have markedly different conclusions about many aspects of the Holocaust. For example, *intentionalists* contend that Hitler came to power intending to murder the Jews and instituted an unbroken and coherent set of policies directed at realizing that goal. In contrast, *functionalists* argue that the Nazi decision to murder the Jews did not originate with a single Hitler decision, but evolved in an incremental and improvised fashion. According to the functionalists, in 1941, Nazi officers in the east, saddled with so many Jews and no place to "park" them, initiated the murders themselves. Only after the killings began did Hitler subsequently approve of their actions.[21]

Other historians differ about the Jews' responses to the persecution. Some argue that *Judenräte*, the Nazi-appointed Jewish councils, which administered life in the ghettoes, were too compliant with Nazi demands. These critics believe the *Judenräte's* failure to warn the ghetto population about their fate was an act of betrayal. Others argue that council members found themselves, or, more accurately, were placed by the Germans, in an untenable and unprecedented situation and were attempting to ease the victims' mental anguish during their final days.

There is an intense and spirited debate about the American response to the Holocaust. I came to the study of this topic with the preexisting supposition that the American Jewish community, by failing to pressure the Roosevelt administration to act, had been responsible in part for the fate of its coreligionists. I quickly realized that this view was simplistic. While American Jewish leaders expended much energy in internecine warfare, it is highly doubtful whether, even if they had raised a sustained outcry, they would have been able to move the Allies to act. Suggestions by some critics that American Jews should have broken with Roosevelt, acted on their own, and used the Jewish vote for leverage, are subject to the fallacy of "presentism"— the application of contemporary standards to the past.[22] Because Jews may have political clout today, these critics believe that they had the same clout fifty years ago.

Over the years, this debate had been hijacked and used for contemporary political ends. Critics from the right wing of the Orthodox movement have accused more acculturated Jewish leaders of not just inaction, but "outright interference with rescue efforts." They believe these leaders wanted Orthodox Jews to die in Europe, rather than come to America.[23] While I was deeply disturbed by these ahistorical attacks, I was equally disturbed by another phenomenon, the tendency to apply the term "Holocaust" to a broad array of injustices and tragedies including racial discrimination, AIDS, abortion, and laboratory use of animals, among other things. Such comparisons trivialize the Holocaust.

Nor did I believe that every genocide—as truly horrifying as it may be— can be labeled a Holocaust. This is not a question of the useless exercise of "comparative pain"—my people suffered more than yours—but of historiography. The Holocaust has certain unique elements that distinguish it from other genocides. However, at the same time, I disagree with those who argue for its utter uniqueness. Nothing can be utterly unique. Over many years of teaching about this topic, I have become increasingly disturbed by how Holocaust education can be more about advocacy than history and the teachers who teach this material more ideologues than pedagogues.

As intense as any of these and many other historiographic debates have become, rarely—if ever—do they falsify data. Deniers, however, distort, falsify, and pervert the historical record and, consequently, fall entirely outside the parameters of any historical debate about the Holocaust.

I had initially assumed that writing *Denying the Holocaust* would be a relatively noncontroversial task. Instead, I encountered unanticipated obstacles. Some scholars contended that, by taking deniers seriously, I was sounding a false alarm about the danger they posed. In fact, I did not consider Holocaust denial a "clear and *present* danger," but rather a *future* danger. Surveys revealed that more people in the United States believed Elvis Presley was alive than believed the Holocaust was a myth. Nonetheless, I did not think deniers were simply purveyors of a "loopy" form of history. Unless their fallacious claims were exposed, they could ultimately pose a more substantial danger. More sophisticated deniers, such as David Irving, had the ability to sow seeds of real confusion about the Holocaust. The greatest obstacle I faced was the glee with which deniers twisted facts, disparaged survivors, and pilloried Jews. In a way, I found it harder to write about deniers than about the Holocaust itself. The Nazis were defeated. Deniers were alive and kicking and reveling in their efforts.

The book was finally published in 1993, shortly after I arrived at Emory University in Atlanta. Much to my utter amazement, on the day of its publication it was featured on the front page of both the *New York Times Book Review* and the *Washington Post Book World*. That was followed by positive reviews in many journals. By 1995, I considered my scholarly work on denial closed. I knew the issue was far from solved. David Irving's books continued to be reviewed in prestigious venues. There were increasing expressions of Holocaust denial in the Arab and Muslim worlds. Even more disturbing was European "soft core" denial, which, rather than deny the Holocaust, equated Israel's policies with those of the Third Reich, labeling Israelis as Nazis.

However, having wallowed in this material for far too long, I believed it was time for me to move on to new fields of research. Then came the letter from Penguin.

# TWO

# THE DEFENSE STRATEGY

Penguin's initial letter was followed by additional inquiries from their lawyers about the sources upon which I had based my critique of Irving. Then, inexplicably, this correspondence ceased. Assuming Irving had turned to other pursuits, I considered this matter closed. During the summer of 1996, as the Atlanta Olympic Games got under way, I spent my time happily mixing attendance at Olympic events with research on my new project, one that had nothing to do with Holocaust denial. Then, in September, as the school year was in its initial throes, Penguin's lawyers wrote again. They informed me that Irving had filed papers indicating his intention to proceed with a lawsuit against Penguin and me.

Shortly thereafter, Helena Peacock, Penguin's general counsel, inquired about the indemnification clause in the contract I had signed with the Free Press, the American publisher of my book. At first I wasn't sure what she meant, but an inspection of my contract revealed that I had agreed that, should my book provoke legal action, the Free Press could essentially leave me on my own. Even though I had written about a controversial topic, I never dreamt I would be sued. Suddenly my predicament seemed somewhat surreal. When I told my lawyer, David Minkin, that Penguin was asking about the indemnification clause, his eyes opened wide and face grew taut. He seemed to be trying to mask his concerns, but the tension in his voice came through clearly as he explained that Penguin might be contemplating shifting the financial burden of the case to my shoulders.

Ironically, travel and research related to writing *Denying the Holocaust* had cost me more than I had earned from it. Virtually all the proceeds—including advance and royalties—had gone to the Hebrew University's Center for the Study of Antisemitism. And the sums were not insubstantial. The advance on the book had earned out, paperback rights were sold to another house, three foreign editions had appeared, and both the paperback and hardcover were in their fourth printing. I realized that this book contract didn't favor me at all. Worse, I now realized that the publishing house could, legally, leave me saddled with substantial expenses related to the lawsuit. Some of my lawyer friends feared that there was even the possibility that Irving could "attach"—legal shorthand for take—my property in the United States if he won. Clearly, all this was no longer a laughing matter.

As a full professor, I earned a respectable income, one that allowed me to own a comfortable home, travel, and know that if I wanted something I could, within reason, afford it. Generally, however, I eschewed material things. I drove a modest car and avoided frivolous purchases. Now I envisioned my savings depleted by this fight.

Although Penguin and I were both being sued, our perspectives on the case were clearly different. Penguin was a worldwide publishing conglomerate with an extensive backlist of classics in the adult and children's book market. It was now a subsidiary of Pearson, one of the United Kingdom's largest public companies, which owned, among other companies, the *Financial Times*. It was the leading publisher of college texts in the world. Though I realized that as a publisher of distinguished literature with an impressive list of authors, Penguin would have an incentive not to settle with Irving, still, I feared that the undetermined but clearly high cost of a lawsuit might make them, and the parent company, wary.

I realized that I needed someone to formulate a legal strategy to suit my interests. As I was contemplating my options, a friend in London who knew about the case called me. He reported that Anthony Julius, an exceptionally smart, first-rate lawyer, had contacted him to say that he would help me— pro bono if need be. Having heard all the right words—exceptionally smart, first-rate, and pro bono—I breathed a sigh of relief. Julius's name rang a bell. I asked if this was the same person who had written *T. S. Eliot: Anti-Semitism, and Literary Form*. This book had been published a few months earlier and all the reviews mentioned that the author, Anthony Julius, was a lawyer in London with clients such as the princess of Wales. My friend laughed. Confused by his laughter, I said nothing, but then I added, as an afterthought, "Isn't he *also* Princess Diana's divorce lawyer?" Still chuckling, my friend remarked that I was one of the few people who would put it in *that* order.

Julius's book on T. S. Eliot was originally his Ph.D. dissertation; he earned a degree while working full-time as a lawyer. When asked why, as a lawyer, he had pursued a Ph.D. in literary theory, Julius responded that many lawyers have hobbies. Getting a doctorate in literary theory was his "golf equivalent." The great poet's appropriation of the degraded discourse of antisemitism to animate his work intrigued Julius. Eliot had turned that which the enlightened world had supposedly discarded—antisemitic speech—into art. Julius, however, believed antisemitism was central—not peripheral, as many critics claimed—to the Eliot texts in which it appears. He was also intrigued by the way legions of critics had ignored or rationalized this aspect of Eliot's work, dismissing it as ironic or merely the cost of entry into the club of modernism. Reviewers vigorously debated the book. One reviewer described it as "the eviction of Eliot from the house of lame excuses." Some reviewers linked Julius's critique of Eliot with his work for Princess Diana, describing him as the ultimate iconoclast, simultaneously challenging two British idols, T. S. Eliot and the House of Windsor. Oxford University's Professor of Poetry, James Fenton, made it the subject of one of his three annual lectures. In "Eliot v. Julius," Fenton posited that "whatever assessment is made of Eliot in the future, the Julius book will have to come into it." With little ambiguity, Fenton asked: "Julius says an antisemite is a scoundrel. What is it that holds us back from saying that Eliot was a scoundrel?"[1]

Still, for most Brits, Julius was better known as Princess Di's lawyer. Julius, a partner in the London firm Mishcon de Reya, first represented Princess Diana when she sued a gym owner for surreptitiously photographing her as she was exercising and then selling the photos to the press. Pleased with Julius's success in this case, Princess Diana asked him to handle her divorce. An unrepentant Diana watcher, who claims to have read everything ever published on the princess, told me that when Diana asked Julius to represent her he protested, "I am not a divorce lawyer. This would be my first divorce case." She apparently responded, "That's all right. This will be my first divorce."

Born in 1956, Julius studied English literature at Jesus College, Cambridge. He joined Mishcon in 1981 and became a partner by 1984. By 1987, he was head of its litigation department. He also taught part-time at University College where he created the course "Law and Literature." I nervously dialed his office prepared to negotiate my way through a phalanx of secretaries. A friendly voice answered, "Anthony Julius." "Is this Anthony Julius's office?" I asked. "This *is* Anthony Julius." Surprised to be connected so rapidly, I stumbled through an explanation of the case. After a few moments he assured me that he was familiar with it. I asked the pivotal question. Would he represent me? Julius assured me that he would be delighted to do so. Having learned that the standard fee for someone of his caliber was over $500 an hour, I told him that I doubted I could afford his fees. Without hesitating, Julius reassured me he would do so pro bono, if need be. I felt a wave of relief. I felt certain that the matter would now be quickly resolved.

## EMORY: DOING THE RIGHT THING

My relief was further heightened when, shortly thereafter, Emory's then–chief legal counsel, a man with the improbable name of Joe Crooks, called to inform me that the president of the university and the Board of Trustees had heard about the case and had allocated $25,000 to help cover my expenses. I was amazed. Though Emory has a substantial population of Jewish students, few of its board members are Jews. The school is loosely associated with the Methodist Church. The board believed, Crooks explained, that my case epitomized academic freedom and raised fundamental moral issues. They wanted to communicate a message that Emory stood squarely behind me. When I relayed this to Anthony, he quickly asked that Emory not publicize the gift. He feared that if Irving knew we had funds—however limited—there was less chance that he would drop the case. Crooks agreed. When I shared news of Emory's generosity with colleagues at other universities, they thought it remarkable that Emory not only had given me the money, but had done so without my asking. "My school would have issued an eloquent statement indicating its support of me," one friend from an Ivy League university told me, "but it would never have come up with cold cash." I slept well for the first time in weeks.

My equanimity dissipated a few days later when I picked up the latest *New York Review of Books*. It contained a review of Irving's *Goebbels: Mastermind of the Third Reich* by the venerated Stanford professor and noted historian of Germany, Gordon Craig. I opened the paper, expecting to find a devastating critique. My optimism quickly faded. The emotional roller coaster, which I seemed to be riding since this experience had begun, plunged to the depths as I read: "Such people as David Irving have an indispensable part in the historical enterprise and we dare not disregard their views." While Craig disparaged Irving's claim that Auschwitz was "a labor camp with an unfortunately high death rate," as "obtuse and quickly discredited," his praise of Irving surprised me.[2] Giving someone with such an "obtuse" notion of Auschwitz an "indispensable part" in the historical conversation would inevitably give these "quickly discredited" views added credibility. If Craig could be beguiled by Irving, how would a judge and jury fare?

## LEGAL LESSONS: THE UNITED KINGDOM VERSUS THE UNITED STATES

In October, I invited Anthony to speak at Emory University. Though I looked forward to hearing him discuss Eliot, I was more anxious to learn about British libel law and even more interested in learning about him. Julius, at five feet ten inches, pale, with closely cropped dark hair, large black glasses, a slight paunch, and friendly smile, hardly looked like someone who had taken on the House of Windsor. He looked and spoke with the literary flair of a university professor. During Anthony's visit, I received a crash course in British libel law. It presumes defamatory words to be untrue, until the author proves them true. The burden of proof is, therefore, on the defendant rather than the plaintiff, as would be the case in the United States. Consequently, had Penguin and I not defended ourselves, Irving would have won by default. I would have been found guilty of libel and Irving could then claim that his definition of the Holocaust had been determined to be legitimate.

In the United States, I would have had another level of protection. American law, founded on the First Amendment right of freedom of speech, stipulates that, in order for public figures—politicians, authors, and others who have placed themselves in the public eye—to win a suit for libel they must prove that the statement was made with "actual malice"—that the author had knowledge of its falsity or exhibited reckless disregard as to whether it was false or not. Irving, as a well-published author and lecturer, would have, in all likelihood, been considered a "public figure" in the United States and would have found it difficult—if not impossible—to sue me.[3] Furthermore, in the United States an author has some degree of protection if she based her critical words on reliable sources and had no way of knowing they were wrong. In the United Kingdom reliance on sources, reliable or not, does not provide a defense.

Anthony explained that in the United Kingdom libel defendants had various legal options. They could argue that the plaintiff was misinterpreting the words in question. This, however, was not the case. My charges—Irving was a denier, Hitler partisan, and right-wing ideologue—were not being misinterpreted. Defendants can also argue that their words were not defamatory, that they were not intended to discredit the subject. Mine, however, were clearly so. Finally, we could claim "justification," that the words at issue were true, even if they were defamatory, so I was justified in writing them. That, Anthony explained, was the path we would pursue.

In legal circles proving the truth of the defamatory words is considered to be the "atom bomb defense."[4] We did not have to prove every detail of my charges. We had to prove the substantial truth or the "sting" of the libel. If a small aspect of my charges was wrong, but everything else was correct, I could still win.[5]

"We will argue," Anthony explained, "that Irving subordinated the truth for ideological purposes and that his comments about the Holocaust were designed to spread antisemitism and engender sympathy for the Third Reich." I felt unexpectedly comforted by his use of the word "we." Though I knew this was common legal parlance, knowing it in theory was different from hearing it, particularly when the "we" was essentially "me."

Anthony assumed Irving would eventually drop the case. "He loves publicity and is delighted to cause you grief. We'll vigorously respond to his charges. We shall change his pleasure into pain." Listening to Anthony convinced me that his Eliot work was hardly a "golf equivalent." He could not abide antisemitism whether it came from T. S. Eliot or David Irving.

Over the next several months, Anthony and his partner, James Libson, explained what needed to be done. They would prepare the pleadings, our presentation to the court of the core issues in the case. At the same time the discovery process would begin. Each party was obligated to turn over to the other side all relevant materials—correspondence, documents, books, and tapes—in its possession. This would be an extensive process. I would have to put my hands on everything I had that pertained to Irving. After that I would have to prepare my witness statement. Since it would "introduce" me to the court, I had to discuss my background, education, and approach to the study of the Holocaust. We also had to select a team of expert witnesses to analyze Irving's claims about the Holocaust and to demonstrate that they contravened the available evidence. Their reports would be submitted to the court in advance of a trial. English courts stipulate that evidence be exchanged before trial to avoid "trial by ambush." We would also present Irving with a list of pretrial interrogatories. Anthony and James were fairly certain that, faced with this unrelenting defense, Irving would retreat.

As our strategy evolved, we not only decided what we would do; we also decided what we would not do. Our objective was not to prove the Holocaust had happened. No court was needed to prove that. Our job was to prove the truth of my words, namely that Irving had lied about the Holocaust and had done so out of antisemitic motives. We decided not to call survivors as witnesses. To have called survivors would have suggested we needed "witnesses of fact"—eyewitnesses—to prove there was a Holocaust. That was our legal reason. In truth, we had another reason. Irving was representing himself because, he said, no lawyer could present his case as well as he could. He would, therefore, cross-examine the witnesses. We did not consider it ethical to subject survivors to cross-examination by a man whose primary objective, we feared, was their humiliation. I recalled how he taunted a survivor who had appeared with him on an Australian radio show. "Mrs. Altman," he had said referring to the concentration camp number on her arm, "how much money have you made out of that tattoo since 1945?"[6] I did not want to risk him ridiculing survivors—even those who insisted that they were eager to testify.

## FILMING MR. DEATH

As the preparations were gaining momentum, Errol Morris, one of America's leading documentary filmmakers, emailed me that he was making a film about Fred Leuchter, the man Zündel had sent to Auschwitz to prove there were no homicidal gas chambers. Morris's *The Thin Blue Line*, had saved the life of a man on death row by showing that the government's case was riddled with holes. A *Brief History of Time*, Morris's film on Stephen Hawking, had won many accolades as had *Fast, Cheap, and Out of Control,* a film about people with unconventional occupations. Morris was intrigued by Leuchter, whose report denying the gas chambers energized Holocaust deniers. Morris told me that if the *Thin Blue Line* was a "movie about false history" the Leuchter film would be "about false history writ large."[7]

Morris and I agreed to meet in Cambridge, Massachusetts, when I was scheduled to give a paper at Harvard on the creation of the Holocaust Remembrance Day ceremony in the Capitol Rotunda. In the face of the growing demands of the lawsuit, doing my research was becoming an impossible task. Though the Harvard conference promised a respite from Irving, I could not resist Morris's invitation to screen a rough cut of his film.

We met at the Inn at Harvard and walked over to Morris's low-key studio in Cambridge's Central Square. We settled into comfortable chairs to watch the film. Leuchter's face filled the screen. He has a high forehead, receding hairline, a long oval pointy face, pasty skin, large heavy black-framed glasses, and a kind of caricatured grinning expression. With his polyester short-sleeved white shirt and tightly hitched pants, he looked like he should have a plastic pocket holder full of pens and a bunch of keys on his belt. He reminded me of the classic nerd, not a man whose junk science had caused neo-Nazis and deniers to rejoice.

Leuchter proceeded to tell his story on film. His father worked for the Massachusetts prison system. By the age of four Leuchter was already accompanying him to visit "all the cell areas, including the death-house area." By his own admission, Leuchter attributed his decision to become an "execution expert" to these father-son excursions. Leuchter drank forty cups of coffee a day, smoked six packs of cigarettes, and hung out at the Dunkin' Donuts in Malden, Massachusetts. He was attached not only to coffee but to a waitress, Carolyn, whom he had recently married.

Leuchter had an old electric chair in the basement of his home. With the cameras rolling, he strapped himself into the chair, put on the helmet through which the electrical current traveled, looked straight into the camera, and smiled. Leuchter excitedly described how the lethal injection system he had designed might be enhanced. Rather than strapping prisoners to a gurney and forcing them to stare at the ceiling, "you could put him in a contoured chair like they have in a dentist's office. . . . You could give him a television, you could give him music, you could put some pictures on the wall." As Leuchter described this user-friendly form of execution, the film cut to a framed Currier and Ives winter scene. Morris, apparently enjoying his "editorial" comment, laughed aloud. He clearly thought that Leuchter possessed the three ingredients he considered key for his films: "sad, sick, and funny."[8] I agreed with the sad and the sick. I found it hard to think of him as funny.

In February 1988, Leuchter had gone to Poland to investigate the "alleged gas chambers" and make a movie about his findings. Zündel paid $40,000 for Leuchter, Carolyn, a cameraman, a translator, and a draftsman to make the trip, which also served as Leuchter and Carolyn's honeymoon. Morris considered calling his movie *Honeymoon in Auschwitz* but eventually dropped that in favor of *Mr. Death*. Morris included portions of Leuchter's film in his documentary. At both Auschwitz and Birkenau, Leuchter chiseled chunks of concrete from the walls of the gas chambers. He also took samples from the walls of the delousing facility in which clothes and objects were fumigated. Leuchter intended to compare the amount of gas residue in each facility. He haphazardly stuffed plastic Baggies filled with chunks from the walls into the front pocket of his hooded sweatshirt. As he gathered his samples, he kept talking to the camera. "Sort of like Mr. Wizard," Morris laughingly observed, referring to the somewhat goofy television character who taught many American children science.

Leuchter smuggled the samples out of Poland wrapped in his dirty underwear. Back in Malden he asked a chemical lab to test them for HCN (hydrogen cyanide). The lab found there was more gas residue in the delousing chamber samples than in the gas chamber samples. Based on this, Leuchter concluded that no humans were gassed at Auschwitz. "Only lice," he declared, "were killed there."[9]

Leuchter had made a number of fundamental mistakes that destroyed the validity of his conclusions. In the fall of 1944, as the Soviet forces approached Auschwitz, the Germans blew up the gas chambers in order to camouflage their genocidal activities. The piles of rubble had been exposed to years of rain, snow, sun, and mud. The water-soluble HCN residue on the chambers' exposed walls and floors had been severely diluted by the time Leuchter arrived with his chisel, Baggies, and running commentary. Despite this exposure to the elements, Leuchter found some HCN traces, indicating that there must have once been far higher levels. But Leuchter made an even more basic mistake. He assumed that because he found higher levels of HCN residue in the chambers for delousing clothing and objects than in the homicidal gas chambers, humans were not killed in the latter. But vermin are far more resistant to cyanide than humans. Therefore, in order to kill them, far higher concentrations of gas are needed for substantially longer periods of time. Therefore, there *should* be more gas residue in a clothes de-lousing chamber than in a homicidal gas chamber. Furthermore, when humans are packed tightly into a room—such as they were in the gas chambers—lower amounts of the gas will kill them more rapidly than in other circumstances. Given these conditions, it is surprising that he found any gas residue at all in the homicidal gas chambers.

I kept waiting for the film to explicate the fallacies of Leuchter's arguments. I waited for him to note that according to Alabama assistant attorney general, Ed Carnes, Leuchter was a *"self-styled* [emphasis added] 'execution technology' expert," whose views on the gas-chamber process were not only "unorthodox" but who also would "make money on both sides of the fence" in capital murder cases.[10] If a state refused to hire him to work on their execution system, Leuchter would testify in court on behalf of an inmate in that state that the system might malfunction.[11] I knew that Morris generally does not introduce other voices into his films and lets the main characters speak for themselves. Still, I assumed he would not let these claims go unchallenged. I waited in vain. When the film ended, Morris turned to me with an expectant look. Without hesitating, I blurted out, "Your film is in trouble. In fact, it's dangerous. Viewers might assume you're espousing Leuchter's views." Morris's eyes darkened. I explained that while critics might understand Leuchter was a nut, innocent viewers would not. Morris, possibly stung by the strength of my objections, dismissed my concerns and assured me that everyone would grasp how eccentric Leuchter was. I doubted he was correct. I suggested that he ask Robert Jan van Pelt, an expert on Auschwitz, to elucidate the absurdity of Leuchter's claims. Van Pelt had just coauthored a major study of the history of Auschwitz. He might rescue Morris from a potential disaster.

I knew that my response was governed, in great measure, by my own situation. I felt entrapped in a legal nightmare, while Morris considered Leuchter's claims as sort of weirdly funny. One of America's most talented documentarians was, however inadvertently, helping Irving make his case. As I walked to my hotel, I felt very lonely.

## A CONSPIRACY OF GOOD

My response to Morris was probably exacerbated by something unrelated to his film. Right before coming to Cambridge, Anthony had called to say that the case had taken already far longer than anyone had anticipated. James and Anthony could no longer work pro bono. They were willing to work at reduced fees, but needed substantial amounts to pay for experts, researchers, and other staff, particularly if we went to trial. When I asked Anthony to define "substantial," he somewhat reluctantly said probably more than a million dollars. My heart sank. Anthony promised to prepare a budget and I resolved, in good southern tradition, not to think about it until it arrived.

A few days later, my ability to ignore this issue abruptly ended as I was leaving my home for a weekend seminar organized by the Wexner Heritage Foundation. I was climbing into the taxi to go to the airport when a FedEx truck pulled up in front of my home. The driver ran over and handed me a large envelope from Anthony. I took out a multipaged document. I quickly turned to the last page and blanched. The bottom line read $1.6 million.

I generally loved participating in the Wexner Foundation's activities and had been looking forward to the weekend as a bit of an escape from the case. The retailing legend, Leslie Wexner, had created the foundation to educate Jewish communal leaders. Wexner, together with his wife Abigail, believed that Jewish life needed leaders who were both educated in Jewish history and tradition and knew how to think "outside the box." Adhering to Leslie's commercial philosophy that "retail is detail," the foundation's programs were meticulously executed and were models of adult education. I had been teaching for the foundation for over ten years. At this seminar I was scheduled to participate in a series of panels about strategies for lessening in terdenominational Jewish strife. That topic quickly faded into the background as word of my predicament quickly spread. Participants inundated me with questions.

The founding president of the foundation, Rabbi Herbert Friedman, a tall man with an Einstein-like shock of white hair, pulled me aside. Friedman had been a United States Army chaplain during World War II. He became profoundly troubled by the myriad of Jewish survivors languishing in Europe—some were being housed in former concentration camps. Many wanted to enter Palestine but the British refused them permission. Friedman commandeered American army trucks and, with the help of Jewish soldiers, transported survivors to Italian ports where they boarded ships for Palestine—among them the SS *Exodus*—and tried to outrun the British blockade. After the war he went on to a distinguished career in Jewish organizational life.

Friedman, sounding a bit miffed that he had heard about my case via the grapevine and not directly from me, demanded a briefing on the case. He immediately asked how I was planning to raise the money. I told him that I had no idea. "I've always been a giver, never a recipient. I never imagined I would need to solicit funds for my own needs." He peered down at me and declared, in a slightly condescending tone, which, had it come from anyone else, I would have resented. "It's time to get organized." He then added, "Irving set his sights on you, but it's the entire Jewish community and historical truth that he is aiming at."

And then Friedman took charge. He called his long-time colleague and benefactor, Leslie Wexner, and briefed him. Les responded in his characteristically straightforward fashion. He requested background material and after closely scrutinizing it, told Friedman, "This is not Deborah's issue. It's our issue." He then relayed a message to me that I was not to worry about funds. He would give whatever it takes. He and Abigail had only one prerequisite. I must have the best defense. After determining that Anthony was, indeed, at the top of his field and would mount an aggressive defense, Les Wexner committed $200,000 for the fight. Soon a collaboration developed between Wexner and Steven Spielberg, whose own Shoah Foundation was deeply engaged in taking survivors' testimonies. This collaboration resulted in the effective solicitation of a number of $100,000 dollar contributors. Bill Lowenberg, a survivor who lived in San Francisco, whose daughter—a participant in the Wexner programs—had briefed him on the case, called Friedman. He said he would raise 20 percent of the costs and began to contact members of the Bay Area Jewish community. Ernie Michel, a survivor who lived in New York, took out his Rolodex and began to call other survivors. Other people pitched in to help. All this was done quietly and without any publicity or fanfare.

When I saw Les Wexner a few weeks later, I tried to thank him. He rather impatiently brushed off my words of gratitude. "This may be the most important check I have ever written." He then spoke, almost in awe, about the high-mindedness of the other donors. They sought no recognition. They gave to protect the historical record. Rarely, Les mused, had he seen such unselfishness. "They are glad to have the opportunity to nail this guy's lies and distortions." Subsequently, when I saw some of the other donors, they, too, brushed off my thanks and urged me to mount as strong a defense as possible. It was a mind-boggling experience.

Friedman asked David Harris, executive director of the American Jewish Committee (AJC), to house a defense fund. The committee's board agreed and then voted to make a major contribution to the fund. The Anti-Defamation League and the Simon Wiesenthal Center stepped forward to contribute. The AJC's Harris assigned Ken Stern—the organization's specialist on antisemitism and extremism—to assist me in any way he could. Ken, a lawyer, immediately established contact with Anthony and James. In an unprecedented display of organizational restraint, none of these organizations publicized what they were doing. Within weeks other contributions began to arrive. One person quietly called another. Some of the donations were substantial; many were quite small. Most came from Jews. Some came from non-Jews. I did not solicit funds. Wexner had stressed in no uncertain terms, "Our job is to ensure that you have the means to fight. Your job is to fight." When someone called the Wexners to suggest that I follow a particular strategy, they were told in no uncertain terms, "It's between Deborah and her lawyers. She has the best. Let them do their job."

The case was slowly taking over my universe. As Anthony and James had warned, preparing the discovery was very onerous. I had to scour my files for everything that might, however obliquely, relate to David Irving. Together with one overworked research assistant, I reviewed the thousands of pieces of paper I had accumulated while writing the book. Files that I thought I would never seriously examine again were piled high on my desk. Books, some with the yellow Post-its I had used while writing *Denying the Holocaust* still attached to them, were shipped to England. Anthony and James decided that, in order to be able to assure the court that I had fully complied with the discovery process, an American lawyer should review my work. Joe Beck, an Atlanta libel attorney, volunteered to help. I assumed that he would perfunctorily review my work. Once again my assumption was wrong. Joe spent hours with me inspecting my files to ensure that I had sent all relevant material to London.

Then we had to select our expert witnesses. Who, I wondered, would do this tedious job? There seemed to me nothing less gratifying for a researcher than tracing footnotes to see if they told the truth. Anthony reassured me that it was a challenge that would intrigue academics. Moreover, he reminded me, we were planning to pay them well, approximately £100—close to $160—an hour. Worried about the mounting expenses, I observed that historians rarely earn that much money. Anthony told me, with a slight note of reproach in his voice, that this was what witnesses in a commercial case received. "Should we pay historians any less?" Though I was embarrassed by Anthony's question, I nonetheless was about to suggest that maybe we should, when Anthony added, "I want them at my beck and call. If I need something from them in a hurry, I want them to make our case the highest priority. At £100 an hour, they will." I dropped the issue.

Together with Penguin's lawyers, Anthony, James, and I compiled a list of potential experts. We prepared a list of those of Irving's claims that the experts would address, including that Hitler had no role in the Final Solution; that the murder of Jews on the Eastern Front was not sanctioned by Nazi authorities; that there was no overall plan to murder the Jews of Europe; and that gas chambers were not used to murder vast numbers of Jews at Auschwitz and elsewhere. We also needed a lead witness to conduct a historiographic analysis of Irving's writings on the Holocaust and to determine if he observes the generally accepted standards of historical scholarship. Did he honestly cite his sources? Did he tell his readers about evidence that disagreed with his arguments? Did he make it easy for other researchers to check his sources?

We selected Professor Richard Evans of Cambridge as our lead historical witness. Evans, a specialist on German history, would conduct the historiographic analysis of Irving's writings on the Holocaust. We decided that he should not limit himself to only Holocaust-related topics but should pick one non-Holocaust topic in order to determine if it was accurate and reliable. Evans decided to analyze Irving's writings on the Allied bombing of Dresden in February 1945. We considered including another non-Holocaust topic, Irving's writings about Sir Winston Churchill. I thought this a fruitful avenue to pursue because I suspected that Irving's anti-Churchill fulminations would not sit well with a British jury. We turned to Sir Martin Gilbert, but when he proved unavailable, we decided Evans's review of Irving's writings on Dresden would suffice.

We asked Professor Robert Jan van Pelt, the architectural historian I had recommended to Errol Morris, to examine Irving's claims regarding Auschwitz. A Dutchman, van Pelt was a professor at the University of Waterloo's Architecture School in Toronto and was emerging as one of the world's experts on Auschwitz. I also suggested that we ask Professor Christopher Browning, author of *Ordinary Men: Battalion 101* and an expert on the origins of the Final Solution, to prepare a report challenging Irving's assertions that Jews, who were shot after the Germans invaded Soviet territory in the summer of 1941, were victims of rogue actions, not of a coordinated system authorized by the highest echelons of the Third Reich. We also asked him to submit a report on the gas vans and on Operation Reinhard, the killing of Jews in the death camps of Belzec, Sobibor, and Treblinka. Richard Evans asked Peter Longerich, a German-born specialist on Hitler who now taught at the University of London, to analyze Hitler's role in the Final Solution. Because our objective was *not* to prove that the Holocaust had happened but that what I wrote about Irving was correct, we asked the experts to compile the evidence that a fair-minded, objective historian would use to reach conclusions about the Holocaust.

But we also needed political scientists. In *Denying the Holocaust,* I had argued that Irving's Holocaust denial was linked to his extremist political views. In other words, he did not just happen to be a denier, who also happened to be an antisemite and racist. The two—denial and political extremism—were linked. He engaged in the former in order to promote the latter. We asked Professor Hajo Funke of Berlin, a German specialist on extremism, to examine Irving's links to the German radical right and neo-Nazi fringe.

## LONDON 1998: EMINENT LAWYERS AND SKEPTICAL EXPERTS

In early 1998, I flew to London to consult with Anthony and James. Mishcon de Reya's offices are located in Bloomsbury, home of London's most popular tourist attraction, the British Museum. Concerned about depleting the defense fund, I asked Michaela, Anthony's secretary, to find a reasonable hotel.

The one she chose had clearly seen better days. I quickly headed to Mishcon's offices. I cut through Bloomsbury Square and walked through an arcade of shops, used-book stores, and restaurants. It opened onto the commercial bustle of High Holborn and Southampton Row, where Mishcon de Reya occupied a small seven-story building. The offices were modest and functional.

Anthony's office had the familiar chaos of a creative mind at work. Papers covered every available surface and books on art, literature, history, and law filled the shelves. A photo of his four young children stood out on his desk and a poster of the Eliot book hung on one wall. In the far corner of the office a framed newspaper with the headline "Princess Wins Record Libel Settlement" described Princess Diana's lawsuit against a London paper shortly before she died. It was the only indication of his famous client. At the bottom of the page the princess had placed a card embossed with her monogram with a personal note: *"Another victory for the eminent lawyer."*[12]

As I was taking it all in, a young man with curly dark hair, a full build, and an open demeanor appeared at the door. The minute he said, "Welcome," I recognized James's voice. If Anthony looked like a young professor, James looked like a graduate student. While we waited for Anthony, James told me he had graduated from Leeds University, where he studied Arabic. He had spent time in Israel and had joined the firm in 1993. He and Anthony frequently worked together. He had an easygoing, kind, and unpretentious style. I also sensed that, when necessary, he could be tough. Once Anthony arrived, we plunged into discussion of what lay ahead. As we spoke, James took copious notes. Anthony took none.

On the following day, Professor Evans, a compact man of medium build, with dark hair, craggy features, and an intense look—at first glance it seemed like a scowl—joined us. Born in 1947, Evans came from a lower-middle-class family. He attended Oxford and was an expert on nineteenth- and twentieth-century German history and historiography. After reading his book, *In Defense of History,* a challenge to postmodernist critiques of history, both Anthony and I were convinced he was the right choice for lead witness. The book argued that the past "really happened, and we really can, if we are very scrupulous and careful and self-critical . . . reach some tenable conclusions about what it all meant."[13]

I tried—without much success—to make small talk with Evans. He seemed guarded, reserved, and even a bit ill at ease talking to me. Only when

I mentioned other historians did he loosen up a bit. He was a man of very decided opinions—many of them quite critical—about other historians' work. After about an hour, we were joined by Thomas Skelton-Robinson and Nik Wachsmann, two graduate students Evans had hired to help with the research work for his report. Born in Germany, Nik, in his late twenties, had first-class honors degrees in History from the London School of Economics. He was writing his Ph.D. dissertation on prisons in the Weimar Republic. Thomas, a Brit who had lived in Germany for over five years, had graduated with honors from Glasgow University and was writing a dissertation about the student movement in West Germany in the late 1960s. He was quiet and listened more than he spoke.

Anthony asked me to brief them. I stressed that I stood firmly behind what I had written and predicted that their research would prove that Irving had falsified documents. Evans listened closely, but said little. He seemed a bit skeptical. When I talked about Irving as an antisemite and racist, he looked downright uncomfortable. I suspected that he thought me a hyperbolic, American, Jewish woman who was more an ideologue than an open-minded historian. As far as he was concerned, even though he would be our expert witness, the jury on Irving was still out. According to British law the allegiance of expert witnesses is to the court not to those who are paying them. They were to present an objective evaluation of the evidence. However, I worried that our lead witness was beginning his efforts with a decidedly ambivalent attitude toward me and my work. Though I did not doubt that Evans's research would ultimately prove me correct, I left the meeting more than a bit disheartened.

The next afternoon, Evans and I walked to the University of London to hear the historian John Lukacs discuss his new book, *The Hitler of History*, which severely castigated Irving for his depiction of Hitler. Lukacs condemned Irving as an "apologist," "rehabilitator," and "unrepentant admirer of Hitler" who twisted documentary sources. Lukacs criticized reviewers who gave him "qualified praise." Had they inspected Irving's sources they would have found his work replete with "unverifiable and unconvincing assertions."[14] After the lecture Lukacs told me that Irving had written to his agent, threatening to do to any British publisher who published his book what he was doing to me and to Penguin, UK. His publisher was watching my case and would, Lukacs said, decide what it would do based on what happened to me. I told Evans that if Irving was able to cow me into settling with him, other authors would fear criticizing him and no publisher would publish anything critical of him. Evans listened but said little.

By May 1998, the date of my next visit to London, Anthony and Penguin had hammered out the terms of a joint defense. Penguin would carry all the "shared costs" and pay for any expenditure relating to both parties, including experts, barristers, and researchers. I still faced substantial expenses, but this agreement lifted a major burden from me. Their insurer would pay their bills. Anthony pointed out that, if, at some point, the insurer balked and Penguin had to assume some of the expenses, they had immense pockets and could treat these expenditures as business expenses. Then he added, "I told them that if they wanted access to you, they had to accept this arrangement."

One evening a few members of the legal team gathered for an informal dinner in Soho. We were joined by Richard Evans and Chris Browning, both of whom would be serving as our expert witnesses. Browning was in London testifying for Scotland Yard at the war crimes trial of Anthony Sawoniuk.[15] A tall, broad-shouldered, and long-limbed man in his mid-fifties, Browning looks like he belongs on a basketball court more than in an archive. He has rugged features, a wide smile, and a full head of straight hair that seems to be perennially falling in his eyes. He had testified for the Canadian government against Zündel's claims that the Holocaust was a myth.

Exceptionally well liked by historians in this field, Browning had recently become ensnared in a nasty academic debate. In his book *Ordinary Men: Battalion 101*, Browning had argued that the German killers were motivated by a combination of factors. In addition to antisemitism, Browning believed their actions were influenced by their deference to authority, social conformity, and peer pressure. His conclusions had been vigorously attacked by Daniel Goldhagen in his controversial book *Hitler's Willing Executioners*. Goldhagen contended that a uniquely German form of eliminationist antisemitism motivated the killers. In other words, Goldhagen considered the killers "ordinary Germans," while Browning considered them "ordinary men."[16]

At dinner, Browning asked Anthony if he planned to call survivors as witnesses. When Anthony said probably not, Chris recalled that Zündel's lawyer questioned the survivors on topics with which they were least familiar. "He had let them twist in the wind as long as the judge allowed it. He seemed not to be searching for truth, but for humiliation. It was a horrible ordeal for both the survivors and for the spectators."

Evans, who had spent the past two months analyzing Irving's work, began to talk about some of his findings. "Irving's veneer of respectability slips away as you do the research." He admitted that he was surprised by the number of distortions he and his researchers, Nik and Thomas, had already found. "There are simply too many for them to be mistakes. And they always seem to move in one direction: exoneration of Hitler." I recalled Evans's skepticism at our first meeting, a few months earlier. Emboldened by his current assessment of Irving's work, I suggested that, instead of arguing that David Irving is a sloppy historian or bad historian, he posit that he was not a historian at all. Evans dismissed this out of hand. "It is an absurd semantic dispute to declare someone who has written two dozen books about history not to be a historian. No jury will accept it."[17] He said this with a finality that seemed to brook no debate. I thought Evans was wrong, but I did not challenge him.

As James walked me to my hotel after dinner, I told him I was worried about a jury. Might jury members assume that Irving was simply an iconoclastic and somewhat wacky historian? Might they share some of Irving's negative sentiments about Jews and other minorities? Drawing on my legal knowledge, most of which was gleaned from television's *Law and Order,* I added that certainly the lawyers would know which jurors to eliminate through peremptory challenges. James's response was sobering. "We have no peremptory challenges in Britain. The court calls 12 people and that's your jury." Once again I felt as if I had been bushwhacked by a legal system not my own.

## SECOND DISCOVERY: A GOLD MINE

Throughout the summer, the lawyers pored over Irving's discovery list consisting of nearly fifteen hundred items. I was struck not only by its volume but by the number of items that seemed totally unrelated to our case, including reviews of his book, a videotape of the birth of his daughter, and even something on the assassination of JFK. There was also material that seemed to be connected to a case Irving was preparing to bring against the journalist and historian Gitta Sereny, who in 1996 had written a critical review of his book *Goebbels: Mastermind of the Third Reich*. The lawyers took note of those irrelevant items because, as James explained, the loser pays costs. "Eventually we will bill him for the time spent reviewing materials which had no connection to our case." I noted—but hardly shared—James's optimism.

The lawyers did something of far greater importance. They prepared an application for a second set of discovery materials. They included all of Irving's correspondence with leading Holocaust deniers, antisemites, and neo-Nazis. James explained that they were not sure he had actually corresponded with all those on the list they had composed but they figured they would ask and see what it produced. They also requested access to his collection of video- and audiotapes and his personal daily diary. We assumed the diaries would reveal his connections with radical extremists. The tapes would indicate what he said to his admirers away from the media glare.

A pretrial hearing was scheduled for September 1998. The lawyers were scheduled to present our application for these additional materials. I asked Anthony whether I should attend. He said no. My presence might give Irving an inflated sense of importance and make him less inclined to drop the case. I reluctantly agreed.

Pretrial hearings are presided over by a "master," whom James described as a sort of junior judge. Our master was John Trench. I told James that, given the nature of this case, Charles Dickens could not have chosen a more appropriate name. As we anticipated, Irving assiduously fought our application, complaining that this was a "fishing expedition" to force him to disclose his "stock-in-trade." Trench initially seemed sympathetic to Irving and questioned the broad sweep of materials we were requesting. Anthony argued that since Irving was suing me, I had the right to defend myself. In order to prove that I was justified in calling Irving a right-wing ideologue and antisemite, we were obligated to examine more than the historical materials he used in his books. The hearing stretched from one day into the next. James called during the breaks to update me. "Irving is fighting tooth and nail. He described this action as part of a global conspiracy against him and argued that the 'enemies of truth' were out to destroy him."

Despite Irving's protests, Trench eventually acceded to virtually all our requests. It was such a sweeping victory that even Anthony, who generally maintained a studied reserve, allowed more than a trace of excitement to creep into his voice as he summarized the results for me. James did not try to contain his excitement. "We had a fantastic day in court. Irving will have to strip his files bare. A great burden has been placed on him." Trench also took the unusual action of requiring Irving to sign an affidavit that his discovery was complete and compelled him to pay for the costs of the work entailed in the discovery application.

Though Irving's diaries promised to produce a gold mine of material, our right to inspect was strictly limited. Only the lawyers and experts could see them. No one else, myself included, could inspect them. While this stipulation protected Irving from having strangers troll through his personal life, it did not offer him complete sanctuary. Any material we introduced into court became part of the public record. I speculated that surely this would make him drop the case, if only to prevent his private material from being made public. James's response was sobering: "At one time I would have agreed. Now, after months of dealing with him, I am not sure."

At the end of our conversation James told me that Anthony, who rarely engaged Irving in conversation, had approached him during the hearing and said in friendly tones, "This case is too complex and intricate to be heard by a jury. Don't you think it should be heard by just a judge?" Irving agreed. Anthony told Trench that both sides wanted a bench trial. I was delighted. A jury was unlikely to carefully read and digest the reams of detailed historical material the experts were preparing. A judge would more easily wrap his or her mind around some of the tedious and complex historical and scientific arguments. Because there would be no jury, we did not have to make "emotional" arguments but could concentrate on the heart of the matter: forensics and history. I wondered why Irving had agreed. James speculated that Irving may have been pleased to be involved in a case Anthony Julius considered "complex and intricate."

A few weeks later Irving asked Trench to order me to sign an affidavit attesting to the honesty of my discovery procedure. Trench agreed. James believed that he did so because Irving was representing himself. He assured me that it was no big deal. I could complete the affidavit at the British embassy or a consulate. I was leaving for Washington on the next day and decided to go to the British embassy, a campuslike setting adjacent to the vice president's residence. A clerk in a drab antechamber gave me the forms, demanded $52 in cash, and asked me to wait. Finally, I was ushered into a wood-paneled room dominated by a large, ornate wooden desk. A tall man introduced himself as a "vice consul." He removed a book, a small velvet bag, and a round container from a wooden cabinet behind his desk. He asked me to stand, place my hand on the book, and swear that I had faithfully executed the form. I was so startled by this process that only after I finished did I realize that I had probably taken an oath on a New Testament. The vice consul removed a small seal with a worn wooden handle from the velvet bag. He opened the container, dipped the seal into red sealing wax, and pressed hard on the document. This relic from centuries past rather amazed me, as did so many other unfamiliar twists and turns that were coming at me from the British legal system.

## TRYING TIMES

As word of my legal difficulties spread, I began to hear from the *Neinsagers*, the doubters, in the scholarly community. "Why are you doing this?" they asked. Their comments perplexed me. Why would anyone question the reason I was defending myself? I explained I was the defendant, had not initiated the case, and was not "doing" anything to anyone. One of the leading Holocaust historians told me that my biggest mistake was in not ignoring Irving's charges. When I explained that I didn't have a choice, that if I didn't fight Irving would win, the response was "So what?"

There were also some British Jews who worried about my staging a strong defense. One prominent member of the community told me that Irving would get a new lease on life from this case. Some of these doubters feared that Anthony Julius was a Svengali of sorts, orchestrating my tough stance. They warned me that I would turn a has-been author into a media personality. I understood their fears and tried to convince them that I had no other option, but I was deeply unnerved by their comments. Anthony told me to ignore them. "They are wrong. We are right." A trial, he acknowledged, might give Irving a platform, but we would use that platform to decimate his historical fantasies. James, on the other hand, found these suggestions demoralizing in light of the hard and productive work that was being done on the case.

I was particularly upset when a prominent Jewish lawyer in London declared, "Settle. You might have to pass on getting Irving to admit there are gas chambers, but that would be worth avoiding a trial." Unable to fathom signing a statement that "passed" on the gas chambers, I was about to ask what he thought should be my bottom line. Four million Jews murdered?

Three million? One set of gas chambers? Two? Before I could formulate the words, Anthony interceded: "We will not negotiate with an antisemite on historical truth." I said nothing but felt exceptionally well represented. I thought back to the Eliot book. Antisemites, irrespective of their standing in the broader world, were scoundrels and with scoundrels one does not compromise.

Reporters were beginning to ask about the case. In early 1999, over lunch in a small Bloomsbury bistro, I asked Anthony to delineate the topics I should avoid when talking to the press. He looked up from his salad and declared, "All of them. If you don't talk, most reporters will then drop the story, thereby denying Irving publicity and making him more likely to drop the case."

Later that night, I called good friends and told them that Anthony wanted me to keep silent and that I was thinking it over. Joe, an experienced litigator, observed that Anthony was not suggesting what I should do. He was instructing me. I protested that I was used to talking to the press. "I do it well. It's silly not to use my talents." Joe's wife, Amelia, a psychologist who knows me very well, interjected, "Deborah, you hate taking orders from anyone. Anytime. Anywhere." I laughed, acknowledging that her evaluation was, as the British say, "spot on." I recalled that according to family legend my first phrase was "Me do it." We were about to hang up when I said— more to myself than to them—"So much is on the line. And I, who love to lead, must cede control to someone else. I hate that." After a moment's pause, I added, "This is hard, excruciatingly hard."

—•—

# THREE

# AUSCHWITZ: A FORENSIC TOUR

"Don't worry, he's very good. He'll do an excellent job. Believe me the system works," Anthony said as we sat in a Mishcon conference room in the fall of 1998. He was trying to calm my nerves, but it wasn't doing much good. "If *your* legal system worked so well, I wouldn't be in this mess," I snapped in response. "And how's a newcomer going to get up to speed?"

Anthony had just explained that he and James, despite having served as the architects of much of my case, could not present it in court. The British legal system is divided between solicitors, who prepare a case up to trial, and barristers, who present it in court. Only barristers have the right of audience in the High Court. Solicitors may not, except in rare circumstances, speak. I was thunderstruck. Anthony and James knew this case inside and out. Anthony assured me that it was akin to preparing a case and then turning it over to a litigator to argue it in court. His reassurances did not allay my concerns. This case had a moral dimension that distinguished it, I believed, from other "normal" cases. Someone else might bring the legal knowledge, but would they have the same passion and commitment?

## RICHARD RAMPTON, QC

Anthony and Penguin's solicitors had selected Richard Rampton, one of England's leading barristers in the field of defamation and libel to present my case. Anthony described Rampton as someone with "a first-rate mind," no small compliment from a man who did not suffer lesser minds gladly.

Rampton was a queen's counsel or QC, a designation conferred upon the most accomplished barristers. Also known as "silks" because of the ornate silken robes they wear, QCs appear in court with a "junior," a barrister whose job it is to assist them in preparing the case.[1] Penguin chose Heather Rogers as its junior barrister. Anthony, having received "rights of audience" under the new Civil Procedure rules, giving him permission to speak in court, would be mine. I had asked some lawyers whose firms had offices in London to check out Rampton. They quickly reported back that he was a pillar of the London legal establishment. One said, "Whoever picked him, picked the best."

On a cold January morning in 1999, Anthony, James, and I went to meet Rampton. As we walked through Lincoln's Inn Fields, the largest square in London, I remembered it as the site of the "Old Curiosity Shop," a putative legacy from Charles Dickens. We crossed Fleet Street and entered The Temple, a vast enclave of Georgian buildings and gardens where barristers have their "chambers," British parlance for a barrister's office. One Brick Court, the site of Rampton's chambers, had specialized in libel and media law since the 1880s. We pushed open the heavy wood door and entered the dimly lit hallway. The stone staircase was well worn with age. We walked up to the receptionist on the second floor. After a short wait, she told us that Rampton was ready and directed us back down the stairs to his office on the first floor. Given his reputation and the stature of the cases he handled, I expected a formal, buttoned-up person. A man of medium build, with thinning white wavy hair, a gentle face, and rimless glasses, emerged to greet us. He was wearing a slightly rumpled corduroy suit, soft cotton shirt, and narrow yellow knit tie. I estimated that he was in his late fifties. I knew that he had studied classics and philosophy at Oxford. He had a soft, kindly voice with just a bit of a Scottish brogue: "Oh, hello, welcome, please do come in." His natural graciousness immediately put me at ease.

I remarked that Brick Court reminded me of the *Pickwick Papers*. "I feel as if I am entering the Dickensian to discuss the Kafkaesque." He laughed and told me my analogy was not off the mark. "Charles Dickens worked as a law clerk not far from here. About the Kafkaesque. . . . Well, we'll see to that."

Rampton's book-lined office was spacious enough to accommodate a large conference table that extended out from his heavy wooden desk. A roaring fire kept the space warm. On the floor near his desk were piles of books on the Holocaust. I spotted books by our experts as well as Raul Hilberg's classic, *The Destruction of European Jewry.* There were also a number of books by Irving. A horsehair powdered wig festooned with rows of curls sat on a wooden, skull-shaped stand. A black silk robe with immensely wide sleeves hung on the back of the door. The pungent odor of stale cigarette smoke left no doubt that Rampton was a smoker. He offered us tea and scurried about to brew it himself. While he did so, I quickly studied some of the photos on the fireplace mantle. He seemed to have children and grandchildren. In addition to family photos, there was a picture of a man who clearly resembled Rampton in fishing gear. When Rampton saw me studying it, he told me it was of his father, from whom he had gained a love of the sport.

Heather Rogers, Penguin's junior barrister, soon arrived. In her mid-thirties, she had short, dirty-blond hair that framed her face. She wore glasses, a dark gray lawyer's suit, plain white blouse, and no makeup or jewelry. She had a down-to-earth, no-nonsense quality about her. After we settled around the table, Rampton started off by saying, "We must discredit this man as a historian. He is a clever opponent, but he is more clever than he is wise. We cannot afford to underestimate him or to lose this case. It's too important."

It quickly became clear that Rampton was already conversant with the basic historical data. He had obviously spent time reading the Holocaust books piled on the floor. Rampton turned to me: "If we go to trial, I will probably not put you in the witness box. You are being sued for what you wrote. Having you give testimony will not advance our case. It will only divert the judge's attention from the main focus, David Irving." According to British law, Irving could not compel me to give testimony. I listened to Rampton with mixed emotions. I was relieved that I would not have to be cross-examined by a man whose views I abhorred and who certainly would use the opportunity to cross-examine me as a way of "settling scores" for the wrongs he felt he had suffered. At the same time, I was disappointed that I would not be able to openly express my contempt for him. I feared that people would think that I was frightened of facing him.

As the lawyers reviewed various legal details and parceled out assignments—some of which were so technical I felt as if I was listening to a conversation in a language I did not understand—I realized that everybody had a job in this diligently orchestrated effort. Expert witnesses would write reports. Our researchers, Nik and Thomas, would comb through the thousands of pages of documentation we had received from Irving and look for relevant information. Lawyers would oversee this work, prepare the various official documents that had to be submitted to the court, and begin to draft the interrogatories that Irving would be asked to answer. By now, I was accustomed to the fact that I was not leading the charge. But, for a moment I felt that I was a spectator—observing but not participating—in a drama where my work and reputation were on the line. It was all very disconcerting. Afraid that I was impeding the lawyers' progress, I stopped asking to have things explained and sat, rather uncharacteristically, silently by.

Over the next few months I returned to London, the frequent trips quickly becoming a routine. After settling into my hotel, I would go to Mishcon's offices to consult with Anthony and James, read documents, and watch videotapes of Irving's speeches. The expert witnesses and researchers would brief me on their work. In the evening I would pick up take-out food and eat it in my room as I reviewed additional trial-related materials. Then, a day or two later, I would fly back to the United States, where I would disabuse my friends and colleagues of the notion that there was anything high-powered or exciting about these journeys.

In June 1999, I returned to London for a few days. I then flew to Berlin to attend an academic conference. From there I was to continue on to Auschwitz to meet Richard Rampton, Heather Rogers, Robert Jan van Pelt, and solicitors from both Davenport Lyons and Mishcon. The trip was designed to give the lawyers—Rampton in particular—a firsthand encounter with the site. A few months earlier the AJC's Ken Stern, who had become an ex officio member of the legal team, told Rampton that a trip to Auschwitz was a must. Ken, a lawyer who had argued before the Supreme Court, said that he would never consider doing a murder case without having a three-dimensional image of the scene. This, in some way, was a very large murder case. Hearing this, Rampton became terribly pale. "I know it's important," he told Ken, "but I just don't know how I will endure it."

Though I had visited Auschwitz a number of times, I anticipated that this would be a different kind of visit. We would inspect the physical and documentary evidence which demonstrated that Irving's claims about the camp were bogus. I hated being in Auschwitz, but was glad this visit would give me the chance to get to know Rampton a bit better.

Berlin seemed a fitting place to begin this journey as the destruction process that culminated in Auschwitz had its roots there. After giving my paper and looking for relief from drawn-out academic deliberations, I went "sightseeing." For me that entailed going to Jewish- or Holocaust-related sites. While I admire Germany's cultural and scenic beauty, much of which is spectacular, I find it difficult to enjoy. I do, however, always make an effort to see the renowned Pergamon Museum, which contains fantastic artifacts, including the huge Altar of Zeus and the famous Ishtar Gate from Babylon. But on this trip I skipped this visit, going directly to Wannsee Haus, the site of the January 1942 conference at which Reinhard Heydrich, Himmler's second-in-command, explained the logistics of the Final Solution to the directors of the primary government ministries. Heydrich knew that, unless the bureaucrats fully cooperated, it would be impossible to implement the Final Solution. This gathering was probably the only meeting at which the killing process was openly discussed before leaders of the ministerial bureaucracy.

At Wannsee Haus, a villa on the shores of a crystal clear Berlin lake, various documents, including the letters of invitation to the conference and the minutes of the deliberations, are on display in the room where the meeting occurred. I had been there before, but somehow this visit felt very different. I thought of how Adolf Eichmann described this meeting at his trial. According to Eichmann, Heydrich came to Wannsee "expecting considerable stumbling blocks and difficulties." To his surprise and delight, the ministers conveyed a sense of "agreement that . . . had not been expected."[2] The ninety-minute gathering concluded with congratulatory cognac.

After visiting the exhibit, I walked a few hundred yards to the adjacent beach. In what must be one of the world's most dissonant scenes, people were swimming, launching small sailboats, and sunbathing in the shadow of this villa. I bought a bottle of mineral water at the kiosk, found a spot at the water's edge, and, needing to talk to someone who would instinctively understand how the history of this place was linked to the battle in which I was engaged, I called Anthony. I told him I was just "checking in." Then I described my visit to the room where German bureaucrats decided on the process of the Final Solution.

Anxious to visit a site of Jewish life—Jews as subject, not object—I headed for the Oranienburger Strasse Synagogue. Dedicated in 1866 at a ceremony attended by Prussian prime minister Bismarck, it was one of the first synagogues German authorities allowed to be built on a prestigious street rather than on a back alley. A magnificent Moorish structure with a red-

striped yellow-brick-and-brown-stone facade and a gleaming bulbous dome
160 feet above the street topped by a Jewish star, its sanctuary had accommodated over three thousand people. For Berlin Jews, the building symbolized
their freedom to aspire to full participation in the secular world. Set ablaze in
November 1938 on *Kristallnacht,* when hundreds of German synagogues
were destroyed, the synagogue was saved when the local police chief held off
the Nazi attackers and ordered the fire department to save it. Today a plaque
commemorates his bravery. Ironically, the massive sanctuary was badly damaged by British bombers in 1943 and demolished by the East Germans in
1958.

   After years of neglect, the facade and expansive vestibule had recently
been repaired. An open gravel field spread out where the sanctuary once
stood. Pillars marked its precise boundaries. At the far end of this field, in a
style reminiscent of an archaeological site, the bits and pieces of the pulpit
and the Holy Ark, which had been excavated from the rubble, had been
placed in their original position. Some seemed eerily suspended in air. Standing at what once was the entrance to this magnificent sanctuary and looking
out at this contemporary void, I thought of the cognac-drinking bureaucrats
at Wannsee. The absence, not just of the sanctuary, but of the community
whose destruction they had coordinated, was palpable.

## JESUITS, THE WHITE HOUSE, HOLLYWOOD,
## AND THE KILLING FIELDS

The next day I boarded a train to Poland. I found my compartment and took
out the eight-hundred-page report on Auschwitz by Robert Jan van Pelt. I
used the train journey to review it in anticipation of our visit to the camp. As
we approached Krakow, I interrupted my reading with reflections on my
family's history. My father left Germany in his twenties because of its terrible economic situation. Although he had no immediate family in the United
States, he came anyway. My mother's parents had left Poland shortly before
World War I. What if they had not done so? Generally, I find such hypotheticals historically invalid, but as I headed east, it was hard not to engage in
such reveries, if only in passing. As the train pulled into the station, I felt myself overcome by a deep determination to fight with all my heart.

   I arrived in Krakow before the rest of the group. After settling into my

hotel, I called Father Stanislav Musial, a Jesuit I first met in 1989 in the cemetery behind Krakow's sixteenth-century Rema Synagogue. The cemetery
contains the remains of both great Jewish scholars and Jews whose identities
have been obliterated by history. Musial was with a small group of tourists.
When he saw me somberly studying one of the gravestones, he tearfully
said, "I'm sorry that all there is for you to visit here are cemeteries and
killing places."

Father Musial had once served as the secretary of the Polish Episcopate
Commission for the Dialogue with Judaism. In that capacity he had drafted
statements about the role of the Church during the Holocaust. He was
highly regarded by those who took part in Catholic-Jewish dialogues. All that
changed during the debate over a twenty-foot cross erected by Carmelite
nuns at their convent in Auschwitz. Jews strongly opposed the cross, arguing
that it lent the death camp a distinctly Christian character. Musial, who participated in negotiations to try to resolve the problem, broke with many
Polish-Catholic leaders when he wrote: "It can never be sufficiently emphasized that the fate of the Jews during the last war was incomparably worse
than that of any other nation." The Polish primate, Cardinal Jozef Glemp,
took a markedly different stance. Falling back on traditional Jewish stereotypes, he said Jews consider themselves to be a "people raised above all
others" and Jewish power lies "in the mass media which are easily at [their]
disposal in many countries."[3] Other Polish clerics echoed his views. In a television appearance, Father Musial criticized Church leaders for this position
and urged a dialogue with the Jews. Scholars who studied this debate describe Musial's comments as a "notable change of tone," particularly when
one considers that they came from a Polish clergyman.[4] That change of tone
did not endear him to his superiors. Shortly thereafter he was reassigned to
an old-age home for senile women. He wryly observed, "They will pardon
you everything but not attacking the bishops." Many of his fellow priests
shunned him. The Jesuit publishing house refused to let him write the introduction to a book on Jews and Christians in Poland, even though the American professor editing it recommended him. No longer was he invited to
conferences.

We spent the afternoon walking through Kazimierz, Krakow's former
Jewish quarter, whose central square figured so prominently in Spielberg's
*Schindler's List*. Members of Krakow's Jewish community kept stopping

Father Musial to wish him well. When we ordered coffee at the café in the Jewish cultural center, the manager refused to let us pay.

Father Musial seemed to internalize the tragedy of the *Shoah*. Over coffee, he described his shame that in places such as France, Roman Catholic leaders felt compelled, long after the Holocaust, to apologize for the Church's failure to help Jewish victims. This Catholic priest, who had lived most of his life under communism, noted, not without a bit of irony, "French communists did not have to apologize. They had nothing to apologize for."[5] Father Musial found the Church's failure, particularly when compared to the communists' record, "deeply embarrassing."

When we parted, he said, "Be strong." I told him that we both were fighting, but that his battle was much lonelier than mine. I was receiving support from many directions while he was shut out from participating in the very dialogue he had nurtured and was compelled to work in a nursing home for people with dementia. "No," he assured me, "this, too, is God's work. I am quiet with my conscience. Before, my hands were tied. Now, I am free. I can say anything." Musial had spoken truth to power.

After leaving Father Musial, I wandered through Krakow. It was a beautiful day, sunny and clear, the kind of day that I imagined was atmospherically impossible in a place so close to Auschwitz. The city was festooned with yellow-and-white banners, the Vatican's colors, in honor of the forthcoming visit of the pope. I walked to the Vistula River where my grandmother, who came from Krakow, remembered folk dancing with her classmates, recalling these days as a "golden age."

From there I walked to Market Square, the central point of this medieval city. An immense area, it is dominated by a seventeenth-century town hall. I sat down at one of the small folding tables in the square, ordered an espresso, and began to write in my journal when my cell phone rang. The caller identified himself as a member of the White House staff. Assuming that one of my friends was playing a trick on me, I responded, "Yeah. Right." Assuring me that he indeed worked for the White House Office of Presidential Personnel, which handles presidential appointments, the caller suggested that I call back to ascertain that he was legitimate. He then informed me that President Clinton had just reappointed me to a second term on the United States Holocaust Memorial Council. I had just returned to my journal when the phone rang again. A movie producer, who had heard about the case, wanted to know if I had assigned the rights for the film version of my story.

Amazed that he thought the case worthy of a film, I told him that I thought
it premature to even be thinking like that.

The next morning I departed for Auschwitz with Veronica Byrnes, a Mishcon attorney. As we pulled up at the camp entrance, Rampton, Heather,
Robert Jan, and Mark, the Penguin attorney, were waiting. As I emerged
from the car, Rampton announced, "Aha, 'tis the Author of our Misfortune."

We began our visit at the archives. When we entered, the architectural
plans for the crematoria were already spread out on the table. Some of these
meticulous plans had been drawn by inmates, who, Robert Jan pointed out,
signed them with their prison numbers, no names. All I could think of at
that moment was Primo Levi's observation about his time in Auschwitz,
where a number was tattooed on his arm: "Only a man is worthy of a
name."[6]

Robert Jan stressed that every decision about this camp had implications
for the physical plant. If prisoners were to be housed, barracks were needed.
If they were to be stripped of their possessions, storehouses were necessary
for sorting the bounty. And if people were to be killed, a cost-effective
method had to be devised to do so.[7] Looking at the drawings, I remembered
a 1943 photograph of the architects and engineers responsible for designing
and building Auschwitz. Before the war, some had been civilian architects
and town planners. One had trained at Germany's Bauhaus. In the photograph they are seen smiling proudly. In my mind I tried to reconcile the faces
of the men in the picture with the plans in front of me.[8] The existence of
these architectural plans and records is a fluke. This is how it happened. As
the Soviets approached Auschwitz in January 1945, the Germans destroyed
the camp command center, and with it much of the documentation on the
killing apparatus. In the confusion, they forgot about the camp construction
office. Its files housed substantial documentary material, including the working drawings for the crematoria.[9] This set of plans had been used at the
building site. Stained and torn, they have scribbling and penciled comments
on them.

Rampton peppered Robert Jan with questions about doors, windows, el-
evators, and incineration capacity. Sitting in the archives of the world's great
killing fields, I felt like I was observing a dissertation defense. Robert Jan explained that prior to becoming a place for murder, Auschwitz was a concen-

tration camp. Crematoria were needed for the disposal of prisoners' corpses. These structures were designed to conform to the German civilian building code. Thus, the architects were compelled to include dissection rooms, even though Auschwitz authorities had not requested them. Eventually the doctors—Mengele best known among them—put them to use for their medical experiments.

When Birkenau, a satellite camp adjacent to Auschwitz, was designated as a killing center, the two crematoria there, known as cremas 2 and 3, were redesigned (crema 1 was in Auschwitz). The morgues were transformed into gas chambers. In December 1942, Walther Dejaco, assistant to the chief of the Auschwitz building office, drew the changes needed for the addition of the gas chambers. Dejaco, who was high enough in the SS hierarchy to be trusted to make the changes, replaced the corpse chute, originally designed for moving bodies to the morgue, with a staircase. Robert Jan observed, "Dead bodies are slid down a chute. Live people could walk to their death." The staircase led to an undressing room and the undressing room to the gas chamber.[10] In January 1943, plans were also drawn up by Dejaco for two new gas chambers, cremas 4 and 5. Since these were not existing buildings that needed to be redesigned, they were built to function far more efficiently. The entire structure was on one floor so the bodies could be moved directly to the crematorium. The roof over the gas chamber was lower than in the rest of the building, allowing for more economical use of gas. Rampton asked why these facilities could not be morgues. Robert Jan pointed to the heating system and asked, "Why would you heat a morgue?"[11]

The drawings for cremas 4 and 5 called for 30-by-40-centimeter windows through which the Zyklon B was to be thrown. Robert Jan showed us a February 1943 order from the Auschwitz Construction Office for the "production of 12 gas-tight doors [window shutters] approximately 30/40 cm." He then led us from the archives to a small storeroom in which there were three decrepit 30-by-40-centimeter window shutters. The remnants of a gas-tight seal were visible around their edges. The windows closed from the outside, a decidedly impractical arrangement for any room, unless one wanted to ensure that those inside could not open them. The drawings, work order, and remaining windows constituted a simple but stunning example of the confluence of evidence.

Around midday we headed to the cafeteria. Auschwitz is a tourist site and every such site must have a food facility. Conversation was muted.

Everyone studiously avoided discussing what we had just seen. I quietly told Heather, who seemed pale and shaken, that according to Jewish tradition, no object is inherently good or bad. A surgeon will use a knife to save a life while someone else might use it to murder. Architects have used their skills to design great wonders, while the Auschwitz architects used their skills for decidedly different purposes. After lunch we visited Auschwitz I, the concentration camp section of the Auschwitz complex. Throughout the day, Rampton focused like a laser beam on the topic, asking a broad array of questions about the camp.

We were scheduled to spend the night at a hostel in Auschwitz. When we arrived, we learned that there were not enough rooms for all of us. Happy not to have to stay so close to the camp, I volunteered to return to Krakow with Veronica. Robert Jan insisted we all have a drink first. Rampton looked pleased by the suggestion. We piled back into our cars and headed to a local watering hole. Robert Jan assured us it was a good place. "Great vodka. Good food." I told Robert Jan that while I expected him to know a great deal about the camp, I did not expect his expertise to include Auschwitz watering holes. He explained that one could not spend long stays in this place doing research without finding out where to get a good drink.

After a few glasses of wine, Veronica and I headed back to Krakow. We had dinner in the center square of Kazimierz, the old Jewish quarter. Trendy restaurants and jazz clubs were situated next to sixteenth-century synagogues. This was where the Nazis began the liquidation of the ghetto. At dinner I told Veronica that on my trips to London, when I was plagued by jet lag, I watched cricket games even though I did not understand the game. Veronica, a cricket aficionado, explained the rules to me. Midway through her explanation, my mind began to wander and I realized that I wasn't really interested in the game. I needed, just for the night, to forget Auschwitz-Birkenau and its history.

## FORENSICS—NOT MEMORY

The next morning we met at the entrance to Birkenau, the death camp. Robert Jan suggested that we begin by walking around its perimeter. Rampton rather sternly instructed him, "Only ask us to do things which move the case forward. This is not a sentimental journey. It's for forensics." I was startled by how he seemed to be able to so explicitly sever one from the other.

Robert Jan thought the walk worthwhile in order to give us some sense of the enormity of the place. Rampton very grudgingly agreed. I had visited the camp a number of times and had climbed the main guard tower, from which one can see the vast reaches of the camp. However, I had never skirted the perimeter. The walk gave me a far more tangible perspective on its size. As we traversed the camp, I reflected on Rampton's comment about this not being a memorializing trip. Clearly, forensics had to rule the day. We had picked Rampton because he was a first-rate barrister. But I did not understand how a trip to these killing fields could not have some element of memorialization, particularly for a first-time visitor. I tried to convince myself that I should be pleased by his unidimensional focus.

In the women's camp, we stopped at the death barracks. Women destined for the gas chamber were held here until they were murdered. It is a dark, damp room with rows of multitiered barracks and little else. Robert Jan explained that the Germans waited until they had enough people to fill the gas chamber because it operated more efficiently—it used less gas and people died more rapidly—when it was full. In addition, it wasn't economical to fire up the crematoria until there was a substantial number of bodies to burn. Since these inmates were to be killed, they received no food or water. Our normally garrulous group grew quiet. As we exited the barracks, Rampton tripped and let out an expletive. A smoker with a preference for the French brand *Gitanes,* he immediately lit a cigarette. When he finished, he lit another.

We proceeded from the death barracks to the delousing building where clothing was disinfected with Zyklon B, the same gas used to kill people. This was the facility where Leuchter had found a concentration of gas residue higher than in the gas chambers. Rampton closely questioned Robert Jan about Leuchter's findings. As Rampton's questions grew more aggressive, I became decidedly uncomfortable. He seemed to be demanding that Robert Jan prove that people were murdered in the gas chambers.[12] Finally, Rampton asked impatiently, "Isn't it time trustworthy experts did an extensive scientific study of this place?" I was stunned by Rampton's apparent conviction that we needed a scientific study to "prove" the gas chambers were killing factories. Unable to contain myself, I burst out, "Why do we need scientific studies? We have the evidence." Rampton glared at me and, in a tone that conveyed his annoyance, said, "Pardon me, but I need to know." I said nothing, but inside I was shaking. Unable to fathom why Rampton was shooting these questions at Robert Jan, I slipped to the back of the group.

We left the delousing building and proceeded to the remains of crema 4. Emotionally and physically exhausted, I sat down on one of its brick walls. All I could think about was that the trial seemed destined to morph from an examination of Irving's abuse of historical records into a debate on whether or not the Holocaust took place. Worse, there was nothing I could do to change this.

I was frightened. Birkenau is a horrible place in any circumstance. Now it felt outright unbearable. When Heather joined me, I couldn't help but tell her directly, "If this becomes a 'did the Holocaust happen?' trial, I am out of here." I had no idea what I meant by "I am out of here," but I said it anyway, even though there was no way I could halt the legal process at this point. Her response was empathetic. "David Irving is not about honest inquiry. Demonstrating that to the court is what this trial is about." She reassured me that the legal team would not allow the trial to become the debate with Holocaust deniers that I had studiously avoided for years. "Everyone involved in this case recognizes that it cannot be that." Her calm, but determined, manner and her evident empathy gave me some comfort.

We proceeded to inspect the site of the little farmhouses that had served as the first gas chambers. To do so, we had to edge our way across a swampy drainage ditch. There was a narrow concrete ledge with a chain-link fence across the ditch. Trying not to fall into the murky water, I held tight to the fence as I inched my way across. The mosquitoes hovering over the stagnant water took aim and I did not have a free hand to brush them away. By the time I reached the other side, my face and arms were full of red blotches.

Toward the end of the day, when we stood at the ruins of crema 2, I quietly explained that I could not be in this place without an act of commemoration. With Rampton's admonition about this visit having a legal—not a sentimental—objective ringing in my ears, I self-consciously invited the others to join me for a memorial prayer. We gathered round the remains of the gas chambers. I recited the traditional Jewish prayer for the dead, the *El molei rachamim*, "Oh God full of mercy," which asked that those who suffered so at this site be granted a restful peace under the sheltering wings of heaven. After saying it in English, I repeated it, despite being conscious of the time, in Hebrew. I was surprised to hear someone quietly joining me. I looked up to see that Robert Jan had covered his head and was repeating the words. Only then did I realize that he was Jewish. Worried about removing the focus from forensics, I did it all rather breathlessly. No one said anything as we walked to our cars.

As we drove out, we passed the Carmelite convent and the cross. We stopped at the rather sparse hostel where the rest of the group had stayed. While we were sitting in the bucolic garden waiting for everyone to retrieve their luggage, Rampton's cell phone rang. It was his wife Carolyn. I could not help but hear him say, "I have just come from what certainly must be the most awful place on the face of the earth. But we will talk about that when I return." With that he bid her farewell and we resumed the forensics.

A few hours later, after a swim at our Krakow hotel, a desperately needed shower, and change of clothing, we gathered for dinner in a nice restaurant off Market Square. Rampton, who has a passion for good scotch and even better wine, ordered drinks and a number of bottles of wine for the table. No one refused. Though we tried to talk of other things, the conversation kept coming back to Auschwitz. Rampton noted that there was no room in a civilized world for a place like Auschwitz, even as a tourist attraction. He mused that if he had been assigned to make the architectural drawings he probably would have complied. "Because I am a coward," he said. No one said anything as he continued: "Why did I have to see this place? Not to learn about it, but to be appalled by it. . . . In the courtroom I will have to memorialize this place." Mark Bateman, the Davenport Lyons solicitor, said to me in an apologetic tone, "I know some of our questions might have seemed insensitive but we had to ask them in order to prepare for trial." I thanked him for his concern, assured him I understood, and proceeded to down too many glasses of iced vodka.

Early the next morning, we flew back to London. I headed directly for Mishcon's offices, settling into a basement conference room to watch videotapes of Irving's speeches. In one Irving declared that it was time to "sink the battleship Auschwitz." His statements were greeted by laughter from his audience. One tape showed a neo-Nazi rally and march at Halle, a medieval East German city that was the birthplace of Reinhard Heydrich, who chaired the meeting at Wannsee. Rows of skinhead "bully boys" marched in front of Irving. Their leather jackets, metal-studded belts, and Doc Martens stood in marked contrast to his dark suit. Some marchers carried the *Reichskriegsflagge,* the Reich battle flag that is often used by German protestors in lieu of the banned Nazi swastika. When Irving stood up to speak, the crowd inter-rupted his speech with chants of *"Sieg Heil! Sieg Heil!"* Irving tried to quell the chants with a warning that this was not helpful to their cause.

I turned off the tape and sat quietly for a few moments, trying to process these ghastly scenes. Finally, I went up to James's office, and told him I was going to the British Museum to see the Assyrian exhibit. James looked perplexed. "Why visit that exhibit when there is so much material you want to review?" I explained that in the eighth century B.C.E., King Sennacherib built a magnificent palace at Nineveh. He boasted of laying waste to "cities without number in Judah," and receiving heavy tribute from the Israelite king, Hezekiah. "But why," James asked, still puzzled, "visit it *now?*" I told him what my friend Grace Grossman, the curator of a major Judaica mu-seum, said to me before I left for London. "Once the Assyrians tried to de-stroy the Jewish people. Today their remnant is in museums. We're still here. Remember that when you face David Irving."

Shortly after my return home, the *New York Times* ran an article on the case. I knew it was in the offing and awaited it with some anticipation. Anthony and I, believing that it was crucial that the *New York Times* get the story right, decided to talk to the paper. This would be our first high-profile coverage. I turned to the "Arts and Ideas" section, and stared at the headline:

"TAKING A HOLOCAUST SKEPTIC SERIOUSLY"

Irving, a Holocaust "skeptic"? Surely any reporter who did the least bit of research on Irving knew he was far more than a "skeptic." Knowing that headlines often fail to accurately convey a story's content, I read the article. In this instance, the headline truly reflected the substance of the article, which began with a question: "Can a writer who thinks the Holocaust was a hoax still be a great historian?" Written by Don Guttenplan, a London-based freelance writer making his first contribution to the paper, it proposed that the case "poses disturbing questions about the practice of history." Irving had told him that "there were never any gas chambers at Auschwitz." Ac-cording to Irving, this did not make him a denier because his comments "are true." Irving had also told Guttenplan, "It may be unfortunate for Professor Lipstadt that she is the one who finds herself dragged out of the line and shot." Guttenplan seemed unperturbed by Irving's imagery and passed over these rather startling statements.

Guttenplan had also solicited comments from other historians. Raul Hilberg declared, "I am not for taboos." Mark Mazower of Princeton insisted that historians cannot restrict themselves to those with whom they are "intellectually akin." These comments made me wonder how Guttenplan had presented the case to them. I certainly was neither trying to impose a taboo nor silence Irving. In fact, Irving was trying to do that to me. My critique of Irving had nothing to do with intellectual differences, as Mazower suggested. Unless, of course, from Mazower's perspective, my critique of Irving's Holocaust denial and antisemitism somehow rendered us *intellectual* opposites. Though Guttenplan had been told by both Anthony and me of specific instances where Irving had seriously distorted evidence about the Holocaust, he nonetheless depicted this case as two historians slugging it out over historical interpretations. It seemed to me that his reflexive desire to be even-handed or just provocative overrode and obliterated his knowledge of the evidence.

About a week later, Guttenplan called to inquire about our reaction to the article. Anthony minced no words. "Deborah thought it was awful. So did I." Shortly thereafter Guttenplan contacted me to acknowledge that I had "grounds" for being angry with him. He claimed historians were frightened, because of Irving's litigious reputation, to be quoted on the record. Therefore, the article ended up favoring Irving. His first draft, he contended, had more accurately reflected my position. However, his editor at the *Times,* Patricia Cohen, considered it too partisan and engaged, which he interpreted as a demand for more balance. He told me that acceding to her request, and in conjunction with his attempt, "as two Jews trying to be fair," he could see how some readers might think he ultimately bent too far.[13] I was amazed that he was willing to self-censor because he was a Jew and that he attributed the same sentiments to his editor at the paper.

The incident reminded me that what seemed so obvious to *me* about the essence of this case was not readily evident to others, even if they were reporting on it for the *New York Times.*

# FOUR

# OUR OBJECTIVE CHANGES

"A knotted web of distortions, suppressions and manipulations became evident in every single instance which we examined." This was how Richard Evans described, in the opening pages of his expert report, his foray through Irving's writings on the Holocaust. In the next paragraph, Evans admitted that he had been caught unaware: "I was not prepared for the sheer depths of duplicity which I encountered in Irving's treatment of the historical sources, nor for the way in which this dishonesty permeated his entire written and spoken output. It is as all pervasive in his early work as it is in his later publications. . . . His numerous mistakes . . . are calculated and deliberate." Evans and his researchers, Nik and Thomas, who by the time Evans submitted his report in the summer of 1999, had worked on the case for eighteen months, far longer than anyone ever assumed would be necessary, did not have to balance Irving's distortions against his use of legitimate methods of historical inquiry. They did not have to do so because they found distortions in "every single instance [they] examined." After detailing numerous examples of Irving's historical malfeasance regarding the Holocaust and the bombing of Dresden, Evans wrote: "If we mean by historian someone who is concerned to discover the truth about the past and to give as accurate a representation of it as possible, then Irving is not a historian . . . Irving is essentially an ideologue who uses history . . . in order to further his own political purposes." Evans concluded that "not one of [Irving's] books, speeches or articles, not one paragraph, not one sentence in any of them, can be taken on trust as an accurate representation of its historical subject. All of them are completely worthless as history."[1]

As I completed his 740-page report, I thought back to our dinner a year earlier when Evans had so summarily dismissed my suggestion that he tell the court that David Irving is no historian. He had not thought it efficacious to argue that the author of over twenty books on history was not a historian. The encounter with the evidence, however, resulted in Evans's striking about-face and the devastating critique of Irving's work that followed. Evans didn't allow his personal or popular opinion to skew objective information facing him. And this, I reminded myself, is how real historians operate.

Almost giddy with excitement, I dashed off a congratulatory email to Evans with a copy to James. Concerned about sounding like a breathless American, I adopted what I imagined was proper British restraint. "Congratulations on the report. It is quite good." James quickly responded, "What don't you like about Evans's report?" "Nothing," I responded. After a few emails the mystery was resolved. My use of "quite" had in British parlance, damned the report with faint praise. I quickly rectified the situation with a short email: "A stunning historiographic work."

Later, as I crossed the Emory campus, I met my colleague Mel Konner and jubilantly told him that Evans thought Irving was no historian. He was surprised—not about Evans's conclusions—but by my excitement: "You knew Irving wasn't a credible historian when you wrote your book." I felt chastised and even a little naive. Mel was right. Evans had only confirmed what I had long known to be the case. I fumbled for an explanation. "When I first met Evans he suspected that my evaluation of Irving was hyperbolic. Now, after having done the research, he knows I'm right."

My explanation was plausible but not sufficient. I realized that Evans's report constituted a validation of sorts, a subjective response to scholars who dismissed Irving's Holocaust denial as unfortunate quirkiness. Evans's findings also confirmed that settling or ignoring Irving's charges, as some urged, was not an option.

On a more personal level, Evans's report came at a most opportune moment. I felt overwhelmed by the havoc this fight was inflicting on me. I had set my new research aside, filing away the reams of archival material I had collected. My repeated rushed trips to London left me perennially exhausted. Despite repeated reassurances from Herb Friedman, who was still raising money for the defense fund, that I not worry, I *was* deeply concerned that we would not have enough funds to fight this to the end. I worried about leaving my elderly mother while I spent four months in London. Moreover, increasing numbers of survivors kept telling me, "We are counting on you to protect our history." I thought their reactions were overstated. Even if I lost, their history would not be decimated. No one person or group of people could do that. Nonetheless, I found their comments a heavy responsibility. They kept me awake at night. All I could think of was that, because of the vagaries of the British libel system, we might lose. Simply put, I was tired, nervous, and frightened, and Evans's report—in addition to being a great research work—was the boost I needed and it came just at the moment I needed it.

I forced myself to ignore the doubters and wrap my mind around the many colleagues and friends who were unquestionably in my corner. Many people were contributing to the defense fund without even being asked. Emory University—both the administration and my colleagues—continued to offer unbridled support. I had told a colleague that I was planning to use my regularly scheduled sabbatical leave for the trial. She pointed out that the two concepts—sabbatical and trial—were counterintuitive and urged me to request a paid leave. When I mentioned this to the provost, she immediately agreed: "Sabbaticals are not for being on trial. We will treat it as if you are teaching your regular courses, except your venue is a British courtroom." In September, as courses were being scheduled for the spring semester, she called again. "Can you find someone to teach your courses on the Holocaust while you're in London?" She explained that the university administration felt it was not sufficient to just support me. "If your courses are not offered," she continued, "it would be a sort of victory for Irving, depriving students of a chance to study this material." When I called colleagues at other universities to look for candidates, they were amazed. "Your provost offered without your asking? Unbelievable," a friend exclaimed.

And of course, my legal team continued to be the bedrock of support. On the eve of Yom Kippur, Anthony called to wish me well. Paraphrasing the traditional Jewish greeting, he said with a note of solemnity in his voice, "May you be inscribed in both the Heavenly and Earthly Books of Judgment during the coming year."

A few weeks later, Irving sent a settlement offer. His terms were simple. Penguin and I would each have to pay £500 to a charity for the handicapped, withdraw my book from circulation, and publicly apologize. I instantaneously told Anthony to reject it. "The only settlement I'll accept is *his* acknowledgment that he had no grounds to bring this case because everything I said was true. And there's not a snowball's chance in hell we are going to get that," I told Anthony.

While I knew that I would never settle, I feared that Penguin might be tempted. Legal costs had skyrocketed. A three- to four-month trial, which is what the lawyers anticipated, would push the bills into the stratosphere. Penguin's insurer was paying the bills, but at some point they might pull the plug. While we waited for Penguin's decision, Rampton called to tell me that he would represent me if Penguin dropped out and would do so pro bono if necessary. Shortly thereafter Penguin informed Rampton that they were resolute in their determination to fight the case.

I wondered if the settlement offer might indicate that Irving was contemplating dropping the case. If he did so, he could save face by claiming that he could not compete with the formidable forces—a multinational corporation and a putative international Jewish conspiracy—arraigned against him. On his website he described me as the "gold-tipped spearhead of the enemies of the truth, who hired her . . . to destroy me, my reputation, and my legitimacy as an historian."[2] When I asked James about the chances of Irving settling, he said with a look of disgust, "I've given up trying to figure out what this guy will do." As we spoke, I realized my hopes had changed. For the past three years we had mounted an aggressive defense, in part, to convince him to drop the case. Every one of my daily conversations with James or Anthony would, inevitably, contain the question, "Any word on his dropping the case?" Now, as the trial was poised to begin, I found myself hoping he would not. We had gleaned a wealth of damning information from his discovery. If he abandoned the case, it would have to remain private. I could never reveal the antisemitic and racist comments he had made in his diaries and speeches. James also began to talk about his growing ambivalence. "I always try to keep my clients out of court. Trials are unpredictable and expensive. Somehow this feels different." It would also be horrible, he acknowledged, to have access to this damning material and not be able to make it public.

## NOVEMBER 1999: GUNFIGHT AT THE OK CORRAL

The final pretrial hearing was scheduled for early November 1999. Anthony, who had kept me away from previous hearings, called to tell me to come.

The hearing would be before Judge Charles Gray, who would preside in our case. Anthony felt it worthwhile for me to see Judge Gray in action and for him to see that I took this matter seriously enough to come from the United States. The hearing was held in a traditional courtroom, the kind made famous by a host of British dramas. By chance, Irving and I entered the courtroom from opposite sides and ended up facing each other in the well of the courtroom. For a second, I had visions of the Gunfight at the OK Corral. Instead, without acknowledging each other's presence, we each took our seats at large wooden tables, which were but a few feet from one another.

A barrel-chested man, who is well over six feet tall, Irving has a full, almost bouffant, head of graying hair, dark sharp eyes, rough features, a ruddy, rather blotchy complexion, and unbelievably large hands. Most people look small when they stand next to him. His thick eyebrows spike upward in little peaks at the far edges of his eyes, giving him a rather forbidding look. He wore a dark blue, pin-striped three-piece suit and white shirt. He carried a plastic shopping bag full of books and papers. A few minutes later Judge Gray entered and took his seat. A tall slim man, with tinted glasses, a square jaw, and salt-and-pepper hair, Gray wore a double-breasted conservative dark gray suit, court regalia such as wigs and robes having been dispensed with for these hearings. Before being appointed to the bench Judge Gray had been a QC specializing in libel law. Rampton speculated that he had been assigned to this trial because the court authorities knew the media would be watching closely.

As soon as we began, Irving handed Judge Gray a list of items he would be raising in this hearing. Irving appeared to me—a total novice—to be familiar with courtroom procedure. He self-assuredly delineated his objections to our evidence. Evans's report should not be admitted because it sought to define a historian when there was no objective standard for doing so. Rampton responded that Evans's report addressed standards of historiography. There was a modus operandi to which all historians adhere and that, Rampton stressed, does not include lying and falsification of documents. Judge Gray rejected Irving's request.

Irving then challenged Chris Browning's report. In the chaos of managing over one hundred linear feet of documents, a paralegal had inadvertently sent Irving the penultimate copy of Browning's report. Shortly thereafter, she corrected her mistake and sent him the final copy. Irving noticed that in this version Browning had deleted references to certain documents. Irving contended that this proved that Browning had "manipulated documents" and was "guilty of precisely the malfeasance of which I am accused."[3] When Judge Gray decided that this argument was best left for the trial, Irving declared, "Good. Christopher Browning should suffer the humiliation of being asked about this in the witness box." Irving then turned to Rampton and said, "I must commend the defense on the quality of these expert reports." It seemed strange to hear him praising reports—two of which he had just tried to have thrown out—that devastated his claims about the Holocaust. I recalled the Hollywood aphorism: I don't care what you say about me, as long as you spell my name right.

Irving next complained that, in my role as the "willing executioner" of an international Jewish campaign, I had falsely claimed in my book that he had been invited to a conference in Stockholm along with Louis Farrakhan and representatives of the Palestinian terrorist organizations Hamas and Hezbollah. After my book was published I learned that this report was indeed false. In our pretrial submission to the court we did not address this charge, indicating that we did not intend to contest it.

Judge Gray told Irving that it was common in libel cases for the defense not to defend every defamatory statement. Irving was, however, not prepared to let this matter pass. "To be called a rotten historian is one thing; to be called a terrorist is quite another. This charge puts my life in danger. The Israeli secret service has a habit of sticking hypodermic needles filled with nerve gas in the neck of its enemies. People who appear at conferences with representatives of organizations they dislike are their enemies." When the judge again explained that it was our prerogative to ignore this matter, Irving turned to Rampton and issued his own warning. "If the defense does not plead to this, they are the architects of their own misfortune." Completely unfazed by this, Rampton shrugged. I, however, was unnerved. James saw and counseled me not to worry. The situation was akin, he explained, to my having written Irving was a pickpocket, arsonist, and murderer. "If you're wrong about the lesser charge but correct about the other, far more serious, charges, it should not really harm us. The court will be likely to find in your favor. Maybe Irving did not attend this conference, but he has interacted with many other dubious types. Therefore, his presence at this particular conference is probably immaterial." I knew James was trying to ease my concerns, but all I heard were his qualifications: "it should not *really* harm us. . . . *likely* find in your favor. . . . *probably* immaterial." After the hearing we gathered around the large table in Rampton's chambers. "My instincts tell me we are going to go to trial," he soberly said. I felt a surge of adrenaline, then, reflecting on what lay ahead, a terrible sense of foreboding.

Prior to returning to Atlanta, Anthony counseled me to prepare for a trial that would last at least four months, maybe five. Not looking forward to such an extended period of hotel life, particularly in the hotels I had been frequenting, I began to look for a place to live. Just as I was beginning my trek, James called to tell me that the owner of the Athenaeum, a five-star hotel within walking distance of Buckingham Palace and Hyde Park, had heard about my case. Touched by the fight I was waging, he urged me to consider renting one of the hotel's apartments. Housed in a quiet row of Edwardian town houses, the one-bedroom apartments—with their postage-sized kitchens—were beautifully furnished. I would have use of all the hotel's facilities. "As long as you vacate the premises by July, the time of Wimbledon—our high season—we'll be delighted to offer you an apartment at a highly discounted rate," Sally, the hotel's manager explained. I accepted on the spot and reassured her, "If we're still in trial in July, you can carry me out feet first." It was comforting to know that I would be able to return to comfortable surroundings after court each day.

## FINAL PREPARATIONS

Back in Atlanta, friends offered any help and support they could think of. One agreed to look after my house. Another would call my mother every day to talk about the trial. People were so anxious for an assignment that I sometimes invented one. When I assigned one friend to water my plants, she declared, "Now I feel that I'm part of the effort to defeat him." I was scheduled to leave on a Saturday evening. At synagogue that morning, a colleague pointed out that the weekly *Torah* portion was from Exodus: "God instructs Moses to 'Go to Pharaoh' and tell him 'Let my people go.' You go tell David Irving to let our people and our history alone."

I arrived in London early Sunday morning. At the airport I picked up the *Sunday Times* to read on the way into London from the airport. I opened the paper to find a long article on the trial. Irving predicted a complete victory. As soon as I reached my apartment, I called James. Dispensing with niceties, I asked how Irving could predict victory, given what our experts had found. Did he have something up his sleeve? James told me to turn to the front page. It showed former MP, Jonathan Aitken, emerging from jail after serving a sentence for perjury. Aitken had sued the *Guardian* for reporting that he accepted lavish gifts from Saudi Arabia while a cabinet minister. Prior to his trial, Aitken boldly predicted that he would not only be vindicated but that his trial would "cut out the cancer of bent and twisted journalism in our country with the simple sword of truth." Aitken's problem was that the *Guardian* was correct. He lost his libel case and, to compound matters, lied under oath. He ended up being sentenced for perjury.

The next day I joined Penguin's general counsels, Helena Peacock and Cicely Engel, at a small Kensington restaurant. Spending the final pretrial moments with them seemed particularly fitting. In 1995, they had first informed me that Irving was thinking of suing. Cicely told me that when Irving offered to settle, Rampton said, "You must not settle. If you do, none of us will be safe in our beds." I found it remarkable that Rampton put it that way. He could have said, "You must not settle because of the need to fight prejudice and protect minorities." But, he said "none of *us*," indicating that for him this case was about more than addressing Jewish concerns.

We returned to Penguin's offices so that I could meet the firm's managing director, Anthony Forbes-Watson. As we walked to his office, Penguin staff members repeatedly stopped us to wish me luck. A BBC film crew appeared. I listened as Forbes-Watson described Penguin's long-standing tradition of backing its authors. "In the 1950s we defended D. H. Lawrence when the Obscenity Commission wanted to pull *Lady Chatterley's Lover* from circulation. We published Salman Rushdie's *Satanic Verses* after the fatwa, the threat on his life and on us by Islamic clerics. Our defense of Deborah Lipstadt is part of that chain." I felt strange—but admittedly flattered—to hear my case compared to these historic literary battles.

# THE TRIAL

Entering the Royal High Courts of Justice on opening day with Penguin managing director Anthony Forbes-Watson, January 11, 2000.

# FIVE

# "ALL RISE!"

On the morning of January 11, 2000, the lawyers, solicitors, paralegals, experts, and researchers gathered in Rampton's chambers. There was a palpable energy in the room. Rampton wore his special QC court dress—a silk vest and a jacket ornamented with horizontal braids. He busily inspected some files. Heather Rogers, in her frilly barrister's white shirt and black suit, consulted with the researchers. The solicitors conversed with one another as the paralegals answered the incessantly ringing mobile phones. When the clock struck ten, Rampton looked up and declared, "It's time." Having anticipated this day for over four years, I felt like an Olympic runner walking to the track, ready to best my opponent.

Penguin lawyers had suggested that the legal team and I walk shoulder to shoulder along the three-hundred-yard journey from Brick Court to the courtroom on Fleet Street as a gesture of author/publisher cooperation and commitment in this ordeal. Anthony Forbes-Watson, Penguin's managing director, and I fell into step next to each other, with lawyers, experts, and researchers walking behind us. Emerging into the bustle of the street, I spotted a horde of paparazzi in front of the building. We approached from the east end of the street while they were looking west, closely watching passengers emerging from taxis. No one spotted us until a photographer crouching down on one knee glanced over his shoulder in our direction. "Here she comes!" he screamed out, his colleagues turning in one fell swoop. While oversized zoom lenses trained on me, I tried my best to exude confidence. As we approached the entrance, a gaggle of photographers blocked our way,

calling out, "Madam, look this way," or, "No, this way." They kept asking for
a statement, and the more I declined, the more they insisted that I comment
on what it felt like to be at the center of this controversy.

The Royal Courts of Justice—known to Londoners as "The Law
Courts"—is an enormous building with spires, clock tower, steepled but-
tresses, ornamental moldings, and statues of Jesus, Solomon, King Alfred,
and a host of bishops. It dominates the busy London intersection where
Fleet Street meets the Strand. In *QBVII,* Leon Uris aptly described it as
"neo-Gothic, neo-monastic, and neo-Victorian." Despite its architectural
hodgepodge, it is impressive. The 250-foot-long Gothic entry hall is a cross
between a large medieval church and a grand nineteenth-century railway
station. Its massive vaulted ceiling soars 80 feet in height. Stone benches set
into the wall, line the length of the hall. Above them are stained glass windows with the coats of arms of England's lord chancellors. A large clock
hangs from an upper level balcony and is visible from every point in the hall.

Over the years, extensions have been added to the main building. Now
many of the courtrooms are reached through vaulted passageways, meandering corridors, and small courtyards. As I followed the lawyers, I felt as if I
was moving through a maze within a labyrinth, which seemed—given what
I was about to face—an appropriate metaphor. I could hear commotion near
the courtroom. People were trying to convince the court ushers to let them
into the room, which was already filled to capacity. As we pushed our way
through, the crowd began to grumble, as if presuming that we were jumping the queue until someone pointed out that I was the defendant. The
courtroom, in contrast to the building, was relatively modern. There were
three rows of tables. A front-row seat had been reserved for me between
James and Penguin's solicitors. Those permitted to speak in court—Rampton, Heather, and Anthony—sat in the second row. Irving, acting as his own
barrister, would sit at the far end of that row. In front the court stenographer
was arranging her equipment. Her transcriptions would appear simultaneously on the computers that had been placed on the tables.

One entire wall of the room was filled with bright red and blue loose-
leaf binders containing a copy of every document or piece of evidence referred to in the expert reports. In a throwback to previous centuries each
binder is called a "bundle." When I first heard the term, I imagined the documents would be brought to court tied up with string. Chairs along the far
wall had been reserved for the press. At the back of the room were a couple

of rows of seats for the public. Some of these were occupied by my supporters. A year earlier my friend Ursula Blumenthal, whose husband, David, is
my Emory colleague, announced, "When the trial begins, we'll be there." At
the time I insisted that I didn't want anyone there, though I'm not sure why.
Perhaps I feared that Irving's attacks on me would be too unpleasant for
them to witness. Luckily they ignored my protestations because now, as this
saga commenced, being alone seemed unfathomable. Ken Stern, who had
dropped his other work at the American Jewish Committee to attend, was
there as well. Grace, the art curator who had sent me to the Assyrian exhibit,
had come from Los Angeles. Bruce Soll, counsel to Leslie Wexner, had arrived that morning from Columbus.

Irving entered carrying a large stack of books under his arm. He was
wearing the same dark blue pin-striped suit that he had worn to the pretrial
hearing. He stood alone, surrounded by empty chairs, which, under normal
circumstances, would have been occupied by his legal team. He had told
journalists that he had elected to represent himself because this battle concerned his area of specialization. He had, he contended, an advantage over
lawyers. They might know the law, but he knew the topic.

The usher's pronouncement—"Silence. All rise"—brought everyone to
their feet as a bewigged Judge Charles Gray entered the room. Everyone
bowed slightly. He returned the gesture and we sat down. His dark silk robe,
trimmed at the cuffs and neck with white ermine, and the red satin sash
across his neck harkened back to another era. Judge Gray sat on the upper
level of a two-tiered judge's bench that dominated the front of the room, so
high above me that I had to crane my neck to see him. Peering out at the
packed courtroom, he apologized that not all who wished to be here could
be accommodated and promised to seek a larger site.

## BRANDED WITH A YELLOW STAR

Irving began by addressing procedural issues. Prior to the trial, Irving and
Rampton had agreed that the questions relating to Auschwitz would be dealt
with as a separate issue. Irving assumed that this would come at the very end
of the trial, which would give him more time to prepare. Rampton, on the
other hand, thought the Auschwitz phase would be at the end of January
when Robert Jan was scheduled to arrive. After a bit of debate, Irving conceded that he was "perfectly prepared to have Professor van Pelt come over

in the middle of whatever else is going on and we can take him as a separate entirety."[1]

With that settled, it was time for opening speeches. Irving, as the plaintiff, was to speak first. All eyes were on him as he slowly and deliberately arranged his papers on the small podium. He was, he began, not a Holocaust denier. In fact, he argued, he should be credited for drawing attention to the Holocaust by "selflessly" publicizing historical documents he had uncovered in various archives and collections. Then, ignoring the fact that he initiated this case, he declared, "If we were to seek a title for this libel action, I would venture to suggest, *Pictures at an Execution*—my execution." There was a time, he told the court, when his books would annually earn more than £100,000. When his accountant asked what steps he had taken in anticipation of retirement, he said, "my immodest reply was that I did not intend to retire. . . . my books were my pension fund." He expected his royalties to sustain him "beyond the years of retirement." Knowing he lived in Mayfair, one of London's tonier neighborhoods, and having seen, many years earlier, a picture of him climbing into his Rolls-Royce, I assumed that this was indeed correct. That, he claimed, was no longer the case. His career had been torpedoed. Gesturing in my direction, he accused me of being responsible. "By virtue of the activities of the Defendants, in particular of the Second Defendant, and of those who funded her and guided her hand, I have since 1996 seen one fearful publisher after another falling away from me, declining to reprint my works, refusing to accept new commissions and turning their back on me when I approach." I had done this, he continued, as "part of an organized international endeavor."[2]

He promised to expose our nefarious scheme. "I have seen the papers. I have copies of the documents. I shall show them to this court, I know they did it and I now know why." Barely pausing for breath, he whipped off his glasses and accused me of having branded him with a "verbal Yellow Star" by calling him a denier. As a result he was now treated like a "wife beater or a paedophile."[3] Though I expected that he would depict himself as the victim, I was surprised by his selection of the yellow star as the symbol of his professed predicament. I had anticipated that, at least in the courtroom, Irving would modulate his provocative language. The cynicism of his imagery and the conviction with which he used it took my breath away. Aware that reporters were positioned three-deep along the courtroom walls, I fought hard to not allow my face to betray any emotion. Thumping the podium, he proclaimed it ironic that he, of all people, should be called an antisemite, when his publishers, editors, and lawyers had been Jews.[4]

Irving promised that he would prove that the "gas chambers shown to the tourists in Auschwitz is [sic] a fake built by the Poles after the war" and he would use our own experts to do so. In language more reminiscent of a Hollywood B-movie than a British court, he announced, "Perhaps the admission will have to be bludgeoned out of them." Irving predicted that we would be completely unable to prove that he willfully manipulated, mistranslated, or distorted the evidence.[5]

He illustrated his contention that, rather than deny the Holocaust, he had actually brought it to the attention of others, by describing how he had publicized a document containing German general Walter Bruns's description of the mass shooting of Jews during the summer of 1941 in Riga. After the war, Bruns was captured by the British. They secretly taped him telling his fellow POWs how the SS enthusiastically did their job. He told them how, when a Jewish woman, who had been forced to strip to her underwear, walked by on her way to be shot, an SS man commented: "Here comes a Jewish beauty!"[6]

Lightly beating his heart, Irving asked how could it be that he, who had publicized this document, with its detailed descriptions of killings, could be branded a "Holocaust denier"? Irving had, it was true, publicized this document. However, what he did not say was that, when he did so, he had argued that it proved that Hitler had tried to stop the shootings and that the shootings themselves were rogue unauthorized actions and not part of a program coordinated by Berlin.

Irving then plunged into a detailed dissertation on a relatively minor aspect of the trial, my claim that he had illegally taken glass plates of the Goebbels's diaries out of the Soviet archives in Moscow. The torpid nature of this discourse, which seemed interminable, made it hard for me to keep my eyes open. Finally, Irving concluded his over two-hour discourse by returning to the conspiracy against him. "It was not just one single action that has destroyed my career, but a cumulative, self-perpetuating, rolling onslaught from every side engineered by the same people who have propagated the book which is at the centre of the dispute, . . . which is the subject of this action." With that he sat down. He was smiling and seemed pleased with his performance.

Before Rampton began his speech, Judge Gray clarified some of the historiographic issues at the heart of the trial. Irving was arguing that we should be obligated to prove that he actually knew a specific event happened and that he then manipulated the facts. Whereas, we believed that the question was not simply whether Irving knew of a particular fact, but that the fact was readily available in the historical records and he "shut his eyes to it."[7]

## "HE IS A LIAR"

With a nod of his head, Judge Gray indicated that it was time for Rampton to begin. When it came to opening and closing statements, Rampton believed in economy of scale. He rose, arranged his papers, gave his wig a small tug—as if to anchor it on his head—and took a deep breath. He then looked up at Judge Gray and began with our bottom line: "My Lord, Mr Irving calls himself an historian. The truth is, however, that he is not an historian at all but a falsifier of history. To put it bluntly, *he is a liar.*" This case, he continued, was not about competing versions of history, but about truth and lies.

Even before becoming a denier, Rampton continued, Irving had distorted the historical record in an effort to exculpate Hitler. *Hitler's War,* published a decade before Irving began to espouse denial, was riddled with examples of the "disreputable methods" Irving used to exonerate Hitler from responsibility for atrocities against Jews or any other victims.[8] In the introduction, Irving promised his readers that the book contained "incontrovertible evidence" that as early as November 30, 1941, Hitler had explicitly ordered that there was to be " 'no liquidation' of the Jews."

> Himmler was *summoned* to the Wolf's Lair for a secret conference with Hitler, at which the fate of Berlin's Jews was clearly raised. At 1:30 p.m. Himmler was *obliged* to telephone from Hitler's bunker to Heydrich the explicit order that Jews were *not to be liquidated.* [Emphasis added]

Irving based this claim that Hitler had demanded Himmler come to a secret meeting at which he ordered that Jews were not to be murdered on Himmler's phone log for the day. It listed a 1:30 P.M. phone call from Himmler to his assistant Reinhard Heydrich, who was in Prague. Himmler made the following notations in his log about the call:

*Judentransport aus Berlin.* [Jew-transport from Berlin.]
*Keine Liquidierung.* [No liquidation.]

The phone log indicates that Irving's claim that Himmler was stopping the liquidation of the Jews was simply not true. Himmler was ordering that *one* specific trainload of Berlin Jews not be liquidated. In Irving's hands this had morphed from instructions about one train into an order concerning all Jews. His claim that this order came from Hitler, was, Rampton said, also "pure invention." There was no evidence that Hitler had *summoned* Himmler or that he had *obliged* him to call Heydrich. In fact, according to Himmler's log, he first saw Hitler that day an hour *after* the call was made. But the matter, Rampton continued, "gets worse still." Irving had also claimed that on the next day Himmler called SS general Oswald Pohl, overall chief of the concentration camp system, "with the order 'Jews are to stay where they are.' " Irving had based this suggestion that Himmler was ordering that Jews not be deported on Himmler's December 1 diary entry.

*Verwaltungsführer der SS* [Administrative leaders of the SS]
*haben zu bleiben.* [are to remain where they are.]

Rampton observed that the entry made no reference to Jews. It was not Jews who were to remain but administrative leaders of the SS. Irving had replaced *"haben"* with *"Juden,"* enabling him to invent the claim that Jews were to stay where they are. When *Hitler's War* was republished in 1991, Irving corrected his mistake regarding *"Keine Liquidierung,"* acknowledging that it referred to only one trainload. However, Rampton continued, he let the other "imaginative assertions"—that the order came from Hitler and that Himmler instructed Pohl to leave Jews were they were—stand. This was a "monstrous distortion of the evidence in Mr Irving's own hands." This was not an innocent mistake, Rampton insisted, but a deliberate misstatement of the facts.[9]

With that Rampton moved to Irving's "astounding volte-face," his metamorphosis into a Holocaust denier. Rampton traced that change to the *Leuchter Report,* which Irving described as "the biggest calibre shell that has yet hit the battleship Auschwitz" and which had "totally exploded the legend." Rampton paused a moment, apparently to give added emphasis to his next statement: "Unfortunately for Mr Irving, the *Leuchter Report* is bunk and *he knows it.*"

Rampton explained why Irving had so wholeheartedly embraced the report, despite its obvious flaws. "He wanted it to be true. After all, if the Holocaust never happened, then Hitler cannot have ordered it or known about it." That was why Irving had said of his 1991 edition of *Hitler's War*, "You won't find the Holocaust mentioned in one line, not even in a footnote. Why should you? If something didn't happen, then you don't even dignify it with a footnote."[10]

Rampton then posed a more fundamental question. Why did Irving resort to these lies and distortions? Rampton suggested that one could derive a "fair picture of a man's true attitudes and motives from what he says and from the kind of people he associates with and speaks to." Over the past years, Irving had addressed right-wing, neofascist, and neo-Nazi groups. Rampton lowered his voice slightly—forcing everyone in the courtroom to listen very carefully—as he provided an example of the tone Irving adopted at these kinds of gatherings. In 1991, Irving had told his Calgary audience:

> I don't see any reason to be tasteful about Auschwitz. It's baloney. It's a legend. Once we admit the fact that it was a brutal slave labour camp and large numbers of people did die, as large numbers of innocent people died elsewhere in the war, why believe the rest of the baloney? I say quite tastelessly in fact that more women died on the back seat of Edward Kennedy's car at Chappaquiddick than ever died in a gas chamber in Auschwitz. Oh, you think that's tasteless. How about this. There are so many Auschwitz survivors going around, in fact the number increases as the years go past, which is biologically very odd to say the least, because I am going to form an Association of Auschwitz survivors, survivors of the Holocaust and other liars . . . A-S-S-H-O-L-S.

The courtroom was so quiet that when James shuffled some papers, it sounded like an earthquake.

The defendants, Rampton declared, had exposed Irving's fraud and deliberate manipulations. For that they should "be applauded for having performed a significant public service not just in this country, but in all those places in the world where antisemitism is waiting to be fed."[11] With that he ended. He had spoken for about forty minutes.

In the hall outside the courtroom, reporters surrounded Irving, who was happily expounding on his great day in court. Soon a group was also pummeling me with questions. "How did the first day go?" "Will you be giving testimony?" "What did you think of Irving's boast that he is going to win this case handily?" I felt uncharacteristically bewildered, not by their questions, but by the fact that I was not supposed to answer them. Earlier that day, as we left for court, Anthony and James reminded me that we must not appear to be litigating this case in the press. Anthony had stressed how much judges dislike it when participants in a legal action predict what they will ultimately decide. "Above all, they cannot abide defendants who don't talk in court, but talk to the press out of court."

As I contemplated his admonition, a tall woman with long hair, a friendly smile, and a low-tech tape recorder emerged from the crowd. The minute she spoke, I recognized the distinctive timbre and almost melodic quality of her voice. Julie McCarthy, National Public Radio's London correspondent, implored me for a statement for *Morning Edition* and *All Things Considered*, two of my favorite news shows. Standing near her were the *New York Times*'s Sarah Lyall and the London bureau chief of the *Los Angeles Times*, Marjorie Miller. They too had questions. What were the broader implications of this case? How did I feel about Irving? Truth be told, while they had many questions, they wanted me to say something—anything—so that, as Julie McCarthy put it, "your voice can be heard." They had spoken to Irving—some of them at length. From their perspective even a few words from me would give their stories some balance. I was dying to talk to them. I wanted to frame my own case. I wanted them to know I was not afraid. At the very least, I wanted my family and friends back home to hear my voice.

When James emerged from the courtroom, he quickly assessed the situation, and made a beeline to where I was standing. I asked him, "Can't I give them *something,* maybe something inconsequential?" James, unmoved by my entreaties, replied, "Nothing you say today will be *in*consequential." I looked over at Irving enthusiastically engaging the press. Keeping my silence was becoming infuriating. Then, someone grabbed my arm and I jumped at the unexpected contact. A small elderly woman had resolutely pushed her way through the crush. She had a heavily wrinkled face and very sad eyes.

Dressed quite sensibly for a January day in London, she was wearing a plain, light blue wool sweater, dark wool skirt, and sturdy shoes. Her knitted hat was pulled tight over her gray hair. Ignoring the reporters, she thrust her arm in front of me, rolled her sleeve up to her elbow, and emphatically pointed at the number tattooed on her forearm. "You are fighting for us. You are our witness." I heard both encouragement and admonishment in this woman's words. It was as if she was saying: Be strong and of good courage *but, whatever you do, do not fail us.*

Suddenly, what the media thought about the trial seemed inconsequential at best. I left the building, emerging into an appropriately dark, cold afternoon.

# SIX

# IRVING IN THE BOX:
# NOT A DENIER BUT A VICTIM

**"** S aw you on television last night!" It took me a moment to realize that the man in the hotel lobby was talking to me. As I climbed into the cab, a woman cried out, "I'm rooting for you." It seemed that, with pictures of me entering the Royal Courts of Justice on the front pages of London newspapers, my anonymity was gone. The taxi driver offered me a warm "Good luck to you, madam" with my change. Perusing the *London Times* over a cup of bad coffee in the Law Courts snack bar, I felt strange reading a description of myself.

> In front of him [David Irving] sat one of the principal defendants. Professor Lipstadt, whose 1994 book casts severe doubts on Mr Irving's interpretation of the Holocaust, is a well-presented, 54-year-old American with ginger hair, half-moon spectacles and gold earrings, an orange silk scarf swathing her black outfit. She followed Mr Irving's address on a laptop computer, occasionally glancing round at him with what looked suspiciously like wide-eyed incredulity.

Thinking back on some of my feelings that day, I was glad that it was only incredulity that the reporter saw. I was intrigued by the impression Irving had made on a number of reporters. The *Times* described the pin-

striped Irving as looking more like an "international art dealer" than a man
we claimed was a Holocaust denier and an antisemite. The *New York Times*
commented on Irving's "articulate, plausible demeanor."[1]

Entering the courtroom, I stopped to greet Ursula, David, and Grace.
Ursula exuberantly introduced me to a man in the queue: "Meet Professor
Sussman, a professor of microbiology from Newcastle." In a slightly conspiratorial tone she whispered, "I saw him waiting and suspected he was on 'our'
side." Sussman, a nattily dressed, formal man in his sixties, explained that he
was in London on business and impulsively decided to attend. He wished me
"Great good luck." I thanked him rather perfunctorily, marveling at Ursula's
ability to collect people.


## CONSPIRING AGAINST DAVID IRVING

As soon as the judge entered and we completed our ritual of rising, bowing,
and sitting, Irving announced his intention to screen a videotape of a 1994
interview I had given to Australian television when I was there on a book
tour. He explained that it "provides the Second Defendant, Professor Lipstadt, with a chance to express her opinions unopposed." He then paused,
apparently expecting Judge Gray to respond. Judge Gray simply said, "Yes."
Irving continued, "I feel it is appropriate to allow her some minutes of the
court's time in this rather oblique manner to express her opinions. . . . I understand that she will not be testifying in person in this case." Irving paused
again. He seemed to be waiting for Judge Gray to comment about my not
testifying. Judge Gray said nothing. Finally, Irving started the video. The interviewer asked me my opinion of Irving, who was then trying to obtain an
Australian visa. I cringed when I heard myself say, somewhat glibly, that no
"historian takes him seriously." Had I then been thinking forensically, as I
had learned to do, I would have probably said, "No historian takes his claims
about the Holocaust seriously and I would be inclined to check his evidence
on other matters."

Irving asked Judge Gray, "My Lord, I do not know if you consider that
was a useful exercise. I would welcome your Lordship's guidance." Irving
could not have been pleased when Judge Gray told him it was "not very"
useful because it did not address the "specific criticisms of your historical approach." Irving challenged Judge Gray's assessment of the screening. "We
are also concerned with the Second Defendant here. My Lord, I understand

she will not . . . speak and I will not be having a chance to cross-examine her. I think it was a useful exercise because it gave us a chance to see her in action. I think she could have handled herself under cross-examination had she proposed to do so." The judge responded, "I have that point and I have now had the opportunity of seeing her on the interview."[2] Though Judge Gray spoke in a flat expressionless voice, I worried we had made a tactical mistake, allowing Irving to portray me as not only scared of facing him but having something to hide. I also knew that the British could not abide cowards. I passed Rampton a note: "Does my not testifying give him some moral or legal advantage with Judge Gray? Remember, I'm ready to testify." Rampton motioned with his hand that I should not worry. But I *was* worried and—even more so—I was frustrated.

One of Irving's video clips had included the ruins of the Birkenau gas chamber. Irving promised that important revelations were coming. "I do not want to reveal precisely the arguments we will lead on this occasion. We will give the Defence great time to prepare counter arguments and we have spent a great deal of time and money with architectural consultants and so on providing this evidence. I would prefer to leave that evidence—"

Irving's hint of great surprises yet to come brought Rampton hurtling to his feet. He interrupted Irving mid-sentence: "The days are long gone where a Claimant . . . is entitled to keep his rabbits in his back pocket and pull them out when it suits him so as to deprive the other side of due notice. If he is sitting on . . . expert evidence then we must have them."[3] British court procedures did not allow for Perry Mason–type surprises. Neither side could sandbag the other. "I think that is right," Judge Gray replied. I asked James why Judge Gray was so tentative. James explained, "That's British judicial parlance for 'Irving's wrong.' " Nonetheless, this hint of new evidence concerned me. Would the trial become the launching pad for another phony scientific study—a *Leuchter Report* redux.

Irving told the judge that he would begin presenting his case with the issue of his "reputation" as a historian and push the historical issues "away for a while." "How long is the while?" Judge Gray inquired. Irving responded, "As long as is necessary for me to deal with the reputation aspects of the case." Judge Gray noted that he did not think that should take very long, since he had read much material about Irving's reputation in pretrial submissions. Irving responded, "My Lord, you have read it but the Press have not."[4] The courtroom erupted in laughter. Judge Gray, who did not laugh, observed that this exercise was not for the press. He did not want to hear about noncontentious matters, but wanted to focus on issues that were central to the case.

Judge Gray suggested that now was the time for Irving to enter the witness box so he could give his testimony. As Irving strode forward, climbed the three steps to the box, and was sworn in, I reflected on the fact that Irving often insisted that, among historians of the Third Reich, he alone adhered to a high standard of historical accuracy. In 1986, he told an Australian audience that his readers could trust him better than any other World War II historian. "I've got all the documents and the evidence on my side, but they can't even find one page of evidence to attack me, and that is why they're beginning to rant and rave instead."[5] In Canada and South Africa he told his audience: "I don't just tell them my opinions: I back them up with all my evidence and the data that we have in British archives. . . . In a few months time, no one is going to believe these legends any more. The legends are collapsing with disastrous consequences for certain countries in the Middle East."[6] In *Hitler's War,* he wrote that other historians were "incorrigible" and "lazy," failing to "burrow deep" into the documents to find the "real truth."[7] Now, as a result of the case he had initiated, we intended to prove otherwise.

Irving began by vigorously denying our charge that he had extreme right-wing views. After insisting that he had never belonged to a political party, left or right, he slipped, without warning, into a soliloquy on the current situation in England.

> I cannot say that I have applauded the uncontrolled tide of commonwealth immigration into this country. Like most fellow countrymen of my background and vintage, I regret the passing of the Old England. I sometimes think, my Lord, that if the soldiers and sailors who stormed the beaches of Normandy in 1944 could see what England would be like at the end of this century, they would not have got 50 yards up the beach. I think they would have given up in disgust.

The courtroom was very quiet.

Irving described how, over the years, he had received "favourable reviews, the kind of reviews that made publishers line up to publish my books." Then came a turning of the tide. Bookstores refused to sell his books. Publishers reacted in "grief and terror" when he sent them manuscripts. My book, Irving charged, was responsible for this.[8]

## THE ST. MARTIN'S IMBROGLIO

My assault on his career, he charged, took on its most ominous character in 1996. St. Martin's Press, a prominent American publisher, was scheduled to publish his biography of Goebbels. When the news of this found its way into the press, there was an avalanche of criticism about St. Martin's. The publisher defended its decision by arguing that the "loyalties, politics, or personal lives" of their authors were irrelevant. They were only concerned about the historical merits of an author's work. *New York Times* columnist Frank Rich, distressed by St. Martin's stance, interviewed me for an article he was writing on this subject. I insisted that, contrary to St. Martin's claims, an author's reputation counts, particularly if it directly relates to the book's topic. I wondered whether St. Martin's would publish a book on child rearing by Jeffrey Dahmer, the serial killer of young boys. The *Washington Post,* aware of my work on Holocaust deniers, also called and I reiterated my opposition. While my criticism of Irving in these two interviews (these were my only comments on the St. Martin's affair) was strong, others were also critical. The publishing trade journal *Kirkus Reviews* called his book "scurrilously misleading." *Publishers Weekly* described St. Martin's plan to publish it as "repellent." *Library Journal* had also condemned the book and the publisher.[9] Best-selling mystery writer Jonathan Kellerman and Nobel Prize winner Elie Wiesel announced that they would not publish with St. Martin's or give any books published by the house endorsements for a book jacket. Finally about one hundred St. Martin's employees held an unprecedented open forum with the chairman of the publishing house, Thomas J. McCormack. They issued an "impassioned plea" that the contract be canceled. McCormack, stung by this groundswell, checked Irving's current pronouncements on the Internet and was left with a feeling of "alarm and humiliation." He then read the book and described it as an inescapably antisemitic book whose subtext was "the Jews brought this onto themselves." At that point he decided to cancel the contract.[10]

Irving told Judge Gray that St. Martin's informed him that the publishing house had come "under attack from all quarters," including "the Second Defendant." He claimed that St. Martin's had "widely quoted" me in justification of its decision. Frustrated that Irving was successfully feeding Judge Gray a stream of misinformation, I scribbled a note to Rampton. "I did not orchestrate a protest. I spoke to two reporters. And if St. Martin's quoted me, I would know about it." Rampton read my note and nodded. I waited for him to protest. Instead, he leaned back in his chair, pulled his wig over his eyes, and seemed to fall into a deep reverie. Distressed, I asked James why Rampton wasn't protesting? James was calm. "Patience. Our turn will come." Judge Gray asked Irving if St. Martin's actually told him that I was responsible for the cancellation. "No, my Lord, media accounts have linked Professor Lipstadt with this particular event." Judge Gray leaned forward as he demanded more precision. "Media accounts, rather than the American publishers?"[11] Irving somewhat reluctantly acknowledged that it was media accounts. At that point, James whispered, "Our turn just came."

## DEFINING THE HOLOCAUST

When Judge Gray asked Irving to define the Holocaust, Irving protested that he was "quite unhappy" about the word. It was "very elastic" and served too many purposes: "*They* set it as wide as they want when it is a concern, for example, of taking money from the Swiss banks. . . . and *they* set it very narrowly when they then try to snare a writer who is dangerous to them, as they put it."[12] Though Irving never explicitly identified who was moving the linguistic goalpost, there was little doubt that the "they" was the Jewish community.

Judge Gray, still trying to get Irving to define the event, asked if he believed there had been a systematic program to exterminate the Jews. Irving stated, "No, I do not." People had been mass-murdered on the Eastern Front, but, he insisted, these killings were not systematic since they "originated" at a "lower level" in the Third Reich hierarchy. They were not the result of an "Adolf Hitler decision." Moving from the mass shootings to the gas chambers, Judge Gray asked, "Do you accept or deny totally that there was any systematic gassing of Jews in gas chambers, whether at Auschwitz or elsewhere?"[13] Since Irving had previously described the gas chambers as "Hollywood legends," and had proclaimed that he had never seen any "evidence at all that gas chambers existed," I expected him to deny that there had been any systematic gassings.[14] I was surprised, therefore, when he acknowledged that "there was some kind of gassing at gas chambers in Birke-

nau." As Irving said this, Heather proclaimed sotto voce, "We have a concession." She had hardly completed her statement when Irving qualified his so-
called "concession." The killings were not "systematized" because that
"implies that it was conducted on authority from above." There was, he insisted, a "chain of documents" indicating that "Hitler was a negative force in
this matter," i.e. he tried to prevent the killings. One of those documents
was, Irving contended, Himmler's diary entry of November 30, 1941, the
one Rampton had mentioned in his opening. "Liquidation was in the air"
and here was "Hitler intervening in a negative way" in order to save this
trainload of Jews.[15]

Irving vigorously rejected our charge that he behaved in a "disreputable
way as a historian." He denied ever "knowingly or willfully misrepresent[ing] a document or misquot[ing] it, or suppress[ing] parts of the document which would run counter to my case." He said he would be "very
surprised indeed" if the defense could prove this "on even one document."
He rejected our contention that he had greatly exaggerated the Dresden
death toll and insisted that his estimates of the victims of Allied bombing
raids came from reliable sources. He dismissed any mistakes he might have
made about the Dresden toll, because there was "not much difference between 135,000 dead and 35,000 dead. Both of them are a monstrous tragedy
or crime. . . . If you are one of those dead it hurts just as much." Moreover,
any mistakes he might have made in the death toll were not a matter of
"willful misrepresentation, or distortion." Judge Gray, assuming Irving had
completed his answer, began to ask his next question. Rather than answer, Irving looked up in surprise and explained his silence to Judge Gray: "I was
just pausing for dramatic effect."[16] There was a slight twitter of laughter in
the room.

As I left the courtroom for lunch, I found Ursula sitting on a bench with
Professor Sussman. He was weeping. Ursula motioned for me to come over.
Shaking my head no, I pointed at my watch to indicate that we only had an
hour for lunch. The other members of the legal team were already rushing
toward Rampton's chambers. I was anxious to hear their assessment of what
had happened in court. I also knew that I didn't feel like becoming entangled
in what was obviously, for some reason, an emotional moment for Professor
Sussman. Ursula, however, was persistent and when she wants something
even the most resolute of people tend to crumble. I approached, intending
to talk for just a moment. Sussman apologized profusely for his public dis-

play of emotions. He explained that listening to Irving had aroused in him personal and difficult memories. He had been sent as a young child to England from his native Germany. Many of his relatives had not survived. His parents had managed to reach England. Aware that I was in a rush, he said he had just one question. "When my mother, a native of Hamburg, used to recall her life in Germany she would speak of a Gustav Lipstadt. Was he a relative?"

Now I was overcome by emotion. Gustav Lipstadt was my grandfather. I never knew him. My father, who had died when I was in my early twenties, had not told me much about him. He would have gladly told me more had I shown a greater interest. To my everlasting regret, I had not. Suddenly, the legal analysis taking place in Richard Rampton's chambers paled in significance. The only picture we had of my grandfather showed a man with a round full face, goatee, slight wry smile, exceptionally kind eyes, and a very bushy mustache. I had learned that he was a gracious man with a keen sense of humor and a willingness to do the outrageous, or, at the least, what bourgeois German Jews considered outrageous. He used to cross a park each morning on his way to work. A monkey grinder generally situated himself next to the entrance of the park. My grandfather noticed that few people were dropping coins in his can. One morning, on his way to work, he told the man to give him the little organ. He stood there playing it with the monkey at his side. The man's business skyrocketed. I wanted to ask Mr. Sussman all sorts of questions. He, however, insisted that I go off with the lawyers. "That," he said, "is more important." I was no longer sure, but I went.

As we returned from Rampton's office, I saw my friend Grace. When she had been a graduate student at Columbia University in the late 1960s, she had often visited my parents on Manhattan's Upper West Side. She quietly said, "Your father would have been proud of you." Despite my father's German roots and formal demeanor, he too enjoyed doing the outrageous. Every morning he would walk our cocker spaniel, Brandy, for about fifteen minutes. At one point, these walks began to last a half hour or longer. At the end of about two weeks my father explained why. An elderly couple ran the newspaper stand on the corner of Eighty-sixth Street and Broadway, which was on his dog walking route. One morning, my father learned that the wife was ill. My father asked, "How do you take a break in order to go to the bathroom?" When the man explained that he could not leave the stand, my father volunteered to watch the stand for a few minutes each morning. And so this distinguished-looking gentleman with his impeccably trimmed red Vandyke beard, dressed in his business suit, gray homburg, and overcoat, with a dog at the leash, stood on Broadway selling newspapers.

Sussman had provided one link to my family and Grace another. As I waited for the proceedings to resume, I reflected on how my father, who had died too young, and a grandfather, whom I never knew, had so unexpectedly come into this setting. I had expected the trial to expose me to personal stories. I never anticipated that they would be my own.

## IRVING ON HITLER AND HATRED

After lunch Irving returned to the stand. He insisted that he did not "manipulate his sources to his own political and ideological desire to exculpate Mr Hitler." In fact, Irving declared, he "bent over backwards" to mention Hitler's crimes. "He issued the euthanasia order for the killing of the mentally disabled. . . . He ordered the killing of the British commandos who fell into German captivity. He ordered the liquidation of the male population of Stalingrad and Leningrad." But Hitler, Irving added, had also done some things worthy of praise. "He did pick his nation up from out of the mire after World War II [sic] and reunify it and gave it a sense of direction and a sense of pride again which, from the German point of view . . . was something commendable."[17]

Judge Gray asked Irving to respond to our accusation that he blamed what was done during the Third Reich against Jews "upon the Jews themselves." Irving dismissed this as a "gross oversimplification," though he acknowledged that, on a number of occasions, he had said, "If I was a Jew I would be far more concerned, not by the question of who pulled the trigger, but why." Why, Irving asked, did Josef Goebbels, who, he claimed, had not been an antisemite in his early years, become one of the "most criminal antisemites of all times? . . . Is it something in the water? Something must have caused him to change." Judge Gray wanted clarification. "Can I just be clear what you are meaning when you say 'something must have caused him to change,' something done by Jews themselves?" Suddenly Irving seemed to back down a bit. He told Judge Gray he would leave that for someone else to investigate "because I am in trouble as it is, my Lord, and I do not think that one would earn any great kudos for investigating that."[18]

When Judge Gray asked Irving about our allegation that he associated with neo-Nazis, Irving emphatically dismissed it as "guilt by association." At the most, he may have associated with someone who was associated with someone who was an extremist. He compared it to the song with the lyrics: "I danced with a man who danced with a girl who danced with the Prince of Wales." Judge Gray replied, "I understand what you are saying and, indeed, it may well be that this does not turn out to be one of the most important issues in the case." Judge Gray's sympathetic comments were worrisome as I was convinced that Irving's association with neo-Nazis and antisemites was directly linked to his Holocaust denial and was an important aspect of the case.

Judge Gray asked Irving about his connection with Zündel. Irving said that he testified at Zündel's trial because he thought it was "my duty as an historian, as a public citizen, to give evidence . . . it was a mistake, because . . . that has been used as a reason to destroy me."[19]

Judge Gray, having given Irving a chance to respond to our allegations, asked if he had anything to add. Irving said that he had already spoken of the pecuniary consequences of my book on his life. However, "there has also been a more intangible consequence, that I have found myself subjected to a burden of hatred which you cannot quantify, but which is quite definitely there." He offered two illustrations of those burdens. A few weeks earlier at a Los Angeles book fair, a "very notorious member of the Jewish community, one of the most extreme members in the United States with a long criminal record—came up to the stand and screamed that he was going to . . . kill me. 'You're a Holocaust denier,' he screamed as he was led away by the police."[20] Having lived in Los Angeles for many years, I did not doubt that this incident was possible and made a calculated guess about the identity of the culprit. I hated such tactics. They give those who practice them a false sense of bravado and those who are subjected to them—in this case Irving—a chance to play the victim. When a Jewish student in London told me that he was organizing a group to stand outside the courthouse and shout epithets at Irving, I implored him not to. I planned to fight with facts, not taunts.

Irving's second example was more disconcerting. A few months before the trial his disabled thirty-eight-year-old daughter had died. Press reports described it as suicide. After the burial he said the family received an elaborate wreath of white roses and lilies with a card attached that said, "Truly a merciful death." The card was signed "Philip Bouhler and friends." Bouhler had been the Nazi doctor in charge of the program for euthanizing mentally and physically disabled Germans.[21]

His story about Jewish thugs seemed plausible. This one, however, beggared the imagination. I wondered if he had concocted it. As soon as I entertained that thought, I felt guilty for having doubted a man whose daughter had just died in such tragic circumstances. I recalled a meeting a small group of Emory faculty had with the Dalai Lama a few years earlier. When he learned that I teach about the Holocaust, he spoke about how important it was for a people who had been oppressed not to allow themselves to be beset with hatred for their oppressors. I would have to work to keep my anger toward Irving from evolving into hate. David Irving was not worth it.

This was not the first time I had wrestled with these emotions. Recently, when I had been ranting about the turmoil Irving was causing in my life, Anthony had counseled me to take a different perspective. "Relate to fighting Irving as you might to shit you step in on the street. It has no value and is intrinsically unimportant. However, if you fail to completely clean it off your shoes and track it into your home, it can cause great damage." This legal battle was a means of cleaning the shit off my shoes.

I had just finished berating myself for doubting Irving when my sympathies were tested by his concluding remarks. "The kind of hatred that this book has subjected me to [is] something intolerable, something unspeakable and which I would wish no other person to be subjected to."[22] Even though I should have been inured to Irving's tactics, I still marveled at the fact that he seemed utterly convinced that it was my book—and not his words and actions—that were the cause of his troubles.

# SEVEN

# THE CHAIN OF DOCUMENTS

I expected Rampton to begin his cross-examination with an eloquent opening question. He rose, straightened his wig, gathered up his robes around him, took a deep breath, and then said, "This is the most ghastly inconvenient and uncomfortable court I have ever been in. . . . I can hardly stand up. I cannot get at my documents. . . . The witness is miles away from the files that he needs. I can hardly see him because of this pillar and my learned junior cannot see him." The chuckling in the room turned into laughter when Judge Gray responded, "Otherwise you are pretty happy?" In fact, Rampton was not, as he told Judge Gray. "Except for the feeling that I am being boiled alive. . . . Perhaps the authorities at least might pretend that it was midsummer instead of Siberia."[1] Judge Gray promised to urge the authorities—obviously his control over the Law Courts' engineering staff was limited—to lower the heat.

Rampton, turning to Irving, wove the story of the funeral wreath into his opening question. "Mr Irving . . . [that was] an elegiac story that you told us just now—I do not mean that sarcastically at all; it is perfectly true it is—you blame that appalling note on the wreath on Deborah Lipstadt's book, is that right?" When Irving said yes, Rampton observed that if what I had written was true, Irving's misfortunes were his responsibility. I understood why Rampton couldn't ignore the story about the wreath, yet it made me uncomfortable. I was relieved when he moved on.[2]

Rampton, noting that Irving had denied being a Holocaust denier, read from a 1991 speech Irving gave in Canada:

Until 1988, I believed that there had been something like a Holocaust. I believed the millions of people had been killed in factories of death. I believed in the gas chamber. I believed in all the paraphernalia of the modern Holocaust, but [in] 1988, when I . . . gave evidence in the trial of Ernst Zündel . . . I met people who knew differently and could prove to me that story was just a legend.[3]

In 1991 in London, Irving had labeled the charge that the Germans had "factories of death with gas chambers in which they liquidated millions of their opponents," as a "blood libel on the German people."[4] Rampton wondered how Irving could say these things, while claiming that he was not a denier. Irving explained that he did not mean that the whole "story of the Holocaust" was a legend. The legend was about the "paraphernalia, the equipment, the factories of death, and the gas chambers" in which millions died. Most people, he continued, thought of the Holocaust as "people being made to walk to the edge of a pit and being bumped off by soldiers holding rifles." Since he did not deny that such shootings occurred, he should not be branded a denier. Irving failed to mention that, since he claimed these shootings were rogue actions that had not been ordered by Hitler or sanctioned by the Third Reich, he was effectively redefining the Holocaust.

When Rampton asked why he had removed all references to the Holocaust from the 1991 edition of *Hitler's War,* Irving insisted that the word was "offensive, . . . vague . . . imprecise, . . . and . . . should be avoided like the plague." His acceptance in *Hitler's War* (1977), he continued, that Auschwitz was an extermination center was a "lazy acceptance which I now regret." Though he rejected the notion of a "gas chamber Holocaust," he insisted he was not a denier because he believed in the "rest of the Holocaust story, namely the shootings on the Eastern front."[5] Though we had only begun, Irving's courtroom tactics were already trying my patience. A simple question elicited long, meandering responses.

> RAMPTON: How many people do you think—I mean innocent people, I am not talking about bombing raids, Mr Irving, I mean innocent Jewish people do you think the Germans killed deliberately?
> IRVING: You mean like Anne Frank?
> RAMPTON: I do not mind whether they are like Anne Frank or not. How many innocent Jewish people—

IRVING: Well, I mean, she is a typical example and a very useful example to take because everybody has heard of Anne Frank. She was innocent. I have daughters of my own and if what happened to her happened to one of my daughters, I would be extremely angry.

RAMPTON: Oh, I see, so Mr or Mrs Frank might not have been innocent, is that what you are trying to say?

IRVING: But I asked you about Anne Frank; I did not ask about her parents.

RAMPTON: No, I am sorry, Mr Irving. The procedure in this court is that you do not ask questions, I do. I asked you how many—

IRVING: I did not ask a question. I just said, I mean, shall we talk about Anne Frank.

RAMPTON: No, I do not want to talk about Anne Frank.

IRVING: You want to talk about nameless, unspecified Jews so that later on we can say, "Well, I was not meaning those ones, I meant those ones"? The reason you do not want to talk about Anne Frank, of course, is because she is a Jew who died in the Holocaust and yet she was not murdered, unless you take the broadest possible definition of murder.

In the midst of this theatrical absurdity, I couldn't help but recall the Abbott and Costello comic routine, "Who's on First." I started to laugh but Rampton's next comment made me quickly refocus.

RAMPTON: We will get to Anne Frank along down the road, I assure you. . . . I said "deliberately killed." How many innocent Jewish people do you say that the Nazis deliberately killed during the course of World War II? That was my question.

Irving shrugged and told Rampton that he was not an expert on the Holocaust, therefore his answer would have no value.[6]

## "INCONTROVERTIBLE EVIDENCE"?

Rampton reminded Irving that Hitler regularly received detailed reports on the shootings from the *Einsatzgruppen*, the special killing squads. How then, he continued, could Irving contend that Hitler did not approve of the killings? For example, the December 1942 *Report to the Führer on Combating Partisans* (No. 51) listed the number of "Jews Executed" as 363,211. Rampton argued that there was little doubt that Hitler had seen it. The report had been typed in a large font known as the *"Führer* typeface," which Hitler could read without glasses. It was initialed by those who prepared documents for Hitler and marked "shown to the *Führer."*

Irving responded that, if Hitler saw the document he probably paid no attention to it. His concerns were elsewhere. "This is the height of the Stalingrad crisis. Every waking moment he is waiting for news that the fourth army that he sent to rescue the sixth army has broken through . . . the battleship *Scharnhorst* is out on the high seas . . . about to be sunk that same day as it [Report No. 51] is shown to him. He has an awful lot of things on his plate." Irving posited that Himmler might have "slip[ped] a document into a heap to be shown to the *Führer*" so he could later claim that he had told Hitler what was being done to the Jews. After posing this theory, Irving warned Judge Gray, "Attach no evidentiary value to what I just said . . . , because it is literally speculating on the basis of very thin evidence."[7]

Irving's comments about the insignificance of this evidence gave Rampton a chance to bring this excursion back to our objective. "Mr Irving, we are not on this side of the court setting out to prove what did happen, we are only interested in the evidence which a reputable historian would put into the scales and weigh before arrival at a conclusion." Someone in Berlin had retyped this report in the *"Führer* type." Someone had put it in front of Himmler, who signed it. Someone had included it in the select documents placed before Hitler. Someone had marked it: "Shown to the *Führer."* Why, Rampton wondered, if these shootings were merely criminal acts by maverick SS commanders, as Irving claimed, would those closest to Hitler have placed the document before him? Irving, in turn, offered that if Hitler did, indeed, see the report, he "did not care about" these victims. They were Eastern European Jews, whom he looked upon as "a man might look on an ant heap."[8] For once, I thought, Irving had got it just right.

As the afternoon drew to a close, Rampton returned to Irving's claim that Himmler's diary constituted "incontrovertible evidence" that as early as November 1941, Hitler had ordered that there was to be " 'no liquidation' of the Jews." Rampton pointed out that the diary concerned only one trainload of Berlin Jews. Irving explained that when he copied the quote he had made a "silly misreading" of the diary. He had mistakenly put an "e" on "transport," changing it from the singular—one trainload of Jews—into the plural—"trainloads of Jews." In any case, Irving observed, almost dismissively, close to thirty years had passed since he first encountered this diary entry. It was, he suggested, wrong to expect him to remember the precise circumstances of this transcription.[9] Scholars often make transcription mistakes, particularly when working in an archive. I doubted, however, that Irving would have made such a mistake with a document he considered so significant.

When the session ended, I quietly packed up my paraphernalia. Though I had sat silently all day, doing virtually nothing but listening, I was utterly spent and happy to be heading home, as I had already come to think of my London apartment. I was relieved not to see any paparazzi, which made the next morning's newspaper, with a photograph of me exiting the Law Courts, utterly surprising.

The next day's session began with Irving asking permission to introduce some documents he believed would be useful to the discussion of the Himmler telephone log. He began with a 1974 letter he had written to a German historian. It contained a transcription of the log. Irving seemed to be about to explain to Judge Gray that the letter demonstrated just how many years had passed since he first translated the entry, when Judge Gray interrupted him: "You . . . transcribe *Judentransport,* J-U-D-E-N-T-R-A-N-S-P-O-R-T, in the singular, and that is in 1974." I quickly took another look at the document. Sure enough, in this letter Irving had correctly transcribed "transport" in the singular. This proved that his claim that he had committed a "silly misreading" was false. When he published *Hitler's War,* three years later in 1977, he knew that Himmler's phone call to Heydrich concerned just *one* trainload of Jews. Therefore, his assertion in the book that he had incontrovertible evidence that Hitler tried to stop the deportation of the Jews—as opposed to one trainload of Jews—was false and he knew it.

Irving seemed momentarily taken aback by the judge's observation. He stopped, reread the letter, and then, with a slight bow of thanks to Judge Gray, acknowledged, "You are absolutely right, my Lord. You are absolutely right." Despite having been caught by the judge in his own fiction, Irving showed no embarrassment. Without missing a beat, he came up with an alternative explanation. He had not misread the text. He had interpreted the word *"Judentransport"* as transportation of *all* the Jews. He then thanked the judge: "I am indebted to your Lordship for having . . . took [*sic*] me back into the mind set of 26 years ago."[10] While Judge Gray kept his counsel about what he thought of Irving's volte-face about transportation, Rampton did not: "When you come into the witness box to answer questions on oath, you simply pluck an explanation out of the air, do you not?"[11]

Rampton asked Irving to produce the evidence upon which he based his claim that Himmler was "summoned" to the bunker. Without pausing, Irving responded, "My very great expertise on this matter." Rampton, who had been glancing down at his papers, looked up with surprise: "What?" Irving repeated his answer: "My very great expertise on this matter. Do you wish me to elaborate?" Judge Gray, looking somewhat perplexed at Irving's response, suggested he had better elaborate since he was not quite sure he understood the answer. Irving explained that no Reich official could show up on Hitler's doorstep without permission. Himmler, therefore, must have been "summoned." Rampton asked if Himmler wasn't of sufficiently high standing for him to be able to place a call to Hitler and ask if he could come in to tell him something. Irving agreed that he was. In that case, Rampton wondered, why had he used the word "summoned"? "Because then Hitler would have said all right, come and see me."[12] Once again, I marveled at the *hutzpah* of Irving's explanation. Hitler's putative response of "come and see me" justified the word "summoned."

Rampton next asked about Irving's claim that, after having been "summoned," Himmler was "obliged" to call Heydrich to order the cessation of the killings. The call to Heydrich was placed, according to Himmler's diary, at 1:30 P.M., one hour *before* he met with Hitler. There was no documentary evidence to prove that Himmler saw Hitler before making the call. Rampton wondered who "obliged, that is to say, compelled Himmler to make this call?" Irving's answer was unequivocal. "His own inner conscience. That was why I used the word 'obliged.' Otherwise I would have said 'ordered.'" Rampton rather laconically observed that Irving's answers hardly constituted the "incontrovertible evidence" he had promised his readers. Moreover, Rampton admonished Irving, "when we say 'evidence' we mean 'evidence' not 'inference.'"[13]

Rampton next challenged Irving about his claim that he had "misread" the word *"haben"* as *"Juden,"* transforming Himmler's December 1 diary entry from the "administrative leaders of the SS are to remain where they are" to "Jews are to stay where they are." His explanation was fundamentally flawed because it left *"Verwaltungsführer der SS"* (administrative leaders of the

SS) hanging in midair meaning nothing. Irving had submitted to the court the page on which he had taken notes about the December 1 diary entry. The notes showed that he had whited out *"Juden,"* and replaced it with the word *"haben."* The correction had been made, he said, with a typewriter that he disposed of some ten or fifteen years earlier. "That is how early I realized my error," Irving told Rampton.[14] Irving's explanation, however, created another conundrum for him. He had just introduced evidence with a correction that he made on a typewriter he had disposed of ten to fifteen years earlier. In other words, Irving had discovered his mistake and corrected it on his notes, well *before* the publication of the 1991 edition of *Hitler's War.* His failure to correct the "mistake" in the book, Rampton charged, was deliberate. "You wanted to keep this picture of benign, magnanimous Adolf Hitler holding up his arm to save the Jews before the public," Rampton said. Irving denied that it was deliberate and dismissed it as "a pretty meaningless sentence." Rampton shook his head back and forth as Irving made his case. He looked decidedly unconvinced.[15]

## SELECTED QUOTATIONS AND PERVERTED MEANINGS

Rampton, continuing his assault on Irving's "chain of documents" that purportedly demonstrated Hitler's magnanimous behavior toward Jews, returned to the Bruns report that Irving had cited in his opening speech. In April 1945, the British had recorded German general Walter Bruns describing for his fellow POW German officers a mass shooting of five thousand German Jews in Riga. Irving had argued on the first day of the trial that if he were a denier he would not have repeatedly quoted this document.[16]

Rampton acknowledged that Irving was right. He *had* cited the Bruns report on a number of different occasions. However, Rampton continued, he had cited it in a way that completely skewed its meaning. According to the document, Bruns had told his fellow German prisoners that, after witnessing the shooting he protested to the SS officer at the site, Altemeyer, telling him that the victims represented "valuable manpower," which should not be wasted. Altemeyer transmitted Bruns's complaint to Berlin. Altemeyer subsequently reported to Bruns that Hitler had issued new orders: "The mass shootings of this kind must no longer take place in the future. . . . They are to be carried out more discreetly." According to the Bruns report, Hitler knew and essentially approved of the killings.

But Irving had propagated, Rampton charged, a very different and dishonest interpretation of the Bruns report in 1992 in a speech he gave at the California-based Institute for Historical Review. Knowing that Rampton was considered a meticulous professional, who never entered court without being exquisitely prepared, I was surprised when he momentarily could not recall the name of the institute. He hesitated until Heather quickly reminded him. At that meeting, Rampton continued, Irving had also told his audience that Bruns had protested the killings and then an "order comes back from Hitler, 'these mass shootings have to stop at once,' so Hitler intervened to stop it."[17] In an article in the *Journal of Historical Review,* Irving had repeated this misinterpretation when he wrote that Hitler ordered that such mass murders were to stop forthwith.[18] What Irving had done was include the first half of Hitler's order—the mass shootings must stop—but omit the second half of Hitler's orders—that they are to be carried out more discreetly. When Rampton asked him why he had only told his audience about half of Hitler's order, Irving replied that he did not write books about the Holocaust. He wrote about Adolf Hitler and such a report would probably have "bore[d] the pant[s] off" his readers. Furthermore, Irving continued, he had discounted the reference to Hitler's order because "evidence shows" that he issued no such order. Rampton challenged Irving's claim. There was no evidence that Hitler had *not* issued the order. There was, at best, only "an absence of evidence." Irving glared at Rampton.

> IRVING: I hate to remind you of the basic principle of English law that a man is innocent until proven guilty; am I right?
> RAMPTON: Hitler is not on trial, alas.
> IRVING: Is Hitler somehow excluded from this general rule of fair play?[19]

I almost fell out of my chair. For a moment, everyone in the courtroom—Judge Gray included—seemed stunned. Rampton pressed on, demanding that Irving admit that his rendition of Hitler's order—including only the first half and leaving out the second—was "completely dishonest." Irving insisted he had done nothing wrong and had provided his listeners and readers with the essential part of the information. Judge Gray turned toward Irving and offered him some advice: "Read it through to yourself again . . . And consider that answer, Mr Irving." Irving stood his ground. He could "see no objection" to his summary of Bruns's report. Judge Gray, sounding a bit frustrated, intervened again. "Can I put it to you straight, as it were, because this is the suggestion? . . . That what you have said . . . namely the renewed orders that such mass murders were to stop forthwith, totally perverts the sense of Bruns' conversation in captivity because Bruns makes clear that Altemeyer said that the killings were to continue?"[20] Irving stood his ground. For a moment, Judge Gray looked like he was considering saying something. After a moment's consideration, he sat back and did not press the point.

At lunch I sat next to Rampton and asked him about his courtroom "tactics." Were there certain stylistic things he did that I, as a novice, might not notice. He told me that he makes a point of not looking at witnesses when cross-examining them. "You'll see that I look away from Irving even as I am asking him direct questions." He had two reasons for doing so. "If you look at someone directly for long periods of time you tend to develop a relationship with him. And that's the last thing I want with Irving." There was another reason. "I want to telegraph a message of how little I think of him and his enterprise." Rampton then reminded me of how he had stumbled over the name of the Institute for Historical Review. "Did it scare you when I could not remember its name?" I admitted it had bothered me, particularly since the IHR figures so prominently into Irving's denial activities. Smiling, Rampton explained that he had not forgotten the IHR's name. "This was my way of showing how insignificant an organization I think it is."

After lunch, Rampton continued to cross-examine Irving about evidence that, we argued, stood in sharp contradiction to his claims about Hitler. On December 12, 1941, right after Germany declared war on the United States, Hitler spoke to the Nazi Party's highest political and administrative leaders. He reiterated his "prophecy" of January 1939—if Jews precipitated a world war they would experience their own annihilation. He had repeated this threat on previous occasions. This time, however, he added an addendum. *"The world war is here, the annihilation of Jewry must be the necessary consequence"* (emphasis added).[21] It seemed quite clear that Hitler was saying: "War has come. The annihilation of the Jews is about to be a reality." This was yet another indication of Hitler's culpability. Rampton noted that Irving, in his book *Goebbels,* had quoted other portions of this speech, but had conveniently omitted this critical element.

When the questioning for the week ended, I felt completely drained. Just then a reporter approached me. I politely reminded him that I was not talking to the press. "Oh, I know that," he said, "I want to tell *you* something." Irving had just been approached by a woman who told him that her parents had been gassed at Auschwitz. Irving told her, in earshot of a number of reporters, "Madam, you may be pleased to know that they almost certainly died of typhus, as did Anne Frank."[22] I winced. The reporter continued, "Why would anyone be 'pleased' to hear their parents died of typhus while imprisoned in a concentration camp?" I shook my head. Even if I had been able to freely speak to him, there really was nothing to say.

I was anxious to return to my apartment, cook dinner, and collapse with a good book, preferably one having nothing to do with the Holocaust. As I was leaving, Ninette Perahia, a friend of the Blumenthals and wife of the concert pianist, Murray Perahia, approached to invite me to join her family that night for an informal supper. "Pasta in the kitchen" was how she described it. I demurred. Once again, Ursula insisted: "Come. You look like you could use a night off." And once again, against my better judgment, I agreed to go. A few hours later I met the Blumenthals at the Green Park tube station on Piccadilly. We traveled to the outskirts of London and, as we approached the Perahia home, two exuberant young boys came running out to greet us.

As we walked up the path and entered the house, we were enveloped by the sounds of Bach: *The Goldberg Variations*. It took me a moment to realize this was not a CD: this was the real thing. Grammy award–winning concert pianist Murray Perahia, whose own family had been scarred by the Holocaust, was in the next room, practicing for his forthcoming concert at New York's Lincoln Center. Not wanting to disturb him, we stood in the vestibule enjoying our own private world-class concert. As the rich sound of the music being played by one of the greatest Bach interpreters of our time washed over me, my exhaustion dissipated. Slowly the memory of Sussman's tears, the old lady with the number on her forearm, and Irving's response to the woman whose parents had died in Auschwitz began to recede from my memory, if only for the moment.

# EIGHT

# THE HOLOCAUST: RANDOM KILLINGS OR SYSTEMATIC GENOCIDE?

In order to accommodate the many spectators who wanted to attend the hearing, Judge Gray managed to move the trial to Courtroom 73, the largest courtroom in the building. With its white walls, blond tables, and standard-issue office chairs, it looked like a small university lecture hall circa 1960. Given its rather nondescript character, I reflected that if Agatha Christie's *Witness for the Prosecution* had been filmed in this room it never would have become a classic, Tyrone Power and Marlene Dietrich notwithstanding. On the front wall, behind the judge's bench was a large gold royal coat of arms, lending the room its only official character. The multitiered public gallery in the back could accommodate about sixty people.

Janet Purdue, the courtroom usher, was a gregarious, dark-haired, heavy-set woman of about forty, with a muted Cockney accent. Precisely at 10:25 A.M., she opened the doors. Directing people to their seats and checking press credentials, she deftly managed the hubbub. When the seats were filled, she closed the doors, leaving some people protesting in the hall. When Janet strode by my table, her black court gown flowing behind her, I suggested she let the people in the hall stand. She sternly admonished me: "No one stands in my court." I quickly resolved not to tangle with her. Judge Gray presided over the case. Janet clearly presided over the courtroom.

Irving began by telling the judge that when he presented his case during the previous week, he had not adequately expanded upon his reputation as a historian. Judge Gray reassured Irving that he had "produced enough" particularly since this was "an action on Professor Lipstadt's book," not on his reputation. Irving insisted that his reputation was relevant because "the sources on which that book draws have been part and parcel of this campaign to destroy my legitimacy." Judge Gray conceded that his reputation was relevant up to a point. "If Professor Lipstadt has jumped on board a sort of bandwagon of critics of yours . . ." As soon as Judge Gray said "bandwagon," Irving's eyes opened wide. Pumping his fists in affirmation, he loudly interjected, "Use that phrase!" Irving may have been pleased by Judge Gray's word choice. I was not. I feared it might suggest an unconscious contempt for Irving's critics. Judge Gray ruled that if Irving could prove I was part and parcel of a conspiracy that supplied me with information, the defense would have to justify my reliance on that material.[1]

Irving next complained—yet again—that I was not going to submit myself to cross-examination. I knew my testimony would not advance our case, but I was increasingly worried about remaining silent. I rarely shied away from a fight, even when logic dictated I should. I passed Rampton a note: "Remember: I'm ready to testify." He crumpled up the paper and shook his head as if to indicate that I was telling him something he already knew.

Irving, announcing that he had information that would challenge Robert Jan van Pelt's credibility, asked whether he was obliged to disclose it to the defense. Judge Gray explained that, if it related to issues being analyzed, it had to be disclosed. Irving begrudgingly said he would comply, even though it was like "playing poker with the other person having a mirror over your head." This brought Rampton to his feet. Litigation, he protested, was not poker. "All the cards have to be on the table." Irving, sounding a bit wounded, insisted that he deserved praise, not criticism. "I do not think . . . any party in an action has ever made a fuller discovery than I have, including the disclosure of my entire diaries." Judge Gray nodded in agreement: "I think that is fair . . . I think that is right."[2] Behind me I heard Anthony quietly fume, "His diaries? He fought their release tooth and nail." I was surprised— and somewhat annoyed—that Judge Gray seemed unaware of this.

## CORNFLAKES AND APPLIANCES

Not that I had any time to reflect on Judge Gray's attitude. Irving reentered the witness box and Rampton continued his questioning. He began with the

World War II Bletchley Park intercepts Irving had submitted as evidence. Bletchley Park, fifty miles north of London, was the site of Ultra, the top-secret decryption project that broke Germany's Enigma codes. Among the decrypts were reports from units on the Eastern Front describing the massacres of Jews. In August 1941, one general boasted that thirty thousand Jews had already been murdered in his region. Based on these types of communiqués, British intelligence experts had concluded by September 1941 that there was "evidence of a policy of savage intimidation if not of ultimate extermination." Churchill, facing the ultimate Hobson's choice, said nothing publicly—despite the fact that it would have alerted some of the victims to their fate—because it would have also tipped off the Germans that the British had broken their code.

One of the decrypts Irving had submitted described how, in November 1941, 940 Berlin Jews had been dispatched to Riga on a train equipped with 3,000 kilos of bread, 200 kilos of peas, 300 kilos of cornflakes, 47,200 *Reichsmark*, flour, nutriments, soup powder, and spices. A few days later another intercept reported that a trainload of German Jews from Bremen had also been dispatched to Riga with *"Geräte"* ("appliances"), which Irving translated as tools of their trade. These decrypts proved, Irving argued, that Jews were being resettled equipped with food to satisfy their immediate needs, tools of their trade, and a substantial supply of cash. They constituted a "dent in the image" of the Holocaust and countered the perception of "wretched victims . . . stuffed into trains, with no food and water for three or four days, and shipped across Europe to their deaths."

Rampton asked Irving what proof he had that the supplies were intended for these Jews. Irving shrugged his shoulders and calmly said, "None whatsoever," and then added that it "would be perverse to assume that it was not." I contrasted Irving's conviction that the supplies on the train proved that Jews were being resettled, with his insistence that only a Hitler-signed document would prove that the German leader ordered the Holocaust. Rampton reacted similarly, declaring Irving ready to "leap to conclusions in favor of the SS and the Nazis on every single occasion." These intercepts, Rampton continued, rather than constitute a "dent in Holocaust perception," simply indicated that the trains had food and cash, some of which may have been for these Jews, prior to their being shot. Then, to prove his point, Rampton showed Irving a communiqué reporting that, on November 25, 1941, eight days after the cornflakes-laden train left Germany,

2,934 Jews from Berlin, Munich, and Frankfurt had been executed at Kovno. "Is it likely that that is where your train load of 944 well provisioned Jews wound up?" Irving conceded, "It is not impossible."[3]

Irving's next answer surprised me. Rampton had asked how many Jews were shot on the Eastern Front. Irving responded, "At least half million and probably as many as one and a half million." His previous estimates had been, at most, hundreds or thousands. I passed Anthony a note: "Why is he conceding such a high death rate?" Anthony wrote back: "I think that he is playing (as he sees it) a tactical game of retreat and advance, in order to continue his practice of appealing to multiple audiences—to deny a bit for the deniers, and to admit a bit for the court and the (rest of) the civilized world. But don't worry this game is bound to fall apart as the trial unfolds, because under cross-examination it is impossible to maintain alternative positions."

Rampton must have seen Irving's tactics similarly. He insisted that Irving affirm that the Jews to whom he referred had been "disposed of by shooting." Though Rampton did not say so, I knew he wanted to prevent Irving from subsequently attributing their deaths to war-related privations. Irving gave a qualified answer. They were shot, but not on orders from Berlin. Berlin "put the Jews and the other victims on the trains and sent them to the East with the food and equipment to start a new life. Once they arrived the system broke down and the murderers stepped in."[4]

Rampton, noting that reports on the killing of vast numbers of Jews were transmitted to Heydrich, Himmler's second-in-command, asked Irving if these messages weren't "evidence of some kind of system operating at the behest . . . of the authorities in Berlin"? Judge Gray echoed Rampton's query: "Berlin *must have* known that the shootings were continuing on, as you [Irving] would accept, a massive scale. To that extent would you accept it is systematic?" (emphasis added). Though I firmly believed history should not be adjudicated in the courtroom, I was beginning to sense that, when dealing with a man like Irving, the courtroom offered certain advantages. Here, when the judge or opposing counsel asked a question, evasiveness and imprecise answers would not suffice.

After some hemming and hawing, Irving conceded that these killings were systematic. But before I could even absorb the implications of this concession, Irving qualified his answer. They were like Vietnam's Mi Lai, where American soldiers massacred civilians. In war, Irving contended, these things happen. "They are subsequently covered up by the people in charge." As a

baby boomer and sixties protestor, I remembered Mi Lai well. In fact, I had
met one of the American helicopter pilots who had tried to stop the massacre. I knew, therefore, that Mi Lai was an entirely different matter. While
the American soldiers hid their offense, the Germans left a paper trail. There
was a consistent flow of information from the Eastern Front, including an
*Einsatzgruppen* report that listed: "Executions carried out 137,346," of whom
98 percent were Jews. "Do not these things jump out at you, Mr Irving?" Instead of answering, Irving brushed Rampton's query aside. "This is of great
interest to a Holocaust historian, but not to an Hitler historian."[5]

Rampton ignored his comment and continued to present Irving with evidence that the murder of the Jews on the Eastern Front was well known to
the highest authorities in Berlin. In early 1942, the head of the SS in Minsk
told civilian officials that a "complete liquidation of the Jews" was not currently possible "because the ground is too frozen to dig pits . . . [for] mass
graves." Nor, the official continued, could a "complete eradication of the
Jews" occur now "because workers were still needed from among the[m]."[6]
Once again, Irving belittled the significance of the evidence, describing it as a
"poor substitute for the real thing"—hard evidence that Hitler had ordered
it. Irving's refusal to consider the historical evidence in these documents
gave Rampton the opportunity to refocus the court's attention on our central argument: "What is your task as a historian, Mr Irving? . . . Is it not to
give an objective, fair, interpretation to the cumulative effect of all the evidence? You will not draw the obvious conclusions from the evidence before
you, simply because you have not got a piece of paper signed by Adolf Hitler
saying, 'Do it.' "[7] For Irving cornflakes on a train meant Jews were to be happily resettled and a message from Himmler to Heydrich not to shoot one
trainload of Berlin Jews constituted incontrovertible evidence that Hitler
gave the order to stop the killings.

Rampton became more insistent: "[Was] what the SS were doing in the
East . . . to a total of perhaps 1.5 million [Jews] . . . done on the authority of
and with the knowledge of at least Heydrich in Berlin?" Irving responded
most matter-of-factly: "Yes, quite clearly." Rampton looked relieved: "At long
last I have a concession that Heydrich authorized and knew about shootings
of these hundreds of thousand of Jews in the East." Irving protested that it
was not a concession because he had said this "all along."[8]

*　*　*

Rampton asked Irving to examine a copy of Himmler's diary entry from December 18, 1941. Irving protested that the document was irrelevant because he did not have access to it when he was writing his books. Judge Gray acknowledged that there was "a lot of force" to Irving's argument, but added a caveat. If the defense introduced a document with which Irving was unfamiliar, but which pointed unequivocally in a particular direction and Irving denied that it did, we could then argue that Irving was not objective when shown a new document.[9] Judge Gray's ruling illustrated that Irving faced a problem of his own making. If he rejected documents that unequivocally proved him wrong, he would prove me correct, namely that he discounted evidence that disputed his preexisting conclusions. If he accepted these documents, he would have to admit he was wrong about the Holocaust. I was beginning to see how the strategy Anthony had laid out for me years earlier was playing itself out. The historical evidence would box Irving in between his lies and the truth. Though this moment passed without fanfare, it was of significant tactical importance.

On December 18, 1941, Himmler recorded the topics he discussed with Hitler. Next to *"Judenfrage"* (Jewish Question), he entered Hitler's response: "To be exterminated as partisans." Rampton next read from the December 1942 *Einsatzgruppen* Report No. 51, which listed 363,000 Jews killed. He contextualized the two documents. In December 1941, Hitler said liquidate the Jews. "Then, low [*sic*] and behold . . . just over a year later, comes along a report from the East saying that just that has happened." Irving quietly answered, "Yes." Rampton continued, "The probability that Hitler saw that report and was, therefore, what shall we say, implicated in the murder of all those 363,000 Eastern Jewish is confirmed, is it not?" Irving agreed. "Yes, there is no contention between us on that point."

I was about to turn to James and happily proclaim another concession, when Irving qualified his answer. Hitler *had* ordered the Jews killed, but "as part of the partisan combating." Rampton was prepared for Irving's maneuver. Report No. 51 included the information that, in addition to the 363,000 Jews who were killed, 14,000 "partisan accomplices" had been killed. If Jews were partisans why were the two listed separately? Rampton answered his own question. "This is put coldly and bluntly, a record of the number of Jews deliberately executed for the reason that they are Jews." Irving quietly acknowledged that this was a "reasonable supposition."[10]

Rampton contrasted Irving's answer in the courtroom with a statement he had made at a 1986 Australian press conference. He had declared that the Jews were the victims of a large number of "rather run-of-the-mill criminal elements which exist in Central Europe." These criminals "acted on their own impulse, their own initiative."[11] Irving insisted that there was no contradiction between his concessions in court and his statements in Australia. Apparently caught off guard by Irving's claims, Rampton could only manage a "What?" Irving argued that these documents proved that the "mindless criminals on the Eastern front who carried out these killing operations had a motive of their own to do the killing even when they were ordered by Berlin or by Hitler's headquarters to stop." Judge Gray interjected, "That . . . is not really the point is it?" Irving apologized. "Oh, I am sorry. I must have missed the point that Mr Rampton is asking about." The judge instructed Irving, "Just focus on the question. What is being put is that what you said in 1986 about these men on the Eastern front having acted on their own impulse is at any rate now known by you not to be right, because in fact it was authorized at the highest level, namely by Hitler?" Entrapped by the very chain of documents that he claimed exonerated Hitler, Irving conceded, "Certainly Hitler sanctioned the killing of the Jews on the Eastern front . . . the non-German Jews, and that has never been a matter of contention for me." His earlier statments, were, he said, attempts "to explain the mentality of the people who are [sic] doing the killing on the Eastern Front."

As the clock moved toward the lunch adjournment, Rampton was intent on preventing Irving from retreating from his concession about Hitler's approval of the killings on the Eastern Front. "My suggestion is this, that those words you used in Australia . . . suggest[ed] to the audience that this killing of the Eastern Jews on a vast scale went on without the knowledge or approval of Hitler and his cronies." I sighed with relief when Irving responded, "If that impression is given, it is the wrong impression."[12] There were no retreats and we went to lunch.

As we sat in the subterranean conference room in Rampton's chambers munching crustless white bread egg salad and smoked salmon sandwiches, the researchers were almost giddy with excitement. They reviewed every aspect of Irving's various concessions, as well as his attempts to deny that they were concessions. Years of their work were paying off. In contrast, Rampton was very quiet. I watched him nurse a glass of French Burgundy. As lunch was ending, I told him that on the previous evening the paralegals had taken me out for dinner and that, while we walked back to the underground,

Laura Tyler said something that deeply touched me. "Working on this case makes me feel as if—at a very young age and the very start of my legal career—I'm making a difference. The problem is that, after this, commercial cases will feel so petty." Rampton looked at me quizzically. I feared he thought Laura unprofessional for failing to grasp that a life in the law meant mundane cases, occasionally punctuated by more interesting ones. Instead he said, "But Deborah, that's true for all of us." He sounded a bit hurt that I needed to be told that.

When we resumed deliberations, Irving told Judge Gray that his Australian remarks that the shootings were conducted by rogue officers had been made fourteen years earlier, suggesting, it was not fair to hold him to these views. As soon as Irving made this point, Heather—who had an uncanny ability to put her hands on the precise document at precisely the right time—handed Rampton a piece of paper. When she saw me watching, she passed me a copy. The paper contained two statements by Irving. In a 1992 letter to the head of the IHR, the California-based denial institute, he wrote: "My position remains unchanged, that there were certain Mi Lai–type atrocities by troops in Russia, that the gas chambers and factories of death are Hollywood legends." The second excerpt came from his 1992 presentation to the IHR conference: "We have to accept there were Mi Lai–type massacres, where SS officers . . . machine gun[ned] hundreds if not thousands of Jews." This was precisely in line with what he had said fourteen years earlier in Australia. When Rampton finished reading these statements, Irving declared, "I am accused of being consistent, am I?" Rampton grabbed the linguistic opportunity. "Yes, you are. You are accused of consistently and knowingly reducing the extent of the responsibility for these massacres. . . . The words 'Mi Lai–type massacres,' mean . . . these massacres were done by criminal gangers [sic] unauthorized in the East without the approval, consent or knowledge of the people in Berlin." Irving, all traces of bravado gone from his voice, conceded, "That is correct."

Rampton admonished Irving that, had he bothered to do the research done by other historians, he could have known it was wrong before he said it. Irving, sounding a bit forlorn, protested, "I am not a Holocaust historian." "Then why," Rampton demanded, "are you making a categorical assertion that they were simply unauthorized gangster killings?"[13] Irving insisted he had only been answering a question from the audience. Irving was still responding when Rampton began to shuffle through his papers. Ostensibly, he was looking for a document. I suspected, however, that he was trying to convey how little credence he accorded these explanations.

## RAMSHACKLE AND HAPHAZARD KILLING OPERATIONS

For years Irving's mantra had been that the absence of a document, because no document exists in which Hitler explicitly says "we are liquidating them," proves that Hitler did not know about the liquidations. Now Rampton reminded Irving that Report 51 with its 363,000 death toll had the notation: "Presented to Hitler." Irving conceded that Hitler might have looked at it, but, if he did, he saw it only as a "footnote," something inconsequential. Judge Gray looked startled. "It is quite a simple document, and it is referring to the killing by shooting of 300,000 Jews. Well, you have to be quite a man to just pass over that . . . ?" Irving told Judge Gray that Hitler had bigger things on his plate. He was primarily concerned with his army's woes at Stalingrad. Judge Gray seemed unpersuaded: "He is not going to notice a document telling him 300,000 . . . innocent civilians were being shot by his army?"[14]

On the next day Rampton reminded Irving of a letter he had written in 1989 to West German historian Rainer Zitelmann, in which he contended that no serious historian can now believe that Auschwitz, Treblinka, and Maidanek were factories of death, "all the experts in scientific forensic evidence is to the contrary." Rampton accused Irving of having no evidence to "contradict the probability" that these camps were extermination facilities. Irving quietly concurred: "I have no evidence to contradict the probability." Judge Gray interrupted to ask Irving, "Does that mean that you now resile from the view you expressed in your letter?" This question produced an exchange that made my head swim.

> IRVING: No, my Lord. I am just confirming the way he put the
> statement. I have no evidence to contradict his statement because I
> have no evidence, period.
> RAMPTON: Then will you accept it is a probability then?
> IRVING: No. That is a different thing entirely. I do not want to sound as
> though I am a bit of an eel on this but . . . I do not want to sound
> slippery; I just do not want to be nailed down in one corner where

later on you will hold it up dripping and slithering next day and say, "Look what you said yesterday."

JUSTICE GRAY: But, you see, you said to Dr Zitelmann that it was clear to you that no serious historian can now believe that Treblinka and some other camps were [death factories].

IRVING: Quite. They were purpose-built factories of death; in other words, [they] had no other purpose than that.

JUSTICE GRAY: Oh, I see.

RAMPTON: . . . This is getting a bit like a fourth form debating society, I fear—a moment ago you said to me that you had no evidence to contradict the probability that these were purpose-built extermination facilities.

IRVING: Yes, because I have no evidence, period.

RAMPTON: No, but you write in this letter: "All the experts in scientific forensic evidence is to the contrary." . . . What is the expert and scientific (forensic) evidence that contradicts the probability that Treblinka was a purpose-built extermination facility?

Rampton kept demanding that Irving explain what evidence he was referring to in the letter. Irving protested that he could not remember the exact details of a letter he wrote eleven years earlier. Judge Gray, in what seemed to be an effort to help Irving, asked if, when he made these statements about the other camps, he was "extrapolating from Auschwitz"? Irving, looking a bit like a man who had been thrown a lifeline, agreed that he indeed was doing that. Rampton immediately jumped in: "But how could you extrapolate from Auschwitz, Mr Irving? It has never been proposed by anybody, so far as I know, that the Nazis used hydrogen cyanide anywhere outside Auschwitz to kill people with, has it?" Irving lifted his arm, made a large arc in the air, as if to give added emphasis to his words, and, with evident frustration, angrily proclaimed:

This is what I find so puzzling. We were told that this is part of [*sic*] system . . . and yet, apparently, they used cyanide here, petrol gas there, diesel fumes there, bullets in yet another place, bulldozers, hangings, shootings—it appears to have been a totally ramshackle and haphazard operation. A total lack of system.[15]

Irving sounded almost insulted that we would ascribe to the Third Reich—a supposed bastion of organizational efficiency—such an imprecise operation.

On the following day the question of gassings at the other camps came up again. Irving again protested that he was not an "expert on that" and did not know. This time, Rampton did not let Irving's answer go unchallenged. "A man in your position does not enter the arena waving flags and blowing trumpets unless he has taken the trouble to verify in advance what it is that he is proposing to say." When Irving repeated his familiar refrain, "I am not a Holocaust historian," Rampton exploded, "Why do you not keep your mouth shut about the Holocaust?" Irving grinned, as if he were pleased to have gotten under Rampton's skin. "Because I am asked about it." He then shifted his gaze to the public gallery and added with a half-smile, "It apparently obsesses people."

Rampton, continuing to place before the court statements by Irving that were at odds with the available evidence, noted that in 1989, Irving had said, "I am prepared to accept that local Nazis tried *bizarre* methods of liquidating Jews. . . . They may have *experimented* using gas trucks . . . [which was] a very inefficient way of killing people" (emphasis added). How, Rampton wondered, could Irving have described the gassings as "local bizarre experiments"—thereby implying that the operation was on a small scale—when a June 1942 SS report stated: "Since December 1941 . . . 97,000 [Jews] were processed [gassed] by three trucks." Irving's response left me dumbfounded: "It's a very substantial achievement when you work it out with a pocket calculator." The normally unflappable James looked up in shock. Judge Gray asked, "Is it very limited and experimental?" Irving insisted he could not answer that question because he did not have access to the June 1942 report when he said the gassings were "limited and experimental." I wondered if he had forgotten the judge's ruling that we could ask him about a historical document, even if he did not have it at the time he made the statement. Judge Gray had clearly not forgotten. He instructed Irving, "Answer the question even so." Irving very quietly said, "Not on this scale. This is systematic."[16]

I turned to James and, momentarily forgetting he was nursing a sore arm as a result of a bicycle accident, hit him in the shoulder with my fist as if to say, "*Yes!*" I then turned to scan the gallery to see if other people had grasped what a major concession this was on Irving's part. An older woman

I knew to be a survivor was watching me. The corners of her mouth lifted slightly in a sad smile.

## DONALD CAMERON WATT: STRANGE TESTIMONY

Irving had asked Donald Cameron Watt, the distinguished London School of Economics Emeritus Professor of International Relations, to testify on his behalf. Watt refused and Irving subpoenaed him, leaving Watt no choice but to appear. On the day of Watt's testimony, Anthony arrived in court wearing a big smile. Clearly pleased about something, he made a beeline for my seat. He had received a call from one of the leaders of the British Jewish community, who had counseled me not to mount a response to Irving's charges. Suspecting that Anthony was pushing me into it, he had urged me to find some way to settle. I feared he had called Anthony with another round of complaints. I assumed Anthony had told him off with a witty but sharp bon mot and that this was the source of his satisfaction. I was wrong. The man had apologized and told Anthony he had been completely wrong to oppose what we were doing. His friends, who had shared his doubts, had also changed their opinion. I was impressed, not only by this man's forthrightness, but by Anthony's great pleasure at his phone call. I recalled how, at the time, Anthony had declared that he simply did not care what these people thought. He may not have cared then, but he certainly cared now.

I saw that Robert Jan, who was scheduled to begin testifying the following week, had arrived in court. I went over to welcome him. As I was returning to my seat, I saw him go over to Irving, amicably shake his hand, and begin an animated conversation that looked, from my perspective, very friendly. I watched them closely inspect a large aerial photograph of Auschwitz that Irving had placed on an easel next to his table. Irving was pointing something out as Robert Jan nodded intently. I turned to Anthony, pointed at this confab, and said, "What's that all about?" Anthony shrugged. He clearly was not going to waste any energy on this and, from the way he looked at me, thought that I shouldn't either. In any case, Janet had given her customary holler, calling the court to order.

When Watt entered the witness box, Irving resumed his role of barrister. Watt, a large, almost burly man in his seventies, spoke with a pronounced upper-crust British accent. With his somewhat rumpled suit, he looked and sounded like the prototype of the Oxbridge don in a British novel or a character in *Masterpiece Theatre*. He began, at Irving's request, by describing his Oxford education: "I indulged myself in the usual activities of undergraduates. That is to say, I wrote, I played opera, I ran the Poetry Society." I smiled at his description of these as "usual" undergraduate activities.

Then Watt began to assess Irving's work. I anticipated that, as an expert on World War II, he would not have kind things to say about Irving. I was wrong. Watt, speaking directly to Judge Gray, declared that, even if one disagrees with Irving's view of history, "it has to be taken seriously. He is after all, the only man of standing, on the basis of his other research, who puts the case for Hitler forward and it seems to me that it is mistaken to dismiss it." This endorsement startled me. I knew that in 1968 Watt had written a substantial introduction to a book Irving had edited and wondered whether he did not, therefore, feel a bit hamstrung about openly criticizing him. Nonetheless, given that Watt had been sent Evans's report, I was surprised by his seemingly unqualified praise. It was his next comment, however, that made me sit up ramrod straight. "I hope that I am never subjected to the kind of examination that Mr Irving's books have been suggested [*sic*] to by the Defence witnesses. . . . There are senior historical figures . . . whose work would not stand up . . . to this kind of examination." Did Watt believe that these senior historians had engaged in the same distortions we had found in Irving's work?

I was on the verge of despair when Watt's assessment of Irving became more critical. He told Irving that his claim that Himmler had conducted the killings without Hitler's knowledge was not supported by any historical information. "To assume that Himmler and his minions went beyond the limits of what Hitler had approved, seems to assume something inherently improbable and out of keeping with all we know of Himmler's relationship to Hitler." Seemingly untroubled by Watt's critique and delighted to be questioning this historian, a smiling Irving leaned toward the witness box and, in a tone that was more reminiscent of chitchat at a cocktail party than courtroom testimony, said, "Himmler's brother actually told me the same. He said, I cannot imagine Heinny would have done this on his own." Irving's use of Himmler's family nickname, "Heinny," was striking in its familiarity.[17]

Watt's criticisms left me unnerved. I would have expected him to praise, not castigate, our efforts. I wondered if I was not witnessing a certain "Old School" closing of the ranks around Irving. Watt seemed to have forgotten that Irving was trying to silence me and pull my book from circulation.

Rampton, convinced that Watt had said nothing substantive that could harm us, chose not to cross-examine him.

## A QUICKIE CONVERSION TO HOLOCAUST DENIAL

When Irving returned to the stand, Rampton reviewed Irving's conversion to Holocaust denial. In his diary, Irving recorded how, after arriving in Toronto for the Zündel trial, he spent a few hours reading Leuchter's report and declared himself much "impressed." The next day, he left for some sightseeing in Niagara Falls. Upon his return, he testified in court that Leuchter's report convinced him that "the whole of the Holocaust mythology is . . . open to doubt." In light of the importance Irving gave the report, his cursory examination of it and his failure to do any subsequent research was noteworthy. Rampton, using surprisingly blunt language, wondered if, as an historian and an expert witness, it did not behoove him "to keep your trap shut" until he had properly investigated the matter? Rampton accused Irving of venturing into an area of history "of which he had absolutely no knowledge whatever, making world-shattering statements" without having done the requisite research.[18]

Had Irving done some research, he might have discovered Leuchter's mistaken assumption that it took 3,200 parts of HCN per million to kill humans, when in fact it took far less. On the basis of this wrong calculation, Leuchter had contended that the residue from such a large amount of gas would have spread through the sewer system poisoning the entire camp; that the guards would have had to throw so much Zyklon B into the chamber that they themselves would have been poisoned; and that the *Sonderkommandos*—the inmates who removed the bodies—would have had to wait twenty-four hours before entering the chambers. All these claims were wrong, because it actually took only 10 percent of what Leuchter had assumed was necessary to kill humans.

Irving pulled himself up to his full height, threw back his shoulders, and, appropriating an almost military bearing, emphatically declared, "I am banned from visiting Auschwitz or the archives. I am the only historian in the world who is not allowed to set foot in the Auschwitz archives." Judging by the tone of his voice, he seemed to consider this ban a badge of honor. Rampton reminded Irving that the Auschwitz ban was not issued until eight years after he testified in Toronto. Why, in those eight years, did he never bother to visit the archives? Irving, chuckling, said he probably would have been banned earlier if he had tried to visit: "It is like the big casinos in Las Vegas. They do not want the big winners to come."[19] I heard someone in the gallery gasp.

## CROOKED JEWISH FINANCIERS

The videos and other materials in the second batch of discovery materials contained a cache of Holocaust-denial statements Irving had made in private off the record gatherings. As is often the case when one is speaking to groups of followers, he spoke a bit more frankly in these settings. In fact, at a "soirée" in Kentville, Canada, right after Zündel's trial, Irving told his audience how pleased he was that "we are such a small circle . . . today because I can talk, . . . more frankly." Irving told Judge Gray that statements made extemporaneously at private gatherings should be given less import than his written books. Judge Gray was not persuaded. "It seems to me . . . that you have been far more unrestrained in your assertions about Auschwitz when speaking at these various talks."[20] Rampton, in an effort to illustrate that Irving's private statements were far more revealing of his true thoughts and motives than those crafted for publication, read one of these "private" utterances:

> Hundreds of millions of innocent people have been bamboozled . . . for a purpose. . . . [E]very time a Jewish financier, a John Gutfreund, the Salomon brothers or Ivan Boesky or . . . Michael Milken . . . is caught with his hands deep in the till and he has . . . undoubtedly bilked hundreds of thousands of investors out of every penny they have got. . . . These financiers have laughed . . . because they can afford it. . . . When you . . . realize that they are Jewish, then the invitation is that the man in the street should say: Yes, but they have suffered, haven't they? They did have the Holocaust.

Judge Gray, with a bit of an edge in his voice, asked Irving, "So the Holocaust is a kind of a lie dreamt up in order to excuse crooked Jewish financiers?" Irving, looking somewhat uncomfortable, protested that he was "not put[ting] it like that." "What," a seemingly unpersuaded Judge Gray asked, "are you saying if not *that?*" Irving claimed he was simply repeating other people's opinion that the Holocaust "legend" protects Jews from criticism for their "activities in the world of finance, or because of their brutality on the West Bank or whatever."[21]

It was not just what Irving said in these small gatherings that we found significant, but the way his audience responded. Rampton noted that when Irving said that "more people died on the back seat of Edward Kennedy's car at Chappaquidick than ever died in a gas chamber in Auschwitz," they laughed. Rampton looked up from the page in front of him: "Laughter, Mr Irving?" His audience also laughed when Irving said that Elie Wiesel did a "Cook's tour of the different concentration camps." Irving protested that they were laughing at the "spurious survivors . . . those trying to climb on the Holocaust bandwagon." Why, Rampton wondered, would a serious matter such as someone falsely claiming to be an Auschwitz survivor provoke laughter? Irving explained, "Because there is something ludicrous . . . something pathetic about it."

Rampton had another explanation: Irving's audience were so "deeply antisemitic" that they reveled in Irving's words, which were "redolent of animosity, hostility, contempt, spite . . . just like Dr Goebbels [sic] articles." Irving quickly shot back, "Just like Winston Churchill talking about Adolf Hitler." Irving's equation of Goebbels with Churchill brought this British courtroom to attention. In the gallery, I saw Churchill's official biographer, Sir Martin Gilbert, paying rapt attention. Rampton's face grew flushed. Sounding for a moment like his client was Prime Minister Churchill—not Penguin or Lipstadt—he said, "Mr Churchill rallied this country to the flag during the war by being spiteful and beastly about Adolf Hitler. The difference is, unlike Dr Goebbels, Winston Churchill had a very good reason to be spiteful."[22] With that the second week of the trial ended.

As I left the courtroom, I reflected on the fact that in my many years of studying antisemitism, I had encountered people like Irving. I knew them, however, more in theory than practice. I did not anticipate—though I probably should have—the world of difference between reading about antisemitism and hearing it up close and personal. My inability publicly to denounce his statements was growing more and more frustrating.

Relieved that there were no paparazzi outside the building, I headed toward the underground when a distressed Ursula caught up with me to breathlessly tell me about an Australian reporter who had been sitting near her in the gallery. "She has exceptionally blond hair and gold wire-rimmed

glasses. She's in her thirties. I overheard her extolling Irving to a group of reporters, comparing him to Churchill and bemoaning how he had been
wronged by you." Feeling as if I could not deal with another issue, I
shrugged my shoulders and reassured her, "It's probably nothing."

That night, I gained, quite unexpectedly, another perspective on the trial.
I went to see Michael Frayn's *Copenhagen,* a play about the mysterious 1941
visit of Werner Heisenberg, the head of Germany's nuclear fission research
project and originator of the "uncertainty principle," to his mentor, the Dan-
ish physicist Niels Bohr. Some historians assume that Heisenberg was trying
to extract information from Bohr about the hydrogen atom. Frayn, who has
a more sympathetic theory about Heisenberg's trip, posits that he was trying
to make a deal with Bohr. Germany would not build a bomb if Bohr promised that the Allies would not build one either. Frayn also suggested that
Heisenberg sweetened the deal by offering to help Bohr, the son of a Jewish
mother, escape the deportations that would inevitably occur in Denmark.[23]

I was troubled by Frayn's suggestion that there was a moral equivalency
between Bohr's research and Heisenberg's work for the Nazis. Interested in
learning more about the play and the playwright, I bought a book with the
text of the play and an essay by Frayn. When I returned home, I brewed a
cup of tea and settled in to read it. I started by flipping to the bibliography to
see the sources upon which Frayn had relied. Among those listed was Irving's book on the German bomb program.[24] Suddenly the playwright's approach to the incident—both sides were equally guilty—made more sense.
As I prepared for bed, I realized how insidious Irving's influence is, even
when it was not direct or obvious.

# NINE

# QUEUES AND GAS CHAMBER
# CONTROVERSIES

The crowd that gathered each morning outside Courtroom 73 included a mix of Holocaust survivors and their children, history buffs, retirees, lawyers, courtroom junkies, teachers, and students. Intermingling with them were a contingent of Irving supporters. My friends also came to root for me, some intentionally, others on the spur of the moment, and their number increased as the trial progressed. One morning I spotted Betty, a friend and a child of survivors, who had just arrived from Milwaukee. "I read a news report a few days ago about Irving's supporters being present. It made me nuts. So I decided I'll be there too." Her friend, Sarah, having had the same reaction, planned to arrive that afternoon from Israel. Anthony, impressed by this growing stream of visitors, took to greeting me each morning with the question "And what country do your friends represent today?"

This was not a typical British queue. Three and four people vied for a single seat and rushed to it as soon as the doors opened. Rampton arrived around 10:20. The crowd would barely give an inch. Adopting his most curmudgeonly style—something he did well—Rampton would push his way through, muttering all the while. An ardent rugby fan, Rampton dubbed the crowd the "scrum," after the tight formation players use to protect the ball carrier. As people waited, strange configurations developed. One morning a young man in a "White Power" T-shirt stood next to a survivor. The survivor had taken off his jacket. I wasn't sure if he did so because of the heat in the crowded hallway or to ensure that his tattooed number was visible. As I walked by, someone gestured toward them and whispered, "Auschwitz tattoo trumps T-shirt. Correct?"

I had gotten used to seeing a beautifully coiffed, smartly dressed woman of about forty every morning in the queue. During the previous week she had sat right behind Irving, chatting with him during the breaks. When one of my friends, who had just arrived, asked for an update, the woman enthusiastically complied: "Oh, Irving's beating them on everything. He's doing great." When I heard what had happened, I dubbed this mysterious woman "Brunhilda."

I soon forgot about her when Irving rose to introduce a newspaper article about a lawsuit a Holocaust survivor had brought against an insurance company. According to the article the insurance company settled the suit because it feared the "jury will be sympathetic to a man who has survived a Nazi concentration camp." Irving asserted that this was the argument he had been making in his "rather heated remarks" about Jewish "fraudsters and racketeer[s] in the United States." Judge Gray told Irving he did not think the insurance company's decision and Irving's remarks were equivalent. The insurance company was concerned about a jury's sympathy with the victims, while Irving, Judge Gray observed, had contended that Jews who get into legal trouble "use the Holocaust as a kind of shield against their own criminality." Irving insisted that both instances dealt with the special "insulation" survivors enjoy. With that he turned his back to Judge Gray, faced the gallery, and added a postscript: "We all have the utmost sympathy with victims of the Holocaust and that includes myself, and I want to say that here."[1] The man with the tattoo on his arm glared.

Rampton then announced that Robert Jan van Pelt would begin testifying the following day. Since Robert Jan was scheduled to attend a Holocaust conference in Stockholm later in the week, Rampton suggested that court adjourn on that day and reconvene on Friday, when we did not usually meet, to accommodate Robert Jan's schedule. Irving amicably agreed.

## FABRICATING EVIDENCE AND FUMIGATING CADAVERS

With preliminaries completed, Rampton turned to Irving's 1989 press conference launching the British edition of Leuchter's report. A reporter had asked Irving whether he thought evidence used at Nuremberg had been fabricated. Irving had replied, "Oh, we fabricated a lot of evidence" and then illustrated his point by telling the story of the Nuremberg testimony of Marie Vaillant-Couturier, a French-Catholic resistance fighter who was interned in Birkenau. She described for the international tribunal how camp inmates died from thirst, starvation, beatings, insufficient clothing, illness, and gassings.[2] According to her, inmates who were punished received fifty blows with a stick. The beating was administered by a swinging apparatus manipulated by an SS man.

Vaillant-Couturier testified that, when SS officers needed a servant, they would accompany the woman commandant of the camp to the women's camp to choose an inmate. They made their choices when prisoners were being disinfected because then the women were naked. She also testified that one of the camp barracks was used as a brothel for the SS. Prisoners who had been in other camps had reported to her that the same brothel system existed in their camps.

Irving had told reporters at his press conference that the American judge on the Nuremberg Tribunal, Francis Biddle, was so appalled by her testimony that he wrote in his private diary: "I don't believe a word of what she is saying. I think she is a bloody liar." But, Irving asserted, Judge Biddle kept these sentiments to himself and, therefore, her testimony entered the official record unscathed.

Rampton asked if Judge Biddle had actually called her a "bloody liar." Irving admitted this was his "gloss," but insisted it was a legitimate gloss because Judge Biddle was "fed up" with this woman's "implausible" testimony. Rampton took out a copy of the relevant pages of Biddle's diary. After summarizing the various punishments Vaillant-Couturier had described, the American judge started a new paragraph. He summarized her description of the brothel and her claim that "all the other camps used the same system." Biddle then wrote: "(This I doubt.)"

Rampton put down the page, looked up at Irving, and accused him of having taken a "side note"—Biddle's reference to her comments about brothels at other camps—and inflated it into "general doubt" about her entire testimony. Irving insisted that Biddle was rejecting her *entire* testimony, not one small aspect of it. Then he turned to Judge Gray and said he was willing to "concede, for what it is worth," that his comments about Biddle's doubts came "four or five . . . or possibly even ten years" after he examined the judge's diary in the Collection of Nuremberg Trial Documents at Syracuse University in New York State.

For the first time since the trial began, I thought Irving had made a good point. If so much time had passed between his visit to the archive and his press conference, then his failure to recall precisely what the judge wrote was understandable. But then I heard a commotion behind me. Heather was excitedly whispering in Rampton's ear as she hurriedly ruffled through her files. She pulled out a document, circled something on it, and handed it to Rampton. He studied it for a moment and then, somewhat offhandedly, resumed his cross-examination: "Tell me when you went to Syracuse?" Irving offered to check the precise date. Rampton, all traces of offhandedness suddenly gone from his voice, suggested he not bother. Gesturing to the document Heather had handed him, Rampton noted that in December 1999, shortly before the start of the trial, Irving had responded to our Statement of Case. In it he had written: "I originally read Judge Biddle's papers . . . in 1988."[3] I suppressed a smile. Irving had—yet again—entrapped himself. The press conference at which he said Biddle called Couturier a "bloody liar" was in 1989. In other words, in contrast to the testimony he had just given, there had not been "four or five . . . even ten years" between his examination of Biddle's diary and the press conference. There had been one year. I wondered if Irving had forgotten what he wrote or, so accustomed to having his distortions go unchallenged, reflexively assumed he could get away with this.

But Rampton wasn't quite finished. In his diary, Irving recorded how, after his 1988 visit to the Biddle archives, he drove directly to Toronto to give a speech. We had the text of that speech. Irving had told his audience that Biddle had written *"All* this I doubt." Irving's first distortion occurred but a few days, not years—as he had just claimed—after reading Biddle's diary.

Irving, no longer able to claim that his distortions were a result of the lapse of years, now insisted that his addition of "All" was not a distortion because Biddle was clearly referring to all of Vaillant-Couturier's testimony. Judge Gray—who generally waited for Rampton to finish before asking his questions—intervened: "Yes, but he did not say *that.*" After telling Judge Gray that he added the word "All" to make Biddle's comment more literate for an audience, Irving shrugged his very large shoulders and added, "Frankly, I do not think there is very much mileage to be made out of that."[4] Judge Gray said nothing.

*    *    *

Turning to the *Leuchter Report,* Rampton observed that Leuchter's fundamental mistake—the assumption that it took far more poison gas to kill humans than to kill vermin, when, in fact, the reverse was true—was not the
only flaw in his methodology. He had hacked great lumps of concrete out of
the walls and, upon returning from Poland, sent them to a lab to be tested
for hydrogen cyanide. He did not, however, tell the lab where these samples
came from. The lab pulverized them for the tests. When Jim Roth, the
chemist who conducted the tests, learned the samples were from *gas* chamber walls, he declared that his findings were meaningless because hydrogen
cyanide has a surface reaction. According to Roth, by crushing these large
samples, the lab had severely diluted any hydrogen cyanide residue.* After
Rampton read the chemist's critique, Irving scowled angrily and announced,
"I am not just going to annihilate evidence from Dr Roth, I am going to exterminate it when the times comes."[5] I was intent on ignoring Irving's verbal
assaults, but his use of "annihilate" and "exterminate" left me reeling.

If, Rampton asked Irving, these were not homicidal gas chambers, as he
claimed, how could there be *any* traces—however infinitesimal—of hydrogen cyanide in Leuchter's samples? Irving, rather nonchalantly, answered
that the traces were there because the room was used "for fumigating objects or cadavers." I almost fell out of my chair. Rampton's eyes opened
wide. Sounding stupefied, he said, "Fumigating cadavers? . . . What makes
you say *that?*" Judge Gray also seemed caught off balance: "I am sorry, this
seems a crude question, but what is the point of gassing a corpse?"[6] A twitter
of nervous laughter greeted the judge's question. Irving, sounding annoyed
at having to explain something so obvious, replied that the corpses needed to

---

*When Errol Morris interviewed Roth for *Mr. Death,* the chemist had said that the HCN
would "probably not . . . penetrate more than 10 microns. Human hair is 100 microns."
Though he qualified his observation with the word, "probably," the HCN most likely pene-
trated far deeper than 10 microns. However, his argument about severely diluting the sample
is valid. Richard Green, a physical chemist with a Ph.D. from Stanford University, noted another serious problem with Leuchter's so-called methodology. He gave the lab samples of
vastly different sizes. The HCN concentration was certainly not homogeneous. Therefore, by
studying different-size samples, the results of any test become highly suspect. Richard
J. Green, "Expert Report," *IvP&DL,* Court of Appeal, 1996-I-No. 1113. See: http://
www.holocaust-history.org.

be gassed because they were full of vermin. Rampton observed that these corpses were about to be incinerated and hardly needed gassing.

Rampton also wondered why, if the room was intended for objects and cadavers, did the door have a thick glass peephole with an internal protective grill? Guards did not have to observe objects. Corpses could not break the glass. As usual, Irving had an explanation. This was a standard air-raid shelter door; therefore it came with a peephole. "It is rather like the ATM machines which have a little Braille pad on them, whether or not it is even a drive-by ATM machine. . . . Obviously drivers are not blind, because that is the cheapest way to make ATM machines."[7] Irving's explanation—though a bizarre analogy—sounded logical. But it was wrong. The door was not produced on an assembly line. The Auschwitz construction office had requested the peephole.

Irving then proposed another explanation. The room was an air-raid shelter. Rampton, unable—or unwilling—to mask his cynicism, declared, "Now it is an air raid shelter, is it? . . . It is either a cellar for gassing corpses, Mr Irving, or else it is an air raid shelter?" Irving's response came quickly: "Did I say either or?" Rampton observed that if this was a shelter, it was far too small to accommodate the inmates. Irving suggested it was for the SS. Rampton thought it absurd for a "whole lot of heavily armed soldiers [to] run two-and-a-half or three miles from the SS barracks to these cellars at the far end of the Birkenau camp" and to do so "before they got squashed by the Allied bombs."[8] I recalled how six months earlier we had walked from one end of Birkenau to the other. Though I did not know it then, the walk *had* a forensic purpose.

Rampton then turned to another document in the Auschwitz archives. In February 1943, camp building authorities had complained to Topf, the company that built the crematoria equipment, that they needed the ventilation blower "most urgently." "Why," Rampton wondered, "the urgency if it is a mere air raid shelter or a delousing chamber?" Irving now had a series of hypotheses. There was a typhus epidemic. The building inspector would not approve the installation without the ventilation system. The words "most urgently" did not mean anything at all. After listening to these explanations, Rampton added his own: "We want to start the big extermination program in March, get on with it."[9]

As the day drew to an end, Judge Gray asked Irving if he had done archival research on the gas chambers. Irving said that due to the machinations of his opponents, archives were generally closed to him. Judge Gray, sounding quite sympathetic, declared, "Really almost every avenue, you say, has been closed to you for one reason or another?" Looking pleased, Irving shook his head in affirmation. I was unnerved by Judge Gray's apparent sympathy for Irving. Did he really think that Irving had been prevented from doing the proper research? Had he forgotten that Irving's public declaration that he would scour archives for evidence on Auschwitz was made in 1988 and that Auschwitz had only banned him in the mid-1990s?[10]

### HOLOCAUST JUNKETS AND COKE IN A BOTTLE

Soon it was time for Robert Jan to take the stand. Despite the macabre nature of his work, Robert Jan projects a boyish air. At scholarly meetings, for instance, he is the one who invariably knows the best nightspot in town. He had once showed up with his hair dyed a bright shade of orange. But a very different Robert Jan appeared in court. His usual design-school garb of leather jacket, turtleneck jersey, and jeans—all black—had been replaced by a finely tailored stylish dark gray three-piece suit with a perfectly fitting vest. The vest had a shawl collar. A pair of dark suede shoes and a dark blue tie with a yellow flower motif completed the ensemble. For a moment I found it hard to resolve that this dazzlingly dressed man standing in front of me was one of the world's experts on Auschwitz and its killing apparatus.

In his report Robert Jan had, by meticulously cross-referencing a broad array of evidence, completely demolished Irving's claims about Auschwitz. He had built his case on prisoner testimony, German documents, blueprints, physical evidence, letters by camp administrators, bills of lading, work orders, and drawings by *Sonderkommandos*. His report not only laid waste to Irving's claims, but was a stunning example of what historians do. They do *not*, as Irving kept demanding, seek a "smoking gun," one document that will prove the existence of the gas chambers. They seek a nexus or convergence of evidence. I waited with some anticipation to see how Irving would attack this.

As the clock neared 10:30, Robert Jan walked over and placed a five-volume set of small books on my desk. He said, "This *Tanakh* has been in our family for generations. I shall take my oath on it." He then opened a folder, carefully removed a cloth yellow star, which his grandmother had worn during the war, and an envelope that contained the last letter his family received from his uncle in Westerbork, the concentration camp where Dutch Jews were held prior to deportation. "His name was Robert," he added with a tiny catch in his voice; "I shall carry his letter and my grandmother's star into the witness box." And then, as he was about to walk away, he told me about his talk with Irving the previous week. Irving had shown him an aerial picture of Birkenau that, he claimed, his experts had *just* taken. When Robert Jan looked at the picture, he saw a series of crosses and stars in the field near the gas chamber ruins. I knew about those symbols. They had been placed there by a group of Polish teenage visitors and were removed in 1998. Clearly, the picture that Irving had shown Robert Jan had not "just" been taken. Either he had been lied to or he was lying to Robert Jan, a man who had repeatedly visited Auschwitz.

Before Robert Jan was called to the stand, Irving rose to complain that, despite the fact that the rules of Civil Procedure called for complete equity between the parties, he stood "alone," facing "powerful [and] wealthy litigants." Pointing in our direction, he accused us of wresting control of the case away from him. We had, he charged, maneuvered to have Robert Jan testify early in the trial, rather than toward the end, thereby driving "a cart and horses" right through his preparations. This adjustment of the schedule was particularly galling, Irving declared, because it was done to accommodate Robert Jan's "Holocaust junket to Stockholm." Looking directly at Judge Gray, Irving asked why he was tolerating the court "being held hostage" to Robert Jan's travels.[11]

Rampton, already on his feet, was shaking his head in somewhat theatrical dismay. He reminded Judge Gray that on the first day of the trial, Irving had agreed to this schedule. Heather had already pulled out the first day's transcript. Rampton read Irving's words: "I am perfectly prepared to have Professor van Pelt come over in the middle of whatever else is going on." Moreover, Irving had answered extensive questions about Auschwitz on the previous day. The topic was already on the table.

Judge Gray declined to alter the schedule, but he reassured Irving, "I am very conscious of the burden that is being placed upon you. It must be gigantic." He insisted he was making a special effort to look after Irving's interests because he was a litigant in person. I sat there frustrated and even more annoyed. Irving had brought the case. He had chosen to represent himself because he felt no lawyer could do as good a job. Now Judge Gray was bending over backward to accommodate him. Behind me I heard Rampton muttering as he waited. When Judge Gray recognized him, he said, "True it is there is an inequality of resources; true also it is, however, that my clients are defending a suit brought by Mr Irving. It reminds one of the old French proverb: 'These animals are very naughty. They defend themselves when they are attacked.' " Irving angrily turned to Rampton: "That proverbs cuts both ways, Mr Rampton." Judge Gray, anxious to defuse matters, declared, "Yes, well that is enough of that."[12]

Irving began by asking Robert Jan if he was "deeply moved" when he first visited Birkenau. "More than moved. I was frightened." With a bit of a chuckle, Irving said, "Ghosts of the dead were still all around?" Robert Jan assured Irving that it was not a matter of ghosts—in which he did not believe—but the "awesome responsibility" of studying Auschwitz.[13] Irving, rather abruptly, turned to Judge Gray to warn him that some of his questions might seem "frightfully obtuse." He was, he explained, "laying a bit of trap . . . which will be sprung either before or after lunch."[14] Irving smiled mischievously.

He then began to question Robert Jan about Himmler's July 1942 visit to Auschwitz. Robert Jan explained that this visit coincided with the Nazi hierarchy's decision that Auschwitz play a central role in the Final Solution. Consequently, immediately after the visit, camp authorities ordered a dramatic increase in the crematoria's incineration capacity. There would soon be more corpses to burn and, if the rate of incineration was not adequate, the backlog of bodies would prevent the smooth functioning of the killing process. Irving suggested that Robert Jan was seeing the sinister when a more benign explanation would suffice. Typhus had ravaged the camp in 1942. Camp officials increased the incineration capacity because they were anticipating another epidemic. Sounding a bit like a professor admonishing a student for a really dense answer, Robert Jan dismissed Irving's theory as "absurd, . . . absolutely absurd."[15] The increase would boost the monthly incineration rate to 120,000 bodies, he explained, while the camp's projected population was 150,000. For Irving's explanation to make sense, in one month an epidemic would have to kill four-fifths of Auschwitz's population and the Germans would have to repopulate the camp with 120,000 people. This exceeded the absolute worst-case epidemiological scenario.

Irving, shifting his line of questioning, challenged Robert Jan to explain how 120,000 bodies could be incinerated monthly. This was, Irving dismissively noted, "four times [the capacity of] Wembley stadium," the famous London soccer arena. Declaring that it took 30 kilograms of coke to burn just one body, he held up his aerial photograph of the camp—the one with the stars and crosses—and asked Robert Jan where were the "mountains of coke?" Robert Jan explained that under normal circumstances it took significant fuel to burn one body because getting the "oven going . . . takes a hell of a lot of energy." However, the Auschwitz ovens were kept hot, reducing the energy needed to incinerate subsequent bodies. The Auschwitz ovens had been designed with precisely that energy savings in mind. In 1943, Rudolf Jährling, a civilian engineer at Auschwitz, had calculated that 4,200 kilos of coke were needed to run one crematorium for twelve hours under normal circumstances, but only 2,800 if it was in constant use. Jährling estimated that, in these circumstances, less than 8,000 kilos of fuel—3.5 kilos per corpse—were sufficient for twelve hours for all the crematoria in Birkenau. Irving, lifting the water bottle from his table, scornfully asked, "Do you really, sincerely believe that you can burn one corpse with enough coke that you could fit in one of these water bottles?" Robert Jan affirmed that, based on German documents, he did.[16]

## GAS CHAMBER TOURS: THE TESTIMONY OF ADA BIMKO

Then Irving began a concerted attack on the eyewitnesses who had attested to seeing gas chambers. He began with Ada Bimko, who later in life was known as Hadassah Rosensaft, a Polish-Jewish doctor who had been imprisoned at Birkenau, where she worked at the medical bloc. At a 1945 war crimes trial, Bimko testified that women, who had been held in a barracks prior to being sent to their death, were marched naked to the gas chamber. They were sometimes allowed to wrap themselves in blankets. On one occasion, when Bimko was sent to retrieve these blankets, an SS officer offered to give her a "tour" of the gas chamber. In addition to showing the chamber, he took her to the area above it, which housed the ventilation system for extracting the poison gas. He explained that the two large cylinders in the corner contained the poison. The gas, he continued, passed through the pipes into the gas chamber below.[17]

This explanation made no sense. In the crematorium she visited, Zyklon

B was thrown through the windows, not piped in from above. Irving dismissed her testimony as pure invention. "She was now in British hands . . . and they have asked her to write a statement . . . because they needed to hang these criminals." Robert Jan saw things quite differently. While Bimko's explanation was wrong, her description of what she saw corresponded precisely to the ventilation system in cremas 4 and 5. Pipes in the attic floor extracted the gas from the chambers. The cylinders probably contained the ventilator. Her explanation was based on what the SS man had told her. When Robert Jan speculated that the SS man was mocking her, Irving admonished him: "Your imagination is not evidence in this court room and I would ask you to adhere to what you know." Rampton jumped up. "That is not right. His motivation for the way he wrote the report is under attack. What he thinks she may have meant by what she said is directly relevant." Judge Gray agreed. Robert Jan added that Bimko had described a system that was only visible from inside the attic. Given Bimko's precise description she was "a very reliable witness, even if she did not know what [the pipe] was used for."[18]

This exchange felt personal. I knew Bimko, who had been appointed by President Carter to the United States Holocaust Council. I was present when the designer of the Holocaust Museum described how visitors would pass through a boxcar used to transport Jews to the camps, Bimko stood up and emphatically declared that she had once been forced into such a car. Nothing could ever compel her to enter again. As a result, the design plan was reworked and visitors who wish can circumvent the car.

Irving, still deprecating Bimko, accused Robert Jan of having included her testimony in his report as "a bit of spice." "Sorry?" Robert Jan asked in some confusion. Irving, seeming to enjoy the moment, repeated his charge. "As a bit of spice. . . . As one more statistic." The distressed look on Robert Jan's face became one of disgust when Irving bemoaned the "unfortunates" who were hanged on the basis of Bimko's testimony.[19] I reflected that among those "unfortunates" was the commandant of Bergen-Belsen, Josef Kramer, who had been in charge of the crematoria in Birkenau during the murder of Hungarian Jewry and, in that capacity, had selected people for the gas chambers. Another "unfortunate" convicted at that trial was Birkenau doctor, Fritz Klein, who, when asked how he could reconcile his Hippocratic oath with sending people to the gas chamber, had replied, "I am a doctor and I want to preserve life. And out of respect for human life, I would remove a gangrenous appendix from a diseased body. The Jew is the gangrenous appendix in the body of mankind."[20]

## NO HOLES, NO HOLOCAUST: THE TRAP

Irving next began to question Robert Jan about the testimony of *Sonderkommando* Henryk Tauber. Tauber had described how a SS officer on the roof of crema 2 or 3 would lift the cover over a hole in the roof, drop the Zyklon B gas pellets into a wire-mesh column, and close the cover. Irving began pressing Robert Jan about the dimensions and position of the holes and the columns. Then throwing back his shoulders, Irving looked up from his papers and loudly asked:

> Professor van Pelt, we are wasting our time really, are we not? There were never any holes in the roof. There are no holes in that roof today. . . . They cannot have poured cyanide capsules through that roof. . . . You yourself have . . . looked for those holes and not found them. Our experts have stood on that roof and not found them. The holes were never there. What do you have to say to that?

Before Robert Jan could answer, Irving turned toward Judge Gray and said, "My Lord, you may apprehend that the trap is now sprung and it would be a pity to put the mouse back in its cage." With a quizzical look, Judge Gray asked, "The trap is what you have just asked?" "Precisely," Irving triumphantly declared. "There are no holes in that roof. There were never any holes in that roof. All the eyewitnesses on whom he relies are therefore exposed as liars." Robert Jan protested that the roof was "absolutely a mess," having collapsed in fragments when the gas chambers were blown up. Irving was "pretend[ing] to be talking about a piece which is intact. It is not."[21]

Despite Robert Jan's protests, Irving had grabbed the momentum, insisting that had there been "holes in the roof, which are the cardinal linchpin of the Defence in this action, they would have been found by now. . . . So their eyewitness evidence collapses because these people are exposed for the liars they were [*sic*]." Robert Jan was about to say something when Irving glanced at the clock on the wall: "My Lord, it is four minutes to four. Unless Mr Rampton wishes to say something to repair the damage at this point. . . ."

Anthony Julius, the architect of my legal defense, was known to the British as Princess Diana's lawyer. I knew his name as the author of the compelling *T. S. Eliot, Anti-Semitism, and Literary Form.* The book was his Ph.D. thesis, something he earned while working full-time as a lawyer. *(Photo courtesy of Deborah Lipstadt)*

James Libson, a partner at Mishcon de Reya, worked with Anthony to build my defense. He mused about how rare it was to have "a case that is both so close to one's heart and in which justice is so central." *(Photo courtesy of Deborah Lipstadt)*

*Left:* The three-thousand-seat sanctuary of Berlin's Synagogue Oranienburger Strasse. Dedicated in 1866, in the presence of Chancellor Bismarck, it was protected during *Kristallnacht* (1938) by the local police chief. *(Photo © Stiftung Neue Synagoge Berlin—Centrum Judaicum)*

*Right:* All that remains of the Oranienburger Strasse sanctuary after being damaged by Allied bombs. Visiting this site, immediately prior to going to Auschwitz to meet my defense team, vividly reminded me of the Jewish life that had been destroyed by the Holocaust. *(Photo by Margit Billeb © Stiftung Neue Synagoge Berlin—Centrum Judaicum)*

*Left:* In the Auschwitz gas chamber barrister Richard Rampton, facing camera, aggressively questioned expert witness Robert Jan van Pelt, in black, about evidence for the gas chambers. I protested Rampton's line of questions. He was not pleased. *(Photo by Omer Arbel)*

Walking behind my defense team in Birkenau shortly after my "altercation" with Rampton. *(Photo by Omer Arbel)*

*Right:* At crema 2, we inspected the remains of the gas chamber roof. Deniers attempt to argue that there were no holes through which to insert Zyklon B. *(Photo by Omer Arbel)*

Both perpetrators and survivors describe how, in cremas 4/5, the Zyklon B was thrown in through windows. The Auschwitz archives contain a February 1943 work order for "12 *gas-tight* doors of 30/40 cm." and architectural drawings of the cremas with windows of this dimension. We found this 30/40 cm. window in Auschwitz. Remnants of the gastight seal remain and the handle is on the *outside,* an impractical arrangement unless one wanted to prevent those inside from opening it. This is a stunning example of "confluence of evidence." Architectural drawings, documentary evidence, testimony, and relics all coincide.
*(Photo by Omer Arbel)*

A portion of the documentation gathered by the defense team for the case. A copy of every document mentioned in an expert report was deposited with the court. Ultimately there were close to one hundred linear feet of documentation. *(Photo courtesy of Deborah Lipstadt)*

Judge Charles Gray in his courtroom regalia. Prior to becoming a judge, Gray had been a distinguished QC (Queen's Counsel) specializing in libel. Rampton surmised that Gray was chosen to hear this case because of his expertise in libel law. *(© Julia Quenzler)*

Upon entering the court on the first morning of the trial, David Irving predicted to the assembled reporters and photographers that he would be victorious. *(Associated Press)*

Lunch in barrister Richard Rampton's chambers. Rampton has intense interests in the classics, music, history, literary theory, and good wine. *(Photo courtesy of Deborah Lipstadt)*

During the trial, I lost sleep worrying that Judge Gray might issue an "evenhanded" judgment. After a series of such nights, I was useless at an early-morning meeting in Anthony's office. *(Photo by James Libson)*

Mr Irving points with a broad brush

When Irving told the judge that he was building his case with a "broad brush," Richard Rampton sketched this cartoon. *(Courtesy of Richard Rampton, QC)*

On the day of closing arguments, the tedium of having to listen to Irving's three-hour summation was disrupted somewhat when he—inadvertently, I assumed—addressed Judge Gray as *mein Führer*. When I left the Law Courts the photographers asked how I was doing. I told them I was happy to be any place *but* the courtroom. *(Photo by David Minkin)*

When the defense team gathered at a pub near the Law Courts after closing arguments, there was a celebratory atmosphere. It was as if, one expert observed, we were emerging from a "cosmos of death." *From left to right:* Laura Tyler, Tobias Jersiak, Heather Rogers, Deborah Lipstadt, Thomas Skelton-Robinson, and Nick Wachsman. *(Photo by David Minkin)*

In my London hotel apartment the day before Judge Gray's decision was to be announced. The lawyers already knew the outcome but were forbidden from telling me. The excruciating wait was lessened by a stream of reporters and photographers. *(Photo courtesy of Deborah Lipstadt)*

Shortly before I arrived at the Law Courts on the day of the judgment, Anthony told me of our victory. Forbidden from telling anyone until Judge Gray read his decision in court, I found it hard to suppress a smile as I entered the building. When friends called to find out if I knew, I said: "It's a spectacular day here in London." They cheered. *(Martin Hayhow/Getty Images)*

A few days after the judgment, the Wexners, stalwart supporters of my legal battle, hosted the defense team. Leslie Wexner said he felt privileged to have been part of this effort. *(Photo courtesy of Deborah Lipstadt)*

Richard Evans described his experience on the stand. Abigail Wexner and researcher Tobias Jersak listened. *(Photo courtesy of Deborah Lipstadt)*

Irving's comment to a television reporter that the judgment was not a great loss and had been very complimentary to him prompted this editorial cartoon.
*(© Daily Telegraph)*

After the Court of Appeal turned down Irving's third and final appeal in July 2001, Anthony assured me it was "over," I found that hard to fathom. *(Photo courtesy of John R. Rifkin)*

Robert Jan tried to interject but Judge Gray told him to wait "until 10:30 tomorrow morning."[22] With that we adjourned.

I was disappointed in Robert Jan's half-hearted protest about Irving's claim that the holes were the "cardinal linchpin" of our case. The holes did not even figure in our case. I felt as if he had really been caught off guard. Anticipating that the press would feature this in their reports, I grimly acknowledged to myself that Irving had orchestrated this well. As we exited the courtroom, I told Anthony how distressed I was. He dismissed these concerns: "It doesn't matter. It's one day's testimony. The judge won't be affected by it. And the press *really* doesn't matter."

I awoke the next morning and immediately checked some of the newspapers piled at my door. The *Times* carried the headline "Irving Disputes 'Lurid' Atrocity Stories." It featured Irving's claim that the eyewitness evidence had been "totally demolished" because there were no discernible holes in the roof. In contrast, the *Guardian*'s headline read: "Author Tells of Massive Proof for Gas Chambers." The paper emphasized Robert Jan's convergence of evidence. The BBC story was all that I had feared. "The existence of homicidal gas chambers at Auschwitz was completely fictitious, historian David Irving has told London's High Court." According to the BBC, Irving claimed that "eyewitness evidence of the chambers was 'totally demolished' because there were no holes in the roof to insert poison. The historian said his theory—based on research by revisionist historians—'blows holes in the whole gas chamber story.' " Toward the end, the report mentioned—almost as an afterthought—Robert Jan's contention that there was a "massive amount of evidence" about the camp's extermination activities.

At that point, I decided that rather than spend the next hour reading every newspaper report, I should stick to my daily ritual. I grabbed my shorts and T-shirt and headed for the gym. I had made a practice of beginning every day with an intensive early morning cardiovascular workout and a weightlifting session. About five years earlier I had lost a significant amount of weight. Keeping fit was a high priority for me. Shortly before I left for London, I had resolved that, irrespective of whatever this trial did to my head, it would not affect my body. My forty-five minutes on the treadmill and fifteen minutes lifting weights constituted both a physical and mental workout. I could not publicly speak, but by keeping in shape I could telegraph to friends, enemies, reporters, and myself that I was coping. A verse in Deuteronomy (4:9) teaches: "Above all, take utmost care and scrupulously watch out for yourself." I had no choice but to let others take care of my legal battle. Only I could take utmost care of myself.

### NUBILE YOUNG WOMEN

Irving began the next day's session by announcing that there were no more "hidden booby-traps or mines." Clearly enjoying the moment, he smiled at Robert Jan and said, "I am sure that the Professor will appreciate advance notification." Robert Jan scowled as Irving continued, "One would have expected the researchers at the other end of the spectrum to have been . . . frantically looking for those holes to prove us wrong."[23]

A sparring match about the holes occupied much of the day. Slowly, Robert Jan regained some of the initiative that he seemed to have lost the previous day. When Irving challenged the existence of the holes, Robert Jan cited the 1944 American aerial photographs of the gas chambers in which the holes were visible. When Irving claimed that the negatives had been altered, Van Pelt responded that Nevin Bryant, supervisor of cartographic and image processing at California's prestigious Jet Propulsion Laboratory, used NASA technology to enhance the pictures. He found no alterations. When Irving asserted that the holes in the picture were shadows, Robert Jan cited drawings by *Sonderkommando* David Olère, who, upon liberation, sketched the gas chambers. The sketches, Robert Jan noted, were fully corroborated by the architectural plans in the Auschwitz Central Construction Office and the aerial photos.

Olère's drawings included the hollow wire-mesh columns into which the Zyklon B was dropped through the roof. These wire-mesh columns were in a staggered arrangement. Both Olère's drawings and the American photos showed this arrangement. When Irving contended that Olère's memories could have been shaped by photographs that "were splashed all over the press," Robert Jan asked Irving for press photographs showing the gas chamber plans.[24] When Irving ignored Robert Jan's challenge and quickly abandoned this line of questioning, I assumed that he had none. He just lobbed one of his many theories.

Irving's next query left me utterly perplexed. Did Olère have "a prurient interest in the female form?" Robert Jan looked equally bewildered. Irving continued, "In almost every single one of these pictures he has drawn . . . there are naked women full frontal . . . and there is no reason whatsoever that he should have made these pictures in that way unless he intended to sell them." Irving continued, "Is it likely that nearly all the females who became victims of the bestialities of the Nazis in Auschwitz were nubile, young and attractive?" Robert Jan, his face reddening in anger, insisted, "No, it is not very likely."[25] As the two men went back and forth, I opened Robert Jan's report to see if the women in Olère drawings were indeed "nubile, young, and attractive." When I realized what I was doing, I rapidly closed the file, disgusted with myself for having taken Irving's accusations seriously.

Irving resumed his attack on *Sonderkommando* Tauber, accusing him of having given testimony that was so bizarre, it sounded "almost Talmudic." According to Irving, Tauber had testified that he had seen a prisoner "chased into a pool of boiling human fat." As Irving poked fun at Tauber, I sat comparing Tauber's actual testimony with Irving's putative summary of it. The difference was staggering. Tauber had testified at the war crimes trial:

> [T]he SS chased a prisoner who was not working fast enough into a pit near the crematorium that was full of boiling human fat. At that time the corpses were incinerated in open air pits, from which the fat flowed into a separate reservoir, dug in the ground. This fat was poured over the corpses to accelerate their combustion. This poor devil was pulled out of the fat still alive and then shot.[26]

Robert Jan countered Irving's attacks on Tauber by noting that his descriptions of the gas chamber and crematoria were corroborated by the architectural plans. Irving speculated that the Polish judge who took Tauber's testimony placed the plans in front of him while he testified. Robert Jan asked Irving for evidence that the Polish judge had done this. Irving moved right on. Moreover, Robert Jan continued, Tauber had described aspects of the gassing and incineration procedures that were *not* on the plans. Robert Jan concluded his defense of Tauber with the observation that, even if the Poles had put the drawings in front of him, these were very technical documents. Tauber could not have made "up a story which matches point for point information in the blueprint of a very technical and specialist nature."[27]

Irving, continuing his attack on the eyewitnesses, demanded to know, Why, if so many people have survived, "it is always the same old gang who come forward and give the evidence?" His choice of words—"same old gang"—felt like a fingernail scraping across a blackboard. Robert Jan argued that there were only a handful of people who had seen the gas chambers and survived. Their testimony, however, was explicit and trustworthy. Irving disagreed, describing them as "highly suspect" and their testimony as "scattered, skimpy and . . . questionable."[28]

### AIRTIGHT DOORS AND FIELD KITCHENS

Some of Robert Jan's most devastating testimony came from the perpetrators. Hans Stark, a member of what was known in Auschwitz as the camp Gestapo, had testified at a war crimes trial about the gassing process:

> As early as autumn 1941 gassings were carried out in a room . . . [which] held 200 to 250 people, had a higher-than-average ceiling, no windows, and only a specially insulated door, with bolts like those of an airtight door [*Luftschutztür*]. . . . The room had a flat roof, which allowed daylight in through the openings. It was through these openings that Zyklon B in granular form would be poured.

Stark had told the court that, because the Zyklon B "was in granular form, it trickled down over the people as it was being poured in. They then started to cry out terribly for they now knew what was happening to them."[29]

Given the compelling nature of this testimony and the fact that it came from a perpetrator, I assumed that Irving would deem it wise to simply not cross-examine Robert Jan about it. I was wrong. Zeroing in on the word *"Luftschutztür,"* he charged that the translator should have used the "totally harmless" "air-raid door" instead of the rather "sinister airtight door." Robert Jan dismissed Irving's criticism about one word and pointed out that the entire paragraph was quite sinister. I was surprised when Judge Gray weighed in. "This is in the context of gassings in 1941 and Zyklon B being poured through holes in the roof. . . . You cannot possibly say, Mr Irving . . . that Hans Stark is describing an air raid shelter on the basis of this passage can you?"[30] Irving said he was trying to show how translations could skew meanings. Judge Gray's face betrayed no response, but I doubted he was impressed with this argument.

In his report Robert Jan had cited a September 1942 permit obtained by Auschwitz commandant Rudolf Höss for use of a car to inspect *"Feldöfen"* ("field ovens") in the vicinity of Auschwitz. The permit and the extensive documentation about the trip were yet additional links in the chain of evidence of the killing process. The German authorities, intent on disposing of evidence of the mass killings, wanted the corpses in the graves burned. Höss was going to inspect the incineration grids. Before questioning Robert Jan about the permit, Irving handed him a translation of it. Robert Jan glanced at the document and immediately noted that the word *"Feldöfen"* had been translated as "field kitchens." Robert Jan complained that this document had "nothing to do with kitchens . . . but with incineration ovens." Judge Gray, who knew German, asked who had translated the word *"Öfen"* as "kitchens"? Irving, sounding rather apologetic, explained that he had done the translation at 2 A.M. the previous morning. Given the hour, there was an "element of stress."[31] I was skeptical about Irving's explanation, but did not think the whole issue amounted to very much. I noticed that Thomas, one of our researchers, who had been paying very careful attention to this exchange, suddenly buried himself in his laptop. He seemed to be searching for something.

## ONE ELEVATOR—HALF A MILLION CORPSES

Later that afternoon, Irving tried to chip away at Robert Jan's contention that five hundred thousand people had been gassed in crema 2, the building that had been altered to include gas chambers. The bodies were taken from the basement gas chambers by elevator to the crematoria ovens one floor above. Irving's point of attack was the single elevator in the building. I was not surprised by this line of questioning because a few days earlier, when Irving had been in the witness box, he had announced that he would use the issue of the elevator to "get revenge on Professor van Pelt."[32] Irving declared it far-fetched to believe that this one elevator could have moved so many bodies. Robert Jan explained that in early 1943, camp authorities, aware that there would be bodies to burn, ordered the elevator's capacity doubled from 750 to 1,500 kilos. Judge Gray asked what this meant in practical terms: "That would be how many corpses?" Robert Jan calculated "20, 25 corpses" per load. Irving immediately interjected: "The same question of course is how many people you can pack into a telephone box."[33] I felt a mix of incredulity and disgust.

Irving argued that, if the elevator was piled with corpses "six or seven high, . . . the doors would not close." Robert Jan, speaking very deliberately, said, *"There were no doors."* Irving who had been studying a paper on his small lectern, looked up in surprise: "There were no doors?" He pursed his lips and then, after a moment's thought, smiled slightly—one could almost see the light bulb go off over his head—and, in a rush of words, said, "That would be even worse then. The bodies would presumably get jammed against the side of the lift shaft if they piled them too high." Once again Irving had unself-consciously turned his argument around. First the problem was that the doors wouldn't close. Then it was that there were no doors.

Irving kept pressing Robert Jan about the elevator, demanding some "back-of-the-envelope" calculations to determine how long it would take to load two thousand bodies, go up one level, remove them, and return to the bottom. Robert Jan, eyes flashing, declared, "I do not do back-of-the-envelope calculations."[34] Irving insisted. Robert Jan turned to Judge Gray as if he was expecting him to intervene. The judge said nothing. Robert Jan, having no choice, began to calculate in a rather lackluster fashion. At the most, he estimated, it would take ten minutes for the elevator to be loaded, go up one floor, be unloaded, and return to the first floor. Irving challenged Robert Jan's calculations. For what seemed like an unbearably long time, the two debated the procedure for loading and unloading bodies. The room was warm, but I felt chilled. Finally the session ended. Instead of immediately packing up my books and papers, as I usually did, I sat ruminating, until I felt a pat on my shoulder. It was Rampton. He said nothing, but looked sad.

James Dalrymple, writing in the *Independent,* described his reaction to the session. "In the train that night, to my shame, I took out a pocket calculator and began to do some sums. Ten minutes for each batch of 25, I tapped in. That makes 150 an hour, which gives 3,600 for each 24-hour period. Which gives 1,314,000 in a year. So that's fine. It could be done. Thank God the numbers add up. When I realized what I was doing, I almost threw the little machine across the compartment in rage."[35] His anger reminded me of how I felt when I found myself examining Olère's drawings to see if the women were depicted pornographically. Irving, despite his record of distortions and inventions, had beguiled both of us into taking his theories—if only for a moment—seriously.

## A VIRTUAL TOUR OF THE GAS CHAMBERS

One morning had been set aside for Robert Jan to present a computer-generated re-creation of the gas chambers. The judge began by asking him what there was to be "derived or inferred from the blueprints relating to the construction of the gas chambers." He quickly corrected himself, "sorry . . . which entitles one to infer that provision was made for gas chambers generally and . . . perhaps for the ducts into which these Zyklon-B pellets are alleged to have been poured?"[36] Puzzled, I asked James about this convoluted language. He whispered, "He does not want to suggest that he has already made up his mind about the gas chambers. It's annoying but it's a forensic necessity."

For the next hour, pointer in hand, Robert Jan conducted a seminar on the gas chambers. Mimicking the judge, he too referred to "alleged gas chambers." Robert Jan pointed out that in Auschwitz most architectural drawings were prepared by prisoners who signed them, not with their names, but with their prison numbers. In contrast, the drawings of the alterations for cremas 2 and 3—when gas chambers were introduced into these buildings—were made by SS architect Walther Dejaco, drawing room chief. Since Dejaco rarely prepared drawings, this already signaled that there was something unique about these changes. But it was the changes themselves that indicated an entirely new purpose had been found for this portion of the building. The doors of the room that became the gas chamber were altered to open outward not inward. Robert Jan posited that Auschwitz authorities had learned—based on the Chelmno gas vans—that people run toward the door when gas is introduced into the room. The pile of corpses would have made it impossible to push the door open after the gassing.[37]

Robert Jan also took note of what had been removed from the original plans. There had been a concrete slide on the side of the building leading to the basement. The slide, which had a narrow set of steps on each side, had been designed for stretchers carrying corpses. The steps could each accommodate the people guiding the stretcher. It had been replaced with a staircase. The new staircase was not wide enough for a stretcher with a person on each side. However, it could accommodate people walking in on their own.

Irving had a completely different explanation for the replacement of the chute with steps. The architects might have decided "for matters of taste and decency, to have a clean side of the building where people could go in without having to jostle with corpses that might be infected going down the steps and they decided, therefore, for pure hygiene reasons to move the staircase." I found it hard to imagine that Auschwitz architects were worried about "taste and decency." Robert Jan agreed that Irving's theory might make sense but for the fact that with the slide gone there was no way to get the corpses into the building.[38] If this was still a morgue, as Irving contended, the bodies had to be brought in and transported to the ovens. Irving suggested that the elevator served this purpose. Robert Jan pointed out that this was simply not plausible. In order to reach the elevator, the people carrying a stretcher would have had to go through two doorways, neither of which could easily accommodate a stretcher, and walk over the coke supply. Finally, Robert Jan observed that the head of the Auschwitz construction office had ordered that, in contrast to plans for other buildings, which were readily available to people at the site, access to these plans was severely limited. Why, Robert Jan wondered, such strict secrecy, if the buildings were just morgues?[39]

As we headed to lunch, I caught up with Rampton. Walking into Brick Court, I said, "Do you remember when I got angry in Auschwitz because you challenged Robert Jan about why there haven't been more tests on the gas chambers?" Rampton took a long drag on his *Gitanes* and said, "I remember. *Very well.*" His tone indicated that it had been as unpleasant for him as me. "I was angry," I explained, "because you seemed unsure about the truth of the gas chambers." Ignoring the brisk January weather, he stopped and asked, "Now, do you understand what I was doing?" It all seemed utterly obvious. "You were preparing Robert Jan for cross-examination." "Precisely. I had to ensure he was ready for Irving's challenges."

I wanted to apologize for challenging him. I wanted to tell him how much I appreciated not just the forensic skills, but the passion he brought to this case. Before I could formulate the words, he said, "I think it's time for some good wine. It's the only thing that makes these sandwiches palatable." With that he headed for the wine cellar he maintained in the building. He returned with a bottle of 1995 *Pommard, Les Epenots,* a robust full-bodied Burgundy, and, before passing it around the table, filled two glasses. As he handed me one, he mused, "I think we both need that today."

Later Irving returned to the question of the holes, repeatedly engaging in various incantations of "no holes, no Holocaust." Finally, Irving gripped the small podium in front of him, rose up on his toes, and challenged Robert Jan to go to Auschwitz "with a trowel and clean away the gravel and find a reinforced concrete hole." If the holes were found, Irving proclaimed, "I would happily abandon my action immediately. . . . It would drive such a hole through my case that I would have no possible chance of defending it any further." Robert Jan said nothing. There was silence in the room, which Judge Gray finally filled: "You have made the point and I understand it, that nobody has actually done the excavation work."[40] With that Irving concluded his cross-examination. He looked pleased.

Most of Robert Jan's report had not been challenged by Irving. Nonetheless, I worried that Judge Gray, who periodically complimented Irving on his cross-examination, might think that Irving's various theses—morgues, air-raid shelters, and chambers for gassing objects—were valid "alternative" historical explanations. Would he think that since nobody had "done the excavation work," Irving's attack on the holes was credible?*

## INNOVATIVE CREMATORIA

Rampton rose to reexamine Robert Jan. Rampton referred to the 1942 patent submitted by Topf, the company that built the crematoria, for the specially designed ovens in Auschwitz. Those ovens simultaneously consumed multiple bodies with limited expenditure of fuel. The design called for the simultaneous introduction of both emaciated and unemaciated corpses in order to guarantee continuous high temperatures through the emission of human fat. If only emaciated corpses were incinerated, it was necessary to continuously add fuel. This was precisely the procedure that Tauber had testified the *Sonderkommandos* followed: "The corpses of people gassed directly on arrival, not being wasted, burnt better. . . . During the incineration of such corpses we used the coke only to light the fire of the furnace initially,

---

*Actually some of the excavation work had already begun. In the summer of 1998, a group of researchers from the Holocaust History Project, a group of historians, engineers, physicists, computer specialists, and chemists who demonstrate the fallacy of deniers' arguments, had gone to Auschwitz. They found two of the holes at that time. Subsequent trips in 2000 revealed an additional hole. Daniel Keren, Jamie McCarthy, and Harry W. Mazal, "The Ruins of the Gas Chambers: A Forensic Investigation of Crematoriums at Auschwitz I and Auschwitz-Birkenau," *Holocaust and Genocide Studies,* vol. 18, no.1 (spring 2004): pp. 68–103.

for fatty corpses burn of their own accord."[41] Topf's 1942 patent application provided the thermodynamic explanation for the *Sonderkommandos'* decision to bring different-size corpses to the ovens. The application also demolished Irving's assertion that vast amounts of fuel were needed to burn the bodies. But it did something else: It exemplified why the "convergence of evidence" was such a useful historical method. Prisoner Henryk Tauber would not have had access to Topf's patent application, which was filed in Berlin in 1942. Yet the procedure he and his colleagues followed was exactly what the design stipulated.

Finally, Rampton asked Robert Jan about the elevator. Robert Jan had estimated that the elevator could hold approximately 25 corpses. A letter by Auschwitz's chief architect, Karl Bischoff, from June 1943 listed an incineration rate for crema 2—the crema in which Robert Jan estimated 500,000 people had been murdered—of 1,440 corpses per twenty-four hours. Rampton asked Robert Jan if it was "feasible" for the one elevator in this building to deliver the requisite number of bodies each hour from the gas chambers to the ovens. Robert Jan did the calculations and said, "Yes . . . the elevator could keep up with the ovens."[42] With that Robert Jan ended his testimony.

Two mornings later, Irving spotted Robert Jan in the courtroom and recalled him. He questioned the authenticity of the June 1943 letter, which listed the daily capacity of crema 2 as 1,440. There were some anomalies about the way it was dated, addressed, and numbered. Though Robert Jan considered these objections groundless, Judge Gray seemed intrigued by them. "Taking . . . the points that have been put to you by Mr Irving about the authenticity of this document. . . . Are you doubtful about it?" Robert Jan explained that had the letter only recently been discovered he would be suspicious. But researchers had known of it for over fifty years. Not only was the original available but there was a typed copy of it in another archive. Given that there were two different copies in two different archives, it was highly improbable that they were forgeries. Finally, it listed an incineration capacity that was lower than that German officials gave in postwar trials. Why would someone falsify a document with a lower incineration rate than that which has been attested to under oath by the German eyewitnesses? *"That* is the discrepancy."[43] I turned around to look at Rampton. His arms and legs were crossed and he was gazing downward. From where I sat, I could discern that he was smiling ever so slightly.

As he had done with the elevator "bottleneck," the holes, and so much else, Robert Jan had demonstrated that Irving's were imaginative suppositions with little—if any—evidence to sustain them. I wondered, however, how this crisp analytical forensic exchange sounded to people in the gallery whose relatives had been piled on that elevator.

# TEN

# AN AMERICAN PROFESSOR

A few months before the trial, James called to tell me that a psychology professor from California's Long Beach State University, Kevin MacDonald, was scheduled to voluntarily take the stand—no subpoena necessary—on Irving's behalf. "Who's he?" I asked. James was disappointed: "We were hoping you would know him. He's supposedly a specialist on antisemitism. He wrote a trilogy on Jews and Judaism." I could not fathom how a specialist on antisemitism would voluntarily testify on Irving's behalf, unless, I thought—facetiously—somehow he's for it. Completely perplexed, I headed for the Emory library to retrieve his books.

## HIGH-CLASS ANTISEMITISM

MacDonald had a Ph.D. in biobehavioral sciences from the University of Connecticut and described himself as an evolutionary psychologist. He was the secretary-archivist and a member of the Executive Council of the Human Behavior and Evolution Society, the main academic organization of evolutionary psychologists. He edited the organization's newsletter and had served as program chair of its annual meetings.[1]

I sat on a bench under a large tree outside my office perusing his books. MacDonald considered Jews a genetically distinct group, who conspired in virtually everything they did to gain political and economic advantage over non-Jews. "Judaism developed a conscious program of eugenics to improve scholarly ability . . . with the result that Ashkenazi Jewish IQ is at least one standard deviation above the white mean."[2] According to MacDonald, Jews opposed intermarriage because they wanted to ensure that their group remained closed to penetration from gentile gene pools.[3] MacDonald identified several "very influential intellectual and political movements [that] have been spearheaded by people who strongly identified as Jews." These groups—which, according to MacDonald, included Boasian anthropology, psychoanalysis, the Frankfurt School of Social Research, and New York intellectuals—worked, often covertly, to alter Western societies in order to ensure Jewish continuity.[4] As I worked my way through these books, I periodically had to remind myself I was not reading *The Protocols of the Elders of Zion*.

In order to restore "parity" between Jews and other ethnic groups and to counter the Jewish advantage in the possession of wealth, MacDonald predicted that eventually universities and other institutions would discriminate against Jews in admissions and that governments would impose special taxation on Jews.[5]

Addressing the topic of antisemitism, MacDonald posited that Jews, rather than being victims, in fact provoked it. As long as Jews refused to assimilate, non-Jews would react as any living thing would do when threatened: defend themselves.[6] MacDonald believed that historians commonly "ignore[d], minimize[d], or rationalize[d]" Jews' role in producing antisemitism. Jews were even responsible, in some measure, for Nazi antisemitism. MacDonald argued that it was "untenable" to portray the actions of the Nazis as completely independent of the behavior of Jews.[7] In fact, he posited, Hitler and the Nazis emulated Judaism's evolutionary group strategy. It became a "mirror image of Judaism, with its emphasis on creating a master race."[8]

MacDonald argued that when Jews appear to be divided about an issue, it's a ploy in order to deceive non-Jews. (MacDonald had clearly never witnessed Jews fighting Jews. If he had, he would have known that these fights are very real.) When Jews repudiate their ethnicity, that too is a ploy. "The Jewish radical is invisible to the gentile as a Jew and thereby avoids antisemitism while at the same time covertly retaining his or her Jewish identity."[9] His ideas reminded me of a scene in the infamous 1938 Nazi propaganda film, *Der ewige Jude* (The Eternal Jew), in which a Jew's beard, earlocks, caftan, and skullcap, are progressively removed until he becomes a relatively nondescript—he still has beady eyes and an oversized nose—man in a standard business suit, while the narrator says: *"Hair [earlocks], beard, skullcap, and caftan make the Eastern Jew recognizable to all. If he appears without his trademarks, only the sharp-eyed can recognize his racial origins. . . . It is an intrinsic trait of the Jew that he always tries to hide his origins when he is among non-Jews.* "[10] These assimilated Jews were more dangerous because unsuspecting non-Jews could not protect themselves.

I found it hard to fathom that this man had been teaching at an American university for over fifteen years and had published what could arguably be described as overt antisemitic tomes without anyone—his colleagues in particular—taking notice. In fact, not only had his colleagues not taken notice, his fellow evolutionary psychologists had elected him secretary of the association of evolutionary psychologists. I called Anthony, who had also read MacDonald's work, and told him I considered it high-class antisemitism. Anthony responded quickly: "High-class?" At that point, overwhelmed by the myriad of details confronting me as I prepared to leave for England, I set MacDonald and his theories aside.

## *SLATE* ENTERS THE FRAY

As MacDonald's turn to testify approached, the Internet began to hum. In the last week of January, *New York Times* columnist Judith Shulevitz, having learned about MacDonald's forthcoming testimony, published a series of provocative articles about him in *Slate*. She challenged his fellow evolutionary psychologists to explain how, given his views, they could have elected him secretary of their organization.[11] Stung by Shulevitz's critique, leaders of the organization protested that they had never published his articles in their peer-reviewed journal. Others posted searing critiques of his work.[12] John Tooby, director of the Center of Evolutionary Biology at the University of California, Santa Barbara, and one of the founders of evolutionary psychology, declared that "MacDonald's ideas—not just on Jews—violate fundamental principles of the field." Evolutionary psychologists study the universal design of a species and not individual or intergroup genetic differences, as MacDonald did.[13] Steven Pinker, a member of MIT's Department of Brain and Cognitive Sciences and a well-respected experimental psychologist who has written about various aspects of language and mind, believed MacDonald's work failed basic scientific credibility because he had neither tested alternative hypotheses nor utilized a control group, such as another minority ethnic group. Critics observed that MacDonald made sweeping pronouncements without the necessary expertise to do so. He had no training in rabbinic studies, but dismissed the Talmud as "unnecessary" because it fulfilled no "purely religious or practical need." Though not a population geneticist, he reached sweeping conclusions about the Jewish gene pool. Though not an economist, he made pronouncements about Jews' economic practices. Though not a political scientist, he analyzed Jews' political influence.

Pinker also found it striking that, whereas people are a composite of many identities, according to MacDonald, Jews identified *only* as Jews. This attribute, Pinker observed, made them unique from all other humans and was an ad hominem argument that stood outside the bonds of normal scientific discourse. To try to engage in this argument was, Pinker contended, an obvious waste of time. "MacDonald has already announced that I will reject his ideas because I am Jewish, so what's the point of reacting to them?" Reminding me of my initial reaction to MacDonald, Tooby contended that his work constituted a "Protocols of Learned Elders Zion–like theory." Pinker agreed: "MacDonald's various theses . . . collectively add up to a consistently invidious portrayal of Jews, couched in value-laden, disparaging language. It is impossible to avoid the impression that this is not an ordinary scientific hypotheses."[14]


MacDonald was scheduled to take the stand on a Monday. Ken Stern, who had been coordinating conversations with John Tooby in California and with James and me in London, was bleary with exhaustion when I talked to him late Sunday night. He had taken to referring to MacDonald as "Old Mac-Donald," because, he explained, his ideas belonged on the farm, not in the classroom. We had gathered extensive critiques of MacDonald's work. We downloaded this material to Heather, who would organize it for Rampton's use in court.[15] It was far more than he needed for cross-examination, but I was glad Rampton would have the most compelling evidence in order to demonstrate that MacDonald's theories relied on a coded discourse that was, in essence, antisemitic. When Rampton entered the courtroom on Monday morning, he was grumbling to himself about being inundated with mounds of vile material. Given his foul mood, it did not seem like an opportune moment to discuss "Old MacDonald" with him.

Before MacDonald could take the stand, Judge Gray asked how Mac-Donald's evidence was "really relevant to the issues I have to decide." Irving insisted that MacDonald's testimony would prove he had "been the victim of an international endeavour to destroy his legitimacy as an historian." Gray cautioned him, "Remember the Defendant is Professor Lipstadt and, therefore, it is her activities . . . for which she can be held accountable." Irving said he would prove that I had made myself "part of a broader endeavour." Gray gave Irving an amber light to proceed. "Let us see how the evidence turns out."[16]

MacDonald, a tall, spindly man with an angular face, ascended the steps of the witness box. His tousled brown hair looked like it had not yet recovered from London's winter wind. His dark suit, which seemed too large for his frame, hung awkwardly on him. After taking the oath, he settled into the chair, hunched his shoulders, fixed his gaze on the floor, and seemed—despite his height—to disappear into the box. Irving began by asking MacDonald to describe his work. He said he wrote about Judaism, which he described as a "group evolutionary strategy" and studied the tactics Jewish organizations use to combat views with which they disagree, "such as St Martin's Press rescinding a publication of the Goebbels' Diary."* When MacDonald mentioned the St. Martin's decision, Irving asked him to elaborate on the way the book was "suppressed . . . under pressure from the Jewish community." Irving had barely finished his question when the Long Beach professor—sounding rather energized—interjected, "Yes, from the Anti-Defamation League." Given Judge Gray's warning to Irving that he had to demonstrate that I was directly involved in the St. Martin's decision, this was not the most prudent reply. Judge Gray quickly made that point, cautioning Irving that this episode was only relevant if he could establish my link to the cancellation. Irving assured the court that he would demonstrate that St. Martin's had "quoted the Second Defendant as an authority for their decision" and that this cancellation was "part of a group strategy."

Irving asked MacDonald whether he had seen anything in the evidence that led him to believe that "the Second Defendant had made herself a part of this endeavour?" MacDonald took out the *Washington Post* article on the St. Martin's imbroglio. It proved, MacDonald concluded, that I "was literally part of the pressure on St. Martin's." I smiled in anticipation of how Rampton would handle the cross-examination of MacDonald. He would certainly

---

*MacDonald was referring to Irving's biography of Goebbels.

ask him to demonstrate how my response to a reporter's query constituted proof that I was part of an organized effort to silence Irving.

## A STUDENT'S PAPER AND A PROFESSOR'S SUGGESTION

Irving seemed to have forgotten his promise to prove that St. Martin's had quoted me when they decided to cancel the contract. Instead he handed MacDonald a student paper on David Irving. The paper, by a Canadian student, reviewed Irving's evolution as a Holocaust denier. Not a particularly distinguished product, it had been sent to me after the publication of my book by the Canadian representative of the Simon Wiesenthal Center, who warned me in a cover letter that it contained "comments that neither you or I would use." The student, ignoring the notion of free speech, had argued that Irving "should not be allowed to disseminate his message of hate as freely in other public forums" and that the "ultimate response was to cease providing him with a forum to convey his skewed version of history. . . ."[17] I found the student's extreme suggestions fanciful and was inclined to toss the paper. However, I decided to file it on the outside chance that some of Irving's quotes, which the student had unearthed, might someday prove useful. I had forgotten about it until the research assistant helping me gather materials for my discovery found it in my files. As soon as Irving raised the topic, I scribbled a note to Rampton: "The paper was sent to me. Unsolicited. I had nothing to do with writing it. Gray should know that." Rampton stretched out his arm in my direction, and motioned in a way that I understood to mean that I should calm down and not worry, he had it all under control. MacDonald was particularly exercised by the student's attack on Irving's legitimacy as a historian. Turning to Judge Gray, he complained that "despite the fact that he is regarded among historians as important . . . there *are* attempts to curtail his freedom of speech." I found MacDonald's use of the passive voice—"there *are* attempts"—telling. MacDonald had seamlessly moved from a student's verbal hyperbole, which even the representative of an activist organization found extreme, to concluding that this paper constituted proof of secretive attempts to curtail Irving's freedom of speech.

Judge Gray asked MacDonald, "How does that establish that Professor Lipstadt is part of this conspiracy to discredit Mr Irving?" MacDonald responded, "The only linkage . . . is the *Washington Post* interview." Judge Gray, in a slightly more insistent tone, asked again, "What has this [student paper] to do with the *Washington Post?*" Irving jumped to his witness's defense: "My Lord, this document was from Professor Lipstadt's own discovery." Judge Gray pressed the California professor: "It is a document that she was sent, apparently unsolicited, by the Simon Wiesenthal organization. What does that prove against her?" The look on MacDonald's face seemed to suggest he thought the answer was obvious. Shaking his head back and forth, he began with some hesitation: "Well, OK, this document—there is not . . ." Then he stopped, as if to collect his thoughts. After a moment, he said in a rush, "My impression was that David Irving has a general complaint about persecution by Jewish organizations and that is what I thought we were addressing here." Gray leaned toward MacDonald, as if he was about to say something. Then, apparently deciding otherwise, he sat back and quietly said, "I see. Thank you."[18]

Next, Irving asked MacDonald about a letter Holocaust historian Yehuda Bauer, who had suggested all those years ago that I write a book about Holocaust deniers, sent to me after he read an early draft of *Denying the Holocaust.* I was expecting Irving to single it out. Two years earlier, when he found it in my discovery materials, he had posted it on his website. Anthony and James, livid at this breach of privilege—discovery materials were private until introduced into court—demanded that Irving remove it. Bauer praised the manuscript and then offered a number of suggestions for strengthening it. He suggested that I expand my discussion of Irving in order to make clear to readers that he was the mainstay of contemporary Holocaust denial in Western Europe. I thought Bauer's suggestion valid and, in an effort to find a bit of additional material on Irving, contacted various archives and libraries. They sent me articles by and about Irving. I wove them into the manuscript.

Judge Gray encouraged Irving. "This seems to me to be more relevant than the general sort of evidence that the Professor was giving earlier." Distressed, I wrote Rampton another note. "It is standard operating procedure for scholars to circulate their manuscripts prior to publication. Bauer was hardly the only one who read and commented on it." I knew I sounded defensive, but I hated that my actions were being painted as something sinister.

Irving seemed energized by the judge's comments. His voice grew louder as he reminded MacDonald that I had described him as "dangerous." Glancing over his shoulder at the press gallery, he asked, "In what way am I dangerous . . . ? Am I the kind of person that *they* think I [*sic*] may place a bomb in their letter box or what kind of danger are *they* referring to?" I was struck by how Irving glided from what *I* had written in my book to what *"they"* thought. MacDonald did the same. "No, obviously, they view you as a danger because of your . . . writings. They think . . . that their version of events [should] be accepted as the truth and that the dissent from certain of these tenets should be viewed as beyond the pale of rational discussion." Irving, looking satisfied, asked, "Finally, in order to pre-empt a question Mr Rampton may wish to ask, do you consider me to be an antisemite?" I was not surprised when MacDonald said, "I do not consider you to be an anti-semite. I have had quite a few discussions with you now and you have almost never even mentioned Jews, and when you have, never in a general negative way."[19] As Irving was bringing his questions to an end, I saw that Rampton was hurriedly making some notes.

## RAMPTON'S RESPONSE

I waited in anticipation—and admittedly some glee—for Rampton's cross-examination. Surely, he would use his rapier-style wit to illustrate that MacDonald did not really grasp what the trial was about. Just as I was con-templating all this, Rampton leaned across his table. In his outstretched hand was the paper on which he had been making notes a few moments earlier. I took it and, after reading the few lines, felt the breath knocked out of me. "You will be *very* cross with me, but I do not plan to ask this witness any questions." I felt blindsided. We had reams of material that I expected Ramp-ton to use to lay waste to the professor's poorly reasoned junk science. I ex-pected him to use the opportunity to demonstrate how Irving and his witness lived in a conspiratorial universe. Compelled to remain silent, I could not make these points. I depended on him to speak for me.

I had barely finished reading the note, when Judge Gray turned to our side of the courtroom: "Mr Rampton." Rampton remained seated and, with-out looking up, mumbled, "I do not think I have any further questions." He omitted the traditional "your Lordship" and did not thank the witness. He could just as easily have been declining an offer of a cup of tea. In fact, Rampton, an unfailingly polite man, would have declined that offer far more graciously. Even Irving seemed surprised by this turn of events. He turned to Rampton as if to ascertain whether he had heard right and then asked

Judge Gray, "Is the witness released, my Lord?" The judge said, "Yes."[20] Mac-Donald, looking a bit startled, turned to Judge Gray and then to Irving, as if to determine precisely what he should do. Irving had told him to expect to be on the stand for a few days. In less than thirty minutes it was over. Looking like a boxer who entered the ring for a much-hyped fight only to be knocked out in the first seconds of the first round, the professor rose, descended from the witness box, and, still shaking his head in surprise, took a seat near Irving.

A few minutes later Gray called a short break. Waves of anger still roiling in me, I turned to Anthony: "We *must* talk." We huddled near the wall of red and blue loose-leaf notebooks. I consciously turned my back to the public gallery so that the press would not see my face. In a voice that was more demanding than inquisitive, I said, "How could Rampton let this guy go without asking any questions?" Anthony, after listening intently, said, "The judge was unimpressed. He thought him an academic schlemiel who didn't understand what this trial was about. Had Rampton questioned him, Mac-Donald would have expounded on his wacky theories. Judge Gray might have thought they had some intellectual gravitas. This was the optimum forensic tactic." For the past four years, every time Anthony, Rampton, or James told me that forensic considerations dictated a certain strategy, I conceded. I wanted to give testimony. They said I should not, so I did not. I wanted to talk to the press. They said not to, so I kept silent. This, however, felt like too much. "This trial," I told Anthony, "is not just about forensics. The press is present. We should have exposed this guy's ideas as antisemitic." Anthony's response was short. "We did not have to. MacDonald did that himself." I was unconvinced but knew it was pointless to say anything else. The moment had passed and the opportunity was gone. I was about to return to my seat when Anthony touched me on the arm and, in a reassuring tone, said, "Trust me, it was the right thing to do."

Just then, Professor Dan Jacobson of the University of London approached us and in a voice laced with sarcasm, laughingly said, "That witness has a small dull mind possessed by a large dud idea."[21] Anthony raised his eyebrows and looked at me over the rims of his glasses. His expression clearly said, "What did I tell you?" Not quite willing to let go of my anger, I said nothing and turned to my computer. I silently acknowledged that maybe—just maybe—Rampton and Anthony were right.

# ELEVEN

# EXONERATING HITLER,
# EXCORIATING THE ALLIES

A fter MacDonald stepped down, Irving reentered the witness box and
Rampton resumed his cross-examination. I was surprised when Rampton began by referring to the permit to inspect *"Feldöfen"* ("field ovens")—the
incineration grids on which the Germans had burned victims' bodies—which
had come up when Van Pelt was on the stand. Irving, who had mistranslated
the word as "field kitchens," had then attributed his mistake to the stress of
doing the translation at 2 A.M. His excuse was hardly convincing. Irving's
knowledge of German was too good to allow for such mistakes, even at 2
A.M. Moreover, his supposed mistake conveniently moved in the direction of
the exoneration of the Germans. I had not, however, given it much thought
because it seemed a small point. Now, Rampton handed Irving a document
and asked him to identify it. Irving acknowledged that it was a translation
of the *"Feldöfen"* document. It had been downloaded from his website on
November 24, 1998. Here too the word had been translated as "field kitchens."
I realized that this was what Thomas had been looking for when the topic
came up a week ago. He had realized that he had seen the same *mis*translation on Irving's website over a year earlier. Clearly, Irving's use of "kitchens"
bore no relationship to the stress of the trial. Irving insisted that he had simply
made the same mistake twice. Rampton, skeptical that Irving would have inadvertently repeated such a basic error, disagreed. "No, Mr Irving. It was a
repetition of a deliberate mistranslation." Irving, ignoring or having forgotten

that he had just acknowledged that his translation was a mistake, now protested that Germans worldwide had emailed him that it was an "entirely acceptable and intelligible . . . [and] plausible translation."[1]

## SWITCHING DATES AND INVENTING WITNESSES: INNOCENT MISTAKES?

Rampton, proceeding with his review of how Irving distorted documents in order to "prove" his preexisting conclusions, turned to a two-day meeting Hitler and Foreign Minister Ribbentrop held with Admiral Horthy, the head of the Hungarian government in April 1943. They demanded that he act more forcefully against Hungarian Jews. Horthy had instituted draconian antisemitic legislation but had not gone as far as the Germans wanted.[2]

On April 16, the first day of the meeting, Horthy protested that he had "done everything which one could decently undertake against the Jews, but one could surely not murder them or kill them. . . ." Hitler assured Horthy that this was unnecessary; the Jews could be placed in concentration camps as had been done in Slovakia. (In fact, Slovakian Jews had not been placed in concentration camps. They had been murdered in Auschwitz, Sobibor, and Maidanek.) The next day, when the topic came up again, Horthy repeated his protests that "he surely couldn't beat them to death." At that point, Ribbentrop said, "The Jews must either be annihilated or taken to concentration camps. There was no other way." Hitler followed Ribbentrop's murderous proposition with a ruthless harangue. Jews should be "treated like tuberculosis bacilli." He declared that "even innocent natural creatures like hares and deer had to be killed so that no harm was caused" and warned that "nations who did not rid themselves of Jews perished."[3]

In *Hitler's War* (1977), Irving presented a convoluted description of this meeting, one that—not surprisingly—painted Hitler and Ribbentrop in a far better light than did the transcript of the meeting. He buried Ribbentrop's statement that Jews had to be either "annihilated or taken to concentration camps" in a footnote, thereby, as Evans observed, "Marginalizing it almost out of existence."[4] Then he justified Hitler's concerns about Hungarian Jews by linking them to the Warsaw Ghetto uprising. "In Warsaw, the fifty thousand Jews surviving in the ghetto were on the point of staging an armed uprising . . . Poland should have been an object lesson to Horthy, Hitler argued." Irving's suggestion that it was the Warsaw uprising that prompted

Hitler's concerns about Hungarian Jewry was a complete fabrication. The uprising began on April 19, 1943, two days *after* this meeting. It could not, therefore, have been a reference point for Hitler.[5] (Furthermore, approximately 1,000 Jews fought the Germans in the Warsaw Ghetto, not 50,000, as Irving claimed.)

But this was not Irving's most grievous misrepresentation of the meeting. According to Irving, on April 17, the second day of the meeting, "Horthy apologetically noted that he had done all he decently could against the Jews: 'But they can hardly be murdered.' . . . Hitler reassured him: 'There is no need for that.' " Irving's readers could have justifiably assumed that Hitler did *not* want them killed.[6]

Rampton asked where in the transcript of the second day of the meeting, April 17, one could find Horthy "apologetically" noting that the Jews could "hardly be murdered" or Hitler reassuring him that there was "no need for that"? Irving protested that he would need to review the transcript to find these quotes. As Irving began to flip through the transcript of the meeting, Judge Gray, rather graciously counseled, "Take your time." Rampton, however, suggested otherwise: "I would not trouble taking too much time, Mr Irving." Time would not help Irving find the quotes on the transcript of the second day because Hitler had said them on the first day. Rampton declared that Irving had moved them to day two in order to give the impression that the meeting had ended on a conciliatory note when, in fact, it had ended on a brutally murderous note with Hitler saying that the Jews must be put down as animals.[7]

Irving protested that Rampton was ascribing a devious motive to what was a "mix up of dates"—something that could happen to any author. Rampton rejected this explanation. "No, Mr Irving. . . . You were concerned that if left unvarnished . . . what Hitler said would appear to be fairly conclusive evidence that he intended the physical annihilation of the Jews." Furthermore, the German historian Martin Broszat had alerted Irving to the "mix up" in 1977. Yet Irving did not fix it in the 1991 edition of *Hitler's War*. Irving responded in the same way that he often did when he had been proven wrong. He dismissed the matter as irrelevant. "Whether it was said on one day or the next day, I do not think is of great moment."[8] Rampton did not respond and announced his intention to move on.

\* \* \*

Rampton next charged that Irving had also engaged in a whitewashing of Hitler's record in his presentation of the 1923 Nazi failed attempt to overthrow the Weimar government. Hitler, as party leader, was arrested and put on trial. According to Irving, a police sergeant had testified that Hitler, incensed by the ransacking and looting of a Jewish delicatessen, sent for the ex–army lieutenant who had led the raid and dismissed him from the party on the spot. "I shall see that no other nationalist unit allows you to join either!" Irving wrote that Göring—apparently amazed at Hitler's admonishments to the looters—"goggled at this exchange."[9]

When Evans and his researchers tried to check Irving's rendition of the event, they discovered significant discrepancies between Irving's version and the testimony given at the trial by a *former* police officer, *Oberwachmeister* Matthäus Hofmann. Hitler had sacked the lieutenant, but not for raiding the deli. He sacked him because he removed his party insignia during a raid on a Jewish store. Moreover, this raid had taken place well before the *Putsch*. Hitler did not send for the lieutenant; he simply happened to be in the room. Irving had made these "adjustments," Evans contended, to make it look as if Hitler had aggressively punished those who engaged in antisemitic activities. Moreover, Irving failed to tell his readers that Hofmann was a long-term member of the Nazi Party, a loyal follower of Hitler, and someone who was, therefore, inclined to be quite biased in Hitler's favor.[10] Finally, Hofmann never mentioned that Göring was present, much less that he "goggled at this exchange."

How, Rampton asked, did Irving know Göring was present or that he goggled? Irving declared, "That was author's license." Rampton responded, "You mean it was an *invention* . . . a piece of *fiction.*" Irving, sounding like he was lecturing Rampton, said, "When you write a book that is going to be read . . . you occasionally help the reader along. . . . Here is Adolf Hitler ticking off an Army lieutenant, one of *his* Nazis, for raiding a Jewish shop and throwing him out of the party for doing it. You would imagine that any other Nazi, like Göring standing nearby, is going to be . . . doing a double take . . . or am I wrong?" Rampton didn't waste a minute: "You are completely wrong." Irving, Rampton charged, had invented Göring's presence to make it appear that Hitler had forcefully reprimanded the lieutenant. Irving insisted that he had drawn a "reasonable inference" when he placed an amazed Göring at the meeting.

Then, repeating the same explanation he had used to justify his addition of "All" to Judge Biddle's comment "This I don't believe," Irving dismissed the matter as "only two words" which did not "make a big difference." Rampton differed: "All your little fictions, your little tweaks of the evidence all tend in the same direction, exculpation of Adolf Hitler."

In his rendition of the *Putsch,* Irving wrote that Hitler had sent "armed men . . . to requisition funds" from a Jewish firm that printed banknotes. Rampton asked what he meant by that. Smiling, Irving replied, "Oh, that was obviously some prank that they carried out." Rampton's voice rose a notch: "A prank?" Irving explained, "He sent them out to go and steal the entire contents of a bank to pay people back." Heather was having difficulty suppressing a smile. Even Judge Gray did not mask his surprise: "He sent them out to *rob the bank?*" Irving responded, deadpan: "It is rather the same way as the great train robbers went to requisition funds." The courtroom erupted in laughter at Irving's Willie Sutton–like perspective on robbing banks. Irving, possibly feeling empowered by the laughter, told Rampton, "I do not know if you have read Noel Coward's poems? This is the way the English write. . . . with a delicate touch."[11] Rampton, employing his own delicate touch, moved on.

## HITLER AND *KRISTALLNACHT:* LIVID WITH RAGE?

Nowhere was Irving's exculpation of Hitler more evident than in his depiction of *Kristallnacht,* the Night of Broken Glass (November 9–10, 1938). During this nationwide pogrom hundreds of synagogues were set aflame. Jewish businesses, shops, buildings, and homes were ransacked. Thousands of Jews were beaten and placed in concentration camps. According to Nazi figures, 91 people were murdered. However, when one takes into account the suicides and subsequent deaths from beatings and mistreatment sustained during the pogrom as well as the death of people arrested during *Kristallnacht* and incarcerated in concentration camps, as many as 1,000 people may have died. Irving argued that Goebbels orchestrated this event and did so without informing Hitler and those closest to him.

The pogrom took place on the fifteenth anniversary of the failed *Putsch.* Nazi Party leaders had gathered to mark the occasion in Munich. A German diplomat in Paris had died from gunshot wounds inflicted by a young Jew. Goebbels and Hitler met earlier in the evening for dinner. According to Irving, Goebbels did not tell Hitler that riots against Jews were already occurring in a number of cities. Hitler returned to his hotel, while Goebbels, addressing the veteran Nazi leaders at the Old Town Hall, told them to take revenge on the Jews for allegedly sponsoring the murder. Violent attacks against Jews spread throughout Germany. Irving claimed that Hitler and Himmler were totally unaware that anything untoward was happening until 1 A.M., when the synagogue next to their hotel began to burn. Heydrich, who had been in the hotel bar, learned of the conflagration and raced to inform them. According to Irving, Hitler was "livid with rage" and Himmler began "telex[ing] instructions to all the police authorities to restore law and order, protect Jews and Jewish property, and halt any ongoing incidents." Hitler was intent on "halt[ing] the madness."[12]

Irving's rendition of events was, we claimed, completely at odds with the documentary evidence. Early in the evening, when addressing the veteran party members at the Town Hall, Goebbels had spoken about the attacks that were already under way: "The Führer had decided . . . [that] such demonstrations were not to be prepared . . . [nor] organized by the party. In so far as they occurred spontaneously, they were, however, not to be opposed or stopped." Rampton asked Irving to reconcile his claim that Hitler and Himmler were totally unaware of these outbreaks until the synagogue next to Munich's Four Seasons Hotel began to burn, with Goebbels's public statement earlier that evening that "the Führer had decided." Goebbels would not, Rampton argued, "lie to a . . . gathering of old party comrades" about Hitler's orders. Irving argued that Hitler assumed that Jews were simply "going to get ruffed [sic] up" but "it got out of hand."[13]

How, Rampton continued, could he argue that Hitler and Himmler were ignorant when Himmler's subordinate, Heinrich Müller, sent a telex at 11:55 P.M. to German police officials informing them that "actions against Jews, in particular against their synagogues, will very shortly take place across the whole of Germany. They are not to be interrupted."[14] Irving dismissed this as of no significance. About an hour and a half after this telex, Himmler and Heydrich sent another communiqué. Irving had described this telex as calling on Germans to "restore law and order, protect Jews and Jewish property, and halt any ongoing incidents." In fact, Rampton observed, it ordered that demonstrations against the Jews were "not to be hindered by the police."[15]

Irving had not only distorted what happened during the pogrom; he also distorted what happened afterward. In *Goebbels,* Irving had written that Hess "ordered the Gestapo and the [Nazi] party's courts to delve into the origins of the night's violence and turn the culprits over to the public prosecutors." Irving had given his readers the impression, Rampton argued, "that anybody found guilty of arson, looting, damage, assault, rape, murder or whatever, was going to prosecuted by the State judicial machinery." In fact, Rampton continued, immediately after *Kristallnacht* the Ministry of Justice announced that those who damaged Jewish property were *not* to be prosecuted. Irving now protested to Rampton that he could not recall twelve years after writing the book what he intended to convey to his readers. Judge Gray was not so easily swayed. Referring to Irving's description of post-*Kristallnacht* events, he said, "If I read that, I think I would be inclined to think that these people were going to be prosecuted by the criminal system of the country."

Irving, no longer claiming he could not remember what he meant, now insisted that many violators had indeed been prosecuted by authorities for their behavior during the pogrom. Rampton disagreed, noting that in February 1939 the party court heard sixteen cases and in only two of them, both involving rapes, were the perpetrators turned over to the criminal courts. As for the other fourteen cases, the party court asked Hitler to quash the charges, even though they included shooting, beating, stabbing, and drowning of Jews. How, Rampton wondered, could Irving reconcile the quashing of these proceedings with his claim that the Gestapo would turn the culprits over to the prosecutors? When Irving insisted that his description of the treatment of the culprits was accurate, Judge Gray disagreed: "On the contrary, Mr Irving . . . . 14 of them never went to the criminal courts. . . . They just got a ticking off for raping and killing."

How come, Rampton wondered, Irving never described this "scandalous manipulation of the justice system" in his book? Irving claimed that to have done so would have filled the book "with 8 pages of sludge." Rampton saw it differently: "If you cannot find enough space to put in the truth, leave it out." Though Irving kept protesting that his rendition was "the truth," Rampton moved to another topic.[16]

## DRESDEN: DEATH TOLL DISTORTIONS

When we first planned our defense strategy, we thought it would be useful to compare Irving's treatment of Holocaust-related topics with a non-Holocaust topic. Evans chose to examine the Allied bombing of Dresden in

February 1945. This was the topic of Irving's first book, *The Destruction of Dresden*. Many historians believe the bombing lacked a military objective and was designed to break the German people's morale. Irving, taking one of the more extreme positions in this regard, declared in a 1990 speech: "The holocaust of Germans in Dresden really happened. That of the Jews in the gas chambers of Auschwitz is an invention. I am ashamed to be an Englishman."[17]

But we did not challenge Irving's sentiments about whether the bombing of Dresden was necessary. We did challenge his claims about the death toll. We were convinced that Irving had significantly inflated the death toll in order to enhance the severity of the Allied bombing. Irving's estimate of the Dresden death toll had gone through various permutations. Initially, Irving believed that approximately 40,000 had been killed. This corresponded to most official postwar estimates. However, over the years Irving gravitated to a far higher figure, sometimes contending that it was as high as 250,000.

Irving attributed his change to his having come into possession of a copy of a March 1945 document known as *"Tagesbefehl,"* or "Order of the Day," 47 (*TB*-47). It supposedly was a "brief extract" from a statement by the police president of Dresden, which listed a provisional death toll of 202,000 as of March 20, 1945. *TB*-47 predicted that the toll would reach 250,000. Irving first saw a copy of the statement in 1964 during a visit to the home of Dresden photographer Walter Hahn. Hahn had a copy that he obtained in a rather convoluted way. He had seen a copy of it in the home of a Dresden doctor, Max Funfack, and had surreptitiously made a handwritten copy from Funfack's copy, which he subsequently typed up. When Irving saw Hahn's copy, he asked for a copy. Hahn's wife typed up additional copies and Irving took one. Richard Evans wryly observed that, based on this carbon copy of a typed copy of a typed copy of a surreptitiously handwritten copy of an unsigned document that was an "extract" from an official police report, Irving changed his conclusion about the death toll.[18]

But even this change was not without its fits and starts. Upon returning from Dresden, with his copy of Hahn's copy of the copy of *TB*-47 in hand, Irving wrote the editor of the *Sunday Times* announcing his discovery, yet expressing some hesitation about its figures. "It remains to be established whether the 200,000 number it contains is . . . genuine." A few days later, Irving's hesitation seemed to have evaporated and he told his German publisher that he was convinced that the death toll was 202,000. He justified his claim by explaining that the "number came" from the then Deputy Chief Medical Officer, "Dr Max Funfack, [therefore] there could be no doubt as to the authenticity" of the document. Three days after telling his publisher the document was genuine, Irving again demonstrated some doubts when he asked the German federal archives to establish the document's authenticity.[19]

Five days after asking the German archives to authenticate *TB-47*, Irving's doubts seemed to have evaporated yet again. The historic Coventry Cathedral, which had been severely bombed by the Germans during the war, was preparing to mount an exhibit on Dresden. Irving advised the cathedral's provost that he had "no doubt" about *TB-47*'s authenticity and suggested that in order "to drive home the impact of the exhibition. . . . the Police President's Report on the Dresden raid [*TB-47*] [be] printed in large type. . . . The casualties . . . it mentions have a shattering impact." He assured the churchman that the document was obtained "indirectly from the Dresden Deputy Chief Medical Officer responsible for the disposing of the victims [who] still live in Dresden."[20] Irving apparently did not mention that this figure of 202,000 had first come from Goebbels, who wanted to arouse the German people into taking a stand against the Allies.

After reviewing this rather convoluted sequence of events, Rampton asked how Irving could urge the provost to include these figures in the exhibit if he was not sure they were reliable? Judge Gray was also puzzled: "Did it not cross your mind that it was a bit suspicious that the figure of 200,040 in *TB-47* was . . . the very same figure which Goebbels was putting into circulation for propaganda purposes?"

Irving insisted the figures in the *TB-47* were accurate because the document came "from somebody who during the war was the Chief Medical Officer of Dresden." Rampton, speaking in a somewhat nonchalant tone, as if he just wanted to ascertain a relatively unimportant fact, asked, This "Dresden Deputy Chief Medical Officer [who] was responsible for disposing of the victims . . . was a Dr Funfack?" Irving answered, "Yes." As soon as Irving said yes, I knew that he had again ensnared himself in his own trap. In Irving's discovery we had found a letter from Funfack to Irving that was written in 1965. Funfack had just read reviews of the German edition of *The Destruction of Dresden* as well as a letter by Irving's German publisher to a German newspaper. Both the reviews and the letter credited Irving with having used information he received from the "then Deputy Chief Medical Officer, Dr Max Funfack" to resolve the question of the Dresden death toll. In his letter,

Funfack insisted that he had never been deputy chief medical officer and had, in fact, been working as a urologist. He had no special information about the death toll. He was "completely uninvolved" in the disposal of the bodies, had "only heard the numbers third-hand" and was "only once present" when bodies were being cremated in *Altmarkt* square. This letter, with its most explicit denials, should have laid to rest any claims about Funfack's knowledge.

Thirty-five years later, in a courtroom while under oath, here was Irving asserting his information came from the deputy chief medical officer who was responsible for supervising the disposal and cremation of all the air-raid victims. When Rampton reminded Irving of Funfack's denials, Irving discounted them, arguing that Funfack's denials could not be trusted because the doctor, an East German, was probably lying in order not to anger Communist authorities who, for reasons Irving failed to explain, wanted a lower figure. (One would have thought that the Communists would have been happy with a higher figure because it made the British and Americans, rather than the Soviets who were not involved in the bombing, look bad in the eyes of East Germans.)

Irving had also ignored other information that should have made him doubt the 200,000 figure. In his discovery, we found three letters from a Theo Miller, a Dresdener whose job it had been to collect bodies after the bombing. Miller soberly and in great detail delineated how the bodies were collected and counted. He concluded that the highest possible toll was 30,000. Trying to demonstrate that Irving's far higher toll was completely far-fetched, Miller asked Irving whether he thought it feasible to "burn in about three weeks 110,000 corpses on a fire-grate of railway rails with a dimension of about 70 × 10 meters?"[21] Irving had failed to include mention of Miller's letters in any of the subsequent editions of his Dresden book. Rampton wondered why "an honest, upright, careful, meticulous, open minded historian does not mention . . . alternative sources?" Irving, discounting Miller's letters, asserted that he could not mention all the information witnesses sent him. Judge Gray was also disturbed by Irving's failure to take account of Miller's letters. He observed that Miller's job was to "record the numbers of deaths at the time. Does that not make him rather a specially valuable witness?"

Irving protested that he received many letters from all "sorts of people who *claim* to have been on the spot." Rampton wondered, "So he is a liar, then?" "No," Irving said, but "I think he is fantasizing slightly." The judge sounded surprised: "He is *fantasizing?*" Irving insisted that he was, but offered no proof.[22]

I found it striking that Irving still insisted that the copy of the TB-47 in his possession was genuine, since in 1977 a man who had been a member of the Dresden police produced a copy of the original TB-47. It listed a death toll of 20,000 with an expected toll of 25,000. Evidently someone in Goebbels's Propaganda Ministry added a zero to each number: hence, the estimate of 200,000 and 250,000. Nonetheless, Irving continued to adhere to a higher death toll. In 1986, Irving told a South African audience that 100,000 were killed in one night. At the *Leuchter Report* press conference he told reporters, "We burned Dresden . . . killing between 100,000 and 250,000." Only in 1995 did Irving reveal to his English-language readers that TB-47 was a product of Goebbels's Propaganda Ministry.[23]

Rampton observed that virtually all historians had, after studying the number of burials, certified deaths, lists of missing persons, and other official sources, estimated a toll of between 25,000 and 35,000. The claims about death tolls of 100,000 and 200,000 had "lost touch with the reality." As the discussion drew to an end, Irving angrily told Rampton, "I am deeply ashamed of what we did." Irving did not know that Rampton was also troubled by the bombing of Dresden, which he believed was not militarily necessary. As the discussion drew to an end, I recalled Evans's observation of how Irving's German publishers resolved the situation. When they republished his book in 1985, on the title page they placed the following description: "a novel."[24]

## TWELVE

# FIGHTING WORDS

"They clamor 'Ours! Ours! Ours!' when hoards of gold are uncovered. And then when antisemitism increases and the inevitable mindless pogroms occur, they ask with genuine surprise: 'Why us?' "[1]

When Rampton read this from Irving's July 1997 *Action Report,* I recalled how a few months earlier, Thomas had come to me one day at the Mishcon offices. With an uncharacteristically serious look on his face, he handed me a file and said, "I've just finished compiling this. You ought to read it." Intrigued, I began to peruse it. It was a compendium of Irving's antisemitic and racist comments and was drawn from Irving's diary entries, letters, speeches, and tapes. I had seen some of them before, but reading them as one corpus was terribly sobering. When I returned the file to Thomas, I told him that I believed that there was no separating between Irving's antisemitism and Holocaust denial. The two were inexorably linked. During the fourth week of the trial it became Rampton's job to prove that to Charles Gray.

### A MAN FROM MARS

Rampton asked Irving if his 1997 statement about Jews clamoring "Ours!" about hoards of gold was not the equivalent of him "saying antisemitism is justified on account of the fact that the Jews are greedy?" Irving, insisting Rampton had it wrong, said he was not justifying; he was explaining. Ramp-

ton proceeded to read an excerpt from an interview Irving had given Errol
Morris for his film on Leuchter. Here too Irving engaged in "explaining."

> "You people . . . have been disliked for 3,000 years. . . . No sooner do
> you arrive . . . in a new country, then [*sic*] within 50 years you are al-
> ready being disliked all over again. Now what is it? . . . Is it built into
> our microchip? When a people arrive who call themselves the Jews,
> you will dislike them? . . . Is it envy because they are more successful
> than us? I do not know the answer, but if I was a Jew, I would want to
> know what the reason is. . . . [T]hat no sooner do we arrive than we
> are being massacred and beaten and brutalized and imprisoned."

Irving had told Morris that he was speaking as an "outsider" who was
trying to understand the situation. "I come from Mars and I would say they
are clever people. . . . I would say that, as a race, they are better at making
money than I am." Rampton looked at Irving with contempt: "That is a
racist remark, of course, Mr Irving." Irving, again insisting that he was explaining, not justifying, told Rampton that these statements were his way of

> investigating the reasons why people may become antisemitic in my
> own rather clumsy and incoherent way. . . . Is it because the Jews are
> better than us? Is it because they play the violin or the piano better
> than us, better at making money than us?

Hearing these words roll off Irving's tongue, so extemporaneously, was
chilling. Rarely, if ever, had I encountered it face-to-face in such a "civilized"
setting and in such an unfettered fashion. Judge Gray interrupted Irving and,
sounding like he too wanted to ensure he was understanding matters, asked,
"That sentence . . . you say: 'If I was going to be crude, I would say not only
are they better at making money but they are greedy.' That is you, Mr Irving,
saying the Jews are greedy, is that right?" Vigorously shaking his head, Irving
insisted that he was putting himself "into the skin of a person who is asking
questions about those clever people." Judge Gray pushed further.

> JUDGE GRAY: Mr Irving, may I just ask you a question. . . . You are
>     saying of the Jews, well, they have been disliked for 3,000 years,
>     they are disliked wherever they go? . . . Then you say: "Well, I do

not know the answer" . . . But then do you not go on to say . . .
Well, look at it "as if I came from Mars"?

IRVING: I tried to stand right back from the planet Earth and look down
on these people.

JUDGE GRAY: "And it appears to me that the reason why they are disliked
is because they are greedy"; is that not what you are saying? . . .

IRVING: . . . I do not know what the reason is. . . . but possible reasons
are—what is the connection between the rise in Swiss antisemitism
and the gold bank business?

JUDGE GRAY: But you are putting that forward as the reason why there is
this dislike of Jews?

IRVING: My Lord, with respect, not *the* reason. . . . One contributing
reason at this moment in time. . . . But I also suggest very strongly
it may be built into our microchip, as I put it. It may be part of the
endemic human xenophobia which exists in all of us and which
civilized people like your Lordship and myself manage to suppress,
and other people like the gentleman [*sic*] on the Eastern Front with
the submachine guns cannot suppress.[2]

I sat transfixed—not at what Irving said—but at the civility of this exchange.

### BABY ARYANS, THEM, US, AND THE BBC

In Irving's diary—which Rampton considered particularly revealing because
it was "Irving speaking to Irving"—we found some ditties Irving composed
to sing to his infant daughter, Jessica. The first was not unlike poems parents
traditionally sing to their children—sweet, silly, and slightly inane. "My name
is baby Jessica, / I have a pretty dressica, / But now it is in a messica." When
I first read this, I had thought of Irving simply as a father engaged in fatherly
things. The next ditty quashed those perceptions. Irving wrote that whenever "mixed-breed" children were wheeled by, he would sing to Jessica:

*"I am a Baby Aryan,*
*Not Jewish or Sectarian,*
*I have no plans to marry,*
*An Ape or Rastafarian."*

Rampton's tone was completely flat. He could have been reading a weather report. The words spoke for themselves; to embellish them would be to detract. Rampton, his voice still on a perfectly even keel, said, "Racist, Mr Irving? Antisemitic, Mr Irving?" Irving accused Rampton of inflating the importance of an innocent poem. Insisting he was not a racist, he said, "I have employed coloured people of ethnic minorities on my staff." Then, gesturing in our direction, he added, "And, so far as I can see, not you or your instructing solicitors have employed one such person." Before Rampton could respond, Judge Gray warned Irving that his comment was not a "very helpful intervention." Irving, ignoring the warning, said, "I am condemned by what I say and you are condemned by what I see. Not once have you had a member of the ethnic minority working on your side." Judge Gray again admonished Irving. "Mr Irving, I just suggested that was not a very helpful intervention. Do not just repeat it."[3] While Irving kept insisting he was not a racist, I thought of his description of Nelson Mandela: a "convicted terrorist who rightly served twenty [sic] years of a life sentence" for planning "real crimes."[4]

In a 1992 speech, describing his visit to Torquay, a city in England, Irving had called it a "white community" where he had seen "perhaps one black man and one coloured family." He had then assured his listeners: "I am not anti-coloured, take it from me: nothing pleases me more than when I arrive at an airport, or a station, or a seaport and I see a coloured family there. . . . When I see these families arriving at the airport I am happy (and when I see them leaving at London airport, I am happy)." Rampton, after reading this excerpt, observed that Irving's comment about colored families had been met with "cheers and laughter." Irving insisted it was just a "cynical little joke" and his audience was responding accordingly. Rampton had a less benign view. He described the audience as composed of "fellow racists who would like to clear these islands of all their black people." Irving, returning to his earlier line of argument, declared: "Mr Rampton, you can take it from me, I am less racist than yourself probably as witnessed by the people I employ."[5] Judge Gray did not look happy.

After a moment's pause, Rampton continued reading from Irving's speech: "But if there is one thing that gets up my nose, I must admit, it is this . . . [when] I switch on my television set and I see one of them . . . reading our news to us." Rampton insisted that Irving explain: "Now who is the 'them' and who is the 'us'?" Without a moment's pause, Irving said the "one of them" was Trevor McDonald, a venerated British newscaster. A native of

Trinidad, McDonald had received an OBE from Queen Elizabeth and was now *Sir* Trevor McDonald. Irving turned to the bench to explain that this was one of his "stock speeches" in which he would start off by talking about how "our people" used to read the news, "but now in the gradual drumming [*sic*] down on television, they have women reading the news." Judge Gray, whose rather delicate features seem to be pulled taut, demanded more precision: "What did you mean by 'them' and 'us'?" Irving, rather matter-of-factly, said he was talking about women. "It is male news and it should be read to us by men." Shaking his head back and forth as if to indicate that Irving's answer would not do, Judge Gray declared himself puzzled: "You said the 'one' was Trevor McDonald . . . but you then said that the 'them' was women. . . . Well, I do not understand."

Irving said he had mentioned McDonald because he subsequently spoke about him in the speech. Rampton kept pushing, demanding to know why do "you say that Trevor McDonald was one of *them?*" Irving, in a tone that suggested that the answer was self-evident, said, "Well, he is someone who is different from us." And then, sounding like he was trying to defuse the entire matter, Irving again described this as a "witty" speech designed to set the "mood of the evening." Rampton was "not enjoying" it. Rampton, who appeared revolted by the suggestion that he should enjoy it, returned to Irving's comments about "them," "us," and McDonald. He read from Irving's speech: "For the time being, for a transitional period, I would be prepared to accept that the BBC should have a dinner-jacketed gentleman reading the important news to us, followed by a lady reading all the less important news, followed by Trevor McDonald giving us all the latest news about the muggings and the drug busts—[rest lost in loud laughter and applause]."[6]

A few days earlier, when Rampton was reviewing this material, he came across this quote in the documents Heather had prepared. His face grew red: "I did not think that man could still shock me. I was wrong." Now Irving insisted that Rampton was missing the point. "This is a funny after dinner speech in the spirit of any stand-up comedian on the BBC." Then, having forgotten—or chosen to ignore—the judge's admonition, he continued: "And as for which of us two is the racist, I can only refer to the fact that I, unlike the members of the Defence team, employ ethnic minorities without the slightest hesitation." Judge Gray, who had been following Irving's words on his computer screen, looked up and quickly swiveled his chair toward the witness box. Scowling, he looked decidedly unhappy. "How many times do I need to tell you not to make that comment? It is inappropriate, futile . . . and is doing your cause no good.'"[7] With that we broke for lunch.

In light of the ugly sentiments that had just aired, it seemed inappropriate to revel in the moment. Nonetheless, I felt a sense of satisfaction that these expressions of racism were now "out of the closet." The conversation at lunch seemed particularly muted. Even the researchers, who usually injected a tone of youthful joviality into our gatherings, were subdued. Everyone seemed a bit shell-shocked.

When we returned to the courtroom, I noticed "Brunhilda" and some other people who had been sitting near Irving in intense conversation with him. As soon as we reconvened, Irving rose and asked to address the court. He apologized for his "unruly behavior on the race matter." Judge Gray, rather kindly, acknowledged that this was all "quite stressful" for Irving, who had been cross-examined for a long time, but—in what I was coming to recognize as British understatement—suggested that such comments were better left "unsaid."[8]

## TATTOOED NUMBERS AND "THE SCUM OF HUMANITY"

During the break a VCR had been set up so Rampton could show a 1992 speech Irving had delivered in Tampa. In the speech Irving had described for his Tampa audience what happened when he spoke in Freeport, Louisiana, about six months earlier. There were a number of Jews in the Louisiana audience. Irving proceeded to lecture them: "You have been disliked for three thousand years. You have been disliked so much that you have been hounded from country to country from pogrom to purge. . . . And yet you never ask yourselves why you are disliked." At that point, Irving told his Tampa audience, a Jew at the Louisiana gathering "went berserk, [and] said, 'Are you trying to say that we are responsible for Auschwitz ourselves?' and I said, 'Well the short answer is "yes." ' I mean he really got my gander up." Again his audience laughed.

When the video was turned off, Rampton asked Irving what was so funny about saying that the Jews are responsible for Auschwitz? Irving described it as "nervous laughter, because they [his audience] had never heard an answer as blunt as that." Rampton noted that the Tampa audience had also laughed when Irving had declared, "I find the whole Holocaust story utterly boring. . . . The Jews keep going on about the Holocaust because it is the only interesting thing that has happened to them in the last three thousand years." Rampton observed, "Very funny, isn't it Mr Irving?" Irving turned to Judge Gray: "95 percent of the thinking public find the Holocaust endlessly boring by now, but they dare not say it because they know it is politically incorrect."[9]

As Rampton prepared to continue reading from the Tampa speech, I spotted the survivor who had rolled up his sleeve so that his number would be showing. Knowing what was coming, I turned away from him. It seemed wrong to watch.

> In Australia there are professional survivors, a woman called Mrs Altman, who will roll up her sleeve and show the tattoo to prove that yes, she was in Auschwitz. . . . And I'll say "Mrs Altman, you have suffered undoubtedly, and I'm sure that life in a Nazi concentration camp, where you say you were, . . . was probably not very nice. And life in Dresden probably wasn't very nice. . . . But tell me one thing," and this is why I'm going to get tasteless with her, because you've got to get tasteless. "Mrs Altman, how much money have you made out of that tattoo since 1945?"

Rampton noted that Irving's comment had been met, once again, with a "jolly laugh." Feeling as if I had abandoned the man with the number on his arm, I turned back toward the gallery. His head was lowered. Again, I turned away. It was easier to look at Irving.

Irving insisted that his criticism of Mrs. Altman, an individual Jew, was not antisemitic. He was not attacking all Jews or even all survivors. Then, seeming to forget that he was not delivering one of his after-dinner speeches, he said, "The burden of my criticism of the Mrs Altmans of this world is that the ones who have been coining the money are the ones who suffered least. . . . Survivors . . . have been turning their suffering into profit whereas people who suffered in other circumstances, like the air raid victims or the Australian soldiers building the Burmese railway have never sought to make money of their suffering."[10]

\* \* \*

Rampton next asked Irving about a description he had recorded in his diary when a group of protestors gathered outside his home. "The whole rabble, all the scum of humanity stand outside. The homosexuals, the gypsies, the lesbians, the Jews, the criminals, the communists, the left-wing extremists, the whole commune stands there and has to be held back behind steel barricades for two days." When Rampton declared this a reflection of "Mr Irving's true mind," Irving angrily insisted that his words were a "literal description" of the protestors and offered to show Rampton the photographs so "we can identify who they are."[11] I wondered how one identified homosexuals or, for that matter, criminals, Jews, and Gypsies from a photograph. I regretted that Rampton did not take him up on the offer. Instead, we ended for the day.

I left the courtroom pleased by our progress but dispirited by the day's exchange. From a forensic perspective I believed we had demonstrated for Judge Gray that Irving's comments about Jews, people of color, and other minorities were an essential part of who this man really was. But Irving's expressions of prejudice and the glee with which he seemed to make them dispelled any feelings of victory.

The events of the day soon faded into the background. I had managed to get tickets to Trevor Nunn's Royal National Theatre production of *The Merchant of Venice* and invited James, Heather, and some friends who had come from Israel to join me. I had made reservations for supper after the play in the theater restaurant. Excited about this break from the tedium of long days in court, I rushed home to get ready. The play was stunning. Nunn remaining true to the text, was sympathetic to Shylock and attributed his vengeance to persecution by the ruling class. By the second act, however, I was finding it increasingly difficult to listen to language that reviled Jews. "Currish Jew." I cringed when Gratiano cursed Shylock as "thou damned, inexecrable dog!" But it was during the infamous third act—"Hath not a Jew eyes . . . If you prick us do we not bleed"—that I began to wonder why was I subjecting myself to two trials, one real and one theatrical, both with antisemitism at their core, on the same day? Worse, this production was set in 1930s Venice, when fascism and antisemitism were on the rise. Reminiscent of *Cabaret*'s Kit Kat Klub, the cast seemed to be primed to break into "*Willkommen.*" Of course, Shakespeare's defendant is gone by the final act; I was determined to last until the bitter end.

## QUEASY ABOUT BLACK CRICKET PLAYERS

When we gathered in the courtroom the following morning, Rampton surprised me by declaring, "We've made our point about antisemitism. When the session begins, I shall ask a few more questions about racism and move on." Distressed, I urged him not to leave the topic until he had questioned Irving about his connections to former Louisiana state legislator and Ku Klux Klan leader David Duke. Irving and Duke had met in Key West on a number of occasions. They played tennis, talked politics, and dined together. They had discussed fund-raising. Duke gave Irving the list of individuals who had contributed more than $100 to his campaign. Irving had edited portions of Duke's book, including his chapter on the Holocaust, which he described as having "many insights" and "a real self-appraisal, and deserves success."[12]

I also urged him to discuss Irving's contacts with the far-right American extremist Willis Carto.[13] Rampton refused: "Neither Duke nor Carto will mean anything to the judge. We've made our point. We can't risk overdoing it." This connection between Irving and these extremists would be relevant to an American audience. I was disappointed at Rampton's decision but knew there was no moving him.

Rampton, turning to Irving's comments about black people, reminded Irving about a 1992 interview he gave on Australian radio in which he said he felt "queasy about the immigration disaster" in Britain. The interviewer asked, "What do you think about Black people . . . on the British cricket team?" Irving replied, "That makes me even more queasy." Rampton asked Irving why he felt queasy. Irving, rather proudly, declared, "Because I am English." I heard a long, low whistle. Janet Purdue, the usher, looked up in horror. I wasn't certain if she was shocked by the comment, the whistler, or both. When Rampton observed that the players were English too, Irving reminisced about the passing of "the England I was born into," lamenting that it was "different from the England that exists now." Rampton, who is Irving's contemporary, responded, "Well, thank goodness."

Judge Gray wanted Irving to clarify his comment about the cricket players. "Is the regret you feel about them playing for England . . . because of the colour of their skin?" Irving responded, "It is regrettable that blacks and people of certain races are superior athletes to whites." Judge Gray did not seem satisfied. "Why is it regrettable?" "Well," Irving answered, "it is regrettable in as much as it is now described as being a racist attitude . . . to point out that there are differences between the species."[14] The minute Irving said the word "species," Anthony sputtered, *"Species?"* Rampton let the moment pass.

The Australian journalist had also asked Irving about his attitude toward racial intermarriage. Irving had answered, "I believe in multi-culturalism." Rampton, eager to pierce the ambiguity of the answer, asked, "Do you believe, Mr Irving, in intermarriage between races . . . ?" Irving proclaimed, "I have precisely the same attitude about this as the Second Defendant. . . . I believe in God keeping the races the way he built them."[15] As soon as Irving said this, I began to pulsate with anger. This was not my view. I was deeply troubled by intermarriage between Jews and non-Jews because it threatened Jewish continuity. Color or ethnicity were entirely irrelevant to me. I wanted Rampton to clarify this, but knew he would not, because these asides by Irving had no impact on the final judgment. Had this happened earlier in the trial, I might have tried to convince Rampton to say something. Now I did not even bother. There was nothing I could do yet again, to prevent another false idea about my beliefs from floating about among the press and the public. I sat there frustrated by both the false statement and my impotence to do anything about it.

Rampton next asked about a speech in which Irving described Lord Hailsham, a cabinet minister, who in 1958 opposed immigration restrictions on people of color, as "Traitor No. 1 to the British cause." Why, Rampton wondered, did Hailsham's failure to stop such immigration make him "Traitor No 1"? Irving, sounding as if he were stating the obvious, said, "He had failed to see ahead to the tragedy which massive immigration would inflict on this country." Then Irving, without pausing, added an aside about Stephen Lawrence, a young black student, who had recently been brutally murdered by avowed racists. "If you ask the family of Stephen Lawrence, you will see the kind of tragedy that has been inflicted on an individual scale by massive immigration into a foreign country."[16] The victim was guilty. I was glad when Rampton's journey through this terrible body of material finally ended.

That night I was painfully exhausted. Rather than read transcripts and documents, as I usually did, I decided to watch British sitcoms, which, despite their silliness, I now found relaxing. James considered this a good sign: "You've come to appreciate the British sense of humor." I found that I had no patience, even for them. I turned off the TV and was headed for bed when my colleague David Blumenthal called: "How are things?" I was surprised by my answer: "Horrible." David's concern was palpable. I quickly reassured him. "From a forensic perspective we are doing well." A deeply empathetic man, David asked, "So what's horrible?" I explained how debilitating it was to listen, not just to Irving's justifications and so-called explanations of his racism and antisemitism, but also to my personal views being misrepresented. "Sometimes I feel," I told him, "I am winning the battle, but losing the war."

A few moments later the phone rang again. It was Ken Stern, who was back in the United States, but following the daily proceedings with a live Internet hookup to the court reporter's computer. I told him I was exhausted and suggested we talk tomorrow. "No, you must go online. You have to read a Reuters article which was just posted." I protested, "I'm too bushed." Ken, an exceptionally sweet person, was uncharacteristically insistent. Half asleep, I went to my computer and found the Reuters dispatch of an interview Irving had given after that day's session. Repeating what he had said in court, he lamented the passing of "Old England" when policemen rode bicycles and "pavements weren't polluted with chewing gum." I wondered why Ken thought the article so crucial. Then I reached the penultimate paragraph. Irving assured the reporter, Kate Kelland, that he could demonstrate he was not a racist by the fact that his "domestic staff" had included a Barbadian, a Punjabi, a Sri Lankan, and a Pakistani. They were "all very attractive girls with very nice breasts."[17] After reading it twice to be sure I had it right, I laughed until I cried. Maybe I laughed and then I cried.

---

# THIRTEEN

# REVOLTING CALCULATIONS

I was certain the next item on the agenda, though relatively small, would be a winner for us. In 1992, the *Sunday Times* hired Irving to go to Moscow to examine a copy of Josef Goebbels's diary, which was stored on glass plates. The diary had been unavailable to researchers until after the fall of the Soviet Union. The *Times,* anxious to avoid a debacle similar to the "Hitler's Diaries" episode, asked Irving to verify that this was truly Goebbels's diary.

### MOSCOW DIARIES: AN ILLICIT BORROWING?

In his diary, Irving described the extensive negotiations he conducted with the director of the Moscow archives to try to get permission to copy some of the plates. Irving, apparently unwilling to await the director's decision, hid one plate outside on a desolate patch of ground during the lunch break. At the end of the day he retrieved it and had it photographed in Moscow. In his diary, he described how he "illicitly borrow[ed]" the plate. The next day he returned it and took two more, according to his diary, "by the same means." However, instead of just keeping them overnight, Irving took them to Munich, left them in the hotel safe, traveled to Rome, returned to Munich, retrieved them, and brought them to England for forensic testing. He returned these plates to Moscow three weeks later. During Irving's second visit the head of the archives permitted him to copy two plates. Irving described them in his diary as the "two slides we legally borrowed."[1] Irving's actions, I had written in *Denying the Holocaust,* constituted a breach of archival protocol and caused archivists to fear that the plates had been damaged. Irving contended that he had broken no agreements and had not harmed the plates.

Irving began by calling Peter Millar, who had then represented the *Times* in Moscow, and asked him if he remembered when "I borrowed two of the glass plates from the archives without permission." Millar recalled it well. Rampton then cross-examined Millar: Was it "clear to you that he knew he should not be taking the plates?" Millar answered, "Quite." Rampton then read a memo Millar sent the editor of the *Sunday Times*. "Irving has taken liberties in our name in Moscow 'borrowing' two plates and taking them out of the country and will shamelessly take more."

When Millar stepped down, Irving returned to the witness box so that Rampton could cross-examine him on this topic. Irving readily acknowledged that his behavior was "illicit and . . . rather shabby." However, given the chaotic situation in the archives, he insisted he had performed a "valuable service" by ensuring that historians would have immediate access to the diaries.[2]

Given Irving's contrasting descriptions of the two borrowings—"illicit" and "legally"—I assumed this would be a slam dunk. We had considered bringing the head of the archive to testify. Because of the cost involved and Irving's descriptions in his diary, we decided that an affidavit by him, attesting to the fact that Irving lacked permission to take the plates, would suffice.

## JOHN KEEGAN: AMBIGUOUS TESTIMONY

Irving's next witness was Sir John Keegan, the distinguished military historian, who after a long teaching career at Sandhurst, the Royal Military Academy, became the defense editor of the *Daily Telegraph*. Keegan, who specialized in the study of twentieth-century wars, is considered to be among the most prominent and widely read military historians of the late twentieth century. His books address both the challenges faced by military leaders and the experience of the individual soldier.

Like Watt, Keegan had declined Irving's invitation to testify and had to be subpoenaed. I had never met Keegan, but I read his work and knew his reputation as one of the leading military historians. I scanned the room to see if he had arrived but did not spot him. When Keegan's name was called, a small man stood up. It was difficult to see how tall he was because he had difficulty standing erect. Walking with a cane, he laboriously made his way to the witness box. I then realized I *had* seen him earlier entering the courtroom, but had not identified him as Keegan. This military historian would, I had assumed, look like a military man—an utterly daft supposition.[3] Most scholars don't "look like" their subjects, nor should they. I asked Rampton if Keegan had been in an accident. Rampton explained that he had tuberculosis as an adolescent. Keegan, who had spent a long time in the hospital, attended Oxford in the 1950s. He was handicapped and walked with a stick. Many of his fellow students were young men, who had recently completed their army service. I wondered if this had influenced his choice of fields.

Keegan, who has an oblong face, dark slicked-down hair, and thick eyebrows, wore a finely tailored double-breasted suit and exceptionally crisp white shirt. A silk handkerchief protruded from his breast pocket. It gave the impression of having been nonchalantly put in place; however the perfect soft folds indicated that careful attention had been paid to its placement. He took his seat in the witness box. Irving deferentially thanked him for coming in spite of his disability. Irving then read excerpts from a 1980 *Times Literary Supplement* article in which Keegan singled out Chester Wilmott's *Struggle for Europe* and Irving's *Hitler's War* as two books in English that "stand out from the vast literature of the Second World War." Irving asked if Keegan still believed that to be true. Keegan said that he did and that if he had to recommend to a beginner two books that would explain the Second World War from Hitler's side and from the Allies' side, he would choose these two books. They were "head and shoulders above all the rest." Keegan described *Hitler's War* as the autobiography that Hitler did not write. I feared that this praise for Irving's book from a British cultural icon would impress Judge Gray. Of course, Keegan's endorsement of *Hitler's War* was not unqualified. He reminded Irving that the same review that praised *Hitler's War* also contained the following sentence: "Some controversies are entirely bogus, like David Irving's contention that Hitler subordinates kept from him the fact of the Final Solution." Keegan also reminded Irving that when he posted this review on his website he neglected to include this sentence.

Irving asked if it was "still your opinion . . . that I am wrong on the Holocaust?" Keegan answered without hesitation: "I continue to think it perverse of you to propose that Hitler could not have known until as late as October 1943 what was going on to the Jewish population of Europe." Upon hearing the term "perverse," I emitted a not quite sotto voce "Yes." Judge

Gray asked Keegan, "Is [it] perverse to say that Hitler did not know about the Final Solution?" Keegan's answer was unambiguous: "It defies common sense."[4]

Irving concluded by asking why, given Keegan's favorable opinion of his writings, "I had to coerce you into the witness box?" Keegan told Irving, "Just because I admire *Hitler's War.* . . . That does not mean to say that I can go further in following you." Then he added, "It seemed to me this was to be a very contentious case. I did not wish to put myself in a position where I might be misunderstood." I wondered where Irving was headed with this line of questioning. His next question resolved the mystery. "Would be it [*sic*] fair to say that you were apprehensive about the repercussions of giving evidence on my behalf?" Irving apparently wanted to use Keegan's testimony to address the putative conspiracy against him. Keegan stressed that he was not giving evidence on his behalf. He was in the court "under subpoena." When Irving kept pushing Keegan, Judge Gray intervened to stop him. "This is a slightly meaningless debate. Sir John is right. He is here compulsorily, not voluntarily. He has no choice but to answer your questions." Irving, possibly reluctant to appear to badger Keegan, apologetically explained that he wished to demonstrate "that there are professional repercussions" for those who advocate these historical positions. Judge Gray assured Irving, "I am not blind to the realities of the position and I understand the point you are putting."[5] I listened to Judge Gray's comments with concern. Was he suggesting that Irving's contention that he was being unfairly persecuted was valid? Did he believe that there were a cadre of historians who would have supported Irving but had been frightened into silence? I thought back to something Guttenplan had told me after the publication of his admittedly skewed article in the *New York Times.* Some historians who wanted to speak out on my behalf were leery of doing so because they feared Irving's litigious reputation.

Rampton, in sharp contrast to his behavior when MacDonald testified, rose, nodded respectfully to Keegan, and said he had no questions. As Keegan carefully descended from the box and took a seat near Irving, I leaned over and told James I was worried about the judge's praise of Irving. Smiling, James reassured me that Keegan could not have been better had he been our witness. In the space of a few minutes, Keegan had declared Irving's theories about the Holocaust "bogus," "perverse," and "defying common sense." James was probably right. But I couldn't help juxtaposing Keegan's praise for *Hitler's War* with Evans's devastating critique of it. Keegan's willingness to ignore what Evans had uncovered starkly illustrated how Irving was still enjoying a reservoir of almost reflexive respect despite his historical manipulations. It was also a testament to how many historians considered his denial an eccentricity, as if, among historians, Irving's denial was the crazy aunt the family sequesters in the attic. Everyone knows she is there, but if you don't shine a light on her, she can be ignored.

After Keegan stepped down, Irving complained that two Canadian newspapers had printed "sinister" articles that inaccurately portrayed events in the courtroom. Furthermore, Irving continued, those articles contained quotations from Evans's report, which, having not yet been introduced in court, was privileged. Someone had apparently leaked it. From the corner of my eye I saw Nik scribble something on a yellow Post-it and hurriedly hand it to Rampton. I wondered if he was the guilty party. Rampton read it, quickly rose, and interjected, "The reason why people have access to Professor Evans's report is that Mr Irving put it on his website."

With little, if any, visible embarrassment, Irving acknowledged that he had posted the report but said he had done so with a password and "a severe health warning, warning people that the entire contents of the report are considered to be libelous." Judge Gray said nothing about this but did reassure Irving that, since he did not read the newspaper, the articles had no impact on him. Irving was not satisfied. Judge Gray might not be affected by them but the "entire public gallery of this court will be." A visibly annoyed Rampton interjected, "If the public's mind is affected adversely to Mr Irving by a fair and accurate report of the proceedings in court, then Mr Irving has only himself to blame."[6]

## COUNTING DEAD JEWS

Our next expert witness, Professor Christopher Browning, had arrived from the University of North Carolina to testify. He is one of the leading experts on the German annihilation policy. When my academic chair was inaugurated at Emory, I selected him as the academic speaker. So too, when we were compiling the list of expert witnesses, I had wanted him to be among them.

Browning's report addressed the Nazi policy of mass shootings of Jews in Soviet territory and the documentary evidence for it. Irving claimed that these killings were the result of rogue actions, which were uncoordinated or approved by the Nazi authorities—Hitler in particular—in Berlin. Irving faced a major problem, however. The *Einsatzgruppen,* the mobile killing units that conducted the massacres, prepared detailed reports on the killings, which they sent to Berlin. The reports, which contained precise death tolls, broken down into men, women, and children, were distributed to high-ranking army, police, and SS officers, as well as diplomats, Foreign Office officials, and even prominent industrialists. Never had a genocidal action been so methodically documented by the perpetrators.[7] Browning relied on these reports to demonstrate that the killings were part of a program that had been carefully coordinated and monitored by Berlin.

Professor Christopher Browning came forward. A tall man with broad shoulders and a full head of straight brown hair, he has an easy manner and a friendly smile. After bantering with Browning about various archives they both had visited, Irving leaned over his podium toward the witness box. Lowering his voice slightly and adopting an almost intimate, "just between us" demeanor, he asked whether Browning had encountered "any particular problems as a non-Jewish historian writing about the Holocaust?" Browning, looking perplexed, asked Irving to explain his question. Irving continued, "Would I be right in suggesting that the Jewish historians regard the Holocaust as their patch?" Irving's tone seemed to suggest that Browning might be more forthcoming with him, another non-Jew. Browning was forthcoming, but not as Irving might have anticipated. Jewish historians had been very accepting of his entry into the field. It "indicated that this was not their patch, if I can use your phrase, but something that was not just important to Jewish history but important to world history."[8] Irving, looking skeptical, reminded Browning of Harvard University's widely publicized search for a professor of Holocaust studies. Browning had been one of the finalists but did not get the job. Hadn't Browning lost out because he was a non-Jew? Browning explained that Harvard's search committee insisted the finalist be someone grounded not only in the scholarship of the Holocaust, but in Jewish history and culture as well. No one on the final list fit this bill. Consequently *none* of the candidates—Jew or non-Jew—got the job.

Despite having made little, if any, headway thus far, Irving appeared happy to be engaging a prominent scholar. Smiling, he explained to Judge Gray, "This kind of discussion is helpful because I do not know Professor Browning, we have never met, and we have never had the pleasure and I am, frankly, interested in finding out what he knows." He planned, he said, to have a general discussion with Browning about the Final Solution and then spend the rest of the day on the *Einsatzgruppen* operations. When Irving announced this agenda, Rampton quietly grumbled, "This is too much." He noisily scraped his chair back and rose to his feet. In sharp contrast to Irving's rather jaunty demeanor, he brusquely declared, "I am not interested . . . in having this court used as . . . an historical forum." Furthermore, he continued, "I heard with some alarm Mr Irving threatening to spend the rest of the day cross-examining about the *Einsatzgruppen* shootings in the East. . . . Mr Irving has made a very clear concession that those shootings happened on a massive scale, that they were systematic and that Hitler authorized them." While Irving had the perfect right to challenge Browning's report, Rampton continued, he could not now "go back behind the concession he has made" and contradict what he had conceded in the witness box. The judge agreed. "Obviously Mr Irving cannot resile from what he has already conceded."[9]

Irving's tone now became decidedly less friendly. "Have not the Jewish people throughout this century . . . constantly proclaimed that they were in danger of being exterminated, or indeed that they were already being exterminated?" He then added with a bit of a sneer, "It has been a kind of ongoing story, has it not?" Browning attacked the question's substance and tone. "When you say 'the Jews have said,' I am afraid that is the kind of formulation that it is impossible to answer. You may find one Jew or another, but that does not mean 'the Jews' have constantly said that."[10]

Finally, Irving turned to the substance of Browning's expert report. In September 1941, one of the *Einsatzgruppen* informed Berlin that hundreds of thousands of Jews had fled into Soviet-controlled territory and described this as an "indirect success" of its work. Describing the Jews' escape as a success, Irving argued, proved there was no plan to "catch all the Jews you could and kill them." Browning pointed out that the officer who wrote the report used the term "*indirect* success." If the objective of the Germans had been expulsion, he would have described it as a "direct success." Browning surmised that the officer was afraid of being considered as "not zealous enough" in killing Jews. Calling attention to the Jews' flight was his way of explaining why his Jewish body count had fallen.

As soon as Browning made his point about the officer's concern that his death tolls were not "high enough," Irving asked if it wasn't likely that these officers had "a tendency to bloat reports or to exaggerate figures." Browning agreed that this was possible. Irving, apparently assuming that he had forced Browning to make a concession, rocked back on his heels, smiled slightly, and suggested that therefore the death tolls in the *Einsatzgruppen* reports were not trustworthy. Browning quickly turned Irving's question on itself. If the officers were bloating death tolls, "they know that Berlin wants big numbers, which would indicate that they perfectly realize they are part of that programme, the purpose of which is to get big numbers."[11]

Irving, in an attempt to challenge Browning's contention that Berlin was behind the killings, cited Himmler's November 30, 1941, diary entry that a trainload of Jews from Berlin was not to be liquidated. Browning pointed out that Himmler was stopping something. You can only do that if it is already under way.[12]

Irving, shifting his argument, now contended that the Germans were killing Jews for legitimate military reasons. In his diary, Himmler had recorded notes from his conversation with Hitler on December 18, 1941, regarding the Jewish question. Jews, he had written, were *"als Partisanen auszurotten,"* to be "annihilated as partisans." Irving insisted that this meant Jews were to be killed *because* they were partisans. Browning, dismissing Irving's explanation as illogical, observed that when the Germans killed partisans, they killed only the partisans. When they killed Jews they killed men, women, and children. What Himmler meant in his diary entry, Browning continued, was "we will kill the one *as if* they were the other." Irving insisted that the word *"als"* meant Jews "are to be liquidated as the partisans they are." Browning thought Irving's interpretation constituted "the sheerest fantasy."[13] Irving reminded Browning that in many of these mass shootings, the Germans first killed Jewish leaders and Jewish males of a military age. There must have been, Irving told Browning, some "military reason" for shooting them. Browning disagreed: "I do not think the 50-year-old Rabbi represents a military threat to the Germans." Irving challenged Browning: "I am older than fifty and I would certainly be capable of pointing a gun at someone." Chris Browning is an affable, easygoing guy. I've known him for over twenty years and rarely have I seen him get angry. Suddenly, for a split second, I saw a very different man in the witness box. There was a piercing look in his eyes as he glowered at Irving and said, in a voice laced with withering contempt,

"If you had a gun. . . . *They* did not have guns."[14] Turning to Judge Gray, he explained that prior to the invasion of the USSR the *Einsatzgruppen* had received orders to murder Jews who held state and party positions. In no way could this be considered a defensive action.

On Browning's second day, Irving handed him a document, which he solemnly described as "a rather sad list . . . a tragic list." Dated April 30, 1943, it was an inventory of possessions taken from Jews: 100,000 wristwatches, 39,000 pocket watches, 7,500 alarm clocks, and 37,000 pens. Browning explained that this was probably a list of items that were taken from Jews about to be deported or from Jews in the death camps. Irving asked Browning to make a "global estimate" of the death toll based on the list. Before Browning could respond, Irving offered his own estimate: "Not everybody had valuable wristwatches or valuable fountain pens, but on the other hand not many people wear two wristwatches, shall we say, so it was probably not less than 100,000 people?" Browning dismissed Irving's attempt to use this fragmentary record to reach a "global" conclusion as illogical. Jews were stripped of most of their property long before they were deported. Right before deportation rings and jewelry were taken. Browning speculated that the items on the list may have been some of the small personal items that they were allowed to keep. "Most Jews would have traded their wristwatches for food and whatever else long before this if they were in desperate straits, which they were. So it does not give us anything approaching a maximum figure."[15]

Despite Browning's answer, Irving seemed pleased by it: "Is it not right, Professor, that our statistical database for arriving at any kind of conclusions for the numbers of people . . . killed in the Holocaust by whatever means, we are really floundering around in the dark, are we not?" Irving, looking very satisfied by his question, proudly glanced in Rampton's direction. Browning, somewhat didactically, explained why Irving's theory was wrong.

We have very accurate lists of the deportation trains from Germany. In many cases we have the entire roster name by name. . . . In terms again of France, the Netherlands, the countries from which there were deportations from Western Europe, we can do a very close approximation by trains, the number of people per train. In the area of

Poland there were at least statistics in terms of ghetto populations and these ghettoes were liquidated completely, so we can come to a fairly good rough figure of Polish Jews. We also have a fairly reliable prewar census and postwar calculations so that one can do a sub-traction.

He pointed out, that with the exception of the Soviet Union—there was no record of how many Jews fled there—historians could provide fairly accurate estimates. Regarding numbers, he continued, there may be differences of opinion, but no "floundering."[16]

Judge Gray asked Browning to estimate the number of people gassed at the smaller death camps. Browning told him that at postwar trials in the 1960s, German prosecutors concluded that approximately two million Jews had been killed at Treblinka, Belzec, Sobibor, and Chelmno. Irving belittled these estimates, suggesting that they were cavalierly made. Browning contended that this was hardly the case. The German prosecutors had, in fact, used the most conservative estimates so that they would not be contested by the defense. The estimates had been made by German historians who had testified at the trial.

Irving kept insisting that the estimates could not be trusted. Finally, Browning turned to the judge and explained precisely how the death tolls at these camps were calculated.

We have a very accurate reduction of the Lodz population, which trains went to Chelmno, when, and we can come very accurately to the number of people deported from Lodz to Chelmno, then one is on a little bit less secure grounds for the various other surrounding towns where we do not have a day by day deduction or a train by train calculation, but we do have statistics of what the populations were there before the whole operation began. . . . We know how many Dutch transports went to Sobibor. We know which regions were cleared that were directed to Sobibor. We had the figures of the Jewish populations in those ghettoes before the liquidation and the number of workers that were shifted to some of the work camps.

When Browning finished, Judge Gray thanked him: "That is very help-ful." Irving, looking a bit deflated, agreed: "Yes."[17]

## HOW MANY PEOPLE CAN A GAS VAN KILL?

Still trying to cast doubt on the death tolls, Irving began to question Browning about Chelmno's gas vans. A few days earlier, Irving had conceded that 97,000 Jews had been killed in three vans between December 1941 and June 1942. Irving seemed to be ignoring that concession when he asked if the number 97,000 was not "wrong by a factor of two or three?" Irving suggested that, if each truck had to drive twenty kilometers, the amount of time as well as petrol for such trips would have rendered them expensive and impractical. Browning pointed out that the vans only drove three, not twenty, kilometers. The distance was so short that the drivers started the motor before they left the courtyard where the passengers were loaded. Otherwise, they would not be dead when they arrived at the site where the bodies were dumped. According to eyewitnesses, different drivers took turns behind the wheel. The trucks, which accommodated, depending on the model, anywhere from 30 to 80 people, could, therefore, have run on a continuous basis.[18] As Browning was explaining this, I noticed Rampton doing some calculations. When he finished, he peered at the sheet and quietly said to himself, "Yes, that's exactly right." He sounded satisfied but looked revolted. When he saw me watching, he pushed the paper across the table in my direction. He seemed to be glad to be rid of it.

*Gassings at Chelmno*
97,000 people killed between December and June [172 days]
97,000 / 172 = 564 people a day
564 / 3 trucks = 188 people per truck per day
188 / 4 [assuming 4 trips a day] = 47 people a trip
4 trips every 24 hours = 6 hours between trips

With simple arithmetic Rampton had shown that there was no logistical problem to gassing 97,000 people in six months.

## ATTACKING THE WITNESSES—AGAIN

Irving, still trying to raise questions about the documentary evidence, said he had the "dubious fortune some time ago of coming into possession" of Eichmann's personal copy of the memoirs of Rudolf Höss, the Auschwitz commandant. In it, Höss described his reaction to the initial gassings in Auschwitz. "It had a calming effect on me, as in the near future we had to begin with mass destruction of the Jews too, and neither Eichmann nor I was clear about how we were to deal with these masses." In the margin of the book Eichmann had written: *"Ich war gar nicht zuständig,"* which could be translated, "This was not at all my jurisdiction." Next to the footnote about these gassings Eichmann had written: *"falsch,"* "false." Irving rather triumphantly told Browning, "In other words, Eichmann, who ought to have known . . . disputes the version given by Rudolf Höss." Browning said Irving was misinterpreting Eichmann's statement: "He does not deny the existence of gas chambers but confirms Auschwitz, but he says that was not my thing."[19]

Irving, who had just been using Höss's memoirs to prove his point, now changed tacks and questioned their credibility. Höss wrote them while in captivity. "When somebody is in captivity on trial for one's life, one might write things, either deliberately or inadvertently, that were not true." Browning observed that Höss had been sentenced to death when he wrote his memoirs. "There is nothing further they can threaten you with."[20]

Midway through the second day, Irving pointed out that Browning had made a mistake in his report. An October 1941 document referred to Jews being deported to "reception camps in the east." Browning had translated camp in the singular rather than the plural. Irving contended that Browning made this mistake because he had "a certain mind-set" and he wanted to depict the Jews' destination as "some kind of sinister place . . . [where] they are going to be bumped off." Browning, once again, skillfully turned Irving's question back on him. His mistake, rather than paint the Nazis in the worst possible light, in fact, made them look better by limiting the document's scope. One sinister camp was not as bad as a series of sinister camps. Rather than pursue this point, Irving posited that Browning's mistranslation proved that researchers often make inadvertent mistakes without intending to do anything perverse. Browning observed that if an author's mistakes were truly inadvertent, they would go 50 percent one way and 50 percent the other. There would not be "a consistent pattern where all mistakes tended to support the position of the man making the mistake." Though Browning did not mention Irving by name, I was certain Judge Gray grasped the allusion. I assumed that Irving, recognizing that Browning had once again entrapped him, would leave the matter. I was wrong. "You mean it is like a waiter who always gives the wrong change in his own favor?"[21] I looked up in surprise. Irving, whose "wrong" explanations tended to always exculpate Hitler and his cronies, had just implicated himself.

Not surprisingly, by this point, all remnants of collegiality were gone. Instead of addressing Browning as "Professor," Irving called him "Witness"—if he called him anything at all. Matters hit a low point when Irving asked Browning whether his book contract with Yad Vashem, the Israeli Holocaust memorial, did not make him a "paid agent . . . of the State of Israel." Browning smiled broadly, "If that was the case, then since I had been at the Holocaust Museum, I would also have been an agent of the American Government [sic] and since I have received scholarships in Germany, I would be an agent for the German government, so I must be a very duplicitous fellow to be able to follow these regimes."[22] By the time he finished, virtually everyone—excluding Irving—was smiling.

As the second day of Browning's testimony drew to a close, Irving continued his assault on eyewitness testimony. Referring to testimony given at the West German trial about Belzec, Sobibor, and Treblinka, he complained that it could not be trusted because it was given thirty years after the fact. Browning acknowledged that testimony given long after an event might have "less specificity." However, he added, "if somebody had [sic] spent six months or twelve months in a death camp, he does not forget the existence of gas chambers." Judge Gray interrupted to ascertain if Irving was challenging the existence of these three camps as killing centers where people were killed by gas. Irving told him, "I accept they were killed at these three camps." He was challenging the "reliability of eyewitnesses."

A perplexed Judge Gray asked Irving to explain what was to be gained by challenging the credibility of the eyewitnesses who reported on these camps if he wasn't challenging what happened at the camps? This was, Irving explained, part of a "general attack on eyewitness evidence which is important for the main plank of my case which is Auschwitz, where we have established . . . from Professor van Pelt that the only evidence one can really rely on is the eyewitness evidence. . . . Rather like Rommel, I am coming round from the rear and attacking . . . the eyewitnesses." A few minutes later he repeated this charge: "I am just alarmed at the notion of building such a major part of World War II history just on the testimony of half a dozen eye witnesses as far as Auschwitz is concerned." At that point, a visibly annoyed Rampton rose: "It is the second time we have had that today. It [the findings on Auschwitz] is built on a mass of evidence, documentary, archeological, eyewitness . . . all of which, as Professor van Pelt puts it, converged to the same conclusion." Irving responded to Rampton by declaring that the "transcript will show what position we reached." Rampton said nothing but as he took his seat, I heard him say to himself, "It will show you are dead wrong."[23]

Irving, still trying to raise doubts about the gassings at these other camps, asked Browning whether his findings about these camps "depend[ed] entirely on eyewitness evidence or is there any documentary basis whatsoever for what you have just told his Lordship?" Browning acknowledged that, while there was documentary evidence for the use of gas vans at Chelmno, there was only eyewitness testimony for the gas chambers in these three camps. Irving, rather triumphantly, declared, "So there is no documentary evidence relating to scale then?" Browning explained that while there was not documentary evidence on the scale or the mode of killing, there was evidence concerning the emptying of the Jewish population of Poland to these three camps, which are located in "teeny little villages which do not accommodate one and a half million people." Irving told Browning that during World War II many British citizens were transported to the small village of Aldershot. The transfer, therefore, of large populations to small villages was no proof of something untoward. Browning forcefully dismissed Irving's analogy. If the people sent to Aldershot had been "deprived of their rights and property, if they had been rounded up with all of the brutality that left bodies lying all the way to the train station, and if they had been sent there and never came back, and if a hundred witnesses from Aldershot said they had been gassed, we would, I think, say something happened at Aldershot."[24] With that Irving ended his cross-examination of Browning.

# FOURTEEN

# LYING ABOUT HITLER

I was bewildered when Judge Gray commenced the fifth week of the trial by complimenting Irving for his questions, which were, he said, "clear [and] almost always to the point."[1] I wondered if Gray had somehow been beguiled by Irving. James, who saw me grimace, leaned over to tell me I was overreacting. I was not so easily comforted, suspecting that Gray did not say something unless he believed it. When I turned and saw how distressed Heather looked, I was even more concerned.

As per usual, I did not have time to dwell on this because it was time for Richard Evans, a graduate of Oxford and distinguished professor of history at Cambridge University, to enter the witness box. An author of numerous books on Germany, particularly its social and cultural history from the mid-nineteenth century to the present, Evans placed special emphasis on historiography, which made him a particularly valuable expert witness for us. He was a man of decided opinions about many things, including other historians. When I first met him two years before the trial, he seemed skeptical about my assessment of Irving as "the most dangerous" denier. Now, as he was about to take the stand, I asked if he still felt the same way. Evans, reflecting on the meeting, which now seemed so long ago, explained that at that time he really knew next to nothing about Irving's work and was influenced by the respect in which he was held by some colleagues in the field. He had been, he acknowledged, somewhat ill at ease because he did not want to compromise his independence and impartiality by being over-friendly with the defendant. Then he paused and, after a moment, added,

"Deborah, you were far *too* kind to him. The historical wrongdoings we have found are more extreme than anything I ever imagined."

## IRVING V. EVANS: AN ANGRY ENGAGEMENT

I anticipated that the Irving/Evans encounter would not be friendly. The other expert reports dealt with specific aspects of the history of the Holocaust. In contrast, Evans had studied David Irving's work itself. By citing numerous examples of Irving's misstatements—if not outright falsifications—of history regarding the Holocaust and the bombing of Dresden, Evans's report called into question the corpus of his writings. Evans's testimony would constitute a direct assault on him as an historian.

Irving began by asking Evans, from what "personal political standpoint . . . do you view people like myself or Margaret Thatcher or John Major?" I was amused by how he grouped himself with two former prime ministers. When Evans said he belonged to the Labor Party, Irving asked, if "the Labor Party dictate[d] your politics to you or do you have any ideas of your own?" Evans, who sounded annoyed at the suggestion that his political views might be "dictated" by Labor, assured Irving that he reached independent conclusions. Irving accused Evans of having had his "knives out in the past for right wing historians or Nazi historians."[2] Evans observed that his reviews criticized historians at both ends of the political spectrum, making him an equal opportunity critic.

Despite the fact that Evans's report did not deal with Irving's racism, Irving used Evans's presence in the witness box to challenge our accusation that he had expressed overt racist sympathies. He handed Evans a packet of pictures of female "ethnics" whom, he said, he employed since 1980 and whom he had paid a "proper salary." Evans, deliberately dropping the packet on the desk in front of him, insisted that it had no impact on the question of whether Irving had displayed racist attitudes and then protested that he had come to answer questions on his report. "So far you have hardly asked a single one." Irving, ignoring Evans's protest, kept pressing him about the question of racism: "What does it take to prove that one is not racist? If one employs coloured people in exactly the same way as one employs whites, one does not prefer them or disadvantage them in any way, one pays them exactly the same amount?"[3] Judge Gray, sounding rather exasperated, urged Irving to move on.

Irving moved on but probably not in the direction the judge hoped. Whereas we had found one racist ditty in his diary, Penguin, he charged, had published entire books with grossly antisemitic passages. He cited John Buchan's *39 Steps*. How, I wondered, was this book, which I knew as a Hitchcock movie, relevant? At a table in the back row Helena Peacock, Penguin's counsel, was studying her watch. She was probably calculating the cost of this rambling exercise. Rampton, shaking his head in great frustration, rose again. Emitting what sounded like a "Harrumph," he protested to Judge Gray:

> My Lord this is a kind of insanity. I feel as though I was in one of Lewis Carroll's books. Mr Irving brought this action in respect of words published by my clients. . . . What can it matter that there may have been some author from the distant past, who . . . might have made a remark as an antisemite?[4]

Judge Gray also seemed somewhat nonplused: "I am trying to give you a lot of latitude, Mr Irving. I think I am perhaps beginning to give you too much." Judge Gray admonished Irving. "If your odds are still on John Buchan, then that is really absolutely, if I may say so, hopeless as a point."[5] Irving, ignoring this rather pointed warning, kept pressing. "Should political correctness not have required them [Penguin] to at least excise these horrendous passages from that book?" It was ironic to hear a man who felt "queasy" about blacks on the English cricket team defend political correctness.

## CHEAP JIBES AND SCHOOLYARD BRAWLS

Irving finally moved to the substance of Evans's report and zeroed in on the sentence that, months earlier, I had found so reaffirming: "I was not prepared for the sheer depth of duplicity, his numerous mistakes . . . and the egregious errors. . . . [which] were not accidental." Irving asked Evans if he began his research convinced he would find "duplicity and distortion." Evans said he was rather surprised at the results that he found. Irving challenged Evans: "Are you going to be prepared to eat your words if we . . . find out that you were misjudging me?" Evans took his hands out of his pocket and folded them across his chest: "Let us see."[6] I was not sure if this was the schoolyard or the Royal Courts of Justice.

Irving, referring to his own claim that no decision was ever made by the Third Reich to annihilate European Jewry, asked Evans if he was familiar with the fact that this is precisely the view espoused by the prominent Holocaust historians Professors Martin Broszat and Raul Hilberg. Evans, insisting that that was "not quite my understanding of what they say," asked Irving for proof. Irving responded, "Well, I believed that you were an expert and this is why you were being paid a very substantial sum by the Defence to stand in the position you are in now." Evans's eyes narrowed, his brow furrowed, his face turned red. His voice was tight and sharp: "[I will] leave . . . aside your cheap jibe about money, which I treat with the contempt it deserves—" Before Evans could finish his sentence, Irving shot back with a reference to what Evans had earned: "It was not cheap from what I hear." The judge pleaded: "This is degenerating and please don't let us let it."[7]

Judge Gray's entreaty notwithstanding, matters only got worse. Declaring his next point "pure gold," Irving warned Evans, "You are going to dislike me over this. . . ." In one of the multitudinous footnotes, Evans had listed a source as the 1977 edition of *Hitler's War*. Irving triumphantly announced that the correct reference for that particular source was pages from the 1991 edition, pages 6 to 7. Evans bent over the desk in front of him and began to ruffle through the book. After a few moments, he looked up and with a bit of "gotcha" in his voice, said to Irving, "It is in fact, I think, 7 to 8, not 6 to 7, so you are wrong there too." Judge Gray, rather plaintively, said: "Come on."[8] I silently echoed his plea.

As we left at the end of the day, Anthony looked perturbed. I assumed he was upset at the glacial pace of the questioning—Irving had covered a mere 35 pages of Evans's 700-page report. But that wasn't what was bothering him. "This was awful. Evans is a professor at Cambridge. He shouldn't come down to Irving's level and let himself be provoked by Irving's cheap jibes."

I set aside my worries about Evans because close friends had arrived from Houston with their three children, one of whom had been my student at

Emory. The weekend was a wonderful respite from the tedium of the preceding week. I invited some of the "younger" members of the defense team to join us for dinner. During dinner, our researchers, Thomas and Tobias, began to delineate for Seth, my former student, some of the various documents they had reviewed while conducting research on the trial. They bemoaned the fact that the manuscript Adolf Eichmann wrote in his cell during his trial in Jerusalem was unavailable. Eichmann had visited the death camps. Had he made reference to gassings in the manuscript? Historians did not know what was in it because after Eichmann's trial, Prime Minister David Ben-Gurion agreed, at the insistence of the prosecuting attorney, Gideon Hausner, that the manuscript be sealed. Given that Eichmann had been in the witness box for thirty sessions, Hausner felt that Israel had no further obligation to publicize his version of history. Recently, Eichmann's son had requested the manuscript, prompting a debate in Israel over what to do with it. Some Israeli historians believed that a German research institute should annotate the manuscript prior to publication, to counter any of Eichmann's false assertions. Other historians argued that it should be released as is and the normal scholarly process should be allowed to occur. Not surprisingly, nothing happened. Seth, rather matter-of-factly, asked Thomas and Tobias, "Well, why don't you ask Israel to release the manuscript?" From the look on our intrepid researchers' faces, it was clear that, despite having unearthed documents in a myriad of unexpected places, they had never considered this option. Seth, the quintessential optimist, said, "I'm sure you'll get it." Tobias jumped up from his chair, ran into my postage-size kitchen, where I was preparing dessert, and said, "Can you ask Israel for the Eichmann manuscript?" Notwithstanding their youthful enthusiasm, I was skeptical that anything would come of the idea. I decided I would make some attempt to get the material, so I could tell them I tried. Then I served dessert.

## NOT SO SELECTIVE QUOTATIONS

On Monday morning, when Evans returned to the stand, I immediately noticed that he had shifted his body so that he was now facing Judge Gray. Irving wasted no time in needling him: "So Holocaust deniers . . . [to] use this favorite phrase of yours, are a form of low academic life or low life . . . ?" Betraying no emotions, Evans said to Judge Gray: "I do not like using phrases like 'low life' or 'low form of life' and, to my knowledge, I have never used those phrases. The problem is not that they are not academic . . . what they are engaging in . . . is a politically motivated falsification of history."[9] Not once during his entire answer did Evans even look at Irving.

In his report, Evans had accused Irving of selectively quoting from documents in order to skew their meaning. With Evans on the stand, Irving turned the tables and accused the Cambridge professor of doing precisely that to him. In 1992, when it became public that the *Times* had hired Irving to go to Moscow to determine the authenticity of the Goebbels diary, the paper faced tremendous criticism. In his report Evans had quoted from one of Irving's speeches in which Irving described the protests as coming from "our old traditional enemies . . . the great international merchant banks are controlled by people who are not friends of yours and mine."[10] Evans considered this comment emblematic of Irving's vituperative language when speaking of the Jewish community. Irving complained that the ellipses Evans had used represented "four sentences, three full stops, four semi-colons and 86 words. . . ." He told the judge that this kind of editing was "highly illuminative and illustrative of this witness's methods."[11] Evans, looking a bit taken aback by the suggestion that he might have manipulated Irving's words, began to flip through his papers in order to find the transcript of the entire speech. After a few moments, Evans looked up from his papers. He seemed to be trying to suppress a smile as he offered to read the omitted words. Judge Gray nodded for him to proceed. According to Irving the editor of the *Times* had faced pressure from

> our old traditional enemies, *pressure not just from the advertising industry, pressure not just from the self-appointed, ugly, greasy nasty perverted representatives of that community, he came under pressure from the international community too because the* Sunday Times, *like many other newspapers, needs international capital to survive and the international capital is provided by* the great international merchant banks.[12]

The words Evans had omitted were more extreme than that which he quoted. Irving could not have been pleased when Judge Gray observed that Evans "might have made his point more strongly, if he put in what he had left out."[13]

## A SURPRISING SETBACK

When I read the beginning of Evans's report, which consisted of a selection of other historians' critiques of Irving's work, I had felt validated—probably unnecessarily so. They made me feel that I was not a lone voice criticizing this man. Irving now began to question Evans in great detail about each of these statements. Judge Gray, concerned about the slow pace at which Irving was moving through the report, urged Irving to proceed to the portions of Evans's report that addressed substantive historical issues. This would help determine his final decision. What other historians said would have little, if any, impact on him. Irving did not move on.

Finally, speaking in a sympathetic voice, Judge Gray acknowledged Irving's legitimate desire to contest this portion of the report as a means of deflecting these attacks on him. The judge, however, assured Irving that he was not going to pay it heed because he was interested in what Evans—not other historians—had to say. Then he added something disturbing:

> Mr Irving . . . I do see your problem and I am actually sympathetic with it. . . . [T]hese opening . . . pages, where the views of other historians about your work are recited at length and in a very critical vein . . . count for virtually nothing . . . and it is . . . unfortunate that they are there because they could be taken to indicate a preconception about the validity of the criticisms.[14]

Judge Gray's warning that these opening pages might cause him to consider the remainder of the report as tainted made my heart sink. Suddenly this section of the report, which provided the judge with a broader context within which to consider my critique, could just as likely harm us.

## PHOTOGRAPHIC DISTORTIONS

Deniers often portray Allied actions against Germans as equal to—if not worse than—German war crimes. This is one of the reasons that they emphasize the bombing of Dresden. Evans had argued that Irving engaged in this kind of imbalance in *Hitler's War* (1991). The book contained three photographs of German victims of Allied bombings—including one of a child clutching an adult's body. There were, however, no pictures of victims of death camps or mass shootings. Irving had also included six photographs of Allied bombing raids on Dresden and Pforzheim, but no photographs of anyone killed by Nazis. There was only one picture of Germany's victims: Jews on a passenger car handing their luggage out of the train windows. The caption read: "Their escorts were all elderly German police officers, with two Latvian police." Irving compounded this imbalance by failing to inform his readers that shortly after arrival, the Jews on the passenger train were shot.

Irving defended his choice of photographs by asking if there were photographs of *Einsatzgruppen* shootings with the same "unimpeachable quality and integrity" as the passenger train photograph? Evans argued that, while quality was important, historians had to give readers a balanced view of the identity of the victims. Irving responded, "Are you suggesting that I should have . . . looked for a more *hackneyed stereotyped* photograph, Professor?" I inwardly cringed at his use of these adjectives to describe pictures of mass shootings. Demonstrating his newfound restraint, Evans ignored the comment and explained that the photograph suggested "how jolly nice this train is at Riga, what a nice time they are having." Irving countered that it demonstrated the "utter banality of this kind of atrocity." Evans, sounding like he was stating the obvious, dismissed Irving's explanation: "Sorry, there is no mention of any atrocity there in the caption at all." Judge Gray, who seemed intrigued by Irving's argument, asked Evans, "How do you react to the suggestion that the reason for not including the sort of pictures you have just been describing is the[ir] utter banality . . . ?" Evans responded, "I find [it] very hard to accept that pictures of . . . people about to be shot by the *Einsatzgruppen* lining up in front of a ditch are banal pictures. It does not matter how many times they are reproduced, they still remain, I think, very shocking."[15] Having seen such photographs many times, I was struck by Evans's observation that, no matter how often he saw them, they remained shocking.

Evans had charged that Irving engaged in the same kind of photographic manipulation in *Nuremberg: The Last Battle*. He placed a caption, under pictures of mutilated German soldiers in the Balkans and of Allied raids on Japan and Dresden, that read in part: "No Allied general is ever called to account . . ." When Irving defended his choice of captions, Evans dismissed this as an attempt to "set up an equivalence between the two sides in order to diminish the importance of the Nazi extermination of the Jews" and to suggest "that what the Allies did was worse than what the Germans did." Irving sounded perplexed: "Worse?" Judge Gray, taking the initiative, answered Irving's question: "Because they got away with it scott-free."[16]

Irving asked Evans if, in his report, he had written that on one night during the war the Allies "*only* killed 17,600 people by burning them alive in 20 minutes?" Evans who resolutely refused to answer any question unless the citation in question was in front of him, bent over to check the pertinent section of his report. While Evans was still reading, Irving, in a rather accusatory tone, elaborated on his previous question: "You are suggesting that killing 17,600 people by burning them alive in the space of twenty minutes is in some way, I do not know, *not* a crime?" Still bent over the desk, Evans lifted up his head and gave Irving a look of contempt. For a moment, I feared he was ready to verbally pounce on Irving. Instead, he stood up straight, faced Judge Gray, and explained the context of his statement. His report contained a section from a 1992 speech Irving had given. In it Irving had estimated that 100,000 had died at Auschwitz, "most of them from epidemics," and then added that about 25,000 were killed by "shooting or hanging." Irving compared this death toll to the suffering of the Germans in the town of Pforzheim.

> Twenty-five thousand killed, if we take this grossly inflated figure to be on the safe side: That is a crime; there is no doubt. Killing twenty-five thousand in four years . . . that is a crime. . . . Let me show you . . . in my book, a vivid picture of twenty five thousand people being killed in twenty-five minutes by us British [in February 1945] in Pforzheim, a little town where they make jewelry and watches . . . . Twenty-five thousand civilians are being burned alive in twenty-five minutes. . . . You don't get it spelled out . . . like that. Except by us, their opponents. . . . When you put things in perspective . . . it diminishes their Holocaust—that word with a capital letter.[17]

This statement, Evans said to Judge Gray, gave the impression "that the Allied bombing of German cities was as bad as or worse than the Nazi killing of Jews in Auschwitz." Moreover, he observed, Irving had compounded this minimization of the Auschwitz death toll by inflating the Pforzheim death toll—as calculated by the city's Statistical Office—by 40 percent. Hence, Evans's comment that the actual death toll was "only" 17,600, not the 25,000, as Irving had claimed.[18]

Evans had posited that Irving's claims about the small number of Jewish victims had originated with one of the earliest Holocaust deniers, Paul Rassinier. Irving challenged Evans, "Have you any evidence at all that I have ever read the words of Paul Rassinier?" Evans dryly responded, "You *did* write an afterword to one of his books, which I find it difficult to believe you wrote without having read it." Irving stared at Evans intently: "Professor, believe. That is all I can say." While looking out at the gallery—and decidedly *not* at Irving—Evans observed, "It does not say much for your responsibility as a historian, Mr Irving."[19]

## BLAME IT ON THE ALLIES

Deniers face a conundrum. They must somehow find a way of explaining—without blaming Germany—the multitude of cadaver-like victims found in the concentration camps at the end of the war. They resolve this by arguing that the Allies—*not* the Germans—were responsible for this suffering. Evans illustrated how Irving had tried to do this in a speech in 1986. He had said: The Allies "bomb[ed] the transportation networks . . . pharmaceutical industry, medicine factories . . . deliberately creat[ing] the epidemics and the outbreaks of typhus and other diseases which . . . were found . . . [in the] concentration camps." As Evans read this quote, I happened to glance at the gallery. A white-haired man in the gallery was wincing. He looked to be in pain.

When Evans finished, Judge Gray asked him, "how do you feel about a historian who says that the person who deliberately created the epidemics was the person who bombed the pharmaceutical factories which might have been able to provide the distribution which might have limited the typhus epidemic?" Evans minced no words: "That is extremely perverse." The epidemics, he argued, were created by the Nazis, who ran the camps in extremely unhygienic fashion.

Irving challenged Evans to explain why, if the Nazis wanted these people to die, they built a whole "system" in the camps to combat the epidemic. Evans explained that these measures were to protect the SS, not the inmates. Suddenly, Judge Gray interrupted Irving. Referring back to Irving's repeated claims that most of the victims died of disease, he cautioned Irving to keep "a slight grip on reality" and asked, "Is it your case that the typhus killed a very large proportion of the Jews who lost their lives?" Irving said, "Yes." Judge Gray continued, "It is difficult in the next breath to say how wonderful the system of fumigating clothes and the like was."[20] I was pleased that Judge Gray had called Irving to account for his mutually exclusive positions. As I left the courtroom, the older gentleman I had noticed wincing, cautiously approached me: "I'm not Jewish. I entered Bergen-Belsen with the British forces in 1945. It galls me to hear him claim that we Allies caused the terrible deprivation we found there." He said nothing for a moment but stood there looking angry. He then pulled himself up, stood almost at attention, and declared, "Get this bastard, madam." With that he marched off, a bit of the old soldier still evident in his gait.

# FIFTEEN

# THE DIARY OF ANNE FRANK: A NOVEL?

Deniers have, over the years, concentrated great energy on attacking the authenticity of *The Diary of Anne Frank* because they believe that by creating doubts about this popular book, which is often young people's first encounter with the literature of the Holocaust, they can generate broader doubts about the Holocaust itself. There are multiple versions of the *Diary*, which, deniers claim, proves it is a fraud. Actually, there are, indeed, a number of versions of the *Diary*. Anne herself had given a reason for this. In 1944, over the radio, she heard a Dutch government official broadcasting from London, urging the population to save letters, memorabilia, and diaries as eyewitness accounts. Anne's response was to rewrite some of her diary entries. She also used the diary as a basis for a novel, *The Annex*. Hence, the different versions.

Deniers also claim that the diary is written in green ballpoint pen, something that was not readily available during the war. In this case, the deniers are seriously bending the truth. There are some minor stylistic marginal notes in green ink. The only ballpoint writing was on two loose scraps of paper included among the loose leaves and have no significance whatsoever in terms of content. Moreover, the handwriting on the scraps of paper differ markedly from those in the diary, indicating that they were written by someone else, an editor perhaps.

By the 1980s, these attacks on the *Diary* had become so widespread that the Netherlands State Institute for War Documentation and the *Bundeskriminalamt*, the German criminal laboratories, tested the diary's glue, paper, and ink. They found them all to be from the 1940s. They compared Anne's hand-writing in the diary to other samples of her writing and found it to be gen-uine. Every test proved this was a genuine World War II–era work by a teenage girl in hiding.[1]

With Evans in the witness box, Irving inevitably raised the topic of the *Diary* and declared that the lab's conclusion regarding the ballpoint ink con-stituted an "ambiguous finding" and raised questions about the *Diary*'s au-thenticity. Evans insisted that there was nothing ambiguous about the finding. Judge Gray interrupted to ask Evans if it would be correct to con-clude that the forensic report, rather than suggesting it was a forgery, actu-ally confirmed it was authentic. "Because it says that there are some sections which were added subsequently, but by necessary inference [it] is saying that most of it was genuine and already there and not in ball point." Evans agreed with Judge Gray's formulation. The Dutch and the German criminal labs had both rejected the notion that whole pages were false "let alone the whole thing being fake or a novel." Irving, sounding a bit miffed, protested, "Have I *ever* said that the whole thing was written in ball point pen?" Evan reminded him, "You said whole pages are written in ball point pen." Judge Gray added, "You said it was a novel, Mr Irving, did you not?" Irving protested, once again: "The third version is a novel, my Lord."[2]

Evans suggested that any difference of opinion about precisely what Ir-ving said about the diary could be resolved by reading the transcript of a 1993 television interview Irving had given: "To me the Anne Frank diaries are a romantic novel, rather like *Gone With the Wind.*" Irving insisted that the court hear the entire interview in order to get the context. Judge Gray's re-sponse wondered, "How can the context really affect what you are saying which is that it is all made up?"

An exasperated Rampton rose and protested "the most frightful waste of time. . . . I have been as patient as I possibly can be, but now I cannot sit here any longer." He told Judge Gray that right before the trial, Irving had been on CNN. Rampton read from the transcript of the interview. "Interviewer: 'Did you say that the Anne Frank diary was a forgery?' Irving: 'Guilty.' Inter-viewer: 'Is it a forgery?' Irving: 'No.'"

Though Irving continued to argue about the *Diary,* Judge Gray was not anxious to hear more. "We have now had enough evidence on the Anne Frank diary. I think we will move on."[3]

## COCKROACHES: A JUSTIFIABLE SLUR?

Referring to the section of Evans's report that delineated Irving's highly derogatory statements about Jews, Irving asked Evans if anyone who criticized Jews was, ipso facto, an antisemite. Evans, referring to an October 1991 speech by Irving, declared, "I do think it is rather over the top to describe the Board of Deputies of British Jews [BOD] as cockroaches." Irving paused for the laughter to subside before insisting that his "lurid language" was a response to the BOD's attempt to stop publication of his books. He handed Evans the minutes of a BOD subcommittee meeting that had deliberated whether to complain to Irving's publisher about his forthcoming book. Irving asked Evans, "[If] pressure was put on my publishers by this body . . . am I *not* entitled to use that kind of language to describe these people?" Evans pointed out that this was a meeting of a BOD *sub*committee, which was attended by precisely five people and, most important, they decided to take no action.

As Evans was explaining this, I noticed Heather calling Rampton's attention to something on the BOD minutes. Rampton quickly rose from his seat. As soon as Judge Gray recognized him, he pointed out that the meeting was in December 1991. Irving made his "cockroach" comment in October 1991. He could not, therefore, have been responding to the BOD's subcommittee meeting. Irving held up a large folio of documents about the supposed global campaign against him, and asked, "Will you accept that, on the balance of probabilities, there are other documents of that nature in that bundle?" Every lawyer around me groaned. Judge Gray articulated their sentiments: "Mr Irving, we must do better than that. . . . If there was in existence a document prior to what you said about the British Board of Deputies being cockroaches, which you say justifies your having said that, then put it to the witness. If you have not got [it] . . . move on." Irving repeated his question: "If an author is aware that such a campaign is being conducted against him . . . is he entitled to use lurid language in private?" Judge Gray looked annoyed: "You have asked that question many times. . . . You have not established the factual premise for it. So, can you move to the next topic . . . ?"[4] Irving, looking decidedly unhappy, complied.

## OUTER SPACE

Evans, himself a consummate researcher, was particularly annoyed by the roadblocks Irving put in the way of other researchers who wanted to check his sources. This was glaringly clear in Irving's handling of the testimony at Hitler's 1924 trial. Rather than point the reader to the precise location of the document on which he based his rendition of events, Irving told readers that his version "is knitted together from eyewitness evidence at the [1924] trial." In his source citation in the Pleadings, Irving cited the eight-thousand-page microfilm transcript without providing either microfilm frame numbers or dates. Consequently, Evans noted in his report, a researcher would have had to read the entire transcript to find the relevant sections.[5]

Irving told Evans that his complaints were unjustified. Evans had used the printed edition of the transcript, which had page numbers, while he used the microfilm, which did not. Evans observed that Irving could have cited frame numbers. Irving responded, "If they do not have frame numbers then you cannot give frame number references." Judge Gray demanded greater specificity: "Are you putting, Mr Irving, that these microfiche did not have frame reference numbers?" Irving removed glasses and, as he twirled them in his left hand, said to Judge Gray, "I . . . leave it exactly the way I said it, my Lord." James looked up from the notes he had been making: "He just blew off the judge." Judge Gray demanded, "What is the answer to my question?" Irving responded, "I put to the witness the possibility that it had no frame numbers in which case I would not have been able to quote them." Judge Gray, who did not sound happy, asked again, "I am asking you a question and I think I am entitled to because I want to know how you are putting your case. Are you making it an allegation . . . that these particular microfiche did not have frame numbers?" Adopting a far more deferential tone, Irving said, "To be perfectly frank, my Lord, it is 12 years since I wrote the book and I cannot remember. But that would be one logical reason why I did not give frame numbers."[6] Judge Gray, a quizzical look on his face, let the matter rest.

Later, Irving returned to the 1924 trial. In his report, Evans had severely criticized Irving for failing to inform his readers that Police Sergeant Hofmann, who had testified at Hitler's trial and whose testimony was the main source of Irving's information, was not only a Nazi Party member, but such a close affiliate of Hitler that the judge disqualified his testimony. Irving challenged Evans, "You suggest that I ought to have known that [Hofmann's testimony was disqualified]?" Evans pointed out that it was in the transcript. Irving demanded, "What evidence do you have that I read those pages of the trial?" Judge Gray wanted more precision: "If your case is, Mr Irving, that you did not ever read Hofmann's testimony, then you should put that because that would be an explanation." Irving responded, "I hope that I was making that point, my Lord." Judge Gray felt otherwise: "You were careful *not* to put it quite that way. You said: 'Have you got any evidence that I had Hofmann's testimony in front of me?' If your case is that you never read it, I think you should put that." When Irving again challenged Evans to prove he had read the testimony, Rampton interjected, "My Lord, I am afraid I think again we are going out into outer space." Rampton reminded Judge Gray that earlier in the trial, when he was cross-examining Irving about the 1924 trial, Irving had said, "I read the entire court transcript which was many thousands of pages. . . ." Irving—with a slight note of urgency in his voice—asked Judge Gray for permission to "clarify this matter"; Judge Gray seemed uninterested: "I think that bears out . . . the correctness of what I said to you. If your case was that you had never read the testimony, then you ought to have put it. But now it turns out that actually you have already conceded that you read the whole thing."

Irving now argued that, given the length of the testimony, he could not be expected to notice all the details. Looking at Judge Gray, he asked, "Has your Lordship any idea of how many words there are on 8,000 pages of transcript?" Evans observed that Hofmann's testimony was only five pages long.

When the session ended, I said to Rampton and Heather, who were removing their robes and wigs, "Two weeks ago he boasted about having read every one of the 8,000 pages of testimony. Today he defended himself by saying it's so many thousands of pages, how could he possibly remember what's there? It's like the elevator in Auschwitz. First, the problem is that it has no doors. Then the problem is that it has doors. Irving's real problem is that for the first time he is being forced to explain his contradictions and he can't."

## A VERY SMALL WORLD

The next day, I spotted Hebrew University professor Shlomo Aronson in the public gallery. Suddenly I remembered my promise to Seth and Tobias about trying to retrieve the manuscript Eichmann had written while in Israel. At the end of the session Aronson told me that the manuscript was in the National Archives, under the control of Attorney General Elyakhim Rubenstein. Daunted by the prospect of getting to Rubenstein, I was inclined to abandon any effort to get the manuscript, when Aronson told me that he attended law school with the attorney general. "Have Rampton write to Rubenstein—lawyer to lawyer—to request the manuscript. Fax that letter to me. *I'll* make sure it gets to the attorney general." I bid Aronson goodbye and told Rampton about his offer. Rampton looked decidedly skeptical about the entire endeavor. He reluctantly agreed to write and asked for the spelling of the attorney general's name. "I think," I said, "it's R-U-B-E-N—" Rampton interrupted, "I do not write an attorney general if I don't know precisely how to spell his name." Feeling a bit sheepish, I promised to obtain the information. Walking out of the courtroom I said to a friend, "Rubenstein's first name is Elyakhim. How the heck do you spell that?"

Finding it difficult to dial up the Internet to retrieve this information, I decided to call my friend Roberta, who worked for Israeli prime minister Ehud Barak. I assumed she would know the proper spelling of Rubenstein's name. Her husband Stuart is a well-known journalist, whom I've known since our teenage days at summer camp. He got on the extension and the three of us had a long conversation about the trial. Finally, warning them that I had a weird question, I asked for the spelling of Rubenstein's name. When they heard why I wanted it, Stuart laughed. "You can do this far more expeditiously. My brother Joshua is his advisor." Within a few minutes I was on the phone with Joshua. "My guess is that he would be willing to release it. He's talked about your trial. Fax me a letter. I will put it on his desk as soon as I receive it." Early the next morning I called Rampton: "Rubenstein spells his name with an 'E.' Here's his personal fax number. Your letter will be on his desk as soon as it arrives. He'll probably say 'Yes.'" Rampton sounded impressed: "How did you manage that?" Rather than explain the path from me to Aronson to Roberta to Stuart to Joshua to Rubenstein, I said, "It's a small world. It's a tiny Jewish world. And it's a microscopic Israeli world."

## THE MADNESS OF *KRISTALLNACHT*

Irving was particularly disturbed by Evans's accusation that he had whitewashed Hitler's role in *Kristallnacht* and contended that he had, in fact, criticized the German leader. To prove his point, Irving read from his section on the pogrom in *Goebbels: Mastermind of the Third Reich:* "Hitler made no attempt to halt this inhumanity. He stood by, and thus deserved the odium that now fell on all Germany." For a moment it sounded as if Irving might have caught Evans in a major error. While Evans paged through *Goebbels* looking for the original quote, Irving pivoted to look at the gallery with a small smile on his face. When Evans looked up from his report, he too was smiling. He suggested that he read the preceding sentence: "20,000 Jews were already loaded onto *[sic]* and transported to the concentration camps at Dachau, Buchenwald, and Oranienburg. Hitler made no attempt to halt this inhumanity. He stood by and . . ." Evans's point was obvious. Irving *had* written that Hitler stood by and for this deserved the odium, but he had been referring to Hitler's behavior *after* the event, not during it. He turned to Irving, something he had rarely done since his first disastrous day on the stand, and like a teacher addressing a recalcitrant student, said: "He did not stand by, Mr Irving, he *ordered* the whole thing."[8]

Irving, attempting to demonstrate that Hitler tried to stop the outbreaks when he learned of them, argued that the telex sent at 2.56 A.M. on November 10, the night of *Kristallnacht,* which called for an end to arson was intended to "halt the madness."[9]* Evans read the telex: "Arson or the laying of fire in Jewish shops or the like may not . . . take place under any circumstances." Irving looked pleased, as if this proved his point: "Pretty emphatic, is it not?" Evans agreed: "Yes. What it is saying is that nobody is to set light to Jewish shops . . . or similar kinds of premises." Then he continued: "It is *not* saying that nobody is to arrest the Jews. It is *not* saying that nobody should smash the shops up. It is *not* saying that nobody should smash up the apartments and houses of Jews." Irving interrupted, "Professor, I have not asked you what it does not say." Ignoring Irving, Evans plowed on: "It does *not* say that nobody should commit arson against many hundreds of synagogues."

When Irving again insisted that the telegram was a call for cessation of the attacks, Evans disdainfully described Irving's comment as a "completely illegitimate misinterpretation and manipulation of this text. . . . Hitler is saying here: '*Go ahead* with burning down synagogues. *Go ahead* with wrecking

---

*The fires were spreading and demolishing both Jewish- and Aryan-owned property. Therefore, the authorities ordered the arson halted.

Jewish shops and smashing up the interiors. *Go ahead* with arresting 20,000 people. *Go ahead* with smashing up Jewish apartments, destroying the furniture, chucking it out of the window, throwing some of the inhabitants out of the window. *Go ahead* with all of that, but don't commit arson on Jewish shops or similar premises.' "[10] As Evans spoke, one by one the defense team abandoned the documents they were reading and notes they were making. They turned to the witness box. I glanced at Anthony. He too was staring at the witness box and shaking his head in affirmation.

## THE DIMENSIONS OF A DITCH

Irving returned to the testimony of Walter Bruns, the German general whom the British had clandestinely taped describing to his fellow POWs the mass shootings at Riga in November 1941. Bruns had described the ditches into which 27,000 Jews were gunned as 24 meters long and 3 meters wide. Irving contended that such ditches could have held only a few thousand people and that the number of 27,000 was, therefore, a vast exaggeration. Evans pointed out that Bruns did not provide the depth of the pits, rendering any calculations meaningless.

Irving, insisting he had expertise about ditches because he dug them to pay for his education, introduced a photograph that showed relatively shallow three-meter-wide pits with soldiers standing nearby. This photo, he suggested, demonstrated that the ditches were not large enough to accommodate so many victims. Evans examined the photo and then, a quizzical look on his face, asked for its origins. Irving acknowledged that it was of British soldiers at Bergen-Belsen or Buchenwald, where "victims of Nazi atrocities" were being buried. However, he continued, it showed "how deep you can dig a pit in circumstances like this." Evans scowled and declared that a picture of ditches dug by British troops had no relevance to pits at Riga. He again insisted that a pit could be any depth. Irving wondered if that answer was "your expert evidence as a pit digger or can we apply some common sense?" The question precipitated the following exchange:

> IRVING: Would you agree, as General Bruns describes, the ditch was 24 yards long and 3 metres wide, and if it was 2 metres deep, that would be 144 cubic metres?

EVANS: . . . No, I do not. They could have dug it any depth they wanted to.

IRVING: We will ignore that remark for the moment and continue with this calculation, . . . So if it was 2 metres deep and if it had straight sides and if there was no back fill—

EVANS: That is three "ifs," Mr Irving.

IRVING: —would you stop interrupting—you would get 1,500 bodies into that pit. . . . So if it was another metre deep, you would get another 750 in, so you can do an order of magnitude calculation, can you?

EVANS: On the basis of those four "ifs," yes, you can do any calculation you like.

IRVING: So you can do a ball park calculation of two or three pits of that kind of size and magnitude would hold of the order of, say, three to 7,000 bodies?

EVANS: Yes, on the basis of those four hypotheticals, yes.

IRVING: Did you bother to do such a check sum before you criticised me?

EVANS: . . . My criticism is that there is no evidence of the depth of the pits. You do not provide any. You simply make all these if, if, if assumptions and then somehow treat them as facts.

At that point, most people—myself included—were finding it impossible to keep a straight face. I felt as it I were watching *Monty Python's Flying Circus*. Then Evans began to lecture Irving: "This is a systematic attempt to undermine the figure given of 27,800 Jews . . . This is typical of your minimisation of the statistics of the numbers of Jews killed in any number of instances." I stopped laughing, as did most everyone in the room. Deeply embarrassed that I had found these pits a source of amusement, I began to envision what, in fact, took place in them. The Germans determined that the ditches could accommodate more people if the victims lay down, head to toe, on top of the bodies of those who had been killed before them. They called this *Sardinenpackung,* or "sardine packing." They also learned that if an adult was holding a child two bullets were necessary to ensure that both were killed. My reverie was interrupted by Judge Gray's order: "On to the next point, Mr Irving. I think we have exhausted that."[11]

★   ★   ★

Finally, Evans's long week in the box ended. The weekend promised an escape from the trial. In a Leicester Square theater every weekend there was a sing-along screening of the Rodgers and Hammerstein classic *The Sound of Music*. People came dressed as their favorite character or object. There were brides, Austrian peasants, yodelers, nuns, and brown paper packages tied up with string. My favorite was a man covered in bright yellow lycra: "Ray, a drop of golden sun." The lyrics appeared on the screen so the audience could sing along. When a particular character appeared in the movie, everyone dressed in that role would rise, face the audience, and recite the character's lines. All this was enough to take my mind completely off the trial.

Then, two-thirds of the way through the movie, the Nazis, who had just "annexed" Austria, appeared. Though these Nazis were more like Keystone Cops than the genuine article, I was quickly brought back to my reality. As I walked through Piccadilly to my apartment, I thought about my experiences with *Copenhagen, The Merchant of Venice,* and, now, *Sound of Music*. I wondered, was I unconsciously choosing entertainment that kept me on focus?

## HITLER'S FINAL WORDS

On the last day of Evans's testimony tempers began to fray. The judge asked Irving, who was moving quickly from one historical topic to the next, to "set the scene . . . [because] I have not spent 30 or 40 years on this." Irving looked up at the judge and, with a smile, said, "I will do it in two lines rather than allow the witness to do it in 25." That brought a strong objection from Rampton: "Mr Irving should stop being so offensive. It does not improve the climate in court and this is a distinguished scholar. . . . Mr Irving ought to mind his tongue, if I may respectfully say so." Judge Gray intervened, "I know tempers run high and they inevitably do, but I think, if one can try and keep it civil on all sides, that does help." Fuming, Irving pulled off his glasses and, looking at Rampton and then at Judge Gray, said, "For seven days and in 750 pages of this report, I have had to listen to the most defamatory utterances poured over my head by witnesses who speak in the knowledge that their remarks are privileged." Judge Gray repeated himself: "Lack of civility is not the way to deal with an attack of the kind that is mounted on you in Professor Evans' report."[12]

Toward the end of the day, Irving questioned Evans about Hitler's Last Will and Testament, which the Nazi leader wrote as the Soviets assaulted Berlin. In it Hitler described Jews as "the race which is the real criminal in this murderous struggle." Despite Hitler's unambiguous comments about Jews, in 1977 Irving wrote the *Sunday Times* that the wording of the will was as "ambiguous as every other document that has ever been produced purporting to prove Hitler's guilt."[13] Evans thought this simply not true and responded by reading the portion of the will in which Hitler predicted that, unlike World War I, this time "millions of Europe's Aryan peoples . . . would not suffer death, nor would hundreds of thousands of women and children be allowed to be burnt and bombed to death in the towns, without the real criminal having to atone for his guilt, even if by more humane means." Evans observed that for Hitler the real criminals were the Jews and the "more humane means" were shooting and gassing. Irving asked whether "the Holocaust was humane which is what you are proposing?" Evans protested: "I am not proposing it. It is *Hitler* who is proposing it." Irving repeated, "You are accepting that the Holocaust was more humane?"[14] Evans again protested this was Hitler's view. Irving again insisted it was Evans's. Suddenly, I heard a loud: *"Jeesus!!"* from the public gallery. I spun around to see my colleague Barbara DeConcini with her hand over her mouth. Her face was beet-red. She seemed to be trying to retract her words by pushing them back into her mouth. Barbara, executive director of the American Academy of Religion, a twenty-thousand-member scholarly organization, had come to the trial with her husband, Walt, my colleague at Emory. I chuckled at her use of this particular expletive since she was a former nun.

# SIXTEEN

# OUR GERMAN CONTINGENT

Once Evans had finished his marathon testimony, I slowly began to fathom that the end of the trial was in sight. Our "German contingent," as I had taken to calling Peter Longerich and Hajo Funke, would be the last experts to testify. Common sense told me that I should have felt unadulterated relief that this five-year ordeal was coming to an end. Yet, I was beset by a gnawing anxiety. It took me a while to sort out my feelings. When I did, I recognized that, though I was increasingly expecting a victory, at least as far as the history was concerned, I was worried that Judge Gray might reach a tentative or even-handed judgment. He might somehow decide that Irving's historical distortions were not deliberate and that Irving was an iconoclastic historian who simply had views that diverged from the mainstream. He might think that Irving's expressions of racism and antisemitism were unconnected to his Holocaust denial. I wanted Judge Gray to unequivocally condemn Irving as a Holocaust denier, antisemite, and racist and to explicitly state that Irving's "mistakes" were premeditated distortions. I wanted it to be clear that my critique of Irving was not about varying historical interpretations—of which there are many—but of truth and lies. Anything less than that would leave Irving free to snatch victory from the jaws of defeat. I wanted a lot.

## ALL ABOUT CONTEXT

Peter Longerich, our next witness and our final historical expert to take the stand, would play a critical role in obtaining the ruling I so wanted. Peter, who was in his mid-forties, wore his hair in a sort of Beatles-like style and tended to speak quietly. Though his English is flawless, he sometimes hesitates while speaking, as if he is pondering his choice of words. He has a rather shy, gentle persona and I worried that his reserved style would not withstand Irving's badgering. He would have to give measure for measure, without being dragged into a verbal sparring match.

A professor at the University of London, with an expertise in the structure of the Nazi system and its decision making process, Longerich had worked for several years at the Institut für Zeitgeschichte in Munich, one of the leading German institutes doing research on the Third Reich. While there, he helped reconstruct the lost original files from the Nazi Party chancellery, the central office of the Nazi Party, which controlled the state bureaucracy. He also wrote both a history of the Nazi Storm Troopers (SA) and an organizational history of the party chancellery. Over the last ten years, his work had increasingly focused on the persecution and murder of European Jews. His most recent work, *Politik der Vernichtung* (The Politics of Extermination), was the first study of the annihilation process that integrated the archival windfall that had become available to scholars after the fall of communism. Browning, whose research was in the same area, considered it "monumental." Peter's report analyzed Hitler's antisemitism and his role in the Final Solution.

He arrived in court on the morning he was scheduled to take the stand, in a stylishly tailored, black, heavy wool, four-button suit that—he proudly informed me when I complimented him on it—he had bought in London's West End. "End of the season sale," he added quietly, as if to justify his extravagance. Peter exchanged pleasantries with other members of the defense team. There was a steely calm about him.

Peter had prepared a report on the term *"Ausrottung"* ("extirpation"). Virtually all Holocaust historians agree that Nazi leaders' use of this term in conjunction with Jews from the summer of 1941 on must be interpreted as an unambiguous euphemism for "physical annihilation." Not surprisingly, Irving took a different view. He contended it meant to literally uproot, as in the enforced emigration—but certainly not the murder—of the Jewish community. To prove his point, he read a speech Hitler gave immediately after *Kristallnacht*. "I look at the intellectual classes amongst us . . . you could *ausrotten* them . . . but unfortunately you need them." Hitler, Irving argued, could not have been referring to actual killings when he used *"ausrotten,"* because the speech was made in "1938 when nobody is liquidating anybody." Before he finished his sentence Peter interjected, "Except the 90 people who just died the night before."* Peter, in a rush of words, which seemed to be designed to prevent Irving from interrupting, added, "This is the most brutal killing which happened in Germany since, I think, the Middle Ages. There are more than 90 people, I would say several hundred people possibly were killed the last night, and in this atmosphere Hitler is giving a press conference and speaks about the *Ausrottung* of intellectuals. . . . Look again at the historical context . . . this is an atmosphere which is dominated by brutality and a kind of absence of public order and law." Judge Gray mused, "It always comes back to context?" Peter vigorously agreed.

Irving offered his own context: "Would [it] not be a parallel if Tony Blair said he wanted to . . . wipe out the House of Lords, would he not say '*ausrotten*' there and would that mean that he wanted to stand them against a wall [and shoot them]?" Peter observed: "[If] Tony Blair just killed 91 Conservative Members of Parliament . . . [and] if he would use . . . the next day the term '*Ausrottung*,' I would look at it and say, 'Well, [that's] a dangerous man.' "

Irving also challenged Peter about the term "*Vernichtung*," which historians generally consider a euphemism for "annihilation." Irving argued that when Hans Frank, the governor of the *Generalgouvernement*, used the word in a speech delivered to his cabinet upon returning to Krakow after hearing Hitler speak in Berlin, he was not referring to murder. Frank told his cabinet of the need for "*Judenvernichtung*" and, complaining about the massive number of Jews being deported to his region, he lamented, "We cannot execute them, we cannot poison them." Irving compared it to a rhetorical question a German general who faced Allied forces in 1944 might have posed: "We have Eisenhower's armies in front of us, we cannot shoot them, we cannot poison them, how are we going to destroy them? The answer is cut off their water supply, cut off the power, deprive them of the shipping lines, the oil." There were, Irving observed, "all sorts of ways of destroying an enemy." Peter once again pierced the cloak of sophistry with which Irving draped his arguments: "In your example you refer to an army, but here it is about the Jews. . . . If I destroy, '*vernichte*,' human beings, and I discuss then the

---

*The official German toll for the night of *Kristallnacht* itself is ninety-one.

methods, whether I should liquidate them, execute them, or whether I should poison them, I think then the context is pretty clear. . . . [Frank] was sure they were going to 'vernichten' the *Juden* because [he] came back from Berlin [where he] heard the speech . . . [only] the method was unclear."[1] As Peter spoke Rampton leaned back in his chair. He crossed his arms across his chest and pulled his wig forward until it was almost covering his eyes. Had I not known better, I would have thought he was taking a nap.

## MAKING LEMONADE

Irving, trying to dispel the notion of Hitler as an unrepentant antisemite, asked Peter if he thought it odd that "an antisemite like Hitler would . . . hav[e] a Jewish chauffeur, Emile Morris?" Peter declined to answer because he had no evidence Morris was Jewish. When Irving demanded an answer, Peter spoke directly to Judge Gray. "If you look into the history of anti-semitism, the greatest antisemites had sometimes Jewish friends. They would say, well, this is my friend, he is an exception, and he is not like others. This is a typical stereotype." Peter had taken a lemon—being forced to an-swer this question—and made lemonade by demonstrating its fallacious foundation. When Peter finished answering, Irving declared, "You are damned if you do and damned if you do not." Irving next contended that Hitler's cook was Jewish. Peter repeated his argument: "You cannot draw conclusions from these personal relationships, because the antisemite would always argue . . . this person is different."[2] When Peter finished speaking, Rampton, who had awoken from his putative nap, took out a blank piece of paper and started sketching.

In his report, Peter had discussed the plan, briefly considered by the Nazis in 1940, of relocating—some would say dumping—four million Jews in Madagascar. Himmler expected that once Germany defeated France and England, the island of Madagascar, operating as a "superghetto," would be a feasible place to park the Jews. Though the plan did not have a killing ele-ment, it would have resulted in massive Jewish losses. Madagascar, off the east coast of Africa, was totally unequipped to support a large urban popula-tion. There were no plans for the infrastructure necessary to provide even the most minimal support for four million people. In essence it was a death warrant for the Jews who were to be moved there.

Irving, however, had a different interpretation of the Madagascar Plan. It proved that the Germans had a benign intention to resettle—not murder—European Jewry. Peter would have none of that. "What they envisaged was that the Jews . . . would perish and [be] put to death by a combination of diseases, epidemics, simply insufficient means for survival, hard labour and things like that." Irving disagreed. The conditions would have been difficult and some Jews might have died, but this was not "quite the same as saying [the Nazis had] a homicidal intent." Peter, speaking with the authority of an historian who had closely studied this material, said, "The difference [was] between the idea to let them perish out there and to immediately kill them by executions or gas."

The judge asked Peter, "The relevant question is [whether] they thought it was feasible?" Rampton looked up from his sketch and listened carefully as Peter said, "In which sense feasible? You mean to provide a place where four million Jews could have a happy life? In this sense feasible? . . . Or feasible in the sense of an SS police state, so to say a big prison, with a high death rate? In this sense I would say, yes, it was feasible."[3]

Irving moved from Madagascar to the shootings in the East. When he argued that Hitler did not know of them, Peter countered by reminding him of Gestapo chief Heinrich Müller's 1941 order that "the Führer should be presented with continuous reports on the work of the Einsatzgruppen" and that "especially interesting" material depicting the activities of the Einsatzgruppen be sent to Hitler.[4] Peter also observed that the Einsatzgruppen reports, which described the murder of hundreds of thousands of Jews, were widely circulated, sometimes to more than fifty people. Given this, Peter concluded, it was "impossible, to argue that the result of the activities of the Einsatzgruppen could be hidden before anybody. . . . It is exactly what he [Hitler] himself demanded. . . . This is what he wanted to hear." Judge Gray summarized Peter's response: "You say he ordered it and it happened." Peter shook his head: "Yes." Irving contended that the absence of Hitler's name on the distribution list, indicated he was not informed of the shootings. Peter dismissed Irving's argument as "inconceivable." Behind me, Rampton, still sketching, quietly whispered, "Perfect." He did not seem to be referring to his drawing.

Peter showed particular disdain for Irving's contention that these killings were orchestrated by Himmler without Hitler's knowledge: "That this whole operation, this enormous operation, killing operation of 6 million people could be started and could be carried out on a large scale with implications, you know, transportation, the building of extermination camps, the involvement of 10,000 people who had to carry out this programme . . . that this could be carried out . . . [against] Hitler's wishes, this whole notion seems absolutely . . . absurd." He concluded, "To argue that this was done behind Hitler's back . . . defies reason."[5] At that point Rampton passed me his completed sketch of a smiling, almost beatific, Saint Peter—who, except for his halo and wings, bore an uncanny resemblance to Peter Longerich. At the end of the day, Anthony, Rampton, and I wended our way out of the Law Courts together. Referring to Irving's contention that Hitler had not ordered the killings, Rampton wondered, "What's the difference between Hitler saying, 'Get rid of them and don't tell me the details' or his saying 'Do it and tell me all about it'?" Anthony observed that Hitler's modus operandi was akin to Henry II's in T. S. Eliot's *Murder in the Cathedral*. Henry did not need to say, "Who will kill Becket for me?" All he needed to say was "Who will rid me of him?" The king's followers, understanding what he wanted, went ahead and murdered Becket.

## AN AUSTRALIAN SIDESHOW: LITERARY HOAXES

That night, upon checking my email, I discovered that some minor espionage had been taking place in the press gallery. A few weeks earlier, Ursula had pointed out a young blond Australian woman, who claimed to be a reporter. After hearing her extol Irving and compare him to Churchill, Ursula cautioned me, "There's something strange about her." I had thought Ursula's imagination was getting the better of her—she revels in a good mystery—and had forgotten about the matter. Subsequently reporters in the press gallery also become suspicious of this woman, particularly when she made what they described as "bizarre" comments about the defense team. After a bit of Internet sleuthing some reporters determined that she was an Australian writer, Helen Darville, who herself had been involved in a major literary hoax.[6] Using the name "Demidenko," Darville had written *The Hand That Signed the Paper*, a fictionalized account of her Ukrainian family's experiences during the Second World War. The book won Australia's two most prestigious literary prizes and subsequent international recognition. One of the judges described it as "a searingly truthful account of terrible war-time deeds [with] extraordinary redemptive power." Not everyone was pleased with the book. Some critics noted that it depicted the German atrocities against Ukrainian Jews as retribution for what the Communists—some of whom were Jews—did in the Ukraine during the Stalinist terror of the 1930s. Even some people of Ukrainian descent were not pleased. The Canadian-Ukrainian writer Janice Kulyk Keefer labeled the book, not only "viciously antisemitic," but "profoundly anti-Ukrainian" for reinforcing the stereotype of the pro-Nazi, antisemitic, drunken peasant savage.[7]

But Demidenko-Darville had more serious problems than critical reviews. She told a television interviewer that she had written the book from her perspective as an ethnic Ukrainian. "I experienced as a Ukrainian-Australian person, a great deal of personal unpleasantness as a result of the war crimes trials." A former classmate recognized her and informed the press that Darville was of British, not Ukrainian origin. Her claim to be writing from a personal perspective was a complete fabrication.[8] Despite this literary scandal, Darville was subsequently hired as a columnist by the *Brisbane Courier Mail*. Her relationship with that paper ended rather quickly, when it turned out that her second column contained Internet material that she presented as her own.[9]

Despite this journalistic record, the glossy magazine *Australian Style* commissioned her to cover my trial. Comparing Irving to Churchill, she portrayed him as a prodigy, who "frequently trips up the Defence," and me as a vacuous American who wears her heart on her sleeve. She bemoaned his "ill-fate," which included—should he lose the case—financial ruin.[10] The *Sydney Morning Herald* was so disturbed by this imbroglio that, breaking standard journalistic practice, it published a critique of her article on Irving before it appeared in the magazine.[11] The whole thing was, admittedly, a sideshow but it provided me with a much welcomed diversion from events in the courtroom.

## COATS IN WINTER AND RATIONALIZED KILLINGS

The next morning Irving challenged Peter's contention that the shootings in the East demonstrated the SS's homicidal intent toward the Jews by introducing an April 1943 memo in which the SS boasted that Auschwitz's monthly mortality rate had dropped from 10 to 8 percent. In an accompanying letter Oswald Pohl, chief of the concentration camps, attributed the reduction in death rate to "better feeding [and] better clothing." If the Germans intended to kill the inmates, Irving asked, why would it reduce the death rate? Peter argued that, rather than indicate a benevolent attitude

toward the camp inmates, the memo showed that the Germans were content with the unnaturally high rate of 8 percent.

Furthermore, Peter added, this report concerned Auschwitz's function
as a slave labor—not an extermination—camp. The Nazi principle for slave
labor was "extermination through work." Prisoners' life expectancy was,
Peter estimated, at most a couple of months. This presented the SS with a
potential problem. If prisoners died too rapidly, they would lack laborers for
the work they had contracted to do for German corporations. The letter reported that prisoners are now allowed to wear a coat, sweaters, and socks—
if they are available—something that had, apparently, previously been
forbidden. To depict this, Peter dryly noted, as a system that cared about
prisoners' welfare was farcical.[12]

Irving asked Peter if he was suggesting that people who died because of
difficult conditions were victims of "homicidal killings." Peter refused to be
drawn into this dialectic. "A killing is a killing," he quietly said. When Irving
kept insisting that these people died from "bad conditions," rather than from
a planned killing program, Peter's face grew red; turning away from Irving,
he said in a clipped tone, "The purpose of the concentration camp was not
to keep prisoners alive . . . the purpose of the concentration camp here was,
clearly, to put people to death. . . . You cannot compare it with a prison or
anything in a civilized country." I was struck by Peter's last statement. The
country and the people responsible for creating these uncivilized places was
his own, Germany.

Irving argued that Peter's claims were irrational: "It does not make
sense, does it, to have a slave labourer who is working for you and work him
to death so you then have to replace him with somebody else because, presumably, his output drops off as he is dying?" This time, Irving was right. It
made no sense unless one was fighting, as Peter described it, a "war of racist
extermination. . . . They worked on the assumption that . . . there was an
endless number of slave labourers who they could force to work for them."
This irrational and completely wrong assumption was the one upon which
the Nazis based the Final Solution.[13]

In his analysis of the *Einsatzgruppen's* activities, Peter observed that
some of the reports "justified" their killings of Jews by describing them as
"retribution." For instance, in July 1941, seven thousand Jews were murdered
in Lvov. The *Einsatzgruppen* report said these shootings were "retribution"
for the "inhuman atrocities" committed by Soviet authorities against Ukrain-

ian nationals.[14] Irving complained that Peter had omitted something significant from this particular *Einsatzgruppen* report. The report included a four-page description of the Soviet atrocities. This description would have explained why the Germans went "berserk" and murdered the Lvov Jews. Peter insisted that there was no connection between what the Soviets did prior to retreating from Lvov and German "retaliation" against the Jews. The Germans did not single out the Jews who might have had some hand in these atrocities. They simply massacred all of them. Rather than constituting an act of retaliation, the massacre of the Jews was "part of the war of racist extermination." To buttress his point, Peter cited another *Einsatzgruppen* report that described how Jewish women had "shown impudent and arrogant behaviour. . . . They tore their own and their children's clothes off their bodies. As provisional retribution the *[Einsatzgruppen] Kommando . . .* shot 50 male Jews." After hesitating for a moment, he then added, "So I think you get a very good insight into this kind of retribution or retaliation."

When Irving continued to pursue this point, Judge Gray interrupted him with a more fundamental question: "I am at a total loss to understand why we are going through the detail of the shooting when you accept that hundreds of thousands of Jews were killed by the *Einsatzgruppen.*" Irving protested that he was doing so because "the witness has left out a four-page description in the most hideous and ghastly detail" of the Soviet crimes that Germans discovered when they arrived in Lvov. Judge Gray, rather uncharacteristically, snapped, "So it served the 7,000 Jews right, did it?" He then pointedly told Irving, "You are not serving your own cause well by taking up time quite pointlessly on these sorts of questions."[15]

Despite Judge Gray's admonitions, most of Irving's subsequent questions to Longerich consisted of small points. Peter, drawing on a meticulous knowledge of the period, had no trouble with them. When Peter finished testifying, Rampton approached to thank him. Peter looked at him and said, not without some bitterness, "The Nazis stole our political identity. And now people like Irving are attempting to steal it again."

# SEVENTEEN

# CAVORTING WITH THUGS OR GUILT BY ASSOCIATION?

In anticipation of Hajo Funke's testimony about Irving's association with various political extremists, we had compiled two large binders from Irving's own diaries, correspondence, and speeches. Irving protested that most of this information concerned nonviolent extremists and, since there was nothing "reprehensible" about that, such material should be excluded. Judge Gray reminded Irving that in our pretrial Summary of Case we promised to demonstrate that Irving was a right-wing ideologue who "associated with right-wing extremists and right wing extremist groups in Germany, Britain and North America. You have regularly spoken at events organized by [them]." Irving dismissed our charges as guilt by association, something that was not a crime. Rampton, not surprisingly, disagreed. This was not a matter of Irving's sitting "in a waiting room in a railway station with whoever might happen to be there but leading a banner-waving bunch of neo-Nazi thugs." Irving more than associated with them. He had "prostituted his skills . . . in the service of . . . a restoration of a kind of Nazi antisemitic ideology."[1]

Judge Gray ruled that we could introduce evidence that Irving had either associated with groups that were themselves right-wing, antisemitic, anti-Israel, or involved with Holocaust denial. Having lost on this point, Irving complained that we were turning the trial into the "most random sort" of shooting gallery by presenting names of neo-Nazis who happened to be in the same room as he. Rampton stressed that he intended to do no such thing. He would show Irving's "intimate relationships over periods of time" with these individuals.[2]

## THE RELEASE OF THE EICHMANN MEMOIRS

That evening, when I returned to my apartment, as I was fishing my key out of my briefcase, I heard my phone ringing. When I opened the door, I had to step over a mountain of pink message slips that the hotel staff had put under my door. Before I could look at them or get to the phone, my computer began to intone: "You've got mail." I checked my email and quickly learned that Israel had just announced that it would release the Eichmann manuscript to us. Suddenly the phone rang again. I picked it up and someone identified himself as Gabriel Bach. While Bach had recently retired as a justice of the Supreme Court of Israel, I also knew his name as an assistant prosecutor at the Eichmann trial. Attorney General Rubenstein had consulted with him about the release of the Eichmann manuscript. "The Eichmann manuscript is on its way to London. Express mail."

The next morning, the release of the diaries was front-page news. I had barely set foot in the courtroom when Tobias accosted me. He excitedly blurted out, "The email version is here. Rampton's clerks are downloading it." I reflected on what Seth's question had produced. I took out my cell phone to let him know that his question had propelled us onto the front page of many papers. When I realized that it was four in the morning for him, I decided this news could wait.

As soon as Judge Gray entered, Irving commented on the release of the manuscript. In a tone of voice that, no matter how often I heard it, irked me, Irving said that, according to the morning papers, the defense was "going to bring in the Battleship Eichmann in a frantic attempt to rescue their position."[3] Irving demanded that Rampton be instructed to give him a copy as soon as possible. Rampton, ignoring Irving's hyperbole, agreed.

## GERMANY: DAVID IRVING'S "POLITICAL PLAYGROUND"

Hajo Funke is a lanky fellow whose long arms and legs seem to be out of proportion to his body. With his sparkling green eyes, Funke often looks like he has just heard a joke and is looking for someone with whom to share it.

He arrived in court on this brisk winter morning sporting a ski cap pulled down to his eyebrows and grinning broadly. Born in Silesia in 1945, he looked more like a schoolchild braving the winter weather than one of Germany's leading experts on the sociological and political roots of Germany's hate scene. Hajo's work in this field was far more than an academic pursuit. I discovered that the previous summer when, on my way to Auschwitz, I visited him in Berlin. On a spectacular June afternoon, over coffee in a café on Unter den Linden, the magnificent boulevard leading to the Brandenburg Gate, Hajo railed against foreigners, such as Irving, who come to Germany to forge common ground with the haters. "They wreak havoc with German democracy. We have to deal with their aftermath. Germany serves as their political playground."

As I watched Hajo chitchat with other members of the defense team, I worried about his less than perfect English. He sometimes translated directly from the German leaving the verb dangling at the far end of the sentence. When he got excited about something, he interchanged subjects and objects and dispensed with any consistency of tenses. Hajo, well aware of his linguistic limits, had asked to testify in German. Anthony and Richard were convinced that using a translator would be cumbersome and would lessen the impact of his testimony. They prevailed upon him to use English and agreed to have an interpreter present, just in case. After taking the oath, Hajo sat down. He arranged his papers in front of him, glanced in the defense's direction, and then, turning to Irving, smiled. He was clearly telegraphing his message: "I'm ready."

In his report, Hajo had noted that when Irving visited Germany prior to unification, he avoided explicit Holocaust denial. Instead he condemned the Allied bombing of Dresden, decried the "unatoned Holocaust" of the postwar expulsion of Germans from former Reich territories, castigated Winston Churchill's policies, questioned German war guilt, and denounced the Nuremberg trials as a sham. In the late 1980s, after adopting the *Leuchter Report,* Irving began to chart a course further to the right and moving to explicit Holocaust denial. He declared that there had never been a gassing of Jews, that six million murdered Jews was a *"Lebenslüge"* ("life lie") by Israel, and that the Holocaust was a means for Jews to financially and politically blackmail Germany.[4] By 1990, Irving was speaking of the gas chamber "dummies" the Poles built for the "damnation and defamation of the German people."[5]

According to Hajo, Irving's new course coincided with the emergence in Germany of more violent extremism, which included frequent verbal and physical attacks on foreigners and guest workers. This extremism, which was rooted in a loose alliance between national conservatives and radical extremists, was hostile to multiracial societies and depicted ethnic minorities as criminals and parasites.⁶ Holocaust denial was useful to this alliance because it rehabilitated the Third Reich's reputation, rendered Nazism a viable political alternative, and inculcated anger toward Jews. Extremists believed that if the Holocaust, which was being used to cast an indelible stain on Nazism, could be exposed as a sham, Nazism could be resurrected. Irving's status as an independent historian served the alliance's needs by elevating it above the image of rabble-rousing, firebomb-throwing, thugs. Christian Worch, one of the more prominent functionaries of the neo-Nazi scene in Germany, believed Irving could help bring "more reserved moderate" elements into the radical sphere. Funke considered Irving a catalyst in the alliance between neo-Nazis and other radical extremists.⁷

During Irving's repeated visits to Germany in the period following unification, his expressions of denial became increasingly explicit. Finally, German authorities petitioned the courts to bar him from lecturing in the country. Irving defended his activities by arguing that his speeches were scholarly, not political, and were protected by civil codes safeguarding freedom of research and teaching. In May 1992 the court ruled against him and noted that he had not only called the "racial murder by the National Socialists a lie," but his speeches stimulated his audience to "express Nazi opinions in public [and] vociferously repeat slogans for a revival of Nazi rule." His "pseudo-scientific" arguments, the court ruled, were designed to help extremists attract people who, while disposed to right-wing theses, were troubled by National Socialist crimes.⁸

Hajo had brought some videotape to illustrate his charges. One tape showed Irving and other deniers at a rally in the Alsatian town of Hagenau. Ernst Zündel, who was also present, had told the audience that "we decent Germans [are] wallowing in the pigsty" of this "base lie against our people which this Jewish rabble *[Judenpack]* has been spreading." Irving then regaled his audience by poking fun at survivors. He claimed that survivors had described a "one-man gas chamber" carried around through the Polish countryside by two soldiers who were looking for the individual Jew who might have escaped deportation.

This one-man gas chamber looked somewhat like a sadan [sic] chair,
I believe, but it was camouflaged as a telephone box, and one asks
oneself: How did they get the poor soul of a victim to enter this
one-man gas chamber voluntarily? Answer: There was probably a
telephone bell inside of it and it rang and the soldiers told him: "I
think that's for you."[9]

Other leading deniers who appeared at these rallies included Robert
Faurisson, the French denier, and Wilhelm Stäglich, author of *The Auschwitz
Myth*. The most chilling of the tapes was of the Halle rally at which the as-
sembled crowd had responded to Irving's speech with chants of *"Sieg Heil!
Sieg Heil!"* It was after watching this speech many months earlier that I had
felt compelled to go see the Assyrian exhibit at the British Museum.

The videotape of a 1990 Munich conference showed a large banner with
the slogan *"Wahrheit macht frei"* ("The Truth Makes You Free"). Rampton
stopped the tape and asked Funke whether the phrase had "any resonance
with some language used during the Nazi period?" Before Funke could answer, Judge Gray interrupted: "I think we all know." I thought back to the
gates to Auschwitz with its slogan, *"Arbeit macht frei"* ("Work Makes You
Free"). A bit later, when cross-examining Hajo, Irving contended that this
phrase had no connection with Nazism but was actually a quote from John
8:32 and dismissed the attempt to link it to the Holocaust as a product of
Rampton's "private obsessions."[10]

Irving was particularly annoyed by Hajo's contention that right wing extremism was often connected with a tendency toward "violence, militancy
and terror." He asked Hajo, "Are you saying that I am a violent, militant and
terrorizing person?" Hajo conceded that Irving had not explicitly called for
or directly instigated violence. This was not his modus operandi. He had,
however, joined forces with groups who "are utterly for violent acts."[11] Hearing this, I was reminded of Hajo's comment the previous summer. "People
like David Irving do not throw firebombs. They throw the words that can
cause others to throw those firebombs."

## HISTORY ON YELLOW PLASTIC

When Hajo's first day of testimony ended, Rampton rose and, holding aloft
a bright yellow computer disk, announced, "I now have the disk of the Eich-

mann memoirs." All eyes in the courtroom were momentarily fixed on
Rampton's hand. He was obligated, he acknowledged, to hand it over to Irving, however, he continued, he had an obligation to the Israeli government,
which had not yet released it to the general public. The Israelis wanted it
only used, in the interim, for trial-related purposes. Therefore, Rampton insisted, it "cannot go on Mr Irving's website." He refused to hand it over until
Irving committed that he would not use it for other purposes or place it on
"anybody's website."

Irving argued that the manuscript was in the public domain and he
could do with it as he wished. Judge Gray asked Irving if he was prepared to
give his "undertaking" not to make collateral use of it. Irving, sounding very
unenthusiastic and a bit annoyed, agreed: "I will give the undertaking not to
make any untoward use of it." The judge gravely shook his head: "No, not
good enough." He then asked again, this time using very explicit language:
"Are you prepared to give me your undertaking . . . that you will not make
use of this tape you are being handed otherwise than for the purposes of
these proceedings and, in particular, will not put it on your website?"[12] Irving, sounding rather deflated, agreed. Rampton then leaned across the
courtroom. In his outstretched hand was a little yellow plastic disk containing a forty-year-old unpublished and unexamined memoir by a man responsible for coordinating the death of millions. I watched in fascination as he
presented it to a man who denied that many of those murders occurred.

When I returned home later that night, I found a large carton on the
dining room table. A quick glance at the return address indicated that it
came from the Archives of the State of Israel. The hard copy of his memoirs
had arrived. The historian in me was itching to read them. Yet, having become so immersed in the details of the killing process—in a way that felt
deeply personal—I momentarily recoiled from this direct connection with
one of the architects of the killing process.

## THE HEROIC NAZI PAST

On Hajo's second day in the witness box, Irving returned to the question of
whether the slogan at the 1990 Munich conference—*"Wahrheit macht frei"*—
was an allusion to Auschwitz's *"Arbeit macht frei."* Judge Gray sat and listened for a while. He looked increasingly troubled. Finally, he admonished
Irving that this topic, which had been covered the previous day, could not be

debated any longer. Rampton quickly rose to his feet and offered to help resolve the matter. He read Irving's diary entry from an October 1989 visit to
Berlin. "At 11 am, a well attended press conference . . . closed with my new
slogan *Wahrheit macht frei*. The lefty journalists got the allusions."[13] Once
again Irving had entrapped himself. His own journal entry revealed that he
knowingly used this slogan as a pun on the words under which millions of
concentration camp inmates had passed.

After Irving persisted in questioning Funke about all sorts of small
details in his footnotes, Judge Gray admonished Irving that his cross-
examination was "achieving virtually nothing."[14] Irving, who seemed taken
aback by Judge Gray's comments, quickly turned to a section of Hajo's report about a dinner party in Munich in 1990. Irving had recorded in his diary
how, on April 20—Hitler's 101st birthday—he had attended a dinner "organized" by Ewald Althans, Ernst Zündel's closest associate in Germany and a
leading right-wing extremist, and attended by an array of extremists and
neo-Nazis, including Wilhelm Stäglich, a member of the *Journal of Historical
Review*'s Editorial Committee and Karl Phillip, a leading German denier.
Most of the guests were Germans, with the exception of Irving and Anthony
Hancock, a major printer and publisher of neo-Nazi material throughout
Europe.

Irving noted in his diary that the dinner ended with a *"Trinkspruch*
[toast] spoken by him [Althans], to a certain statesman whose 101st birthday
falls today. All rose, toasted; I had no glass, as I don't drink." Irving asked
Funke about the party: "From the diary entry, is it evident that . . . I did not
join in this very tasteless toast?" Rampton jumped to his feet to protest Irving's description of the toast. "Mr Irving should not lard his questions with
interpretations like 'this very tasteless event.' There is nothing in the diary
about that." A scowling Irving asked Funke, "[W]ould you consider it to be
very tasteless for a German to offer a toast to Adolf Hitler in the presence of
two English people?"[15] What happened next caught me by complete surprise. Suddenly I heard myself exclaiming: "Otherwise, it would have been
*just fine!*" Unlike my other comments, which were usually whispered to
James, this came out of my mouth at full throttle, something I only realized
when people in the gallery began to laugh. Heather, grinning broadly, gave
me a decidedly un-barrister-like thumbs-up. Rampton nodded his head ever
so slightly in my direction and, apparently satisfied that no further objections
were necessary, sat down. Embarrassed, but also admittedly satisfied that at

long last I had "broken" my silence, I avoided looking in Judge Gray's direction.

When Rampton reexamined Hajo, he asked him to elaborate on the connection between words and violence. Those who commit violence, Hajo explained, need a "kind of encouragement . . . to do the deeds they are doing." Irving's visits provided this form of encouragement. When Rampton suggested that these contemporary "rabble rousers" might be compared to Hitler and Goebbels who never "wield[ed] a club or a gun themselves" but whose words prompted others to do so, Hajo shook his head up and down, indicating a firm "Yes."[16]

Rampton noted that when Irving proclaimed at the Halle rally that he did not fear writing about the war crimes "we, the English, committed against the German people," his words were greeted with applause and cheers. "Does that surprise you, Professor Funke?" "No, not at all," Hajo responded. The people at this rally identified with "the kind of Nazi past, the past of heroic things."[17]

At the Hagenau rally, where Zündel spoke of a *Judenpack,* Irving had regaled the crowd with his story about the "one-person gas chamber." Rampton asked Hajo if this kind of rhetoric was "characteristic of the views and attitudes of neo-fascists in Germany?" Hajo observed that this was not "soft" antisemitism, but was "openly rage-based antisemitism." He then leaned forward in his chair and enunciating carefully, as if to ensure that, despite the somewhat convoluted context of his words, they would be fully understood:

> This full scale of contempt like in the word *Judenpack,* this absolutely cynicism with which Irving is referring to the most deep causing sorrows of the people of the Jewish descent, this kind of extreme radical racist, post Holocaust antisemitism is . . . at the core of these groups that I call neo-National Socialists.[18]

When Hajo finished, Rampton quietly said, "Thank you very much, indeed, Professor." Maybe I was projecting my own feelings, but my Scottish-born, Oxford-educated, fly-fishing, cartoon-drawing, and rugby-loving barrister seemed to be thanking Hajo for far more than just testifying at this trial.

*   *   *

Irving then rose to defend his use of the "one-man gas chamber" anecdote. It demonstrated the "lurid" and "totally ludicrous" eyewitness evidence that has been cited to prove the existence of gas chambers. Moreover, he insisted, he had also spoken at the rally of the appalling horrors undoubtedly suffered by the victims of Auschwitz. Wasn't it "dishonest," he asked Hajo, for the defense to use "just that passage . . . as a representation of my entire speech?" Hajo, who tends to be a mild-mannered man, angrily observed that Irving had not just poked fun at the survivors this one time, but did it "again and again." Citing Irving's promise to form ASSHOLS, an organization of Auschwitz survivors, Hajo insisted that "This cannot be. If you honestly, if you seriously are saying that you realize the trauma of those who . . . survived."[19] Once again in the closing days of this trial, Irving was being called to account. He could not have it both ways—call the survivors liars but deny being a Holocaust denier.

At the end of the day I left the courtroom with James, Rampton, and Heather. As Rampton lit his cigarette, he observed that our worries about Hajo's English had been unnecessary and that the longer he was on the stand, the more he became a prosecutor of sorts, deftly drawing on moral principles that harkened back to Hajo's Jesuit education. I told the others that Peter's and Hajo's testimony had moved me deeply. They seemed to not just be defending historical truth. They seemed to also be defending their country against political predators. James, who had spent countless hours compiling material on Irving's right-wing extremism, believed that Irving considered postunification Germany a fertile field for his politics. "His visits to Germany," James observed, "seem eerily different from his speaking tours in Canada or the U.S."

As we neared the street, Heather observed, "For the past two months we have been living in the Third Reich. During the past few days we have begun to emerge into the present. The question remains: which is more repulsive?"

# EIGHTEEN

# ONE-PERSON GAS CHAMBERS AND WHITE PEOPLE'S POLKAS

**"S**o how do you feel, now that we can see the light at the end of the tunnel?" Anthony smiled at my question, which I posed as I caught up with him on the stairs to the courtroom. Today was the last regular session. We would then recess for a week to prepare for closing arguments. I told Anthony that I was finding it hard to fathom that we were approaching the end. The team that had worked so closely together was about to disband. I expected him to find this a bit maudlin and to protest—a bit too much—that this was how trials worked, a group comes together, works intensively, and then disbands. Instead, with unmistakable melancholy, he agreed it would be hard. "This was a good team and an important battle." Just then Janet called for silence. Anthony looked relieved.

## STRATEGIC TASTELESSNESS

Rampton began by playing a videotape of a 1991 speech Irving had given in Ontario. Irving had repeated for his audience the "one-person gas chamber" anecdote about the telephone booth that, he said, was carried around the Polish countryside by two Germans. Irving claimed that according to "eyewitnesses" the Germans convinced people to get in the gas chamber by ringing the phone inside. His audience laughed. Rampton turned off the tape: "How many eyewitness accounts and who were the people that told these stories?" Irving was emphatic: "Alleged survivors of Auschwitz." "How many?" Rampton demanded. "Certainly one account," Irving responded. That was all Rampton needed. Relying on a rhetorical device he had used before, he repeated one word from Irving's Ontario speech and added his own commentary: " 'Eyewitness*es*,' *plural?*" Irving brushed away his use of the plural. It was just "a slip of the tongue." "It is not," Rampton said. "It is a deliberate exaggeration. . . . You got some good laughs with this little story." Irving defended telling this anecdote. Not only was it a "ludicrous story" but it illustrated how historians selectively use the eyewitness accounts. "They take the ones that they like and they ignore the ones that are obviously baloney." Rampton wondered why a serious historian would recite a story that was "obviously untrue."[1]

And why, he continued, did the Ontario audience find this anecdote so funny? Irving claimed he kept his audience interested "by interlacing the serious documents that you want them to listen to with material to keep them awake." Rampton offered a different explanation. "What you are doing is . . . mocking the survivors and, indeed, the dead from the Holocaust." When Irving insisted he was not mocking survivors, Rampton countered by reading Irving's comments about the stories spread by people who "went to Auschwitz or . . . who believed they went to Auschwitz, or . . . who can kid themselves into believing they went to Auschwitz. . . ." Irving had told his audience that these "little legends" must be treated with "ridicule and . . . bad taste. . . . [But] ridicule alone is not enough. You have got to be tasteless about it. You have got to say things like more women died on the back seat of Senator Edward Kennedy's car at Chappaquiddick than died in the gas chambers of Auschwitz."[2] Rampton pointedly noted that Irving's quip had been met with applause.

Rampton's voice bristled: "Mr Irving, what you are doing here—" Irving interrupted to finish Rampton's sentence: "Mocking the liars." Rampton, looking away from Irving: "Oh yes, Mr Irving, but why the applause?" Irving responded, "Because I am a good speaker, Mr Rampton." His answer caught Rampton off guard. "What?" In a tone suggesting that the answer was self-evident, Irving repeated, "I am a good speaker." Rampton, having regained his footing, had a different explanation: "You are . . . feeding, encouraging, the most cynical radical antisemitism in your audiences." Irving shot back, "Do liars not deserve to be exposed as such?"

The judge interrupted this heated interchange to ask Irving to clarify his statement about survivors: "Are you saying that they have come to believe what they say about their experiences and that is why they need psychiatric treatment? Or . . . that they are collectively telling lies, deliberate false-hoods?" Appearing happy to expand upon his views directly to the judge, Ir-ving described Auschwitz as having become akin to a religion. "As with any religion, there are hangers on, people who believe they were there, people who believe they touched the cloth." Irving admitted he had been tasteless. Rampton interjected, "And your audience absolutely love it. . . . It is music to their ears." Irving stood up straight and possibly forgetting the context of the question, rather proudly responded, "They travel 200 miles sometimes to . . . hear me speak."[3]

Rampton looked like he was about to respond. Then, apparently having decided that Irving's answer spoke for itself, moved on.

## IRVING AND THE NATIONAL ALLIANCE: AN INADVERTENT CONNECTION?

From Irving's diaries and correspondence files, we discovered that, during visits to the United States, he had spoken on a number of occasions at meet-ings sponsored by the National Alliance (NA), an organization whose goal was to build societies "throughout the White world which are based on Aryan values" and to thoroughly root out "Semitic and non-Aryan values and customs everywhere."[4] The NA's founder, William Pierce, authored *The Turner Diaries*, which had become the underground bible of American far-right extremists.[5]

In response to our pretrial interrogatory about his NA connections, Ir-ving had denied ever having spoken at any of their meetings. Rampton now asked Irving to concede that this statement was false.[6] When Irving insisted that it was not, Rampton reminded him of a video we had found in his col-lection that showed Irving giving a speech with an NA banner by his left shoulder. Irving insisted he was completely unaware of the banner's signifi-cance, therefore his denial was earnest.

Rampton looked skeptical, but did not challenge Irving's disclaimer. In-stead he introduced a letter Irving had received detailing the arrangements for a June 1990 speech in Ohio. In the corner were the words "National Al-liance" and the group's logo. Irving insisted he had paid no heed to either one. Once again Rampton looked unconvinced, but did not challenge him.

He then asked Irving to look at a National Alliance bulletin that reported the following: "On October 1st, the Cleveland unit hosted a very successful lecture by the British historian and revisionist author, David Irving. More than 100 tickets were sold . . ." Irving's photograph accompanied the article. Irving, assuming he knew what would be Rampton's question, jumped right in: "Have I ever seen that before? The answer is no." Rampton asked Irving to be patient and assured him that his question would come, but only after several more documents. Rampton continued and read Irving's diary entry about the Cleveland meeting: "Fine meeting, around 150 people, many ethnic Germans. Gate of $500 was agreed plus $1700 book sales." Irving emphatically noted that "there is not the slightest reference either in that diary entry or in any other diary entry . . . to the National Alliance." Rampton reproved Irving in a tone a parent might use with an obstreperous child: "I asked you to be patient. You have jumped in as you so often do." Then, rather nonchalantly, Rampton asked Irving to turn to the next document. As he did, Heather passed a copy of it to me. A quick glance revealed Rampton's strategy. On October 6, 1991, five days after the Cleveland meeting, Irving wrote in his diary: "Drove all day to Tampa. . . . Arrived at the Hotel Best Western. . . . *Turned out the meeting here is also organized by the . . . National Alliance*" (emphasis added). A flicker of surprised recognition crossed Irving's face. "It just goes to show how bad my memory is." Then, trying to extricate himself from this predicament, he continued, "Yes, but it . . . illustrates, does it not, the fact that . . . I had not the slightest notion who these people are." In a tone I had not heard previously, Irving rather plaintively asked Rampton, "Would *that* be a proper interpretation to put on that entry?" Not surprisingly, Rampton disagreed. He reread Irving's diary entry: " '[T]he meeting here—Tampa—is *also* organized by the . . . National Alliance.' In other words you knew that *both* meetings were organized by the National Alliance?" When Irving declared that he learned who the organizers were after the meeting, Rampton reminded him that in the videotape of his speech in Tampa the host opened the meeting by announcing: "On behalf of the National Alliance and National Vanguard Books I would like to proudly welcome Mr David Irving." Rampton, rather solicitously asked Irving, "Do you want to revise your evidence?"[7] I whispered to James, "Did Rampton just ask him if he wanted to admit he had lied?" James smiled. Irving insisted that the man in the video had simply put in a "plug" for his own organization and that he had not "the faintest notion" of who organized this meeting. Rampton declared, "I take leave, . . . Mr Irving, to inform you that I reject every word of that answer."[8]

In 1998, Irving had spoken at yet another National Alliance meeting. A representative from the American Jewish Committee had attended and picked up National Alliance books and tapes. When Rampton asked Irving to look at this material, Irving dismissed it as irrelevant: "What possible relevance [could] whatever leaflet was on the table 100 feet away from me [have]?" Before Rampton could respond, Judge Gray interjected, "I regard it as being relevant to know what sort of an organization it is that you have addressed on three occasions." Irving, looking a bit surprised, turned toward the judge and declared, "My Lord, I object to the suggestion that I was addressing an organization. I was addressing my people who had come from all over Northern Florida to hear me speak. . . . I am sure it was a slip of the tongue, but I would hate it to go on the record unchallenged." Judge Gray ignored Irving's protest. Rampton did likewise. I wished he had asked Irving what he meant by "my people."

In an effort to illustrate what the NA stood for, Rampton took out its *Statement of Belief.* He warned that it sounded like a "modern English American version of Nazi ideology." Irving protested. "What has that got to do with me?" Rampton angrily responded, "You fuel these people with your thoughts about the Holocaust, Mr Irving. That is why [sic] it has got to do with you."[9]

From a section entitled "White Living Space," Rampton read: "After the sickness of multi-culturalism . . . has been swept away we must again have a racially clean area of the earth for the further development of our people." On its website the organization promised the creation of an "Aryan Society" in which young men and women would dance "polkas or waltzes, reels or jigs, or any other White dances, but never undulate or jerk to Negroid jazz or rock rhythms." Rampton asked Irving if the Alliance's warning about the "sickness of multi-culturalism" resonated to him. When Irving said no, Rampton reminded him of his declaration about "feeling queasy" when he saw blacks playing for the English cricket team, his description of AIDS as God's Final Solution against black Africans and homosexuals, and his proposal that a black newscaster be "relegated to reading the news about muggings and drug busts." Irving insisted these were jokes, not "racial incitement." Rampton looked up at Irving over his gold-rimmed spectacles. His raised eyebrows clearly indicated what he thought of Irving's explanation.

Rampton returned to the NA's statement. "We must have White schools, White residential neighborhoods, and recreational areas, White workplaces, White farms and countryside." Again Irving protested, "But what has it [to] do with me?" Rampton angrily insisted, "It has everything to do with you." Before Irving could respond, Judge Gray interrupted: "You say that this is . . . news to you? . . . How [then] do you react to this sort of stuff?" Irving declared, "It is a most appallingly badly written piece of propaganda." Even the unflappable Charles Gray seemed caught off guard. Unable—or possibly unwilling—to camouflage his surprise, he repeated, "Badly written?" The statement, Irving continued, did not "interest me in the slightest . . . and I do not intend to retain it in my memory quite frankly."[10] Rampton stared at Irving for a moment and then rather deliberately laid the NA's manifesto down. He seemed glad to be rid of it.

While questioning Irving, Rampton suddenly asked him if he had been reading the Eichmann manuscript. When Irving said he had not, Rampton suggested that he do a word search for the word *Vergasungslager* (gas camps).[11] That alone would demolish deniers' arguments. Though the manuscript had really come too late to be of much help to us, I knew how grateful Rampton was to the Israelis for releasing it to us. Rampton knew how pleased I was that historians would now have free access to this material. This was, I assumed, his way of signaling our appreciation.

Moving on to a new topic, Rampton asked Irving what he knew of the British National Party (BNP), which opposed nonwhite immigration into the United Kingdom and endorsed repatriation of blacks and Asians already living there. It had links to the National Front, a group with a reputation for ruthless violence against immigrants. The leader of the BNP used to be photographed in jackboots and armband in front of pictures of Adolf Hitler.[12] Irving told Rampton that he knew no more about the BNP than he did about the NA. Rampton asked Irving, "You speak to them, do you not?" Irving responded, "No." Rampton continued, "Or you have done?" Again, Irving responded, "No." Once again Irving walked into a trap of his own making. We had found his correspondence with the BNP in his files. After Irving's second—very unqualified—"No," Rampton asked him to look at a letter that was written on BNP stationery. "British National Party, Yorkshire region. Dear Mr Irving, further to our telephone conversation today, I am writing to confirm that we would be very happy for you to come up to Leeds on Friday 14th September to address a special northern regional meeting."

When Rampton finished reading, Irving protested that this was just like functions in America where a "local functionary of some political group is inviting me to come and address an umbrella body." Judge Gray, who sounded more than a touch annoyed, interrupted Irving's answer: "Mr Irving, *come on*, that is letter [*sic*] on the stationery of the British National Party."

This back-and-forth was followed by one of the stranger and more revealing non sequiturs by Irving. Earlier, in his diary, we had found an entry made while he was in Key West, Florida. "12 midday. Kirk Lyons phoned. Going to London . . . for BNP meeting." Rampton asked Irving about Lyons and his connection with the BNP. After identifying Lyons as an American lawyer and insisting he had no idea of his connection with the BNP, Irving said, "Speaking of my first lawyer, who was Michael Rubenstein who was my lawyer for 25 years . . . and may be familiar to this court." Rampton, looking rather disgusted, responded, "Many of my best friends are Jews too, Mr Irving."[13]

## JEWS AND CRIME

Rampton now turned to the section of Irving's book *Goebbels* that attributed the Nazi propaganda chief's antisemitism to his encounter with Jewish criminals in Berlin in the late 1920s. From then on, Irving wrote, Goebbels "would highlight every malfeasance of the criminal demi-monde and identify it as Jewish." Irving had then told his readers that Goebbels "was unfortunately not always wrong," Jews were heavily involved in crime:

> In 1930 Jews would be convicted in forty-two of 210 known narcotics smuggling cases; in 1932 sixty-nine of the 272 known international narcotics dealers were Jewish. Jews were arrested in over sixty

percent of the cases concerning the running of illegal gambling dens; 193 of the 411 pickpockets arrested in 1932 were Jews.

Irving concluded this section of his book with a startling assertion: "In 1932 no fewer than thirty-one thousand cases of fraud, mainly insurance swindles, would be committed by Jews." Irving accompanied this sweeping indictment of Jews' criminal actions with a footnote containing four different sources.

> Interpol figures, in Deutsches Nachrichten-Büro (DNB), July 20, 1935; and see Kurt Daluege, 'Judenfrage als Grundsatz' in Angriff, Aug 3, 1935 . . . ; on the criminal demi-monde of 1920s Berlin, see Paul Weiglin, Unverwüstliches Berlin . . . and Walther Kiaulehn, Berlin: Schicksal einer Weltstadt.[14]

Rampton began by asking Irving to identify Kurt Daluege, whose article Irving had cited in the footnote. Irving responded, "He was the head of the Ordnungspolizei which is the Order Police in Germany." Rampton's Scottish brogue sounded a bit more pronounced than usual, as he rather casually added, "Yes, Mr Irving. Tell us a wee bit more about him." Irving responded so matter-of-factly that he could have been recounting the man's university activities: "Oh, he was a mass murderer later on. He was in charge of all the killing on the Eastern Front." Daluege had joined the SS in the late 1920s. In 1935 he became chief of police in the Interior Ministry and eventually was in charge of the Order Police, the reserve police units that participated in the murder of Jews in the East. After Heydrich's assassination in 1942, he became acting Reichsprotektor of Bohemia and Moravia. It was under his watch that the infamous Lidice massacre occurred. In 1946, he was executed by a Czech court for these and other crimes.

Rampton, rather drolly, observed, "One should be rather cautious, perhaps, about what one is told by Mr Daluege."[15] Rampton noted that Irving's statistics about Jewish criminal activities came from Daluege's July 1935 press conference at which the Nazi leader told foreign reporters that Jews were criminals. In a subsequent article in Der Angriff, a major Nazi propaganda outlet, Daluege reiterated his accusations about Jews and posited that the "number of cases of fraud in the Reich's capital . . . [were] 31,000 in 1933." Under the Nazis, Daluege wrote, this number had dropped to eighteen thousand but "a considerable part, if not the largest of these fraudulent manipulations are still committed by Jews."[16]

When Evans and his team compared Daluege's statement with Irving's rendition in *Goebbels*, they found dramatic discrepancies. Whereas Daluege had blamed a *portion* of the eighteen thousand cases of fraud on Jews, Irving wrote: "In 1932 no fewer than thirty-one thousand cases of fraud, mainly insurance swindles, would be committed by Jews." Dismissing Irving's mix-up of 1932 and 1933 as irrelevant, Rampton observed that Irving had almost doubled the number of fraud cases Daluege attributed to Jews. Furthermore, Daluege had not mentioned "insurance fraud." Irving, apparently, had invented that. Rampton did not stop there. Though Irving's footnote cited the authoritative-sounding "Interpol figures," this too, apparently, was an Irving creation. There was no reference to Interpol in the DNB press release. Irving also failed to inform his readers that the DNB was not a traditional press agency, but was an arm of Goebbels's Propaganda Ministry.*

"Even assuming, which I do not," Rampton continued, "that this was an innocent mistake on your part to double the number of offences attributable to Jews, do you think it right, when your source is this man Daluege, [to] uncritically simply to take his figures as being right?" Ignoring the fact that Daluege, as a leading Nazi, was not the most unbiased source on Jews, Irving defended him as a reliable source. "He was the head of the German police system. He was in a position to know." Rampton dismissed Irving's explanation. "This is a case of deliberate distortion by you so as to inflate the number of wicked, dishonest Jews in Berlin in 1932. . . . You double Daluege's numbers . . . you have relied on an unreliable source, you have attributed his figures to Interpol and you have spoken about insurance swindles which are not mentioned in Daluege's document."[17]

Irving now insisted that the information on Jewish criminal activities came from the two books cited in the footnote. Nik scribbled a note and passed it to Rampton. Rampton quickly read it and announced, "All the figures, I am told, come from Daluege." Irving, abandoning the two books,

*Interpol, the international crime-fighting organization, was formed in 1923. Its headquarters were in Vienna. In 1938, after the Anschluss, the Germans took control of the organization and moved it to Berlin where they used it, in the main, as a vehicle for the persecution of Jews, Gypsies, and homosexuals. After World War II it was reconstituted as an international organization.

now insisted that he had relied on the German Federal Statistical Office for his figures of Jewish criminal activity. Rampton took a quick look at the clock on the side of the room. It was 12:50. He seemed anxious to make his point before we broke for lunch. He handed Irving a copy of a page from the official German Criminal Statistics. He directed Irving to a line on the ledger that showed there had been, in fact, a total of seventy-four cases of insurance fraud in *all* of Germany in 1932. The thousands of cases of insurance fraud by Berlin Jews alone was clearly a figment of Irving's imagination. Holding this page out in front of him, Rampton said, "Any reputable historian would have gone to this document, as opposed to some rabid Nazi's utterance, to find out what the truth was."

Irving, no longer insisting his figures were correct, now argued that, if he had committed errors about Jewish criminals, they were not deliberate. "You do not establish a reputation by making deliberate errors." Rampton, shaking his head in great—and somewhat theatrical—dismay, said, "Well, I think I have about 25 in my pocket by now Mr Irving and that is the 26th."[18] With that we broke for lunch.

During lunch, Rampton and Anthony got into a debate over deconstructionism, the literary theory that challenges attempts to ascribe an ultimate meaning to a text. Using linguistic analysis, it "deconstructs" the ideological biases that shape literary, historical, and philosophical texts. Rampton challenged Anthony to explain why deconstructionism was not just another version of skepticism and, therefore, was not of particular interest or importance. Anthony argued that, while it may be a form of skepticism, it was also a disciplined method of reading. Though I thought deconstructionism, taken at its most simplistic level, had fostered an attitude of "the text can mean whatever I think it means," I did not participate in the debate. I just sat back, sipped a glass of 1992 *Clos de La Roche, Dujac,* and reflected on the delicious irony of this conversation, of these two men who had spent innumerable amounts of time on this case, only to devote its final moments to a debate about literary theory. Happy that the trial was nearing its end, I knew that I'd miss, not only the legal team, but moments such as these with their fine wines and clever repartee.

After lunch, Rampton asked a few follow-up questions and then, with no fanfare, announced that he was done. Judge Gray reminded Irving that he could reexamine himself. Irving declined. The substantive part of the trial was effectively over. We would gather in two weeks for closing speeches but the nine-week daily court routine was done.

The next day a few of us gathered for a celebratory lunch. Rampton chose Livebait, a fish restaurant in Waterloo, which, with its tiled floors and waiters in big white aprons, was a nice change from London's trendy minimalist restaurants. Over a lunch of Dover sole and carefully chosen white wine, we analyzed the preceding weeks. Rampton praised Hajo for having put Irving on the defensive. "I did not have to cross-examine Irving on his German right-wing connections. You did it for me." He then handed Peter the sketch he had made while he testified. Peter smiled when he saw himself depicted as Saint Peter standing in the witness box. As we talked, drank, and laughed, I could feel the tension dissipating. We were emerging, Hajo said, from a "cosmos of death."

## JUDICIAL RESTRAINT AND LIMITED EXPECTATIONS

I looked forward to continuing this celebratory atmosphere that evening at Shabbat dinner. Generally, I declined invitations because at the end of each week I felt exhausted. This time, I had made an exception in part because the hostess mentioned that one of the guests was a judge at the High Court. "Though he has nothing to do with your case he had to obtain permission from the Lord Justice to attend because you are coming." I thought he might help me deconstruct—in the nonliterary sense—some of the events of the previous weeks.

The judge was affable and the evening informal and relaxed. As dinner drew to an end and the Fortnum and Masons chocolates I had brought were making the rounds, he turned to me and said, "The perception at the Law Courts is that your defense team is doing well. Everyone seems to think you will win." Thinking he might have some inside information, I asked as dispassionately as I could, "What's your source?" Understanding my drift, he chuckled and said, "Oh, no one knows what Charles Gray is thinking. This is strictly the impression of the many people who have attended the sessions." Even his clerks, he added with a wry smile, had found time to attend.

Buoyed by his words, I declared, "I want an unequivocal victory. I want to beat this guy. Bad." The judge suddenly grew serious and, in a cautionary tone, added, "Allow me to give you fair warning: Do not anticipate a rousing condemnation of Irving from Charles Gray. British judges practice judicial restraint. A judge who believes a witness lied will say: 'I did not find this witness helpful.' Everyone at the Law Courts knows this is judicial shorthand for 'He's a liar.' The judge, however, is not going to say so."

My heart sank. I heard the voices of those who had predicted that, irrespective of the outcome, this would be a lose/lose situation. "You might win the battle," they had said, "but lose the war. Even if he loses, he will reinterpret the verdict to make it sound as if the judge found for him." They had warned that Irving would take any ambiguity in the judge's decision and twist it to his advantage. My feelings of an imminent victory evaporated. A restrained judgment would be the equivalent of a defeat.

# NINETEEN

# THE FINAL SCENE

It was with the fear of winning the battle and losing the war that I arrived at the Law Courts for closing arguments. The courtroom was packed. Reporters and paparazzi, whose interest had waned during the closing weeks of the trial, were waiting. The Blumenthals and Ken Stern had returned. They were joined by my sister, niece, close friends from Atlanta and other places. All the regulars—from both sides of the aisle—were present. Once again survivors of the Holocaust were sitting cheek by jowl with Irving's supporters. Extra chairs had been set up. I felt as if I was in a theater where the curtain was about to rise on the last performance of a long-running show. Janet Purdue was happily exerting control. Apparently, having decided that this occasion warranted breaking her rules, she was instructing people where they could stand. She even let some people sit on the steps of the public gallery. One of the paralegals arrived and excitedly announced, "It's bedlam out there. The queue goes out the hall, around the corner, and down the steps."

At 10:25, Janet hurriedly and very purposefully walked to the front of the room—her black gown flowing behind her as if it were trying to keep up with her. She ascended to the top step of the judge's bench and turned to survey the room. The crowd immediately jumped to its feet. She looked at us with a surprised smile: "But I didn't say anything yet." People laughed at their own Pavlovian response and sat down. A few minutes later she reappeared. This time her decided sense of authority left no doubt that it was time to rise. As she emitted her familiar call, she let each syllable linger in the air for an added moment, effectively rendering the one word into three:

*"SI-LEN-CE."* As Judge Gray entered and walked to his seat, his stride bespoke a particular purposefulness. After taking his seat, he looked all around the room, as if he too was assessing the assembled crowd.

The session began, as it always did, with housekeeping. Irving told Judge Gray that he wished to include in his closing arguments comments on the global conspiracy against him. Judge Gray had previously declared the topic irrelevant, unless linked directly to me or to Penguin Books. Irving asked for permission, arguing that it would explain "my state of mind when I am alleged to have made certain remarks about the bodies or the persons concerned." He seemed to recognize that he had not helped his cause with his comments about crooked Jewish financiers, description of the Board of Deputies as "cockroaches," and accusation that survivors tattooed numbers on their arms to make money. This time Judge Gray agreed to Irving's request. "I know the Defendants are not very happy about this but I think I am going to do it anyway."[1]

Judge Gray was right. I was not happy. I did not think his decision would materially impact the judgment, but I worried that we would be subjected to a long excursion through material that would make extreme assertions about my involvement in various diabolical schemes to destroy David Irving. I knew that Rampton, convinced that the judge considered the issue irrelevant, would not respond to these charges about a global conspiracy. Forensically, that was a wise decision, but it would leave Irving's baseless accusations about me to once again go unchallenged.

## RAMPTON: IRVING'S BOGUS HISTORY

It was time to begin. Rampton rose, laid his text on the small podium in front of him, took a deep breath, and slowly scanned the public gallery. He seemed to be looking for someone. Then he began. "If one had read some of the media reports of this trial . . . one might have supposed that Mr Irving had been dragged into this court to defend his freedom of expression as an historian. In fact, of course, that is not so. The history of the matter is quite the reverse." Rampton acknowledged that I had leveled serious accusations against Irving. These charges were so serious that, had they "been untrue, Mr Irving would clearly have been entitled to a large sum of money and an order of the court preventing the Defendants from repeating their accusations. But, the[y] are true in every significant respect."[2]

Rampton estimated that we had presented close to thirty examples of Irving's historical malfeasance. They could not be inadvertent mistakes because they all moved in the same direction: exculpation of Hitler and denial of the Holocaust. Rampton, in his typical economy of style, illustrated his charge with just two examples. Irving's version of *Kristallnacht*—particularly his claim that Hitler, unaware of the event, was "livid" when he learned of it and tried to "halt the madness"—was completely bogus. In fact, Rampton continued, arson—and *only* arson—against Jewish owned shops was halted. "Synagogues, houses, apartments, cemeteries, and, in particular, Jewish people were left to the mercy of the continuing violence."

Irving's claim that the perpetrators were punished was equally false. In fact, Rampton stressed, "nothing could be further from the truth." The authorities exonerated all those who damaged Jewish property and treated with a "rap on the knuckles" those guilty of assault and murder. Only those guilty of sexual offenses—"race defilement"—were prosecuted. Murdering Jews was acceptable. Raping them was not. Irving knew this. He had cited the documents that contained this information. However, he never mentioned it to his readers.[3]

Rampton's second example of falsification of history concerned Hitler's two-day April 1943 meeting with Admiral Horthy of Hungary. Irving's attempt to link Hitler's concerns about Jews in Budapest to the Warsaw Ghetto uprising was a total distortion, given that the meeting occurred two days *before* the uprising. Irving had skewed the tenor of the meeting by saying it concluded with Hitler's declaration that there was "no need for that [the murder of the Jews]," when it actually ended with "Hitler's chilling observation about the need to kill the Jewish 'beasts.' "

These two examples were "but the tip of a large iceberg of numbers of other equally egregious falsifications by Mr Irving." With a bit of rhetorical flourish, he echoed his opening statement delivered ten weeks earlier: " 'Mr Irving is a liar.' The Defendants say, on this part of the case: 'Case proved.' "[4]

## GAS CHAMBER MANIPULATIONS

Irving, Rampton continued, had engaged in the same manipulation and falsification of sources regarding the gas chambers. During the trial, however, he had been forced to retreat. "Mr Irving has been driven, in the face of overwhelming evidence . . . to concede that there were indeed mass murders on a huge scale by means of gassing at Chelmno . . . [and] the camps of Belzec, Treblinka, and Sobibor, and even that there were 'some gassings' at Auschwitz." Irving had also made a "slippery concession" that the gas chambers at Birkenau were used for gassing "objects and cadavers." Rampton declared that "if this were not such a serious matter, it would be hilarious." Why, Rampton wondered, would a room for gassing objects and cadavers have a spyhole in the door? Why would that spyhole be covered with a heavy metal grille on the inside? Why, when the crematoria buildings were transformed in 1942 to gas chambers, were the chutes for sliding bodies to the morgue replaced with steps? Were the "objects and cadavers" supposed to walk down the steps?

Irving's claim that the gas chamber was an air-raid shelter was "equally absurd." The notion of SS personnel running from their barracks one and a half miles to the crematoria, under a hail of bombs, was "just plain daft."[5] Irving had tried to argue that there was not enough fuel at Auschwitz to incinerate all the corpses. When we produced a letter from Bischoff, the head of Auschwitz's building program, demonstrating that the potential incineration capacity was more than sufficient, how, Rampton asked, did Irving react? "Mr Irving's only . . . response was—as ever—to challenge [its] authenticity." When confronted with the information that this letter had been found in the Moscow archives right after the war and had been introduced at war crimes trials in 1948 and in 1971, Irving had posited that the letter was a Communist forgery. That claim was also contradicted by the evidence that the incineration capacity stated in the letter was "significantly lower" than the Soviet's postwar estimates. Why would the Communists create a forgery that was at odds with their own theory about the number of people killed? Rampton closed this section of his summation by dismissing these claims—cadavers and objects, air-raid shelters, insufficient coke, forged letters—as "fragile conjectures based on no significant research at all."[6]

Irving, Rampton declared, was a "right-wing extremist, a racist, and, in particular, a rabid antisemite." Irving had described his own speech at the neo-Nazi rally in Halle, where he had been greeted with chants of *"Sieg Heil"* as "rabble rousing." Rampton quickened the tempo of his words. "Why Mr Irving should have engaged so actively in the promotion of these historical falsehoods? . . . Mr Irving is an antisemite. Holocaust denial . . . is music to the ears of the neo-Nazis and other right-wing extremists to whom he purveys it."

Finally, Rampton addressed a question that still perplexed some of us who had spent too much time and too many years trolling through Irving's words. "How far . . . Mr Irving's antisemitism is a cause of his Hitler apology or vice versa, is quite unimportant. . . . [T]hey have led him to prostitute his reputation as a serious historian—spurious though it can now be seen to have been—for the sake of a bogus rehabilitation of Hitler and the dissemination of virulent antisemitic propaganda."[7]

With that Rampton, who had spoken for less than an hour, ended. As he was about to sit down, he paused and once again slowly scanned the public gallery as if he was looking for someone.

## SOME VERY STRANGE QUESTIONS

Charles Gray spoke next. He noted that in approximately twenty-five different instances, we had charged that Irving engaged in a deliberate distortion of the historical record. Did we believe, Judge Gray asked Rampton, that in the other instances where we had challenged Irving's conclusions, he had also deliberately falsified the record? Rampton responded by describing what Irving did as a deliberate blindness to the evidence. "What he does not like, he ignores." Judge Gray mused for a moment before responding: "So it is a telescope to the wrong eye?" Rampton, pleased with the judge's metaphor, agreed. Any evidence, he pointed out, that contradicts Irving's preexisting conclusions—an aerial photograph showing the holes in the roof or Bischoff's letter on incineration capacity—he dismisses as a forgery. "His denial must have another agenda," Rampton continued, "because it cannot be the product of genuine *bona fide* historical research and contemplation."[8]

Judge Gray introduced his next question with a comment: "It is important that I am absolutely clear what it is that is being suggested. . . . You put it as being deliberately perverse blindness and acting in pursuance of what is, effectively a neo-Nazi agenda. Is that right?" Rampton, who nodded again in affirmation, answered, "He is, at root, deeply antisemitic and a neo-Nazi." Judge Gray pursed his lips and waited for a moment as he seemed to reflect on Rampton's response.

He then posed what he described as his "last question": "If somebody is antisemitic . . . and extremist, [is] he perfectly capable of being, as it were, *honestly* antisemitic and *honestly* extremist in the sense that he is holding those views and expressing those views because they are, indeed, his views?"

I quickly checked the computer monitor to make sure I had heard right. Was Judge Gray suggesting that, if Irving honestly believed his antisemitic and racist statements, they were acceptable? I looked at James expecting him to reassure me, as he so frequently did, and to tell me I was overreacting. Instead, he was shaking his head in dismay. He turned around and locked eyes with Anthony, who looked equally bewildered.

Judge Gray continued. "It seems to me that . . . the antisemitism is a completely separate allegation which really has precious little bearing on your broader and, perhaps, more important case that Mr Irving has manipulated the data and falsified the record or do you say that they are connected in some way?" Judge Gray's suggestion that Irving's antisemitism had "precious little bearing" on our case was stupefying. Irving's antisemitism, we had repeatedly argued, was inexorably linked to his denial. Rampton seemed equally rattled. His initial response was uncharacteristically tentative. "I propose that they probably are connected." After a moment's hesitation, he spoke slightly less tentatively: "I propose that they are connected." Then, regaining his verbal footing, he became quite deliberate. "The bridge between Holocaust denial and the Hitler apology from antisemitism is very easy to build, because what more would an historian who is an antisemite want to do in exculpation of Hitler, which he has been trying to do by telling lies about history for years, what more would he want to do than to deny the Holocaust?"

Judge Gray returned to his original point. "Yes, but he might believe what he is saying. That is the point. That is why it is important." Shaking his head back and forth, Rampton insisted that since there were no good historical reasons for denying the Holocaust, Irving had to have another one. "The most obvious thing for a profound and genuine antisemite to do . . . is to leap into Holocaust denial . . . and to cart it around the world . . . to audiences of other antisemities and neofascists." Judge Gray, seeming to mull Rampton's words over in his mind, mused, "That is another agenda, you would say?" All traces of tentativeness on Rampton's part were gone: "Yes, that is the other agenda . . . the promotion of antisemitism. . . . Given that there is . . . absolutely no proper historical foundation for Holocaust denial, and given that there is evidence that Mr Irving is an antisemite . . . the bridge between the one and the other is very easy to build indeed."[9]

With that Judge Gray called a five-minute recess. Irving's closing statement would follow. I swung around to Anthony and Rampton. Rampton looked perturbed. Anthony, for the first time in the five years I had known him, was speechless. Ken Stern, who specialized in the study of extremists and antisemites, looked like a deer in headlights. I was scared. How could Judge Gray suggest that Irving's antisemitism had precious little bearing on our case? Rampton, sounding more concerned than at any time during the trial, declared, "I fear Charles Gray sees the trees but not the pattern they make." I wondered if he even saw the trees.

As we prepared to resume, I asked Rampton if he had been looking for someone when he scanned the gallery. "No," he replied, "I just wanted the survivors and their offspring to know that I was aware that they were there. This trial has caused them much pain. I wanted to pay them tribute."

## BANQUO'S GHOST, LIARS, AND PORNOGRAPHERS

Irving rose. "This trial is about my reputation as a human being, as an historian of integrity, and—thanks to the remarks made by Mr Rampton—as a father." Penguin and I had tried to drive him "out of business as an historian." This case, he proclaimed, was about free speech. Should he lose, historians would fear asking tough questions about the Holocaust.[10]

He denied that he falsified sources. His interpretation of events might not be the "most probable. But they are never perverse." Our accusation that he deliberately manipulated the evidence was "a foul one." At worst he had made some "innocent mistakes." Some resulted from the many drafts through which he had put his manuscripts.[11] Irving acknowledged having transposed the dates of the Hitler-Horthy meeting but accused us of making far too much out of that error. He declared the testimony of Marie Vaillant-Couturier, who had testified at Nuremberg about brothels at the camps, to be so riddled with "absurdities" that Judge Biddle had dismissed her *entire* testimony. Our charge that he had falsified Daluege's Jewish criminal statistics was "meaningless."[12] Had we checked all of his sources we would have found the statistics he had cited. Not surprisingly, Irving did not provide the court with the sources. He just declared us wrong.

Well into the second hour of his presentation Irving turned to the "international endeavor" against him. His more egregious statements were a response to this effort to destroy him. "[I]f I am accused of certain postures or uttering certain tasteless remarks, these momentary lapses are . . . explicable on the basis of . . . [a] 30 year international endeavor by a group of organizations to destroy my legitimacy as an historian." They were the real defendants, Irving thundered, they had not been in court "but their presence has been with us throughout like Banquo's ghost." I may have started my research with honest intentions, but they led me astray by providing me with a "cornucopia of filth." Raising his long arm and pointing his index finger in my direction, he declared, "She fell in with bad company."[13] My friend Rela, who had come from Philadelphia for the closing, passed me a note: "He can't seem to decide whether you are the powerful queen bee manipulating drones all over the world or a little lamb who was led astray."

Auschwitz, he charged, had "become, like the Holocaust itself, an industry, a big business in the most tasteless way." No one knew the number of victims who had died there or the specific events associated with their death. Suddenly Irving paused, lowered his head, and, in a somber voice, said, "I never forget in anything I have said or written or done the appalling suffering that has been inflicted on people in the camps like Auschwitz." Then, all traces of empathy having disappeared from his voice, he attacked the eyewitnesses who testified to the existence of gas chambers. French *Sonderkommando* David Olère was a pornographer who had portrayed the "victims of the Nazi killers mostly as nubile young females, all naked."[14] Heather winced.

The most outrageous of the liars were those who claimed to have seen holes in the gas chamber roof. Even van Pelt, he claimed, "accepts that those holes are not in that roof slab now." As soon as he said that, Judge Gray interrupted: "I am not sure that is right, is it? I think what he says was that the state of the collapsed roof is so poor now you simply cannot see where those holes would have been if they were there." Rampton, who had developed a close personal relationship with van Pelt, was already on his feet. His eyes were glowering as he charged Irving with a "continuous misrepresentation of the evidence of *my* witness." Irving, looking at Rampton with annoyance, if not contempt, asked, "May I now continue with preferably fewer interruptions?" Judge Gray admonished him: "No, I think that is not fair. Mr Rampton I think has been restrained. . . . that is quite an important misstatement of van Pelt's evidence."[15] Irving looked annoyed as he continued with a defense of his theories about the gas chambers. They *could* have been air-raid shelters. That would explain the peepholes, which were "standard fittings" on gas-tight air-raid shelter doors. Hearing this, Rampton emitted a cross between an angry sigh and a mumble of discontent. Judge Gray stopped Irving mid-sentence and looked at Rampton: "I would find it easier if there were not such an overt reaction to what you are saying on the other side of the court." Rampton, looking very embarrassed, apologized.[16]

## "MEIN FÜHRER": A SURREALISTIC SLIP

Irving began to address our allegations about his "racism and antisemitism" by glancing at the bench with a somewhat conspiratorial smile: "I have the feeling that your Lordship is not overly-impressed by them." Judge Gray quickly disabused him: "Do not get feelings one way or the other about any part of the case, Mr Irving." Smiling a bit sheepishly, Irving shrugged his shoulders: "It was a good try."[17] Irving's comment struck me as a metaphor for his modus operandi. He made a "good try" to prove Hitler innocent, Berlin Jews criminals, gas chambers "Disneyland" creations, and so much else. Until this trial, most of his "tries" had gone unchallenged.

As his speech moved into the third hour, I began to shift in my seat. I was beset by frustration and deep exhaustion. Anthony, who over the past two months had become quite adept at watching my back—in more ways than one—passed me a note: "I fear if he goes on much longer I will have to restrain you from jumping up and saying 'I surrender! I surrender! Please, just stop speaking.' "

The evidence we cited regarding his contacts with German extremists was naught but an attempt to smear him. Such was the case with the 1991 Halle rally. He had arrived shortly before his speech and had spoken for only a few moments when the crowd began to chant "Sieg Heil! Sieg Heil!" The defense, he charged, had made much of these chants, but had ignored the fact that he tried to stop them. "I am clearly heard to say, 'You must not,' because they are shouting the 'Sieg Heil' slogans."

Irving was anxious to distance himself from these chants. That may explain what happened next. After repeating that he tried to stop the chants, he looked at Judge Gray and, instead of punctuating his remarks with "my Lord," as he commonly did, he addressed him as "mein Führer."[18] There was a moment of intense silence as the entire courtroom—Judge Gray included—seemed frozen. Then everyone erupted in laughter. Ken Stern turned to James and said, "This is out of Dr. Strangelove." From behind me I heard someone humming the Twilight Zone theme. Irving, who seemed not to have grasped what had happened, marched on, accusing us of having used "guilt by association" to link him with extremist elements. Our tactics were reminiscent of the "inquisitions conducted by Senator Joseph McCarthy." He attacked Evans's "odious attempts to smear and defile my name which, I hope, will long haunt him in the common rooms at Cambridge." He dismissed his lectures for the IHR or the National Alliance with a "so what?" His spoke before any audience that wished to hear him. He defended his Dresden death tolls. Then, after almost four hours, he requested that Judge Gray award him "aggravated damages for libel and an injunction restraining the Defendants . . . from further publishing or causing to be published the said or similar words defamatory of myself as claimant."[19] With that he ended his speech.

Rampton rose to apologize for his outburst. "I should, at my age, know better. . . . It is sometimes extremely difficult to restrain oneself when one can actually hear the evidence of one's own witnesses being misrepresented." Judge Gray accepted his apology. He seemed ready to rise when he asked Irving, "You are going to forfeit the last word, are you?"[20] I was amazed when Irving agreed. With that the trial ended.

# THE AFTERMATH

Judge Charles Gray reading his judgment to a packed courtroom.

# TWENTY

# JUDGMENT DAY: PHONE CHAINS, PSALMS, AND SLEEPLESS SURVIVORS

After closing arguments I returned to Atlanta for two weeks. The judgment was scheduled to be handed down on Tuesday, April 11. One morning James called to inform me that the lawyers would receive the decision on Monday, twenty-four hours before it would be read in court. I asked, "Can we talk about it or do we have to keep quiet until Tuesday?" He responded, "We can't tell anyone. Including our clients. We can't tell you until one hour before Judge Gray reads it in court." I was annoyed that they would know and I wouldn't. James explained that this arrangement allowed the victor's lawyers to prepare a "cost order," a request that the loser immediately pay a portion of the costs. I grudgingly accepted James's explanation, until he added that because Irving was serving as his own lawyer, he too would receive it on Monday. I did a slow burn. It seemed patently unfair. I had been an observer to so much of this saga, despite the fact that it concerned my work and my reputation. I had been compelled to sit and listen to misstatements about my beliefs. And now Irving—who had instigated this suit—would know the outcome twenty-four hours earlier than I. At the moment, it seemed more than I could bear. Suddenly, five years of pent-up frustration burst forth in one uncensored stream of anguish. A colleague, who had walked into my office, expressed admiration at my "colorful language."

## ADRENALINE AND BANDS OF ANGELS

I returned to London on Sunday, April 9. At dinner I told James and his wife, Ann, of my recurring fear that the judgment would be so restrained that Irving would claim it as a victory. James did not discount my fears. Still annoyed that the lawyers would receive the verdict early, I told James I had devised a scheme. "I'll ask, 'How's the weather?' Depending on the verdict, you can answer either bright and sunny or overcast or dark and stormy." James's dismissive laughter made it clear my plan was a nonstarter.

On Monday a steady stream of reporters and camera crews arrived at my hotel. Aware that the judgment was already in my solicitors' hands, they asked if I had any "inkling" of the outcome. I told them I did not and admitted that it was excruciatingly difficult to remain in the dark when both my lawyers and Irving knew the verdict. Wary of predicting victory, I carefully monitored my words. Even though I could not speak as freely as I wished, it felt liberating not to have to depend on others to speak on my behalf. Though I tried to appear relaxed, the reporter from my "hometown" paper, the *Atlanta Journal Constitution,* saw things differently:

> Over coffee the day before the verdict, Lipstadt—described . . . by the Times of London as a "striking redhead"—was charged up in a way people often are when they find themselves in a favorable limelight. In Britain, as in the United States, she has been widely portrayed as the defender of good against David Irving's bumbling prince of darkness. In the sitting room at her elegant London hotel—Lipstadt's home away from home during the trial—a waitress brought her a small porcelain coffee pot. "Are you nervous?" the waitress asked politely as she set the pot and cup on the table before Lipstadt. "Adrenaline, adrenaline," said Lipstadt, who apparently decided that was all the stimulant she needed and asked for decaf. Each morning during the trial the uniformed doorman wished Lipstadt good luck as she headed off to court. When she returned at night, he asked her how it went. "The concierge told me to be optimistic because there is plenty of time to be pessimistic afterwards," she said, clearly proud of the quasi-family she acquired at the hotel. Lipstadt seems up to the fight, and believes the cause is worth the struggle.[1]

Douglas Davis, Jewish Telegraphic Agency correspondent, asked me what I had been doing since the end of the trial. "I returned to Atlanta to prepare for Passover. I have twenty people coming for *Seder.*" Astonished, he said: "You did WHAT?!" Other guests in the hotel lounge looked up, intrigued to know what I had done that evoked such a response. Davis found it difficult to fathom that, on the eve of the judgment, I was preparing for Passover. The answer to Davis's next query—"Has the trial changed your life?"—seemed obvious. I had been preparing for Passover for years and no one had ever thought that remotely interesting, much less newsworthy.

During the interviews, a number of reporters commented on my "dignity" during the trial. Since I had done nothing but remain silent, I was, at first, perplexed by their reaction. Then I realized that my silence was a dramatic contrast to Irving's behavior. The Reuters reporter recalled how Irving had told her his "domestic staff" included "very attractive girls with very nice breasts."[2] Two months later, she was still "stupefied" by the encounter. The London correspondent for Israel's *Haaretz* described how, when he visited Irving together with his colleague, Tom Segev, Irving told his daughter Jessica, the one to whom he had sung "I am a Baby Aryan," that Segev's baldness was a decidedly Jewish attribute.[3] Compared to that it was hard *not* to appear dignified.

By early evening the media madhouse subsided. Ken Stern arrived from Brooklyn. We shared a bottle of wine and a light dinner, which I prepared in my tiny kitchen, and speculated on the judgment. A lawyer who had argued before the Supreme Court, Ken shared my worries about a tentative and ambiguous judgment. Given Judge Gray's questions on the final day, neither of us knew what to expect. Our conversation was repeatedly interrupted by phone calls from France, Germany, Poland, Israel, the United States, Canada, Mexico, and Australia. I learned that the morning *minyan* at my synagogue would recite Psalm 51—"God, You are right in your sentence and just in Your judgment." Other friends had arranged an international phone chain and email distribution list to spread the word. My cousin, Lady Amelie Jakobovits, known throughout the British Jewish community as "Lady J," called from Poland, where she was accompanying a group of two hundred teenagers on a tour of Jewish sites. "Deborah," she said, "the young people are praying on your behalf."

Around 11 P.M., Ben Meed, president of the American Gathering of Jewish Holocaust Survivors and a survivor of the Warsaw Ghetto, called. A compact white-haired man, Ben's life was the world of Holocaust survivors. "Deborah," he said, "tonight you can sleep soundly because none of us will be sleeping." He did not have to identify the "us." There is a Jewish aphorism: "Things which come from the heart enter the heart." And so it was. I found the notion of survivors unable to sleep as they awaited news of the verdict hard to fathom. After a prolonged silence at my end, Ben, afraid that our connection had been cut, said, "Are you there?" I assured him I was and bid him goodnight. I sat at my desk looking out on the London streets, overwhelmed by it all. The adrenaline was gone.

The first night of Passover is called the "Night of Watching" because Jewish tradition posits that God watched over the Israelites as they fled Egypt. On *Seder* night Jews do not recite bedtime prayers requesting that God keep them safe throughout the night because, tradition has it, God is *already* on guard. I doubted Ben had this in mind when he told me that survivors would not be sleeping but, when I did go to sleep, I imagined myself surrounded by a band of resolute angels, whose lives had been shaped by the Holocaust and its attendant horrors.

## NO MORE WAITING

I arose early the next morning. My workout was determined and deliberate. I avoided chitchat with the other early-morning exercisers. As I walked through the lobby in my sweaty T-shirt and shorts, the hotel staff quietly wished me luck. The bellman gave me a thumbs-up. The concierge showed me that all his fingers were crossed. I carefully timed my preparation so I would arrive at the Mishcon offices precisely at 9:30. I did not wish to arrive early and have to nervously wait in the reception room. I did not wish to be late and delay hearing the news. I fumed as my taxi got stuck in Piccadilly's perennial traffic jam. At 9:30, I was still a few blocks from the office. I called Anthony: "It's nine-thirty. Well?" Laughing, he said, "We won. . . . Big." When I shrieked, the taxi driver hit the brakes. My papers went flying everywhere. I assured the driver all was fine. Anthony continued, "We won on everything except the Goebbels diaries in Moscow." Ignoring the fact that the glass was essentially totally full, I expressed dismay that we lost on Moscow. Anthony reassured me, "It doesn't matter. Wait until you see what the judge has to say about everything else." By then the taxi had reached the office, and I ran off without paying. Embarrassed, I returned and gave the driver ten pounds for a five-pound ride.

Too excited to wait for the elevator, I ran up the stairs. This moment British reserve was thrown out the window. Anthony, James, and I exchanged hugs. Laura Tyler arrived, grinning from ear to ear. We did a little victory dance. Over the preceding months, despite being a paralegal, Laura had assumed tasks usually assigned to lawyers. At strategy sessions she contributed as if she were a full partner in this team, which, in fact, she was. Her work had earned her just desserts. Mishcon had invited her to join the firm upon completion of the law course she would begin in the fall. Michaela, Anthony's secretary, warmly congratulated me and told me she was coming to hear the verdict. I was glad. She had been a stalwart worker throughout this process. James handed me the 355-page judgment. He had already highlighted significant sections of it. "Sit and read. You'll be pleased."

Judge Gray began his findings by praising Irving as a "*military* historian" and describing him as "able and intelligent (emphasis added)." After that it was all downhill for him. Our criticisms of his work were "almost invariably well founded." Irving had "significantly misrepresented what the evidence, objectively examined, reveals." Judge Gray's choice of words to describe Irving's writings about the Holocaust were unambiguous: "perverts," "distorts," "misleading," "unjustified," "travesty," and "unreal." I lifted my arms in victory, looking more like a prizefighter than a professor.

But there was work to do. We had scheduled a press conference for after the judgment. A few days earlier I had drafted a statement to read. I had written it in anticipation of victory, but my fears about an evenhanded judgment compelled me to keep it decidedly reserved. I edited it to reflect the sweeping nature of our victory. I quoted Judge Gray's findings: Irving's "falsification of the historical record was deliberate and . . . motivated by a desire to present events in a manner consistent with his own ideological beliefs even if that involved distortion and manipulation of historical evidence."[4] Never had I enjoyed editing so much. I was still scribbling when James announced that the taxi was waiting.

Photographers and demonstrators were crowded behind police barricades in front of the Law Courts. I asked, "Why all the press?" Anthony, sounding somewhat incredulous at my question, replied, "Deborah, they're here for us." Emerging from the taxi, I grabbed James by the arm and ran toward the building. Aware that I was still under embargo and could not yet broadcast the news, I tried to squelch the satisfied grin on my face and waved at the photographers.

Today's session had been moved to the largest courtroom in the Law Courts. It was packed. Reporters and spectators were standing three and four deep along the walls of the courtroom. As I walked to my seat, people whispered, "Good luck." Someone reassuringly patted me on the shoulder. Once I reached the front table, I turned to scan the room. Ninette Perahia, who had included me in a family supper during the first week of the trial and whose husband, Murray, had provided a musical interlude, was there as was her son, who had clearly ditched school to attend. Behind them a high school teacher, who had regularly attended the trial, held up both hands to show me her fingers were crossed. In the balcony Sir Martin Gilbert, Winston Churchill's official biographer, raised his fingers in a Churchillian V. I returned the gesture. The two gestures, though ostensibly identical, conveyed vastly different sentiments. His meant "good luck," while mine said "victory." It was hard not to give Richard Rampton a bear hug. Instead I took his hand in mine and quietly whispered, "Thank you, so very much." I exchanged smiles with Heather, who had promised me many months earlier as I sat despondent in Birkenau, that this trial would be about proving David Irving is a liar. I wanted to remind her of that moment, but it did not seem necessary.

## AN UNAMBIGUOUS JUDGMENT

Judge Gray entered and began to read his findings. His flat, unexpressive monotone was in striking contrast to the power of the words. I heard someone whisper, "Sounds like he's reading a grocery list." Referring to Evans's "meticulous" report, he declared that "Evans justified each and every one of the criticisms on which the Defendants have chosen to rely." One reporter caught my eye and mouthed the words "Well done." I saw Julie McCarthy slip out of the courtroom and assumed she was going to broadcast to National Public Radio's *Morning Edition*, which would soon begin. I was glad to know that my friends and family would awaken to this news.

Regarding Irving's claim that during the 1924 *Putsch* Hitler sought to maintain order, Judge Gray declared Irving had "embroider[ed] the incident" in order to depict Hitler as "behav[ing] responsibly."⁵ He criticized Irving's reliance on Kurt Daluege's summary of Jewish criminal statistics. Daluege's "enthusiastic membership" in the Nazi Party and his role in the shootings on the Eastern Front, should have made Irving "doubt any pronouncement of his affecting the Jews."⁶

Irving's rendition of Hitler's role in *Kristallnacht* was "at odds with the documentary evidence."⁷ His claim that "Hitler bore no responsibility" for starting the pogrom and that, upon learning of it, intervened to halt the violence, "seriously misrepresents the available contemporaneous evidence" and was "based upon misrepresentation, misconstruction, and omission of the documentary evidence." Irving's account of the trials of the culprits who participated in *Kristallnacht* "fails lamentably" to reveal what a "whitewash it was."⁸

Regarding Himmler's November 30, 1941, diary entry about his meeting with Hitler, there was "no evidence" that Hitler "summoned" Himmler to his headquarters or "obliged" him to telephone Heydrich ordering Jews not to be liquidated."⁹

Irving "perverted" General Bruns's account of the shooting of Jews in Riga. Bruns did *not* say that instructions had come from Hitler that the shootings were to stop, as Irving had claimed. Bruns had said that he had received orders that there should be no more shootings "on that scale" and those that did occur were to be carried out "more discreetly." In other words, Judge Gray observed, "the shooting was to continue."¹⁰

Irving's contention that Hitler did not know or approve of the "whole sale shooting of Jews in the East" and was not complicit in the gassing of Jews in death camps had "a distinct air of unreality."¹¹ Judge Gray was convinced that the shootings were coordinated and sanctioned by the leaders of the Third Reich. "Irving was misrepresenting the historical evidence when he told audiences in Australia, Canada, and the US . . . that the shooting of the Jews in the east was arbitrary, unauthorized, and undertaken by individual groups or commanders."¹²

Irving "materially pervert[ed] the evidence" of the Hitler-Horthy meeting.¹³ Irving's claim that Nuremberg judge Francis Biddle thought Marie Vaillant-Couturier a " 'bloody liar' is a travesty of the evidence."¹⁴ Regarding Dresden, Judge Gray found that Irving's comments about the authenticity of *TB-47* were "reprehensible."¹⁵ Irving had charged that Miller, the Dresden resident who participated in the burning of the bodies and who concluded that the death toll was approximately thirty thousand, was "fantasizing." Judge Gray dismissed this as "absurd."[16] He concluded that Irving's treatment of the historical evidence "fell far short of the standard to be expected of a conscientious historian" and that his estimate of "100,000 and more deaths [in Dresden] . . . lacked any evidential basis and were such as no responsible historian would have made."[17]

Judge Gray believed the "cumulative effect of the documentary evidence for the genocidal operation" of the gas chambers at "Auschwitz [to be] considerable" and "mutually corroborative." He found it "striking" that the eyewitness and documentary evidence were so "consistent." The *Leuchter Report* was insufficient reason for "dismissing or even doubting" the existence of homicidal gas chambers at Auschwitz. Judge Gray concluded that "no objective, fair-minded historian would have serious cause to doubt" the existence of gas chambers at Auschwitz that were used on a substantial scale to kill Jews.[18]

Judge Gray declared it "incontrovertible that Irving qualifies as a Holocaust denier." He had denied the existence of gas chambers at Auschwitz frequently and "in the most offensive terms," including in his telephone-booth-cum-gas-chamber anecdote, comments about Senator Edward Kennedy's car, dismissal of eyewitnesses as liars, ASSHOLS, and the question to Mrs. Altman about earning money from her tattoo.[19]

Irving had "repeatedly crossed the divide between legitimate criticism and prejudiced vilification of the Jewish race and people." His comments confirmed he was an "antisemite" and a "racist." His statements about minorities "provide ample evidence of racism." The ditty he composed for his daughter—"I am a Baby Aryan"—was "undeniably racism," while some of his other statements—his reference to "one of them" reading "our news to us"—were racism of a more "insidious kind." Irving's appearances at gatherings such as the Halle rally demonstrated his "willingness to participate in a meeting at which a motley collection of militant neo-Nazis were also present." The "regularity" of his contacts with the National Alliance confirmed his "sympathetic attitude towards an organization whose tenets would be abhorrent to most people."[20]

Judge Gray's critique became even more pointed when he addressed Irving's claim that, at worst, he had made some inadvertent historical mistakes.

Irving's treatment of the historical evidence is so perverse and egregious that it is difficult to accept that it is inadvertence on his part. . . . Mistakes and misconceptions such as these . . . are more consistent with a willingness on Irving's part knowingly to misrepresent or manipulate or put a "spin" on the evidence so as to make it conform with his own preconceptions. . . . He has deliberately skewed the evidence to bring it in line with his political beliefs.[21]

When Judge Gray turned to Irving's motivation for his Holocaust denial, I was reminded of the disturbing question he had posed on the final day of the trial. Could someone be "honestly antisemitic and an honest extremist?" Judge Gray had then seemed unable to recognize the link between antisemitism, extremism, and Holocaust denial. Now Judge Gray declared that Irving "desire[d] to present events in a manner consistent with his own ideological beliefs even if that involved distortion and manipulation of historical evidence." My fears had obviously been in vain.[22]

We did not succeed in convincing Judge Gray that Irving had engaged in an unauthorized borrowing of the Goebbels diaries glass plates in Moscow. However, Judge Gray continued, what we had proven was of sufficient gravity that this did not have any "material effect on Irving's reputation." Then, after close to two hours of reading, Judge Gray came to the bottom line: "It follows that there must be judgment for the Defendants."[23]

We had won and we had done so conclusively. As Judge Gray left the courtroom, Irving rose, turned to Rampton, stretched out his hand, and, somewhat jovially, said, "Well done. Well done," as if he had just been bested in a rugby match. Rampton rather perfunctorily took his hand but said nothing. I don't know if Irving intended to offer his hand to Anthony. Anthony had pointedly turned his back on him. We had cleaned the dirt off our shoes.

## SWEET BEDLAM

Outside the courtroom bedlam reigned. Irving was nowhere to be seen. Friends and strangers gave me exuberant hugs. Others offered more restrained British expressions of "Well done." Bruce Soll, who had come to London for the opening of the trial and returned for the end, managed to reach Les and Abigail Wexner in Paris. He handed me the cell phone. Their voices were filled with emotion. "We are so proud to have been part of this effort." They had been far more than "part" of it. I tried to thank them, but could not. I gave the phone to Anthony, who briefed Abigail, a lawyer, on the outcome. Ursula called from Atlanta. She had just received a call from Peter, the concierge at the hotel she and David frequented in London. "Madam, it's Peter. *We* won, madam. *We* won!" I managed to call my mother on my cell phone. She had already heard the news and was thrilled. "Your father would have been very proud."

Then, from amidst the crowd a familiar face appeared. I momentarily could not identify her. When she touched me gently on my forearm and said, "Thank you," I realized who she was. I remembered how, on that first day of the trial, she rolled up her sleeve to show me her number. Once again, she transformed a fleeting moment into a more profound one. I turned to the legal team and indicated that I was ready to leave.

As we wended our way through the building, strangers wished us well. Anthony's wife, a journalist, warned me, "There will be camera crews waiting outside. If you say something to one, they will all want statements." I assured her that I would be fine; after all, I had not been fazed by the paparazzi who had appeared off and on for months. As I strode through the 250-foot Gothic entry hall with a celebratory group of lawyers, experts, researchers, and friends behind me, intermittent waves of joy and relief began to cascade through my body. Feeling almost giddy with excitement, I punched the air with my fist and let out, what I thought was a sotto voce "YES!" Only when a couple of bystanders quickly pivoted in my direction and I heard Laura Tyler, who was walking about ten feet behind me, begin to laugh, did I realize that this had been anything but *sotto*. As I approached the exit, my mood quickly changed. The previous three months—if not five years—flashed before my eyes. I thought of all the work that had been devoted to this effort. I thought of the upheaval to my life and the research I had abandoned and students I had neglected. I thought of the survivors. I took a deep breath and, this time, very quietly said to myself, "This chapter of my life is over. This is the last time I walk out of here as *the defendant.*"

I pushed open the heavy wooden doors and gasped at what I saw. The media representatives who had been present when we arrived had been joined by numerous others. Photographers, reporters, and camera crews were straining at the barricades. Some had ladders to enhance their view. There was a sea of microphones and recording devices, some of which were on long poles so that they extended well over the police barricades. Three

London policemen, clad in bright yellow rain slickers to protect themselves from the steady drizzle, stood by to maintain order.

Reporters were shouting, "Give us a statement." "Say something." "We need a quote for the afternoon news." James reminded them that a press conference was in the offing. "But we are on deadline," they responded. It may have been the need to engage in yet one more act of verbal restraint that prompted me to take the next step. It may have been a desire to give the press "something." It may have been the overwhelming emotion of it all. I impulsively hoisted my arm in the air, raised my thumb high above my head and—depending whom you ask—scowled or gave a look of righteous indignation and triumph. I tried to smile, but could not. Maybe it was the subliminal awareness that, even at this moment of joy, so much pain had been caused by this endeavor. Maybe it was the woman in the sweater with the number on her arm.

## IN MY OWN WORDS

Later, in front of a sea of cameras and reporters in the hotel ballroom, I described this not just as my victory but as a victory for all those who fight hatred and prejudice. I paid tribute to Penguin for "doing the right thing" and to the magnificent legal team—lawyers, experts, researchers, paralegals, and even secretaries—who fought this as if it were their own battle.

But I soon learned that some people still did not grasp what this trial had been all about. A reporter asked if I thought Irving's loss would deter other historians from adopting controversial points of view. I reminded the reporter that Irving had sued me and that my issue with him did not concern his "controversial" views, but his lies and manipulations. Another reporter followed up and, in a thick foreign accent that I could not identify, asked, "Will you have pity for Mr. Irving? Or will you force him to pay your costs, probably causing him to be bankrupt?" Well aware that the press conference was being broadcast live in a number of countries, I modulated my answer, but with some degree of umbrage said, " 'Pity for Mr. Irving?' I think you have it backwards. It's my life and work that has been disrupted."

Another reporter asked, "Given all that has happened to you, would you write the same book once again?" Over the course of the past ten weeks, I had thought a lot about this and was prepared for it. I immediately said, "No." My answer caused an audible stir in the room. This time I was the one who paused for dramatic effect. Then I added, "What I would now write would be far more harsh." As a result of the trove of documents we had uncovered, I now knew that Irving's assault on history was considerably more egregious than I had previously imagined.

As we neared the end of the allotted time, one reporter asked, "Have you heard from Holocaust survivors?" I started to relate Ben Meed's admonition that I could sleep soundly because "none of us are sleeping," when suddenly my voice began to tremble and tears welled up in my eyes. The room grew quiet as reporters waited. Drawing on whatever emotional reserves I could muster, I regained control and finished the anecdote. When Penguin's publicist stopped the conference shortly thereafter, I was relieved.

After months of depending on others to articulate my position, I felt liberated. For the first time in a long time, I was in control. After the press conference Richard Rampton approached me. He was smiling broadly: "You are *really very good* at this," he said. "Richard," I teased him, "you sound a wee bit surprised. Remember, answering questions is my stock and trade." I realized that neither Richard nor any member of the defense team had ever heard me "perform" publicly before. James came over to say that Prime Minister Barak's office had been furiously calling Mishcon looking for me. He was in the midst of negotiations with President Clinton but took time out of those meetings to acknowledge this important victory "on behalf of the Jewish people."

Later that day, I returned to my hotel to freshen up for another round of interviews. As I entered the lobby, activity stopped. Other guests were momentarily left in the lurch, as the desk staff, doormen, and bellmen all began to clap. Sally, the hotel manager, came running from her office with a bottle of champagne and a gorgeous array of flowers.

Within a few moments I was on my way to an evening news show. Walking into the studio building, I spotted Professor Donald Watt, who was also scheduled to appear. I recalled Watt's dismissal of Irving's argument that Hitler did not know of the Holocaust as "difficult . . . to accept." After he testified, Watt sent me a letter reassuring me that he had no sympathy for deniers. Smiling, I extended my hand in greeting and said, "Professor Watt? Deborah Lipstadt." Without indulging in any niceties, he blurted out, "Penguin was out for blood." Unsure that I had heard correctly, I mumbled, "Excuse me?" "None of us," he continued, "could have withstood that kind of scrutiny." I said nothing but turned away perplexed.

When I reached the "green room," or its British equivalent, someone handed me the *Evening Standard*. Watt had written an op-ed column, which must have been composed prior to the release of Judge Gray's judgment. Entitled, "History Needs David Irving," its opening line confirmed that I had indeed heard him precisely right.

Penguin was certainly out for blood. The firm has employed five historians, with two research assistants, for some considerable time to produce 750 pages of written testimony, querying and checking every document cited in Irving's books on Hitler. Show me one historian who has not broken into a cold sweat at the thought of undergoing similar treatment.

After praising Irving's ability to ferret out new documents, Watt argued that Irving suffers from the "characteristic faults of the self-taught" and was "seduced by the notion of conspiracies." Watt claimed that other British historians could also be accused of having "allowed their political agenda and views to influence their . . . selection and interpretation of historical evidence."[24] I recalled the fact that Watt had written a lengthy introduction to one of Irving's books and wondered if he felt obliged to somehow defend Irving, even though in his testimony he had been quite dismissive of Irving's theories about Hitler. Shortly before the show began, as the host was reviewing how he would identify each of us, he described Watt as having "coauthored a book with David Irving." Watt sternly corrected him: "That is not correct. I just wrote an introduction." In any case, I found it hard to believe that Watt had actually read the judgment, particularly since his column appeared in the afternoon paper a few hours after it had been handed down. While historians often let politics influence their writing, they did not weave a web of inventions and suppressions, as Irving did. Anyone reading Watt's column might have assumed that I had sued Irving to drive him underground.

After the broadcast, when I left, the young man whose responsibility it was to make sure guests found their way in and out of the rabbit warren of studios and offices, quietly said, "I'm Jewish. Thanks."

As the driver worked his way through the London traffic to the next interview, I phoned my friend Bill Lowenberg in San Francisco. Bill, a Holocaust survivor, is a tough, no-nonsense kind of guy. When he heard about my defense fund, he took responsibility for raising over $100,000. Bill's secretary said, "I am sorry, Mr. Lowenberg is indisposed." I smiled at her delicate euphemism and said, "Just tell him Deborah Lipstadt called." When she repeated my name, I heard Bill's daughter, Susan, yell, "Deborah's on the phone! Someone get my dad." Within a few moments a breathless Bill Lowenberg picked up the phone. "Deborah, Deborah, is that you?" "Yes, Bill. I just wanted you to know that I was thinking of you." Bill's voice, usually so confident, trembled. "We were joyous when we heard the good news. We are so happy." And he began to weep. "Thank you. Thank you. In the name of my family, thank you."

Ernie Michel, another survivor who had spearheaded raising funds for my defense, reacted similarly. "We did it. We did it," he said. I called Rabbi Herb Friedman, who two years earlier had demanded to know how I was going to fight this. I told him, "Without you, I could not have done it."

The day ended with a late-night appearance on *Newsnight,* the BBC's equivalent of ABC's *Nightline.* While James and I sat in the BBC café eating a late supper prior to the show, a bottle of champagne arrived at our table. The waiter said it came from a young couple sitting in the corner. I invited them to join us. They described themselves as "just two members of the British public who very much appreciate what you did."

Irving was in one studio and I was in another. Jeremy Paxman, the host, countered Irving's attempt to reinterpret the judgment. When Irving argued that the judge had not ruled against him, Paxman replied, "Typical of your methods." Paxman then recited a litany of Irving's racist and antisemitic statements. Irving, obviously a bit nonplused, burst out, "You're not Jewish, are you?" When asked by Paxman whether he would, in light of the judgment, "stop denying the Holocaust," Irving responded, "Good Lord, no."[25] As we left the studio, the morning papers arrived. The trial was the lead story on all the front pages.


It was well after midnight when I returned to the hotel. Physically spent, yet bursting with emotional energy, I turned on my computer. I found over three hundred emails from friends, family, and complete strangers. Many were expressions of joy: "HOORAY!!" My research assistant, Maureen, noted that her message would be very short as she was too busy "dancing around the room." An Emory student related that his professor announced the news to his class early that morning. "We all began to whoop and holler. We made so much noise that other professors came in to ask what was going on. Soon their classes were celebrating as well." A colleague had been in O'Hare Airport waiting for a very early morning flight, when CNN broadcast the news. The coffee and bagel he was carefully balancing on his knees went flying as he stood up, threw his hands in the air, and yelled, "Yes." A group of my students from the Wexner Heritage Foundation emailed me: "You taught us well in class and you taught us—and so many others—well in court." Many of the notes were sobering:

> On behalf of my grandmother, aunts, uncles and cousins who died at Treblinka I thank you. . . . Now, enjoy Pesach, because you can doubly enjoy your freedom. Moe Stein

> Dear Dr. Lipstadt,
> Thank you for defending the historical truth of the Holocaust. My father-in-law came of age in a concentration camp, so I have witnessed the physical and emotional scars first hand. . . . Perhaps there will now be a few less such horrors in the world. Sincerely, Gloria Klaiman

> Thank you in the name of my grandparents Bertha and Max Steiner and my uncle Robert Steiner, killed by the Germans in Poland in 1943, and in the name of my great-aunt Paula Weiss, killed by the Croats in 1942. Gratefully yours, Professor Felix Dothan

These messages were very much on my mind as I crawled into bed. They made me feel decidedly uncomfortable, though I could not figure out why. I turned off the light and fell asleep.

Early the next morning, as I prepared for the BBC *Breakfast News,* I hurriedly glanced at the *Daily Telegraph.* The lead headline on the front page was unambiguous:

"JUDGE BRANDS DAVID IRVING A HOLOCAUST DENIER WHO FALSIFIED THE FACTS TO EXONERATE HITLER: RACIST HISTORIAN FACES £2M BILL FOR LIBEL DEFEAT"

Under the headline was a cartoon showing a man in a bookstore inspecting David Irving's new book. Its title: *The Libel Trial That Never Happened.* The lead editorial declared that "this trial has done for the new century what the Nuremberg tribunals or the Eichmann trial did for earlier generations." Irving had "damned himself."

As I waited in the hotel lobby for a car to take me to my next interview, I noticed that Sir John Keegan's column in the *Daily Telegraph* was also devoted to the trial. As I turned to it, I recalled his courtroom testimony that Irving's claim that Hitler did not know about the Holocaust was "perverse." This time, however, Keegan's tone was very different. Keegan opened his column by bemoaning the outcome of the trial. "The news that David Irving has lost his libel case will send a tremor through the community of 20th-century historians." I read the sentence twice to make sure I had grasped it correctly. Apparently Keegan did not think that forcing an academic to defend her scholarly work at tremendous personal and professional costs would upset historians. Keegan then turned to Irving's Holocaust denial. Seeming to discount the repeated outright inventions and falsifications that our experts had documented, Keegan described Irving's denial as "nonsense" that constituted a "small but disabling element in his work." Keegan did not address the fact that Irving's work on Dresden—a decidedly non-Holocaust topic—was riddled with the same falsifications and distortions. Engaging in what sounded to me like armchair psychology, Keegan posited that Irving simply sought to shock people and may "not really believe what he says." How Irving's putative failure to believe what he says made his lies any less egregious Keegan failed to explain. Then, changing tacks and contradicting himself somewhat, Keegan declared that Irving was only guilty of errors of interpretation. The "judge has now decided that an all consuming knowledge of a vast body of material does not excuse faults in interpreting it." Keegan ignored the fact that Judge Gray's devastating judgment had nothing to do with "faults" in interpretation but with outright falsifications.

In one of the stranger parts of the article, Keegan waxed rhapsodic about Irving's appearance. "He is a large, strong, handsome man, excellently dressed, with the appearance of a leading QC," who asked his questions in "a firm but courteous voice." Irving, he declared, "is certainly never dull." Keegan then turned to me. "Prof Lipstadt, by contrast, seems as dull as only the self-righteously politically correct can be. Few other historians had ever heard of her before this case. Most will not want to hear from her again. Mr

Irving, if he will only learn from this case, still has much that is interesting to tell us."[26] The hotel concierge, who noticed me reading the column, said in a stage whisper as he walked by, "Sir John seems besotted with Mr Irving." Then, possibly reacting to the concerned look on my face, he added, "And we at the Athenaeum know you are certainly *not* dull." A bellman, who was walking by, added, "That's right."

Thinking about how Watt and Keegan had leapt to Irving's defense, I wondered if this was not an expression of England's "Old Boys" network, a network that would certainly have more sympathy with someone who attended one of England's more prestigious private schools and looked like a "leading QC" than with an American who also happened to be both a woman and an openly identifying Jew.

My ruminations were interrupted by the arrival of a car from the BBC. The driver peered at me, looked down at the front page of the morning paper, and then looked back at me. Apparently reassured that it was the same person, he emerged from the car, rushed to open the door for me to enter and said, "Madam, someone should have done it to that bloke long ago."

When I reached the BBC studio, all the morning papers were on the table in the waiting area. It was only then that I realized that the trial was the lead headline in every single British daily as well as many foreign papers.

*THE GUARDIAN:*
"Irving: Confined to History as a Racist Liar"

*THE INDEPENDENT:*
"Racist. Antisemite. Holocaust Denier. How History Will Judge David Irving"
"David Irving lost his case—and we can celebrate a victory for free speech"

*THE LONDON TIMES:*
"Racist who twisted the truth"
"David Irving's reputation as an historian is demolished"

Numerous editorials hailed the judgment. The *New York Times* declared that the verdict put an end to the pretense that Irving was anything but "a self-promoting apologist for Hitler."[27] The *London Times* said that "history has had its day in court and scored a crushing victory."[28] The *Sydney Morning*

*Herald* editorialized that Judge Gray's finding that Irving was an "active Holocaust denier, that he is antisemitic and racist, and that he associates with right-wing extremists who promote neo-Nazism" confirmed Irving's "real reputation." Neal Ascherson, in the *Observer,* described Judge Gray's judgment as "one of the most crushing judgments ever dumped over an English plaintiff."[29] The *Fort Worth Star Telegram,* adopting a bit of a down-home Texas style, declared: "Good man, that Judge." The *Economist* expressed the hope that "although Mr Irving will go on talking and writing, fewer and fewer people will be listening."[30] The *Irish Times* believed the judgment "blunt . . . to the point . . . entirely justified and much to be welcomed."[31] Even Helen Darville, the Australian whose true identity had been uncovered by other reporters during the trial and who had written two flattering pieces about Irving, now declared that Irving had been "seduced by Hitler," and dismissed his views on Hitler and the Holocaust as "bunk."[32]

That afternoon, as I crossed Piccadilly Circus, a driver leaned out of his car window, hoisted his thumb in the air, and yelled, "Bravo!" This time I smiled, an unambiguous smile.

# TWENTY-ONE

# ENORMOUS THANKS

An avalanche of messages, phone calls, letters, and emails continued to pour in over the next few weeks. Once again, it was the communiqués from survivors and their children that left me feeling particularly unnerved. Their praise was so effusive and their thanks so personal. It seemed to transcend anything I had done. I had fought a good fight, but their accolades seemed out of scale.

> *Dear Professor Lipstadt*
>
> *You do not know me and we will probably never meet. . . . My mother was killed in Auschwitz. If David Irving had won my mother would have been a victim a second time! So too would everybody else who perished there. I loved my mother very much and have not seen her since April 14, 1939 when I was 14 years old. She was killed on October 23, 1944. Gratefully yours, Anne Bertolina (née Hannelore Josias)*

This letter landed on my desk at a time when my eighty-five-year-old mother was ailing. When I reached the line "I loved my mother very much," I choked up. As a daughter who also loves her mother very much, I could only imagine what it meant to be separated from her at age fourteen and then to learn of her terrible fate. I wanted to tell Anne Bertolina that even if, by some mishap, David Irving had won, her mother would not have been a victim a second time. He had the power to do great mischief, but he did not have the power to do that.

A few days later I flew to Los Angeles to give a talk at the synagogue with which I had been affiliated for over fifteen years. The emotions in this room were palpable, but they paled compared to what happened later in the evening when, as I was taking off my jacket, I found a card that someone must have slipped in my pocket after the lecture. On the back was the following note:

> *Thank you. I was inmate #193061 in Auschwitz and helped to dismantle the gas chambers and crematoria. Ernie Regan.*

When I found that note, I sat looking at it for a long time. It was a stark reminder of both the gas chambers, which Irving had so gleefully denied, and the many people who had been touched—whether it was logical or not that they should be—by this effort.

But not all the letters were from victims. Some came from people with a more ancillary connection to the tragedy.

> *Dear Professor Lipstadt:*
>
> *My husband served with Patton and on a Sunday entered the "camps" at Dachau. . . . He was a hardened combat veteran as were the 3 others who went in with him. They broke down in tears. He recalled an inmate pointing at him and screaming in Yiddish. He had not realized his dog tags, on which he had a tiny Bar Mitzvah mezuzah hanging, were visible. "Du bist ein Yid?" the inmate asked. [Are you a Jew?] When my husband said, "Yes" he was Jewish, more yelling and others gathered. They couldn't believe a free Jew walked the face of the earth, let alone a Jewish soldier! It took him 28 years to tell me this (in Jerusalem at Yad Vashem). He'd buried the memories of what he'd seen that deep. . . . Cordially, Marion Lieberman.*

While many of the letters came from Jews, there were correspondents who made a point of identifying themselves as non-Jews.

> *Dear Professor Lipstadt:*
>
> *British justice is a bit long winded and unemotional: like the mills of god, it may grind slowly but, on occasion, it can grind exceedingly fine. I was a boy during the war, but one thing is ineradicably engraved upon my mind. Not the*

bombing, which had long ceased, but the memory of sitting in a cinema with my mother and sister, weeping together with the rest of the audience, as we saw the first dreadful newsreel pictures of the liberation of Belsen.

Fair-haired and light-eyed, Christian, Goy and stranger, I may be, but I cannot understand how that dreadful creature persuaded some of our children that their parents and grandparents are either liars or fools. There are still plenty of us who will remember until we die, including those who, unlike me, were there.

Sincerely, Ray Waters

Many survivors perceived my fight as protecting them from what has been called a "double dying."[1] I tried to tell these survivors that, even if we had lost, their memories would not have been threatened and that they were giving me far more credit than I deserved. But they were reluctant to hear this. Their accolades left me feeling strangely uncomfortable. Some grew quite angry with me when I asked them not to thank me. "I must," one Dutch survivor declared, "my parents would want me to."

I was not the only one who experienced emotional turmoil after the trial. A few days after the verdict I asked Rampton what it was like to work on this case. Without hesitating, he said, "A privilege." Shortly thereafter he wrote me to tell me that the emotional aftermath was more complicated than he had thought it would be.

I had hoped to be basking in a glowing success and satisfaction. In fact, the aftermath has been, for me, an amalgam of anger and regret. Anger that we (you) were ever brought to what was, in truth, a false confirmation (though it was unavoidable and necessary). Regret that I no longer have daily contact with all the company of friends that the case drew together. A bit as war veterans might feel, I suspect.

Laura Tyler talked about how she had changed. "I have a sense of enormous pride that at such a young age I have done something that is so important to many others. I made a difference." Anthony, ever his iconoclastic self, insisted that "winning this trial was not that important." That is what he said. But after having worked with him for close to five years, I did not quite believe him. He had devoted countless hours to it and he was very proud of the job he and his cohorts had done. Moreover, in my journal I found that early in our fight Anthony had said, "This could well be the most important case I will ever handle." When I challenged him about this, he admitted that he was reacting to some of the posttrial media reports that seemed to draw Irving as a truly significant figure and, consequently, our unequivocal victory equally significant. David Irving was not important; defeating him and demonstrating the bankruptcy of his ideas was.

A few weeks after the trial, James came to Washington to accept an award from the American Jewish Committee in recognition of the work he and Anthony had done for the case. As we walked near the tidal basin enjoying the cherry blossoms, he mused about the "extraordinary" aspects of this case. Even during the biggest commercial litigation cases, rarely does such a large team remain together for such an extended period of time. More than the team distinguished this case for James. "I always advocate for my clients and care about their legal problems, but it is rare to have a case that is quite so close to one's heart and in which justice is so central." In virtually every other legal altercation, there was some accommodation that could be reached between the sides. "Not this time," James continued. "Here there was an absolute difference between right and wrong. We could wholeheartedly be on the side of the angels."

Though I had heard from survivors throughout the trial, only now, in the throes of victory, did I fully understand the extent to which they had been with me. Now my victory was their victory. In some sense it was more theirs than it was mine. While it was my work that had been vindicated, it was their pain, memories, and experiences that, they believed—whether it was logical to do so or not—had been saved from defeat.

Over the next few months there was one email to which I kept returning.

*Friday, April 14, 2000 4:32:32 PM*
*From: paola.castagno*
*Subject: YOU ARE THE GREAT WINNER!*
*To: dlipsta@emory.edu*

*Dear Miss Lipstadt,*

*My name is Paola Castagno, I'm italian, I'm 28 years old and fortunatly i didn't new the II World War.* *

*I red on an italian newsparer that you won agaist David Irving.*

*My grandfather Aldo rimained 8 mounth in Auschwitz (like Disneyland).*

*When he came back in Italy he weighted 34 kilos (for 1.82 mt high).*

*He died 3 year ago. I remember that he cried, thinking Holocaust, after 40 years.*

*He didn't say me nothing about this. So I write to thank you enormously.*

*I know that also my Grandfather thank you for your courage and that you speak about truth. Bey my graet hero!!!*

*Paola Castagno*

*NB: I'm sorry for my English*

I did not feel as if I was anybody's "great hero." Five years earlier David Irving had "taken me out of the line to be shot." Fully expecting me to "crack up and cop out," Irving may well have been surprised when I fought back as I did, ultimately giving far better than I got. I fought to defend myself, to preserve my belief in freedom of expression, and to defeat a man who lied about history and expressed deeply contemptuous views of Jews and other minorities.

For a long time after the court battle was over, I felt pain when I thought of the many people who had watched Irving ravage their memories. I could not fathom what it felt like to have one's experiences not just denied, but deprecated and ridiculed. However, I felt not just pain, but also a certain sense of privilege. I was reminded of the fact that Jewish tradition highly values acts of loving-kindness, including visiting the sick, sheltering the needy, feeding the hungry, and welcoming the stranger. There is, however, one act of loving-kindness that supersedes all the others because it cannot be reciprocated. Taking care of the dead is called *hesed shel emet*, the most genuine act of loving-kindness, because it is then that we most closely emulate God's

---

*Spelling as in original message.

kindness to humans, which also cannot be reciprocated. For five years I had the privilege to do *hesed shel emet,* to stand up for those who did not survive or who could not stand up for themselves. Being able to do that was thanks enough.

I did not choose this field of research in order to perform this act of *hesed.* I did not write my book on deniers expecting to engage in this act. I did not choose this fight. But now, as I look back, I am filled with gratitude. If someone had to be taken out of the line to fight this battle, I feel gratified to have been the one.

# TWENTY-TWO

## THE "JESTER'S COSTUME"

I soon discovered that this case was not yet over. Not surprisingly, Irving chose to appeal the judgment. The lawyers assured me that, given Judge Gray's sweeping decision, there was little likelihood of a reversal and this would be a relatively straightforward matter. Consequently, I was quite sanguine about the process. Once again my expectations proved dramatically wrong.

In England one must secure "leave" or permission to appeal. Irving's first request was made to Judge Gray, who rejected it because his decision had been rooted in history and there was no issue of law to be contested. He also ordered Irving to repay our costs and stipulated that the first installment of £150,000 be paid immediately. In the fall of 2000, Irving—who now had lawyers to represent him—submitted a written request to the Court of Appeal. Irving argued that the trial had been held in an intimidating atmosphere of hysterical press hostility and that Judge Gray's findings contradicted the "weight of the evidence." The expert witnesses, Irving contended, were motivated by bias, large fees, and, in the case of Evans, personal hatred. Shortly thereafter Irving began depicting Evans on his website as a rose-carrying skunk with demurely blinking eyes.[1]

In December 2000, Appeal Court judge Stephen Sedley ruled that, in light of my having called Irving a falsifier of history and a bigot, a "heavy burden" had been placed on the defense and we had fully met that burden. Irving's mistakes were not "casual misreadings of evidence" but "sedulous misinterpretations." Sedley supported Gray's "damning and justifiable finding" about Irving's "misreading of evidence" and wrote that Irving, having "played for high stakes," had lost conclusively. His request to appeal was, yet again, rejected.

Shortly after Judge Sedley's ruling, Irving profiled him on his website. He claimed that the firm to which Sedley had belonged prior to being elevated to the bench had been founded by "a clandestine leader of the Communist Party." According to Irving a significant number of the members of this firm are "evidently Jewish." Judge Sedley, he suggested, might be acting on his "religious instincts" more than the dictates of the law.[2]

In view of Judge Sedley's unrelenting affirmation of Gray's decision, I thought that Irving might cut his losses, rather than risk having yet another court rule against him. Once again I was wrong. Irving requested an oral hearing, arguing that he had new evidence that had been unavailable to him during the trial. He submitted four hundred pages of evidence, including a report by Germar Scheerer, a well-known Holocaust denier who sometimes used the name Rudolf. It argued that the gas chambers were an impossibility. This, apparently, was the startling "new" information on Auschwitz that Irving had dramatically promised would be introduced at the trial but never was. Irving also submitted an affidavit by a Zoe Polanska Palmer, a former prisoner at Auschwitz, who claimed that she never saw anything that looked like a gas chamber or any chimneys belching smoke. The Court of Appeal agreed to hear Irving's claim and a hearing was scheduled for June 2001.

I returned to London to consult with the lawyers. We agreed that we should adhere to the modus operandi we had during the trial and treat this material in a comprehensive fashion. Rampton, Anthony, James, and Heather decided to send it to van Pelt for analysis. Van Pelt wrote a very lengthy response on all the historical and technological arguments in Rudolf's report. Feeling that we needed a chemist to respond to Rudolf's arguments, van Pelt then contacted Richard Green, a Stanford Ph.D. in physical chemistry and a consultant to the United States Army on defending personnel against chemical weapons, and asked him to prepare a report addressing Rudolf's claims.

Green was also an active member of the Holocaust History Project (THHP), a group of researchers who had banded together under the leadership of Harry Mazal, an engineer and expert in computer science, to methodically debunk Holocaust deniers. During the preceding two years Mazal and other THHP members had made a number of exploratory visits to

Auschwitz, where they carefully examined the remains of the roof of crema 2. Using computer modeling and mathematical analysis, they found what they believed to be three of the four holes. Van Pelt asked a professional engineer to review these findings. He found them so compelling that we appended both Green's analysis and the THHP's report on the holes to van Pelt's second report and submitted it to the Court of Appeal.

As I awaited the appeal hearing, I learned some disconcerting news. Prior to the trial, Irving had threatened the British publishers of John Lukacs's *The Hitler of History,* that if they published this book, which so excoriated him, he would do to them what he was doing to me. Weidenfeld & Nicolson shelved the book for three years. I was delighted when, nine months after Gray's judgment, the book appeared in the United Kingdom. My delight was short-lived when I read the British reviews. Reviewers complained about the "significant emendations" to the section on Irving and decried the fact that the publisher had "toned down" the American edition. What emerged, the *Guardian* believed, was a "much less incisive attack on Irving." The *Observer* declared that, had the book appeared without the changes, it would have been a triumph of "free speech over a bully." Weidenfeld & Nicolson were not alone in their lack of publishing fortitude. Heinemann, a division of the publishing giant Bertelsmann, had contracted to publish Evans's expert report. Suddenly, on the eve of publication, it cancelled the contract because, I was told, of its fear of a libel suit. Though another publisher stepped in, I was disheartened by these developments.[3]

Sometime after the trial, the historian Richard Breitman, who was doing research on the Nuremberg trials, sent me a copy of a memo he found in the National Archives in Washington. It provided some added insight into Irving. In 1969, former Nuremberg prosecutor Robert Kempner sent a memo to FBI director J. Edgar Hoover, describing how, during a recent trip to Germany, he had been visited by David Irving, a "young man, who made a nervous and rather mentally dilapidated impression" and who voiced many "anti-American and anti-Jewish statements." Irving told Kempner that he was planning to visit Washington to check whether "the official record of the Nuremberg trial was falsified." Kempner, who dismissed this notion as "nonsense," was troubled because Irving could have easily checked the Nuremberg record in London. It was not this, however, that prompted Kempner to write to Hoover. "Completely unsolicited, he stressed twice very emphatically that Sirhan Sirhan did the right thing in killing 'that big fat-faced' Kennedy. If he, Irving, were an Arab, he said, he would have done the same thing, because of Robert Kennedy's alleged pro-Israel remarks."[4]

This occurred two decades before Irving espoused Holocaust denial. It seemed to begin to answer the question Rampton had raised in his closing argument: what came first—Irving's denial or his antisemitism?

In mid-June 2001 we reconvened in Court 73 for the appeal hearing. I asked Harry Mazal, who had come with his wife, Jerry, to join van Pelt and Evans at the experts' table. Given the time and energy that he and his THHP colleagues had devoted—quietly, privately, and voluntarily—to this case, it seemed highly appropriate. Irving entered wearing, what appeared to be, the same suit he had worn for the ten weeks of the trial. He was accompanied by "Brunhilda" and his barrister, Adrian Davies, a man in his forties with a round, very white, soft pudgy face, thick neck, and, I soon discovered, a high-pitched nasal voice.

When the court usher (Janet Purdue was nowhere to be seen) called "Silence," the tribunal of three lord justices—Mantell, Buxton, and Pill—entered. Davies began by arguing that Irving might be a sloppy historian, but he was not a deliberate liar. He had simply arrived at "reasonable alternative positions" regarding the evidence. He then began to chronologically plow his way through much of the material covered in the trial. The judges demonstrated amazing patience. I had none, particularly as the first day dragged into the second and the third. Soon the appeal hearing had metamorphosed into a minitrial. When I complained to James about the exceptional leeway the court was giving Irving, he explained that British courts traditionally give unlimited time to oral arguments, particularly when one party has represented itself. Furthermore, he continued, given the court's sensitivity to the high-profile nature of this case, it did not want to be seen as penalizing Irving.

Toward the end of the second day of the hearing, Davies, sounding rather agitated, announced: "Milords, we are withdrawing the Polanska Palmer and Germar Rudolf affidavits." I was completely flummoxed by this.

This was the evidence on which Irving had hinged his appeal. Moreover, we had expended significant money and energy refuting it. I tried to gauge Irving's reaction. His large frame was hunched over his desk, as he busily scribbled notes. He had a nervous little smile on his lips but his eyes were focused on the papers in front of him.* The lord justices looked perturbed.

When the session ended, Harry Mazal, who, together with his colleagues, had invested hours of research on what he called the "idiot affidavits," bemoaned the fact that their work had been in vain. Smiling, Rampton counseled him, "Wasted energy? You've sunk their case without firing a shot." Irving's lawyers, Rampton speculated, probably recognized that Rudolf's report would be demolished by our rebuttal. This would have dealt Holocaust deniers a grievous blow.

Later that night the defense team gathered at the Ritz Hotel. Harry and Jerry had planned a celebration dinner. Richard and James assured everyone that victory was in the offing. Harry and I refused to get our hopes up but a couple of hours of good food, drink, and company forced us to relax. When Harry rose to give a toast, he still had the withdrawn affidavits in mind. "Sun Tzu's *Art of War,* which was written over twenty-five hundred years ago, says: 'To fight and conquer in all your battles is not supreme excellence; supreme excellence consists in breaking the enemy's resistance without fighting.' "

Finally, after two more days of arguments by Davies, the hearing ended. Four weeks later I returned to hear the court's decision. About an hour before court, I met Anthony and James in their offices. They handed me the judgment. "It's over. We won. Conclusively and completely." I looked at them and asked, "What's next?" James laughed: "Believe it. It's over. It's done. He can't do anything to you." When I looked skeptical, James continued, "Now we press him for reimbursement of our costs."

---

*I am not sure why he was smiling or what he was scribbling, but in a subsequent posting on his website he claimed that because of Court of Appeal rules, he was *"not allowed* to introduce any new evidence whatsoever." He then goes on to say "we might even have had difficulty introducing the new 1,000-page Rudolf affidavit." Irving fails to inform his readers that the affidavit—which was not 1,000 pages—*had* been submitted to the court three months earlier and the court *had* accepted it. He does not mention that it was withdrawn by his barrister to the consternation of the lord justices. David Irving, "The Lipstadt Case," http://www.fpp.co.uk/ActionReport/AR19/items/recent.html (accessed January 2, 2002).

A few minutes later we left for court. Irving's place was noticeably empty. I kept waiting for him to rush in at the last moment but he did not. Within a few moments the three judges entered. Lord Justice Pill, speaking extraordinarily softly, said that Justice Gray's ruling—which they praised for its "comprehensiveness and style"—stood. The appeal was rejected. The lord justices criticized Irving for withdrawing his so-called "new" evidence at the last moment. After the lord justices ordered that Irving pay our costs, they rose and left the room. I looked at James in a somewhat tentative fashion. Smiling he said, "Deborah, it's over. Believe me, it's over."[5]

As the legal team rose to congratulate one another, I reflected on the fact that this battle was fought by Jews and non-Jews, in the common conviction that antisemitism and extremism are evil dangers to society. Our all-encompassing victory notwithstanding, this was not the last battle against deniers or, for that matter, against antisemites, because antisemitism itself cannot be "defeated." It will wither away, or not—probably the latter—of its own accord. Since antisemitism and, for that matter, all forms of prejudice are impervious to reason, they cannot be disproved. Therefore, in every generation they must be fought.

As we began to press Irving for our costs, some newspapers tried to uncover the source of his funds. This was of more than passing interest, because British law stipulates that third parties who fund libel actions can be dunned for costs if the party they supported loses. The *Observer* obtained a copy of Irving's list of 4,017 contributors, over half of whom lived in the United States. A former U-boat commander, currently "a tax avoidance specialist" living in Hawaii, had on one occasion asked Irving to meet him in Amsterdam where he handed him a paper bag with $50,000 in cash. Another supporter was a Floridian, who loaned Irving $45,000. Two contributors—one from Sweden and another from Switzerland—had loaned him over $25,000. Irving told the paper that if he were ordered to reveal the names of his supporters, "I'll come straight back here and destroy all the files."[6]

The press also uncovered the identity of "Brunhilda," who had consistently been at Irving's side. She was a former Australian beauty queen who, in 1991, had married a New Zealand financier, Sir Frank Renouf. She had told Sir Frank, who was almost thirty years her senior, that she was the Countess Griaznoff and that her father was dead. When the couple honey-

mooned in Australia, Sir Frank discovered that her father—a truck driver—
was very much alive.[7] After six weeks of marriage, Sir Frank left his wife,
who continued to call herself "Lady Renouf."

After the appeal she introduced Irving to Prince Fahd bin Salman of
Saudi Arabia, the son of the governor of Riyadh and nephew of King Fahd.
The prince, who had recently accompanied his father on a trade mission to
England, where he met the queen and the prime minister, invited Irving to
his estate in Surrey. A few days later, in a phone call from Riyadh, the prince
agreed to support Irving. But, according to Renouf, tragically, the following
day, the generous and fit prince died suddenly.[8]

Our effort to recoup some of the funds we had expended on this effort
turned out to be far more complex than I anticipated. In March 2002, Irving
paid Penguin a small portion of their costs. Irving claimed he was now bankrupt and could neither pay the rest of their costs nor any of mine. I was
skeptical about this claim because he continued to travel regularly to the
United States, sell his books at his lectures, and live in London's upscale Mayfair neighborhood.[9] A court-appointed trustee took Irving's books, papers,
and other personal items to determine if they had any monetary value. We
informed the court that we had no interest in Irving's personal papers or any
other personal items.[10] Despite this disclaimer, Irving—ever the model of historical accuracy—accused me of trying to take his "lifetime possessions,
properties, and rights."[11] We were only interested in those items that might
have some monetary value. We thought a university or archive might be interested in purchasing them. That way we would avoid putting them on the
open market and attracting collectors of Nazi memorabilia. The defense
fund was long depleted and we still owed Rampton a significant amount of
money for conducting the appeal, a cost that Penguin had rather unexpectedly left for me to carry.

There were some documents of interest to historians. Our researcher,
Tobias Jersak, and the appraiser whom we asked to evaluate the collection,
discovered that it contained Third Reich–era material—including diaries, letters, and notes by various German leaders—that were not in other archives
or libraries. These included the notes made by Field Marshall Wilhelm Keitel, the Chief of Germany's *Wehrmacht* in his cell at Nuremberg. In it Keitel
admitted to having knowledge of the crimes against the Jews. We knew of
no other historian who had a copy or who had been able to examine it. Unsure of how Irving might have gotten this, we speculated that Keitel's family,

trusting Irving to treat the field marshall's legacy well, had given him access to this document. Irving also had obtained portions of the diary of Nazi State Secretary Herbert Backe, who was head of the Ministry of Agriculture and Nutrition. Backe was one of those primarily responsible for the low food rations given to Jews. Here too we assumed that Backe's widow or members of his family had allowed Irving to see the diary and copy those portions in which he was interested. Tobias and the appraiser also found telephone logs, letters, and photographs that they believed could constitute evidence of Irving's extensive contacts with deniers in other countries and with Nazis and their family members.

Aside from these documents, about whose provenance some of the lawyers expressed concerns, the rest of the collection seemed to be of limited value. It reminded me of the material that languishes on eBay, for example, a bronze bust of Goebbels. *Irving v. Penguin and Lipstadt* had been a battle over historical—as well as my personal—integrity. It had been one we could not afford to lose. This would have been a battle over documents and money. Despite the fact that we almost certainly would have won, it did not seem to be worth our time and effort. In June 2004, after consulting with James, Laura, and Danny Davis, Mishcon's specialist on bankruptcy and insolvency matters, I decided not to pursue the matter. As I left their offices after making my decision, I knew that this was the right decision. However, I felt a sense of disappointment that unless Irving decided to share these documents, historians would not have access to them. It seemed strange to be ending this long imbroglio feeling that I had somehow failed my colleagues.

When I climbed into a taxi to go to my next appointment, the driver asked me if I was in London on business or pleasure. When I explained why I was there, he immediately recalled the case. "Haven't heard much from or about David Irving since your trial. Seems to me that for most Brits he's toast, burnt toast. Well done." I wasn't sure if his last two words referred to Irving's condition or the job a wonderful team of people had done.

As my life began to take on some semblance of normalcy, I tried to make sense of what we had accomplished. We had won an overwhelming victory. Virtually all the claims posed by Holocaust deniers prior to the spring of 2000 had been demolished. David Irving had been far less formidable a foe than any of us imagined. His fanciful claims had crumpled under the simple weight of the facts.

However, even as I felt gratified by this, I knew that Holocaust denial arguments—including those discredited in court—continued to have a lease on life. Deniers, such as Hutton Gibson, the father of filmmaker Mel Gibson, repeated Irving's claims about the amount of fuel needed to dispose of bodies and the impossibility of gas chambers. His son engaged in what I considered "soft core" denial. When asked by *Reader's Digest* about his father's comments regarding the Holocaust, Gibson said, "My father never lied to me in his life." He responded to the question "The Holocaust happened, right?" by saying, "Yes, of course. Atrocities happened. War is horrible. World War Two killed tens of millions of people. Some of them were Jews in concentration camps." Then he added a strange and rather telling non-sequitur. "In the Ukraine, several million starved to death between 1932 and 1933." This ambiguous answer reminded me of David Irving's definition of the Holocaust, which posits that virtually no Jews were targeted by the Nazis for "murder." Many simply lost their lives and the Holocaust was no different and certainly no worse than what happened in the Ukraine in the 1930s, under the Soviet regime. From Gibson's statement I could only conclude that he does not really believe that European Jewry was singled out by the Germans to be completely annihilated. Gibson repeated these views in an interview with Diane Sawyer. "Do I believe that there were concentration camps where defenseless and innocent Jews died cruelly under the Nazi regime? Of course I do; absolutely. It was an atrocity of monumental pro portion."[12]

Once again Jews died—as opposed to being deliberately murdered. And once again Gibson fails to make any mention of the Final Solution as an attempt to annihilate European Jewry. It was particularly disconcerting that Gibson made these comments during the publicity campaign for *The Passion of the Christ,* a film that many critics considered not only a dangerous distortion of the historical record but one that was capable of arousing anti-semitism.

Holocaust denial has proliferated in the Islamic world, particularly in the Middle East. Palestinian leader Mahmoud Abbas (Abu Mazen), who was the secretary-general of the PLO Executive Committee, wrote in his book *The Other Side: The Secret Relationship Between Nazism and the Zionist Movement* that the six million figure was "peddled" by the Jews, and that the actual number may be even fewer than one million. When he became prime minister of the Palestinian Authority, he was asked to clarify his comments. Rather than repudiate them and acknowledge that they were false, he said that he wrote the book when the Palestinians were at war with Israel. "[T]oday I would not have made such remarks . . ." Abdel Aziz Rantisi, who served as the "general commander" of Hamas until his assassination by Israel in April 2004, expressed his outrage at the Zionists' success in spreading the propaganda of the "false Holocaust" and claimed that no one has clarified how the "false gas chambers worked." Maintaining a consistent level of historical accuracy, Rantisi decried the fact that David Irving "was sued" because of his Holocaust denial.[13]

Holocaust denial is not the only form of false history that is gaining ground in the Muslim world. Yasser Arafat has repeatedly denied any historical connection between the Jewish people and the land of Israel. Increasingly the myth of the blood libel has been spread, as has the perennial myth of world Jewish domination. The manuscript museum at the famed Alexandria Library recently exhibited *The Protocols of the Elders of Zion*. The Egyptian weekly *Al-Usbu* interviewed Dr. Yousef Ziedan, the director of manuscripts at the library, in conjunction with the exhibition. Regarding the Holocaust, the weekly quoted Dr. Ziedan as saying, "[A]n analysis of samples from the purported gas chambers has proven that these were sterilization chambers, without a sufficient quantity of cyanide to kill."[14]

A different kind of historical distortion was evident in Europe during the buildup to the Iraq war. The grotesque equation of President George W. Bush and Prime Minister Ariel Sharon with Hitler—irrespective of how much one opposes their policies—constituted a gross whitewash of Nazi crimes. Equally troubling was the use of Nazi motifs to attack Israel's policies. Nobel laureate Jose Saramago compared the situation of the Palestinians with the Jews in Auschwitz. When asked whether there were gas chambers in Gaza, he said, "I hope this is not the case. . . . But what is happening is more or less the same." British poet Tom Paulin declared that Jewish settlers in the West Bank are "Nazis and racists . . . [who] should be shot dead."[15] While these metaphysical attacks on Jews may not cause physical harm, they leave Jews terribly dispirited and prompt them to question their place in a supposedly enlightened Europe. For me, they were a stark reminder that while I might have won a single solitary battle, the struggle against the distortion of history—particularly inconvenient history—is ongoing.

One day, anxious for some escape, I decided to go rent some videos. On impulse—and apparently having forgotten that I was looking for an escape—I selected Charlie Chaplin's *The Great Dictator* and Mel Brooks's *The Producers,* two highly effective spoofs on Adolf Hitler. The clerk—who, much to my amazement, actually knew something about films—asked: "You interested in comedy or Hitler?" I shrugged my shoulders and said, somewhat tentatively, "Both, I guess."

While I was watching the films, I recalled a manuscript Anthony had written during the trial. He had been asked to deliver a series of endowed lectures at the University of London on Jewish art. Regarding artists who attack their opponents with irony and ridicule, he had written: "To defeat your adversary and bury him is one thing. To dress him in a jester's costume and have him perform for you is another, more crushing blow. He survives to give witness to his own powerlessness."[16] This is what both Chaplin and Brooks did to Hitler.

At that point, I understood not only my choice of movies, but also what was and was *not* important about my battle. Repeatedly during the trial, David Irving was left exposed, not just as a falsifier of history, but as an irrational and foolish figure. Since the trial, whenever his name appeared in the press, it was almost invariably accompanied by some variation on the adjectival phrase "the Holocaust denier whom the court branded a racist, an antisemite, and a falsifier of history."[17] Ultimately, however, he was not important. Defeating him, however, was. And therein is a lesson that can be learned by all who fight the purveyors of hatred and lies. Though the battle against our opponents is exceptionally important, the opponents themselves are not. Their arguments make as much sense as flat-earth theory.

However, in dramatic contrast to flat-earthers, they can cause tremendous pain and damage. Some of them use violence. Others, as Hajo Funke said in Berlin as we sat in the shadow of the Reichstag, use words that, in turn, encourage others to do harm. It was words that motivated those who blew up the Murrah Building in Oklahoma City, dragged an African-American down a logging road to his death, tortured a young homosexual in Wyoming, stabbed a Jewish student to death on the streets of Crown Heights, blew up Israeli families about to celebrate the Passover Seder, and flew planes into the World Trade Center.

We must conduct an unrelenting fight against those who encourage—directly or indirectly—others to do these things. But, even as we fight, we must not imbue our opponents with a primordial significance. We certainly must never attribute our existence to their attacks on us or let our battle against them become our raison d'etre. And as we fight them, we must dress them—or force them to dress themselves—in the jester's costume. Ultimately, our victory comes when, even as we defeat them, we demonstrate not only how irrational, but how absolutely pathetic, they are.

———◆——

Deborah Lipstadt's momentous courtroom victory over David Irving is one of those great moments in legal history when truth, justice, and freedom of speech are all simultaneously served. Truth does not, of course, need a judicial imprimatur to be validated. Regardless of what any court might rule, David Irving's denial of the Holocaust will always be a lie and Deborah Lipstadt's exposure of Irving's lies will always be the truth. Justice, on the other hand, is not nearly as absolute and uninfluenced by human evaluation as is truth. Justice is often in the eye of the beholder, since it is a function of perception, attitudes, experience, education, and values. The great American judge Oliver Wendell Holmes Jr. once scolded his law clerk for complaining that a particular legal decision was not "just." "Our job," Holmes told his clerk, "is not to do justice; it is to apply the law." How much better it is, however, when justice is done by applying the law, as occurred in this case.

Truth and justice are sometimes served only by compromising freedom of speech, as when nations ban Holocaust denial speech, racist speech, sexist speech, or other forms of bigoted falsehood. Had David Irving been the defendant in a case seeking to censor his lies, and had he lost, it might be argued that the loss compromised principles of free speech. But Irving was the plaintiff here. It was he who was trying to censor Lipstadt's truth by suing her for defamation. Had he won, it would have been a defeat for truth, justice, and free speech. Thankfully, he lost—and he lost resoundingly and unambiguously. Truth, justice, and free speech won, and won big. Yet "some journalists called the verdict "a blow to free speech."[1] This is an absurd conclusion. Freedom of speech includes the right to expose lies, as Lipstadt did. It does not grant immunity from criticism to bigots like Irving. The marketplace of ideas must be open to all, not just neo-Nazis. Indeed, one reason why false and offensive speech is permitted in most liberal democracies is precisely because the best answer to bad speech is good speech, rather than censorship. Absent an opportunity to respond to the falsehoods spread by the likes of Irving, it would be more difficult to make the case for permitting racist liars to pollute the marketplace of ideas. Indeed, before Irving lost his case, several publishers had refused to issue books critical of Irving, out of fear of his bringing expensive and time-consuming lawsuits. *That* was a chilling of free speech. The chill was thawed by Lipstadt's victory *for* freedom of speech.

We live at a time when Holocaust denial, Holocaust trivialization, and Holocaust minimization are increasingly being used as part of a larger antisemitic and anti-Israel agenda. Hard-core deniers are supported and praised by people such as Noam Chomsky and Norman Finkelstein, while those who seek justice for Holocaust survivors are condemned by Finkelstein and his ilk. Chomsky has, in defending his absurd view that there are no "anti-Semitic implications in denial of the existence of gas chambers, or even denial of the Holocaust," added the following pregnant words: "whether one believes it [the Holocaust] took place or not." And he has praised Robert Faurisson, a hard-core Holocaust denier, as a scholar whose "findings" that the Holocaust did not occur were "based on extensive historical research." Chomsky's statements provide substantive support for the "finding" that the Holocaust is a debatable issue or a fraud. Perhaps on Planet Chomsky, but not in the real world, in which Nazi butchers murdered millions of Jewish children, women, and men. In a similar vein, Norman Finkelstein has praised the Holocaust-denying David Irving as a "good historian" who has made an "indispensable" contribution to our knowledge of World War II.[2]

At the other end of the political spectrum are people such as Patrick Buchanan, who have defended Nazi war criminals including Klaus Barbie, Karl Linnas, and the SS killers buried at Bitburg and expressed skepticism about Holocaust claims, doubting whether Jews were gassed at Treblinka.[3]

The work of keeping the memory of the Holocaust alive is thus not completed. Lipstadt's victory was the most important courtroom defeat for Holocaust denial in recent history. But the struggle must persist, on university campuses, at the United Nations, in the media, in publishing houses, and wherever ideas are important. There is no excuse for silence on this important issue. The truth must be spoken again and never silenced. Deborah Lipstadt led the way. She has proved that the best response to Holocaust denial is not futile attempts at censorship, but rather active exposure of the falsehood of these bigoted claims. When Holocaust deniers speak their lies, we must respond with the truth—with the facts, the evidence, and the documentation. Truth and justice are on our side. Lipstadt has shown us that freedom of speech is also on our side. So let us exercise our collective right to tell the truth and to expose falsehood. Lipstadt has done her job, and so has the court, and they have done it well. Now it is our job to continue the never-ending quest for truth, justice, and freedom of speech.

# ACKNOWLEDGMENTS

My legal struggle stretched out over six years—the "My Day" in the title is highly euphemistic. A cadre of people assisted me, both in the courtroom and in places far from it.

I had an exceptional legal team. The architects of my defense, Anthony Julius and James Libson of Mishcon de Reya, were more than stellar solicitors and fierce advocates on my behalf. They became—and remain—friends to whom I turn for wise counsel. People often ask about "turning points" in this case. A crucial one was when they agreed to represent me. They were skillfully assisted by Mishcon's Juliet Loudon, Laura Tyler, Veronica Byrne, Harriet Benson, Michala Barham, and Pippa Marshall. In the aftermath of the trial, Mishcon's Danny Davis has been a source of very wise and generous counsel. Richard Rampton is not only a uniquely gifted barrister, but the quintessential mensch. I wish we had met under different circumstances, but I am ever so grateful to have him in my life. Heather Rogers, Penguin's junior barrister, showed great legal acumen and an uncanny ability to retrieve a document at precisely the right moment. Of equal importance was the emotional support she offered me at crucial junctures. Penguin's legal representatives, Mark Bateman and Kevin Bayes of Davenport Lyons, were important members of this team. On this side of the Atlantic, Joe Beck of Kilpatrick Stockton offered his services with his typical giving spirit. My own lawyer and good friend, David Minkin of Greenberg Traurig, acting as a true advocate, was often more zealous in protecting my interests than I. His colleague Steve Sidman was exceedingly gracious as well.

Penguin, UK stood shoulder-to-shoulder with me during the trial. While it was the right thing for a publisher to do, I know that many publishers would not—and have not—supported their authors.

Our experts, professors Richard Evans, Christopher Browning, Peter Longerich,

Robert Jan van Pelt, and Hajo Funke, constituted the historian's ultimate dream team. Appalled by Irving's cavalier treatment of the historical record, they made an exceptional commitment to this endeavor. I am delighted that three of their reports have been published to deservedly stellar reviews.* Our researchers, Nikolaus Wachsmann, Thomas Skelton-Robinson, and Tobias Jersak, were critically important components of our research team. We could not have done this without them.

Leslie and Abigail Wexner, demonstrating the exemplary leadership which has become their hallmark, spearheaded the drive to create a defense fund. The contributors to this fund, who gave quietly and with no fanfare, were convinced that this was their fight as much as it was mine. Much of the fundraising effort was coordinated by Rabbi Herb Friedman, Michael Berenbaum, Phyllis Cook, Robert Goodkind, Miles Lehrman, William Lowenberg, and Ernie Michel. Bruce Soll was and is a wonderful troubleshooter and treasured friend.

The American Jewish Committee, the Anti-Defamation League, and the Simon Wiesenthal Center were all forthcoming with their assistance. The American Jewish Committee volunteered to house the defense fund and to coordinate the myriad of details associated with it. David Harris, AJC Executive Director, encouraged its expert on extremism, Ken Stern, to become an ex-officio member of the legal team. Ken calmed me down, cheered me up, and shared his wise counsel. The AJC is lucky to have him as a member of its team. I am lucky to have him as a friend. The AJC's Rebecca Gutman attended a National Alliance meeting, a less than hospitable setting for anyone who does not share its abhorrent ideology, to hear Irving's lecture.

In London, Daniel Levy, Sally Bulloch, Jonathan Critchard, and the staff at the Athenaeum turned a hotel into a home away from home. Many people—close friends and complete strangers—came to London for the trial. Far too numerous to name, their presence in the courtroom was like balm in Gilead. During my long absence from home, friends and neighbors performed a range of tasks—from fixing my mailbox and paying my bills to regularly calling my mother—allowing me to focus on the task at hand.

Emory University was resolute in its support. Without waiting to be asked and with no fanfare or publicity, it stepped forward. As an institution committed to academic excellence and moral engagement, Emory, under the leadership of then-president Bill Chace, was appalled by Irving's distortions of history; attempts to quash my academic freedom; and antisemitic, racist, and extremist rhetoric. I am saddened that Joe Crooks did not live to witness the outcome. Throughout the trial,

---

*Richard Evans, *Lying About Hitler* (New York: Basic Books, 2001), Peter Longerich, *The Unwritten Order: Hitler's Role in the Final Solution* (Charleston, S.C.: Tempus, 2001), Robert Jan van Pelt, *The Case for Auschwitz* (Bloomington, Ind.: University of Indiana Press, 2002).

colleagues, staff, and students inundated me with support, exemplifying what it is that I treasure about this institution.

That support continued after the trial. Emory College and Graduate School supported my work on this book. In addition, the University agreed to house a Web site, www.hdot.org, to ensure that the documentary record of the trial would be available for research. This was made possible by the support of the Revson Foundation and its then-president, Eli Evans, who originated the idea. This important scholarly resource is now a joint effort of Emory's Institute for Jewish Studies, Woodruff Library, and Information Technology Division. The AJC's Ken Stern was a critical asset. Among those who helped plan *hdot* were Mark Semer of Kekst and Company, Dan Yurman, Nancy Slome, Michael Berenbaum, Ken McVay of Nizkor, Shelly Shapiro, Gail Gans of the ADL, and David Goldman of Hatewatch. At Emory the expansion and upgrade of *hdot* has been supported by Dean Robert Paul and overseen by Naomi Nelson, Carole Meyers, Alan Cattier, David Lower, Marcia Wade, John Ingersoll, Leah Wolfson, and Maureen MacLaughlin. Maureen not only designed educational modules for *hdot* but also tirelessly checked my sources and worked assiduously to make order out of the chaos which often surrounds me. She has been a critically important asset and genuine partner in this book.

Historians will long be indebted to Israel's then-attorney general, Elyakim Rubenstein, and his advisor, Joshua Shoffman, for facilitating the release of the Eichmann diaries and to Seth Kornfield for suggesting that we ask for them.

My agent, Gary Morris of David Black and Associates, was determined to find the "perfect" editor for this book. And so he did. I could not have asked for more—or imagined that I would ever find as much—in an editor, as I did in Julia Serebrinsky. At Ecco, Gheña Glijansky, Amy Baker, Jill Bernstein, Amy Taylor, Chris Goff, Diane Aronson, and David Falk's enthusiasm for this project was infectious.

Jamie McCarthy stepped forward as soon as he learned of this legal battle. He was subsequently joined by Harry Mazal, Danny Kerem, Richard Green, and the other members of The Holocaust History Project. They were exceptionally forthcoming with their time and expertise. Dan Yurman's daily media digest allowed people throughout the world—myself included—to track media coverage of events in the Royal High Court of Justice. The Nizkor Project created a very helpful media record of the trial coverage.

I am deeply grateful to those who read and commented on portions of this manuscript, including Shalom Goldman, Anthony Lewis, Amelia Kornfeld, Joe Kornfeld, Nessa Rapoport, Rachel Rosenblit, Melissa Faye Greene, Marcella Brenner, David Minkin, Glenda Minkin, Laurie Patton, and Ronald Harwood. Dori Kornfeld of Houston's Yetter and Warden provided wise editorial and legal counsel. My wonderful friend Grace Cohen Grossman, in her characteristically generous fashion, carefully commented on every line. Helen Epstein reminded me what it is an author of a memoir owes her readers. They all helped make this a better book. The shortcomings which remain are, by and large, a result of my refusal to heed their advice. In addition, I was assisted by Cynthia Forland, Neil Reinstein, Dana Adler, and Arlene Robie. Rebecca E. Rubin worked tirelessly on the photographs and illustrations.

In the midst of the writing of this book, I unexpectedly had to have a series of operations. (I may well have been the only one who considered this turn of events 'unexpected.') A coterie of people did more than "just" help my body heal. They ensured a healing of spirit. I remain incredulous, even now, when I reflect on their righteousness. It is impossible to list them all, but I would be remiss if I failed to thank my friends at the Wexner Foundation who provided wonderful care when I took ill. In Atlanta, Glenda Minkin and Laurie Patton oversaw a myriad of details to ensure that I was safely transported home. When I was, friends in Atlanta and my colleagues at Emory University, particularly the faculty and staff of the Religion Department and Institute for Jewish Studies, cared for me as they would a member of their family. My enduring thanks to Dr. Art Safran and to the Emory University Hospital medical staff and, in particular, to Drs. James Robeson and Shelli Bank.

My family is fiercely proud of me and my accomplishments. Their love and support sustains me. Rarely, if ever, during this long, drawn-out affair did I feel that I was fighting alone. All those who reached out to me were and are a blessing. It is to them and, above all, to those who suffered so terribly during the Holocaust that I dedicate this book.

Deborah E. Lipstadt
Atlanta, GA
September 24, 2004, Erev Yom Kippur

# NOTES

## PROLOGUE: THE LETTER

1. The law, under which Zündel was convicted, was eventually declared unconstitutional by the Canadian Supreme Court. Second Zündel Trial, *Her Majesty the Queen vs. Ernst Zündel*, District Court of Ontario, 1988, pp. 45–46, 88, 186.

2. *Irving v. Penguin, Limited & Deborah Lipstadt* (hereafter *IvP&DL*), Day 1 (January 11, 2000), p. 98.

3. David Irving, "On Contemporary History and Historiography: Remarks Delivered at the 1983 International Revisionist Conference," *Journal of Historical Review (JHR)*, vol. 5, nos. 2–4 (winter 1984): pp. 274–75.

4. David Irving, Statement of Claim, *IvP&DL*, September 5, 1996.

5. Neal Ascherson, "Last Battle of Hitler's Historians," *Observer* (London), 16 January 2000; "The battle may be over—but the war goes on," *Observer* (London), 16 April 2000; Jonathan Freedland, "Court 73—where history is on trial," *Guardian* (London), February 5, 2000; Stephen Moss, "History's verdict on Holocaust upheld," *Guardian* (London), April 12, 2000; Richard Evans, *Lying about Hitler* (New York: Basic Books, 2001), pp. 185–93.

6. *IvP&DL*, Third Supplemental Discovery List: Tape 190: Irving at Bayerische Hof, Milton, Ontario, October 5, 1991 as cited in Richard Evans, *David Irving, Hitler, and Holocaust Denial, Expert Opinion, IvP&DL* (hereafter *Evans Report*), 1.5.5, p. 15. *Evans Report* available at www.hdot.org, "Evidence" (accessed February 20, 2004).

## CHAPTER 1: A PERSONAL AND SCHOLARLY ODYSSEY

1. Deborah E. Lipstadt, *Beyond Belief: The American Press and the Coming of the Holocaust* (New York: Free Press, 1985), 172ff.

2. *Institute for Historical Review (IHR) Newsletter* (October 1988), p. 7; Lipstadt, *Denying the Holocaust,* Chapter 8.

3. Michael A. Hoffmann II, "The Psychology and Epistemology of 'Holocaust' Newspeak," *JHR*, vol. 6 (1985–86), pp. 267–78. *IHR Newsletter* (April 1988), p. 1. *Evans Report*, 3.5(a), pp. 174–89.

4. The IHR was also associated with Noontide Press and the Legion for the Survival of Freedom, Inc., all of which were linked to Willis A. Carto. Mark Hosenball, "Spotlight on the Hill," *New Republic*, September 9, 1981, p. 13.

5. For a more thorough discussion of Holocaust denial and political extremism in Germany, see Hajo Funke, *David Irving, Holocaust Denial, and His Connections to Right-Wing Extremists and Neo-National Socialism (Neo-Nazism) in Germany, Expert Opinion, IvP&DL* (hereafter *Funke Report*) available at www.hdot.org, "Evidence," (accessed August 28, 2004).

6. The deniers' attempt to drape themselves in scholarly respectability is illustrated by Arthur Butz's *The Hoax of the Twentieth Century*. In this heavily footnoted academic-looking book, the Northwestern University professor of electrical engineering contended that gas chambers were an impossibility and described the Holocaust as "a myth perpetrated upon the world by the most powerful group on earth" for Zionist ends. Arthur Butz, *The Hoax of the Twentieth Century* (Newport Beach, Calif.: 1976), pp. 247–48.

7. For Irving's version of his youth and his legal travails, see www.fpp.co.uk/Legal/PQ17Libel/Backfround220170html (accessed August 27, 2004); David Irving and Kai Bird, "Reviewed vs. Reviewer," *New Statesman*, May 8, 1981, pp. 23–26. From 1977, Irving claimed that there were a chain of documents proving that Hitler repeatedly intervened to help the Jews. David Irving, "On Contemporary History and Historiography. Remarks Delivered at the 1983 International Revisionist Conference," *JHR*, vol. 5, nos. 2, 3, 4 (winter 1984), pp. 251–88. *Evans Report*, 4.3(a), pp. 220–22.

8. The prominent historian Hugh Trevor-Roper first thought the diaries genuine. Other scholars were dubious, but *Stern* did not allow them to closely inspect the diaries. By the time of the press conference Trevor-Roper also had developed doubts. Harris, *Selling Hitler* (New York: Pantheon, 1986), pp. 323, 327, 338–59.

9. *Evans Report*, 3.4(a)31, p. 125.

10. Second Zündel Trial ("The Irving testimony"), *Her Majesty the Queen vs. Ernst Zündel*, District Court of Ontario, 1988, 9471ff.

11. Interview with David Irving on Radio Ulster, June 23, 1989, *Evans Report*, 3.3(c)12, p. 99. David Irving, "Preface," *Auschwitz: The End of the Line: The Leuchter Report—The First Forensic Examination of Auschwitz*, Fred Leuchter (London: Focal Point, 1989). *Evans Report*, 3.4(d)33, p. 164.

12. David Irving, *Hitler's War* (London: Hodder & Stoughton, 1977); idem. *Hitler's War* (London: Focal Point, 1991). For a comparison of the 1977 and 1991 editions of *Hitler's War*, see *Evans Report*, 3.3(a), 3.3(b), pp. 89–99.

13. "History's Cache and Carry," *Guardian*, July 7, 1992.

14. Nigel Jackson, *The Case for David Irving* (Cranbrook, Australia: Veritas, 1994), p. 85; "This Week," November 28, 1991, *IvP&DL*, K3, Tab. 12, pp. 7–8. Irving's speeches, articles, diaries, and letters regarding his political activities and sentiments were compiled and submitted to the court by the Defense. They are available in "David Irving: A Political Self Portrait" (hereafter *Irving: Self Portrait*) 1.2/G, www.hdot.org, "Evidence" (accessed June 25, 2004).

15. A. J. P. Taylor, "Hitler the Opportunist," *Observer*, June 18, 1978; Hugh Trevor-Roper, "Hitler: does history offer a defence?" *Sunday Times* (London), June 12, 1977; Paul Addison, "The Burden of Proof," *New Statesman* (London), July 1, 1977, p. 46 as cited in *Evans Report*, 2.5.8, p. 44.

16. John Charmley, *Churchill: The End of Glory* (London: Knopf, 1993), p. 675, note 51 as cited in *Evans Report*, 2.5.13, p. 47. John Lukacs, *The Hitler of History* (New York: Knopf, 1997), pp. 28n, 229.

17. *Die Zeit*, October 6, 1989 as cited in Lukacs, *Hitler of History*, p. 181. For examples of other historians' evaluations of Irving's work see *Evans Report*, 2.5.8–23, pp. 44–65.

18. *IvP&DL*, Day 16 (February 7, 2000), p. 4.

19. Lukacs, *Hitler of History*, pp. 229–30.

20. Charles W. Sydnor Jr., "'The Selling of Adolf Hitler: David Irving's *Hitler's War*," *Central European History*, vol XII, no. 2 (June 1979), pp. 169–99.

21. Christopher R. Browning, "Beyond 'Intentionalism' and 'Functionalism': The Decision for the Final Solution Reconsidered," *The Path to Genocide: Essays on Launching the Final Solution*, ed. Christopher R. Browning (New York: Cambridge University Press, 1992), pp. 86–121. For a summary of these two positions see Michael Marrus, *The Holocaust in History* (New York: Meridian, 1989), pp. 34–51.

22. Douglas Wilson, "Thomas Jefferson and the Character Issue," *The Atlantic*, pp. 57–74, November 1992.

23. David Kranzler, *Thy Brother's Blood* (Brooklyn: Mesorah, 1987), pp. 68–69. M. J. Nurenberger, *The Scared and the Doomed: The Jewish Establishment vs. the Six Million* (Oakville, New York: Mosaic Press, 1985), p. 31.

## CHAPTER 2: THE DEFENSE STRATEGY

1. "Eliot v. Julius," *The New Yorker*, May 20, 1996, pp. 29–30.

2. Gordon A. Craig, "The Devil in the Details," *New York Review of Books*, September 19, 1996.

3. The public figure defense is based on *New York Times v. Sullivan*, which the Supreme Court heard in 1964. Four black ministers placed a full-page ad in the *New York Times* that claimed that the arrest of the Rev. Martin Luther King Jr. in Alabama for perjury was part of an effort to destroy King's efforts to integrate public facilities and encourage African-Americans to vote. The Montgomery city commissioner, L. B. Sullivan, filed a libel action against the *Times* and against the ministers, who were listed as endorsers of the ad, for defamation. Though the Alabama courts decided in his favor, the Supreme Court reversed the ruling. It held that the First Amendment protected the publication of all statements, even false ones, about the conduct of public officials except when statements are made with actual malice (with knowledge that they are false or in reckless disregard of their truth or falsity). *New York Times v. Sullivan*, 376 U.S. 254 (1964), Docket Number: 39. Argued: January 6, 1964. Decided: March 9, 1964 http://www.oyez.org/oyez/resource/case/277/ (accessed September 16, 2004).

4. David Swarbrick, "Defamation," February 24, 2002, http://www.swarb.co.uk/lawb/defGeneral.html (December 2, 2003).

5. Edwards v Bell (1824) 1 Bing 40–3 at 409, as cited in The Hon. Mr Charles Gray, "Judgment," *IvP&DL* (London, 2000), 4.7 available at www.hdot.org (accessed June 15, 2004).

6. David Irving at Tampa, Florida, October 6, 1995, as cited in *Irving: Self Portrait*, 1.4/A.

7. Errol Morris to Deborah Lipstadt, email, "Fred Leuchter/Holocaust Denial," August 16, 1997.

8. Anthony Kaufman, "Errol Morris and the Accidental Nazi," www.indiewire.com/film/people/int_morris_990127.html (accessed September 15, 2004).

9. Mark Singer, "The Friendly Executioner," *New Yorker*, February 1, 1999.

10. Tony Rogers, Associated Press, October 24, 1990.

11. Memorandum from Ed Carnes, Alabama Assistant Attorney General, to all Capital Punishment States, July 20, 1990; Shelly Shapiro, *Truth Prevails*, (New York: The Beate Klarsfeld Foundation and Holocaust Survivors & Friends in Pursuit of Justice, 1990), pp. 17, 21, 22; Lipstadt, *Denying the Holocaust*, p. 170.

12. The paper had accused her of pocketing the proceeds from the auction of her designer dresses. Anthony proved that the funds went to charity and won Diana the biggest cash settle-

ment ever given to a member of the royal family. The princess had placed her note so that it became part of another headline. The composite headline now read: *"Chief Rabbi Says: Another Victory for the Eminent Lawyer!"*

13. Richard Evans, *In Defense of History* (New York: W. W. Norton, 1999), p. 290.

14. Lukacs, *Hitler of History,* pp. 26, 132, 178, 229–30.

15. Sawoniuk was charged with hiding his role in the murder of Jews in the village of Domachevo in Nazi-occupied Belarus in 1942. The prosecution alleged that Sawoniuk led "search and kill" police squads that hunted down those who escaped the massacre of the town's two thousand nine hundred Jews in September 1942. According to the prosecuting QC, Sawoniuk not only did the "Nazi's bidding, but carried out their genocidal policy with enthusiasm." At the trial, Sawoniuk's attorney tried to get Browning to confirm that his client had no choice but to act as he did. Browning offered a number of possible ways in which he could have behaved otherwise, but made clear that he could do no more than speculate about Sawoniuk. What was important was the testimony of witnesses who were there and knew him. Jay Rayner, "Painful History Lessons Begin in Court 12," *Guardian,* February 14, 1999. http://www.guardian.co.uk/nazis/article/0,2763,191260,00.html (accessed March 22, 2004).

16. Daniel J. Goldhagen, *Hitler's Willing Executioners* (New York: Knopf, 1996); Christopher Browning, *Ordinary Men: Reserve Police Battalion 101* (New York: HarperPerennial, 1998).

17. Richard Evans, conversation with author, London, May 27, 1998.

## CHAPTER 3: AUSCHWITZ: A FORENSIC TOUR

1. Timothy Daniell, *A Literary Excursion to the Inns of Court in London* (London: Wildy & Sons Ltd, 1971).

2. *Documents on the Holocaust: Selected Sources on the Destruction of the Jews of Germany and Austria, Poland and the Soviet Union,* ed. Y. Arad, Y. Gutman, and A. Margaliot (Jerusalem: Ktav, 1981), pp. 249–61. Christopher Browning, "Wannsee Conference," *Encyclopedia of the Holocaust* (New York: Facts on File, 1990), pp. 1591–94.

3. John T. Pawlikowski, "The Auschwitz Convent Controversy: Mutual Misperceptions," *Memory Offended,* ed. Carol Rittner and John K. Roth (New York: Praeger, 1991), pp. 65–66.

4. Wladyslaw T. Bartoszewski, *The Covenant at Auschwitz* (New York: G. Braziller, Inc., 1990), p. 50.

5. In fact, during the early years of German occupation, French Communists were relatively silent about antisemitism, treating it as a by-product of capitalism. During the war they were active resistance fighters and, in that capacity, did help some Jews escape deportation. Susan Zuccotti, *The Holocaust, the French, and the Jews* (New York: Basic Books, 1993), pp. 139–40.

6. Primo Levi, *Survival in Auschwitz* (New York: Touchstone, 1993), p. 42.

7. Debórah Dwork and Robert Jan van Pelt, *Auschwitz: 1270 to the Present* (New York: W. W. Norton, 1996), page after p. 320.

8. Ibid. p. 334.

9. Copies of those documents were also stored in Berlin at the SS headquarters. When the Allies bombed that structure, they were destroyed. Ibid. page after p. 320.

10. Ibid. p. 324.

11. Ibid. plate 18.

12. Polish authorities conducted various studies on the Auschwitz killing apparatus. In 1945, they found traces of cyanide in crematorium ventilation covers and bags of hair. In 1994, they found traces in the delousing room and gas chambers. They also tested areas of the

camp where no Zyklon B had been introduced. They wanted to ascertain whether there was random cyanide content in the walls or, because the camp had been fumigated, cyanide residue remained. They found none. Jan Markiewicz, Wojciech Gubala, Jerzy Labedz, "A Study of the Cyanide Compounds Content in the Walls of the Gas Chambers in the Former Auschwitz and Birkenau Concentration Camp," *Problems of Forensic Science,* vol. 30 (1994), p. 19ff. as cited in Robert Jan van Pelt, *Expert Opinion, IvP&DL* (hereafter *Van Pelt Report),* part 4, sec. 9, pp. 545–50. *Van Pelt Report* available at www.hdot.org, "Evidence" (accessed February 20, 2004).

13. *New York Times,* June 26, 1999; D. D. Guttenplan to author, London, October 12, 1999.

## CHAPTER 4: OUR OBJECTIVE CHANGES

1. *Evans Report,* 1.6.1–1.6.2, 6.2.1, pp. 19–20, 739.

2. David Irving, *Action Report,* 1999, http://www.fpp.co.uk/Inner/Circle.html (accessed September 15, 2004).

3. The penultimate version of Browning's report referred to the report by Kurt Gerstein, who served as the head of the Technical Disinfection Department of the Waffen SS, where he worked with various toxic gases, including Zyklon B. In his report, Gerstein described a gassing he had witnessed in the summer of 1942. Browning included the disclaimer that aspects of Gerstein's report were clearly exaggerated and provided one such example. He contended, however, that the exaggerations did not invalidate other confirmable aspects of the report, which were, in fact, far more important. The final version of Browning's report, the version that should have been given to Irving, contained a more complete listing of Gerstein's exaggerations. Browning wished to deprive Irving of the opportunity to suggest that he was being selective or repressive in his use of this evidence. Christopher R. Browning, *Evidence for the Implementation of the Final Solution, Expert Opinion, IvP&DL* (hereafter *Browning Report),* 5.4.1.3ff, pp. 50–52. *Browning Report* available at www.hdot.org, "Evidence" (accessed July 5, 2004).

## CHAPTER 5: "ALL RISE!"

1. *IvP&DL,* Day 1 (January 11, 2000), p. 5.

2. *IvP&DL,* Day 1 (January 11, 2000), pp. 14, 16, 20–22.

3. *IvP&DL,* Day 1 (January 11, 2000), pp. 22, 26.

4. *IvP&DL,* Day 1 (January 11, 2000), pp. 49, 51–52, 62.

5. *IvP&DL,* Day 1 (January 11, 2000), pp. 28–30.

6. *IvP&DL,* Day 1 (January 11, 2000), pp. 42–46.

7. *IvP&DL,* Day 1 (January 11, 2000), pp. 86–88.

8. *IvP&DL,* Day 1 (January 11, 2000), pp. 89–90.

9. *IvP&DL,* Day 1 (January 11, 2000), pp. 91–94. David Irving, *Hitler's War* (1977), pp. xiv, 332; idem. *Hitler's War* (1991), p. 427; Evans, *Lying about Hitler,* pp. 78–82.

10. *IvP&DL,* Day 1 (January 11, 2000), pp. 95–98.

11. *IvP&DL,* Day 1 (January 11, 2000), pp. 98–101.

## CHAPTER 6: IRVING IN THE BOX: NOT A DENIER BUT A VICTIM

1. *The Times* (London), January 12, 2000; *New York Times,* January 12, 2000, p. 1.

2. *IvP&DL,* Day 2 (January 12, 2000), pp. 111–13.

3. *IvP&DL,* Day 2 (January 12, 2000), p. 114.

4. *IvP&DL,* Day 2 (January 12, 2000), p. 117.

5. *IvP&DL*, Audiocassette 88: Irving press conference in Brisbane, Queensland, March 20, 1986, side 2 no. 107–126 as cited in *Evans Report*, 1.6.7, pp. 22–23.

6. David Irving, "David Irving on Freedom of Speech," Victoria, British Columbia, October 28, 1992, http://www.fpp.co.uk/speeches/speech281092.html (accessed September 12, 2004).

7. David Irving, *Hitler's War*, pp. xii, xxii, 6–7 as cited in *Evans Report*, 2.32–2.3.3, pp. 30–31.

8. *IvP&DL*, Day 2 (January 12, 2000), pp. 147–50.

9. *Publishers Weekly*, March 25, 1996, pp. 25, 75, April 8, 1996, p. 17; *Library Journal*, April 15, 1996, p. 70.

10. *Washington Post*, March 25, April 3, 4, 1996.

11. *IvP&DL*, Day 2 (January 12, 2000), pp. 133–34, 150.

12. *IvP&DL*, Day 2 (January 12, 2000), pp. 154–55.

13. *IvP&DL*, Day 2 (January 12, 2000), pp. 156–58.

14. David Irving at Clarendon Club, London, November 15, 1991, K3/11; David Irving to Tom Marcellus, January 16, 1992, K3; 11th IHR Conference, October 11, 1992, p. 22, K3/13. *IvP&DL*, Defendants' *Closing Statement* (hereafter *Closing Statement*), 5.iv.a.l.2–9, pp. 1–5. *Closing Statement* available at www.hdot.org (accessed March 21, 2004).

15. *IvP&DL*, Day 2 (January 12, 2000), pp. 158, 164, 168.

16. *IvP&DL*, Day 2 (January 12, 2000), pp. 174, 175, 179.

17. *IvP&DL*, Day 2 (January 12, 2000), pp. 201–2.

18. *IvP&DL*, Day 2 (January 12, 2000), pp. 204–6.

19. *IvP&DL*, Day 2 (January 12, 2000), pp. 207–8, 214.

20. *IvP&DL*, Day 2 (January 12, 2000), pp. 215–17.

21. *IvP&DL*, Day 2 (January 12, 2000), p. 217. Helen Darville, "Irving's Berlin," *Australian Style*, March 2000, pp. 83–91 http://www.uq.net.au/~enhdemid/irving.html (accessed November 15, 2003).

22. *IvP&DL*, Day 2 (January 12, 2000), p. 217.

CHAPTER 7: THE CHAIN OF DOCUMENTS

1. *IvP&DL*, Day 2 (January 12, 2000), pp. 218–19.

2. *IvP&DL*, Day 2 (January 12, 2000), p. 219.

3. *IvP&DL*, Day 2 (January 12, 2000), p. 225; David Irving at Calgary, Canada, September 29, 1991, *IvP&DL*, K3/9 as cited in *Closing Statements*, 5.iv.a.l.1, p. 2.

4. *IvP&DL*, Day 2 (January 12, 2000), p. 229. David Irving at Clarendon Club, London, November 15, 1991, *IvP&DL*, K3/11, as cited in *Closing Statements*, 5.iv.a.l.2, p. 2.

5. *IvP&DL*, Day 2 (January 12, 2000), pp. 225–26, 230, 239–46.

6. *IvP&DL*, Day 2 (January 12, 2000), pp. 232–34.

7. *IvP&DL*, Day 2 (January 12, 2000), pp. 264–65.

8. *IvP&DL*, Day 2 (January 12, 2000), pp. 266, 276.

9. *IvP&DL*, Day 2 (January 12, 2000), pp. 289–91.

10. *IvP&DL*, Day 3 (January 13, 2000), pp. 7–8.

11. *IvP&DL*, Day 3 (January 13, 2000), p. 30.

12. *IvP&DL*, Day 3 (January 13, 2000), pp. 34–37.

13. *IvP&DL*, Day 3 (January 13, 2000), pp. 37–42.

14. *IvP&DL*, Day 3 (January 13, 2000), p. 17.

15. *IvP&DL*, Day 3 (January 13, 2000), p. 74.

16. *IvP&DL*, Day 1 (January 11, 2000), pp. 46–47.

17. *IvP&DL*, Day 3 (January 13, 2000), pp. 83–88, 101.

18. David Irving, "Speech to IHR Conference," October 1992, *IvP&DL*, K3/13/24 as cited in *Closing Statements* 5(i)d.2, pp. 20–24. See also David Irving, "Introduction to the American Edition of *Hitler's War*," *JHR*, pp. 415, n. 7 as cited in *Closing Statements*, 5(i)d.2, p. 22.

19. *IvP&DL*, Day 3 (January 13, 2000), pp. 91–93.

20. *IvP&DL*, Day 3 (January 13, 2000), pp. 96–99.

21. *Closing Statements*, 5(i)e.B3.18, p. 32.

22. *Sunday Telegraph* (London), January 16, 2000; *Jewish Telegraphic Agency*, January 18, 2000; *Chicago Tribune*, January 23, 2000. (According to some reporters, the woman said her grandparents died in Auschwitz. The reporter who spoke to me said "her parents.")

CHAPTER 8: THE HOLOCAUST: RANDOM KILLINGS OR SYSTEMATIC GENOCIDE?

1. *IvP&DL*, Day 4 (January 17, 2000), pp. 10, 11.

2. *IvP&DL*, Day 4 (January 17, 2000), pp. 18–19.

3. *IvP&DL*, Day 4 (January 17, 2000), pp. 46–60. For a discussion of British treatment of German decodes regarding the Holocaust, see Richard Breitman, *Official Secrets* (New York: Hill and Wang, 1998), Chapter 6.

4. *IvP&DL*, Day 4 (January 17, 2000), pp. 62–63. For other instances of assertions by Irving that these were ad hoc killings see *Closing Statements*, 5.ix.b, p. 2.

5. *IvP&DL*, Day 4 (January 17, 2000), pp. 64–69.

6. Christopher R. Browning, *Evidence for the Implementation of the Final Solution, Expert Opinion, IvP&DL* (hereafter *Browning Report*), 4.2.8, p. 16. *Browning Report* available at www.hdot.org, "Evidence" (accessed February 22, 2004).

7. *IvP&DL*, Day 4 (January 17, 2000), pp. 79–80.

8. *IvP&DL*, Day 4 (January 17, 2000), pp. 86–88.

9. *IvP&DL*, Day 4 (January 17, 2000), p. 89.

10. *IvP&DL*, Day 4 (January 17, 2000), pp. 94–96.

11. *IvP&DL*, Day 4 (January 17, 2000), pp. 102–3. According to Irving, members of these Eastern European ethnic groups had seen their homes and families bombed and took revenge on the Jews. As Evans observed in his report, Irving never explained how Allied bombing raids on Germany could have turned these people against the Jews. Audiocassette 8: David Irving Press Conference, Brisbane, March 20, 1986, 445–58. Audiocassette 89: Terry Lane, ABC 3LO Radio, interview with David Irving, March 18, 1986, as cited in *Evans Report*, 3.4(c)1–3, pp. 134–35.

12. *IvP&DL*, Day 4 (January 17, 2000), pp. 102–8.

13. *IvP&DL*, Day 4 (January 17, 2000), pp. 110, 113–14, 115, 122.

14. *IvP&DL*, Day 4 (January 17, 2000), pp. 153–57.

15. *IvP&DL*, Day 5 (January 18, 2000), pp. 138–40.

16. *IvP&DL*, Day 6 (January 19, 2000), pp. 42–45, 47–51.

17. *IvP&DL*, Day 7 (January 20, 2000), pp. 25, 41–43, 47–48. D. C. Watt, "Introduction," *Breach of Security*, ed. David Irving (London: W. Kimber, 1968), pp. 15–42.

18. *IvP&DL*, Day 7 (January 20, 2000), pp. 114–25.

19. *IvP&DL*, Day 7 (January 20, 2000), pp. 128–29.

20. *IvP&DL*, Day 7 (January 20, 2000), pp. 141–42, 160–63.

21. *IvP&DL*, Day 7 (January 20, 2000), pp. 183–85.

22. *IvP&DL*, Day 7 (January 20, 2000), pp. 185–89, 192.

23. This idea was suggested by Thomas Powers in *Heisenberg's War: The Secret History of the German Bomb* (New York: Knopf, 1993). For a less benign view of Heisenberg's activities see Jeremy Bernstein's *Hitler's Uranium Club: The Secret Recordings at Farm Hall* (Woodbury, N.Y.: AIP Press, 1996).

24. David Irving, *The Virus House* (London: W. Kimber, 1967).

CHAPTER 9: QUEUES AND GAS CHAMBER CONTROVERSIES

1. *IvP&DL*, Day 8 (January 24, 2000), pp. 6, 7.

2. For Vaillant-Couturier's testimony, see Nuremberg Trial Proceedings, vol. 6, forty-fourth day, Monday, January 28, 1946, Morning Session, http://www.yale.edu/lawweb/avalon/imt/proc/01-28-46.htm (accessed August 26, 2004).

3. *IvP&DL*, Day 8 (January 24, 2000), pp. 14–23. Irving's *Nuremberg: The Last Battle* contained a photograph of Vaillant-Couturier with the following caption: "Credibility Problems." The caption stated: "As Madame Marie-Claude Vaillant-Couturier . . . testified about her ordeal as a Communist interned at Auschwitz, Judge Francis Biddle notes that he does not believe her." David Irving, *Nuremberg: The Last Battle* (London: Focal Point, 1996), picture caption after p. 182. For a summary of Irving's various statements regarding Vaillant-Couturier's testimony see *Closing Statements*, 5(i)p, pp. 72–75.

4. *IvP&DL*, Day 8 (January 24, 2000), pp. 24–27.

5. *IvP&DL*, Day 8 (January 24, 2000), p. 62.

6. *IvP&DL*, Day 8 (January 24, 2000), pp. 86–87.

7. *IvP&DL*, Day 8 (January 24, 2000), p. 135.

8. *IvP&DL*, Day 8 (January 24, 2000), pp. 88, 141–42.

9. *IvP&DL*, Day 8 (January 24, 2000), pp. 145–49.

10. *IvP&DL*, Day 8 (January 24, 2000), pp. 178–79.

11. *IvP&DL*, Day 9 (January 25, 2000), pp. 6–9.

12. *IvP&DL*, Day 9 (January 25, 2000), pp. 10–13.

13. *IvP&DL*, Day 9 (January 25, 2000), p. 47.

14. *IvP&DL*, Day 9 (January 25, 2000), p. 81.

15. *IvP&DL*, Day 9 (January 25, 2000), p. 141.

16. *IvP&DL*, Day 9 (January 25, 2000), pp. 141–51.

17. *IvP&DL*, Day 9 (January 25, 2000), p. 164. For Bimko's testimony see *Trial of Josef Kramer and Forty-four Others (The Belsen Trial)*, ed. Raymond Phillips (London: W. Hodge, 1949), pp. 16, 66, 68, 742.

18. *IvP&DL*, Day 9 (January 25, 2000), pp. 166–68.

19. *IvP&DL*, Day 10 (January 26, 2000), p. 63.

20. Robert Jay Lifton, *The Nazi Doctors* (New York: Basic Books, 1986), pp. 15–16, 232. For a slightly different version of this quote see Ella Lingens-Reiner, *Prisoners of Fear* (London: Gollancz, 1948), pp. 1–2.

21. *IvP&DL*, Day 9 (January 25, 2000), pp. 186–87.

22. *IvP&DL*, Day 9 (January 25, 2000), p. 193.

23. *IvP&DL*, Day 10 (January 26, 2000), pp. 4, 22.

24. These wire-mesh columns were attached to the four structural columns supporting the roof. Since two of the wire columns were on the east side of the structural columns and two on the west side, they formed a staggered arrangement. *IvP&DL*, Day 10 (January 26, 2000), p. 43.

25. *IvP&DL*, Day 10 (January 26, 2000), pp. 52, 53.

26. *IvP&DL*, Day 10 (January 26, 2000), pp. 78, 100. Testimony of Henryk Tauber, as quoted in Jean-Claude Pressac, *Auschwitz: Technique and Operation of the Gas Chamber* (Paris: CNRS Éditions, 1993), pp. 489, 494. See also *Van Pelt Report*, part 2, sec. IV, p. 190.

27. *IvP&DL*, Day 10 (January 26, 2000), pp. 78, 86.

28. *IvP&DL*, Day 11 (January 27, 2000), pp. 147–49.

29. *Those Were the Days: The Holocaust As Seen by the Perpetrators and Bystanders*, ed. Ernst Klee, Willi Dressen, and Volker Riess; trans. Deborah Burnstone (London: Hamish Hamilton, 1993), pp. 252–55.

30. *IvP&DL*, Day 10 (January 26, 2000), pp. 94–95.

31. *IvP&DL*, Day 10 (January 26, 2000), pp. 99–103.

32. *IvP&DL*, Day 8 (January 24, 2000), p. 144.

33. *IvP&DL*, Day 10 (January 26, 2000), p. 184.

34. *IvP&DL*, Day 10 (January 26, 2000), pp. 184–86.

35. James Dalrymple, "The Curse of Revisionism," *Independent* (London), January 29, 2000.

36. *IvP&DL*, Day 11 (January 27, 2000), pp. 10–11.

37. *IvP&DL*, Day 11 (January 27, 2000), pp. 16–44.

38. *IvP&DL*, Day 11 (January 27, 2000), pp. 47–50.

39. *IvP&DL*, Day 11 (January 27, 2000), pp. 48–50, 87–89.

40. *IvP&DL*, Day 11 (January 27, 2000), pp. 148, 151–52.

41. *IvP&DL*, Day 11 (January 27, 2000), pp. 162–64.

42. *IvP&DL*, Day 11 (January 27, 2000), p. 189.

43. *IvP&DL*, Day 13 (February 1, 2000), pp. 16–17.

CHAPTER 10: AN AMERICAN PROFESSOR

1. Kevin B. MacDonald, *The Culture of Critique: An Evolutionary Analysis of Jewish Involvement in Twentieth-Century Intellectual and Political Movements* (Westport, Conn.: Praeger, 1998); idem., *Separation and Its Discontents: Toward an Evolutionary Theory of Anti-Semitism* (Westport, Conn.: Praeger, 1998); idem., *A People That Shall Dwell Alone: Judaism as a Group Evolutionary Strategy* (Westport, Conn.: Praeger, 1994).

2. Kevin MacDonald, "Shulevitz' Yellow Journalism," Culturebox, *Slate Magazine*, January 27, 2000. http://slate.msn.com/id/73780/#ContinueArticle (accessed September 3, 2004).

3. Ibid.

4. Kevin MacDonald, "Witness Statement," par. 3. http://www.csulb.edu/~kmacd/statement_court.htm (accessed March 3, 2004).

5. MacDonald, "Shulevitz' Yellow Journalism."

6. MacDonald, *Separation and Its Discontents*, pp. 177–78. After the trial, MacDonald replied to critics on his website that German Jews' "lack of assimilation" at the time the Nazis came to power "created a volatile situation in which exclusionary policies on the part of the Germans would be one likely outcome." Kevin MacDonald, "Replies to Donald Schwartz," http://www.csulb.edu/~kmacd/replies.htm (accessed August 15, 2004).

7. Kevin MacDonald, "Statement on Trial Testimony," www.ihr.org/jhr/v19/v19n1p56_MacDonald.html, see also: http://www.csulb.edu/~kmacd/media_flyer.htm (accessed August 17, 2004). After the trial, MacDonald attacked Evans for having written in 1989, "Nazi antisemitism was gratuitous: It was not provoked by anything. . . . It was born out of a

political fantasy." He described this as a "dogmatic statement," which makes no attempt to determine the factual basis of antisemitism. Kevin MacDonald, "Reply to Tooby & Shulevitz," http://www.csulb.edu/~kmacd/tooby.html (accessed August 17, 2004).

8. MacDonald, "Shulevitz' Yellow Journalism."

9. MacDonald, *Separation and Its Discontents*, pp. 177–78; idem., *Culture of Critique*, p. 92.

10. Fritz Hippler, *Der ewige Jude: ein dokumentarischer Film* (Deutsche Filmherstellungs- und Vertriebs G.m.b.H., 1938). See also Stig Hornshoj-Moller, "Der ewige Jude," http://www.holocaust-history.org/der-ewige-jude/stills.shtml (accessed January 2, 2004).

11. Judith Shulevitz, "Evolutionary Psychology's Anti-Semite," Culturebox, *Slate Magazine*, January 24, 2000. http://slate.msn.com/id/1004446/ (accessed March 14, 2004).

12. For some of the discussion MacDonald's testimony generated, see http://www.h-net.org/logsearch/. Keywords: MacDonald, Lipstadt, Irving.

13. John Tooby email to Deborah Lipstadt, January 30, 2000.

14. Steven Pinker, "Battling Bad Ideas," January 27, 2000, www.psych.ucsb.edu/research/cep/slatedialog.html (accessed August 12, 2004).

15. Judith Shulevitz, "On Fighting Bad Ideas," Culturebox, *Slate*, January 25, 2000. August 12, 2002. http://slate.msn.com/id/1004469/; Judith Shulevitz, "MacDonald vs. Culturebox, Continued," Culturebox, *Slate*, January 27, 2000. http://slate.msn. com/id/1004480/ (accessed September 15, 2004). "Slate Magazine Dialogue On: How to Deal with Fringe Academics," *Center for Evolutionary Psychology*. Homepage. N.D. http://www.psych.ucsb.edu/research/cep/slatedialog.html (accessed September 15, 2004).

16. *IvP&DL*, Day 12 (January 31, 2000), pp. 6–7.

17. *IvP&DL*, Day 12 (January 31, 2000), pp. 9–16.

18. *IvP&DL*, Day 12 (January 31, 2000), pp. 15–17.

19. *IvP&DL*, Day 12 (January 31, 2000), pp. 18–24.

20. *IvP&DL*, Day 12 (January 31, 2000), pp. 24–25.

21. Dan Jacobson, "The Downfall of David Irving," *Times Literary Supplement*, March 12, 2000.

## CHAPTER 11: EXONERATING HITLER, EXCORIATING THE ALLIES

1. *IvP&DL*, Day 12 (January 31, 2000), pp. 26–28.

2. *The Destruction of Hungarian Jewry*, ed. R. Braham, vol. 1 (New York: Pro Arte, 1963), docs. 86, 92. See also Debórah Dwork and Robert Jan van Pelt, *Holocaust: A History* (New York: W. W. Norton, 2002), pp. 172–73.

3. *Staatsmänner und Diplomaten bei Hitler*, ed. A. Hillgruber, vol. 2, p. 256, as cited in *Evans Report*, 4.3(h)(ii)3, pp. 441–42.

4. Irving, *Hitler's War* (1977), p. 872; idem., *Hitler's War* (1991), pp. 541–42; *Evans Report*, 4.3(h)(iii)A, p. 443.

5. Irving, *Hitler's War* (1977), p. 509, as cited in *Evans Report*, 4.3(h)(iii)C1, pp. 446–47.

6. Ibid.; repeated in David Irving, "Hitler and the Jews," *Spectator*, September 30, 1978 (correspondence column).

7. *IvP&DL*, Day 12 (January 31, 2000), pp. 41–42.

8. *IvP&DL*, Day 12 (January 31, 2000), pp. 43–49, 56.

9. David Irving, *Göring: A Biography* (New York: Morrow, 1989), p. 59; *Evans Report*, 4.3(b)(ii), pp. 225–26.

10. *Evans Report*, 4.3(b)(iii)–(v), pp. 226–30.

11. *IvP&DL*, Day 12 (January 31, 2000), pp. 63–73.

12. David Irving, *Goebbels: Mastermind of the Third Reich* (London: Focal Point, 1996), pp. 276–77.

13. *IvP&DL*, Day 12 (January 31, 2000), pp. 88–90.

14. *Evans Report*, 4.3(c)(ii)(F)9–11, pp. 265–67.

15. *IvP&DL*, Day 12 (January 31, 2000), pp. 110–11. What this telex did halt were attacks that endangered German property, the looting of Jewish shops and dwellings, and assaults on foreigners, even if they were Jews. *Evans Report*, 4.3(c)(ii)(F)1–4, pp. 262–63.

16. *IvP&DL*, Day 13 (February 1, 2000), pp. 59–69.

17. David Irving at Dresden, February 13, 1990, *Closing Statements*, 5(iv)(a)(ii)15, p. 8.

18. *Evans Report*, 5.2(d)(i)–(iii), pp. 508–23. See also Richard Evans, *Lying about Hitler*, p. 154.

19. *IvP&DL*, Day 13 (February 1, 2000), pp. 83–89.

20. *IvP&DL*, Day 13 (February 1, 2000), pp. 91–93.

21. Theo Miller to Irving, February 7, 25, 26, 1965, as cited in *Evans Report*, 5.2(d)(iii)(E)1–5, pp. 537–40.

22. *IvP&DL*, Day 13 (February 1, 2000), pp. 135–43.

23. *Evans Report*, 5.2(d)(v)1–5, pp. 552–54. For a list of Irving's widely varying estimates of the Dresden death toll, see *Closing Statement*, 5(vii)(a)1.1–1.3, pp. 1–3.

24. *IvP&DL*, Day 13 (February 1, 2000), p. 159. *Evans Report*, 5.2(f)4, p. 572.

## CHAPTER 12: FIGHTING WORDS

1. *IvP&DL*, Day 14 (February 2, 2000), p. 84.

2. *IvP&DL*, Day 14 (February 2, 2000), pp. 88–96.

3. *IvP&DL*, Day 14 (February 2, 2000), pp. 96–100.

4. David Irving, "David Irving on Freedom of Speech," Victoria, British Columbia, October 28, 1992, http://www.fpp.co.uk/speeches/speech281092.html (accessed January 12, 2004). Mandela was imprisoned for twenty-six years.

5. *IvP&DL*, Day 14 (February 2, 2000), pp. 105–7.

6. *IvP&DL*, Day 14 (February 2, 2000), pp. 108–12.

7. *IvP&DL*, Day 14 (February 2, 2000), pp. 112–13.

8. *IvP&DL*, Day 14 (February 2, 2000), pp. 113–14.

9. *IvP&DL*, Day 14 (February 2, 2000), pp. 130–33. David Irving at Tampa, Florida, October 6, 1995, "Irving: Self-Portrait," 1.4/A, K3, Tab. 20, pp. 16–19.

10. *IvP&DL*, Day 14 (February 2, 2000), pp. 138–39. David Irving at Tampa, Florida, October 6, 1995, op. cit.

11. *IvP&DL*, Day 14 (February 2, 2000), p. 145.

12. Irving's Diaries, December 8–13, 23, 30, 1994, "Evidence of David Irving's Right Wing Extremism" (hereafter *RWE*), sec. 004, *IvP&DL*, www.hdot.org (accessed January 12, 2004). David Duke, *My Awakening* (Newport Beach, Calif.: Noontide Press, 1998), p. 245. In 1994, Duke sent Irving a list of four hundred people who had donated over $100 to his campaign. Irving noted in his diary that there were "some names I recognize." After "weed[ing] out those names," possibly because they were already on Irving's own list, he proclaimed it "time to get to work on milking the David Duke list." Immediately after the bombing of the Oklahoma City federal building, Irving and Duke checked whether they had a "Jimmy [sic] McVeigh" on their mailing lists. If Irving found such a name he intended to go directly to the FBI. I found it striking that Irving even suspected that he might find McVeigh among his supporters. Irving

diary, October 31, 1994; November 1, 1994; May 8, 1995; December 8–13, 23, 1994; January 6–7, 1995; November 15, 1997. *RWE*, sec. 004, *IvP&DL*, http://www.hdot. org/nsindex.html (accessed March 12, 2004).

13. *Spotlight*, which was published by Carto, featured articles such as "Famous Gas Chamber Victims Living Well" and "White Race Becoming an Endangered Species?" Carto's Noontide Press published *The Protocols of the Elders of Zion*, *Mein Kampf*, and Henry Ford's *The International Jew*. Irving met Carto and corresponded with him. After one such meeting he reassured Carto that "you . . . and the rest of the gang are nice guys and I'll punch anyone in the nose who says different." Publicly Irving tried to keep his distance. During the Zündel trial, when Carto told Irving that he would "make a song and dance in *The Spotlight* about the trial," Irving "panicked" and instructed him "to lay off any publicity" because he was then "in mid-deal in New York on two books and any publicity here of the Toronto testimony could sink the deal."

Eventually Irving seemed to grow less concerned about his Carto links. In 1994, Irving told Carto that he might consider becoming editor of the IHR's *Journal of Historical Review*. Though he never took the position, he warmly endorsed the publication: "It is sincere, balanced, objective, and devoid of polemics. It presents the enemies of truth with a serious opponent. . . . [L]ong may . . . the Journal stay unchanged—staunch and unflinching." David Irving, "A Radical's Diary," *Focal Point*, March 8, 1982, p. 13; Irving to Willis Carto, November 18, 1994, Interrogatories, October 1999 draft, p. 68; Diary of David Irving, April 28, 1988, May 4, 1994, Interrogatories, October 1999, pp. 67, 75. For Irving's endorsement of the *IHR*, http://www.ihr.org/other/endorsements.html (accessed July 12, 2004).

14. *IvP&DL*, Day 15 (February 3, 2000), pp. 10–15.

15. *IvP&DL*, Day 15 (February 3, 2000), p. 17.

16. *IvP&DL*, Day 15 (February 3, 2000), pp. 20–22.

17. Kate Kelland, "British Historian Refuses to Tame Views," Reuters, February 4, 2000.

CHAPTER 13: REVOLTING CALCULATIONS

1. Irving Diaries, June 10–11, 1992, July 2–3, 1999. *Closing Statements*, 5(viii)(a), pp. 1–6.

2. *IvP&DL*, Day 15 (February 3, 2000), pp. 46, 51, 55, 69, 74–75.

3. Daniel Snowman, "John Keegan," *History Today*, May, 2000, http://www.findarticles. com/p/articles/mi_m1373/is_5_50/ai_62087850 (accessed September 15, 2004). I knew that Keegan had not participated in a war because of a physical disability; I did not know that it was so severe.

4. *IvP&DL*, Day 16 (February 7, 2000), pp. 4–9.

5. *IvP&DL*, Day 16 (February 7, 2000), pp. 12–13.

6. *IvP&DL*, Day 16 (February 7, 2000), pp. 16–20.

7. *The Einsatzgruppen Reports*, ed. Yitzhak Arad, Shmuel Krakowski, and Shmuel Spector (New York: Holocaust Library, 1989), pp. xiii–xv. Turkey has not yet made the documentation regarding the Armenian genocide fully available to researchers.

8. *IvP&DL*, Day 16 (February 7, 2000), pp. 35, 36.

9. *IvP&DL*, Day 16 (February 7, 2000), pp. 43–44.

10. *IvP&DL*, Day 16 (February 7, 2000), p. 51.

11. *IvP&DL*, Day 16 (February 7, 2000), pp. 59–60.

12. *IvP&DL*, Day 16 (February 7, 2000), p. 118.

13. *IvP&DL*, Day 16 (February 7, 2000), pp. 136–37. There was no question about these reports' authenticity. After the war, the Allies discovered them in the Gestapo's Berlin headquarters. At the 1947 *Einsatzgruppen* trials, the officer who compiled the reports identified them.

The defendants, whose fate was determined in great measure by these reports, did not dispute their authenticity.

14. *IvP&DL*, Day 16 (February 7, 2000), pp. 142–43.

15. *IvP&DL*, Day 17 (February 8, 2000), pp. 4–11.

16. *IvP&DL*, Day 17 (February 8, 2000), pp. 12–13.

17. *IvP&DL*, Day 17 (February 8, 2000), pp. 20–22.

18. *IvP&DL*, Day 17 (February 8, 2000), p. 83. This issue came up again later that day when Rampton reexamined Browning, pp. 200–204.

19. *IvP&DL*, Day 17 (February 8, 2000), pp. 64–67.

20. *IvP&DL*, Day 17 (February 8, 2000), p. 70.·

21. *IvP&DL*, Day 17 (February 8, 2000), p. 111.

22. *IvP&DL*, Day 17 (February 8, 2000), p. 115.

23. *IvP&DL*, Day 17 (February 8, 2000), pp. 153–56, 180.

24. *IvP&DL*, Day 17 (February 8, 2000), pp. 181–82.

## CHAPTER 14: LYING ABOUT HITLER

1. *IvP&DL*, Day 18 (February 10, 2000), p. 6.

2. *IvP&DL*, Day 18 (February 10, 2000), pp. 21, 30.

3. *IvP&DL*, Day 18 (February 10, 2000), pp. 57–61.

4. *IvP&DL*, Day 18 (February 10, 2000), pp. 101–2.

5. *IvP&DL*, Day 18 (February 10, 2000), pp. 102–4.

6. *IvP&DL*, Day 18 (February 10, 2000), pp. 120–23.

7. *IvP&DL*, Day 18 (February 10, 2000), p. 134.

8. *IvP&DL*, Day 18 (February 10, 2000), pp. 146–47.

9. *IvP&DL*, Day 19 (February 14, 2000), pp. 14–15.

10. *Evans Report*, 3.4(d)50, p. 168.

11. *IvP&DL*, Day 19 (February 14, 2000), p. 54.

12. *IvP&DL*, Day 19 (February 14, 2000), p. 55. David Irving at Clarendon Club, London, September 19, 1992, "Irving: Self-Portrait," 1(B) 1.7(c)(1.7/T) www.hdot.org.

13. *IvP&DL*, Day 19 (February 14, 2000), p. 57.

14. *IvP&DL*, Day 19 (February 14, 2000), pp. 95–96.

15. *IvP&DL*, Day 19 (February 14, 2000), pp. 141, 149.

16. *IvP&DL*, Day 19 (February 14, 2000), pp. 152–53.

17. David Irving at Latvian Hall, Toronto, November 8, 1992, videotape 190, *Evans Report*, 3.4(a) 12–14, pp. 113–14.

18. *IvP&DL*, Day 19 (February 14, 2000), pp. 155–56.

19. *IvP&DL*, Day 19 (February 14, 2000), pp. 184–85.

20. *IvP&DL*, Day 19 (February 14, 2000), pp. 206–9.

## CHAPTER 15: *THE DIARY OF ANNE FRANK*: A NOVEL?

1. The historians and forensic specialists who tested the diary found some corrections in various colors, some of which were clearly made by Anne herself, others made by her father, who renumbered some loose pages at the bottom. The colors, which include black ink, pencil, red, and green, concerned spelling corrections, page numbering, and the like and were not contextual. *The Diary of Anne Frank: The Critical Edition*, Prepared by the Netherlands State Institute for War Documentation, ed. David Barnouw and Gerrold van der Stroom (New York: Doubleday, 1989), pp. 160, 163–64.

2. *IvP&DL*, Day 20 (February 15, 2000), pp. 67–68.
3. *IvP&DL*, Day 20 (February 15, 2000), pp. 76–81.
4. *IvP&DL*, Day 20 (February 15, 2000), pp. 95–99.
5. Irving, *Göring*, p. 518, footnote reference for p. 55, as cited in *Evans Report*, 4.3(b)(iii), pp. 226–27. See also *Pleadings*, IV, p. 14, *IvP&DL*.
6. *IvP&DL*, Day 18 (February 10, 2000), pp. 160–61.
7. *IvP&DL*, Day 20 (February 15, 2000), pp. 200–1, 203, 213.
8. *IvP&DL*, Day 21 (February 16, 2000), p. 78.
9. Irving, *Goebbels*, p. 277.
10. *IvP&DL*, Day 21 (February 16, 2000), pp. 88–94.
11. *IvP&DL*, Day 22 (February 17, 2000), pp. 36–40.
12. *IvP&DL*, Day 23 (February 21, 2000), pp. 164–65.
13. David Irving to Harold Evans, *Sunday Times* (London), September 14, 1977, as cited in *Evans Report*, 4.3(j)(v)2, p. 485.
14. *IvP&DL*, Day 23 (February 21, 2000), pp. 183–84.

## CHAPTER 16: OUR GERMAN CONTINGENT

1. *IvP&DL*, Day 24 (February 23, 2000), pp. 42–46, 94–96.
2. *IvP&DL*, Day 24 (February 23, 2000), pp. 100–4.
3. *IvP&DL*, Day 24 (February 23, 2000), pp. 108, 113.
4. Peter Longerich, *Hitler's Role in the Persecution of the Jews by the Nazi Regime, Expert Opinion, IvP&DL*, Section 15.6, p. 57.
5. *IvP&DL*, Day 24 (February 23, 2000), pp. 151–56, 184.
6. Dan Yurman, "Helen Darville Returns," Online posting, February 27, 2000, Holocaust on Trial list; idem., "Counting Coup: Discovering Helen Darville," Online posting, March 1, 2000, <hot-l@nizkor.org> (accessed July 23, 2004).
7. Janice Kulyk Keefer, "Multiculturalism: Could the Demidenko Scandal Have Happened in Canada," *The Sydney Papers* (winter 1996), pp. 74–75.
8. Paul Gardner, "The Demidenko/Darville Affair: Media Summary," September 18, 1995. http://www.nizkor.org/ftp.cgi/people/d/darville.helen/press/press-summary (March 26, 2004).
9. Cassandra Pybus, "Helen Darville aka Helen Demidenko—Update," *Australian Humanities Review*, February 1997. http://www.lib.latrobe.edu.au/AHR/emuse/demidenko/demiupdate.html (accessed August 19, 2004).
10. "Irving's Berlin: Helen Darville Speaks with David Irving," *Australian Style*, March 2000.
11. Robert Manne, "Tears for David Irving," *Sydney Morning Herald*, February 28, 2000, p. 7, http://www.geocities.com/fairfax_are_yellow/manne.html (accessed September 15, 2004).
12. *IvP&DL*, Day 25 (February 24, 2000), pp. 32–34.
13. *IvP&DL*, Day 25 (February 25, 2000), pp. 48–49, 51–52.
14. Peter Longerich, *The Systematic Character of the National Socialist Policy for the Extermination of the Jews, Expert Opinion, IvP&DL*, sec. 2.3.1–2.4.2, pp. 16–19.
15. *IvP&DL*, Day 25 (February 25, 2000), pp. 94–97.

## CHAPTER 17: CAVORTING WITH THUGS OR GUILT BY ASSOCIATION?

1. "RWE," and "Irving: Self-Portrait," *IvP&DL*, www.hdot.org (accessed February 4, 2004); *IvP&DL*, Day 26 (February 28, 2000), pp. 133–37, 143–47.

2. *IvP&DL*, Day 26 (February 28, 2000), pp. 149–52.

3. *IvP&DL*, Day 27, (February 29, 2000), p. 2.

4. *Funke Report*, 3.2.10, 3.2.27–30, 3.3.6, pp. 23, 30–31, 34.

5. "Irving: Self-Portrait," 4/B; *Funke Report*, 5.1.8, 5.3.12–13, 5.3.19–20, pp. 54, 63–64, 66.

6. *Funke Report*, 3.1, 5.9, 8.3, pp. 19–20, 101–4, 135.

7. *Funke Report*, 5.7, 8.7, pp. 93–101, 136.

8. *Funke Report*, 6.1–6.4, pp. 106–09.

9. This film was shown on Day 27. Rampton read out this quote on the following day. *IvP&DL*, Day 28, (March 1, 2000), pp. 190–91.

10. *IvP&DL*, Day 27, (February 29, 2000), pp. 60, 93.

11. *IvP&DL*, Day 27, (February 29, 2000), pp. 147–48.

12. *IvP&DL*, Day 27, (February 29, 2000), pp. 162–65.

13. *IvP&DL*, Day 28, (March 1, 2000), pp. 69–70.

14. *IvP&DL*, Day 28, (March 1, 2000), p. 92.

15. David Irving, Diary entry, April 20, 1990, as cited in *Funke Report*, 5.3.35, p. 72. *IvP&DL*, Day 28 (March 1, 2000), pp. 98–99.

16. *IvP&DL*, Day 28, (March 1, 2000), pp. 152–53.

17. *IvP&DL*, Day 28, (March 1, 2000), pp. 184–85.

18. *IvP&DL*, Day 28, (March 1, 2000), p. 194.

19. *IvP&DL*, Day 28, (March 1, 2000), pp. 199–200.

CHAPTER 18: ONE-PERSON GAS CHAMBERS AND WHITE PEOPLE'S POLKAS

1. *IvP&DL*, Day 29 (March 2, 2000), pp. 14–15.

2. *IvP&DL*, Day 29 (March 2, 2000), pp. 16, 22–27.

3. *IvP&DL*, Day 29 (March 2, 2000), pp. 35–37.

4. "What Is the National Alliance?" http://www.natall.com/what-is-na (accessed September 15, 2004).

5. "'Turner Diaries' introduced in McVeigh trial," *CNN Interactive*, April 28, 1997, http://www.cnn.com/US/9704/28/okc/ (accessed July 2, 2004).

6. *IvP&DL*, Day 29 (March 2, 2000), pp. 38–39.

7. *IvP&DL*, Day 29 (March 2, 2000), pp. 40–49.

8. *IvP&DL*, Day 29 (March 2, 2000), pp. 49–51.

9. *IvP&DL*, Day 29 (March 2, 2000), pp. 57–58.

10. "What Is the National Alliance?" op. cit.; *IvP&DL*, Day 29 (March 2, 2000), pp. 57–58, 59–63.

11. *IvP&DL*, Day 29 (March 2, 2000), pp. 33–34.

12. For recent changes in BNP strategies see: "BNP: A Party on the Fringe," BBC, Friday, August 24, 2001, http://news.bbc.co.uk/1/hi/uk/1507680.stm (accessed September 15, 2004).

13. *IvP&DL*, Day 29 (March 2, 2000), pp. 72–76.

14. Irving, *Goebbels*, pp. 46–47, as cited in *Evans Report*, 5.4(b)2–6, pp. 692–94.

15. *IvP&DL*, Day 29 (March 2, 2000), pp. 94–95. Lidice, the Germans claimed, had assisted Heydrich's assassins. It was razed to the ground and some 200 male inhabitants and approximately 70 women were murdered. The remaining 198 women were sent to Ravensbrück concentration camp, where many of them died. Kurt Daluege was hanged in Prague on October 24, 1946. The brutal destruction of Lidice had a tremendous impact on Allied opinion about Nazi Germany. In the United States the Office of War Information used it, rather than Jewish deaths, to illustrate Nazi brutality.

16. *Evans Report,* 5.4(b)8–14, pp. 696–98.
17. *IvP&DL,* Day 29 (March 2, 2000), pp. 97–101.
18. *IvP&DL,* Day 29 (March 2, 2000), p. 101–6.

CHAPTER 19: THE FINAL SCENE
  1. *IvP&DL,* Day 32 (March 15, 2000), p. 3.
  2. *IvP&DL,* Day 32 (March 15, 2000), pp. 5–8.
  3. *IvP&DL,* Day 32 (March 15, 2000), pp. 9–13.
  4. *IvP&DL,* Day 32 (March 15, 2000), pp. 13–16.
  5. *IvP&DL,* Day 32 (March 15, 2000), pp. 21–23.
  6. *IvP&DL,* Day 32 (March 15, 2000), pp. 28–30.
  7. *IvP&DL,* Day 32 (March 15, 2000), pp. 30–34.
  8. *IvP&DL,* Day 32 (March 15, 2000), pp. 44–46.
  9. *IvP&DL,* Day 32 (March 15, 2000), pp. 46–49.
 10. *IvP&DL,* Day 32 (March 15, 2000), pp. 50–55.
 11. *IvP&DL,* Day 32 (March 15, 2000), pp. 78–83.
 12. *IvP&DL,* Day 32 (March 15, 2000), pp. 104–8.
 13. *IvP&DL,* Day 32 (March 15, 2000), pp. 111, 115, 124, 141.
 14. *IvP&DL,* Day 32 (March 15, 2000), pp. 144, 147, 158–59.
 15. *IvP&DL,* Day 32 (March 15, 2000), pp. 162–63.
 16. *IvP&DL,* Day 32 (March 15, 2000), p. 171.
 17. *IvP&DL,* Day 32 (March 15, 2000), p. 184.
 18. *IvP&DL,* Day 32 (March 15, 2000), p. 194.
 19. *IvP&DL,* Day 32 (March 15, 2000), pp. 197–217.
 20. *IvP&DL,* Day 32 (March 15, 2000), pp. 218–22.

CHAPTER 20: JUDGMENT DAY: PHONE CHAINS, PSALMS, AND SLEEPLESS SURVIVORS
  1. "No Libel Found in Holocaust Suit," *Atlanta Journal Constitution,* April 12, 2000.
  2. Kate Kelland, "Hitler Historian Refuses to Tame Views," Reuters, February 4, 2000.
  3. "Where Are All Their Holes?" *Haaretz* (Israel), February 4, 2000.
  4. Deborah E. Lipstadt, "Statement," April 11, 2000, http://www.mishcon.co.uk/inp/inp_a/inp_a_pr/inp_a_pr04003.htm.
  5. The Hon. Mr Charles Gray, "Judgment," *IvP&DL,* (hereafter: J) 13.12.
  6. J 13.13.
  7. J 13.16.
  8. J 13.15, 13.18, 13.20.
  9. J 13.21.
 10. J 13.24.
 11. J 13.26.
 12. J 13.58.
 13. J 13.44.
 14. J 13.49.
 15. J 13.120.
 16. J 13.122.
 17. J 13.51, 13.126.
 18. J 13.72, 13.77, 13.80, 13.84, 13.91.

19. J 13.95.

20. J 13.104–05, 13.106, 13.113–14.

21. J 13.143–44.

22. J 13.163.

23. J 13.167, 14.1.

24. D. C. Watt, "History Needs David Irving," *Evening Standard*, April 11, 2000, p. 13.

25. "Irving Defiant over Libel Defeat," *BBC News*, April 12, 2000, http://news.bbc.co.uk/1/hi/uk/709996.stm (accessed September 9, 2004).

26. John Keegan, "The Trial of David Irving and My Part in His Downfall," *Daily Telegraph*, April 12, 2000, p. 28.

27. "History in Court," *New York Times*, April 14, 2000.

28. "History and Bunk," *Times* (London), April 12, 2000, p. 23.

29. *Sydney Morning Herald*, April 14, 2000; *Observer*, April 16, 2000.

30. "The Big Lie," *Fort Worth Star Telegram*, April 13, 2000; *Economist*, April 15, 2000.

31. "Holocaust Denial," *Irish Times*, April 12, 2000.

32. Helen Darville, "Darville Dumps Irving," *Courier-Mail* (Brisbane, Australia), April 20, 2000.

## CHAPTER 21: ENORMOUS THANKS

1. Alvin H. Rosenfeld, *A Double Dying: Reflections on Holocaust Literature* (Bloomington: Indiana University Press, 1980).

## CHAPTER 22: THE "JESTER'S COSTUME"

1. David Irving, *Action Report*, November 20, 2000. http://www.fpp.co.uk/Legal/Penguin/experts/Evans/RadDi201100.html (accessed March 22, 2004).

2. David Irving, *Action Report*, December 23, 2000.

3. Tim Adams, "Memories are Made of This," *Observer*, February 24, 2002; *London Evening Standard*, January 29, 2001; Dominick Donald, "One Hundred Hitlers," *Guardian*, February 10, 2001.

4. Robert M. W. Kempner to J. Edgar Hoover, March 1, 1969, National Archives, RG 65, Entry A1-111, Box 4. In an interesting postscript the files also indicated that in October 1945 Hoover instructed that Kempner, who had been a special employee of the FBI from 1942 to 1945, was not to be reemployed by the bureau. No reason was indicated.

5. *Judgment*, In the Supreme Court of Judicature, Court of Appeal (Civil Division), On Appeal from the Queen's Bench Division, Before: Lord Justices Pill, Mantell, and Buxton, *IvP&DL*, July 20, 2001.

6. David Irving, *Action Report*, October 31 2001. *Observer*, March 3, 2002.

7. She claimed that the title was legitimate because she had previously been married to a man whose mother hailed from a line of White Russian aristocrats. *The Age* (Australia), December 3, 2002.

8. *Observer*, March 3, 2002. For other details of Renouf's activities see *Independent*, April 23, 2003; *The Age* (Australia), December 3, 2002, May 7, 2003, http://www.theage.com.au/articles/2002/12/02/1038712883644.html (accessed March 18, 2004).

9. "Holocaust Denier Made Bankrupt," *Guardian*, March 5, 2002; "Failed Libel Action Costs Irving His Home," *Guardian*, May 22, 2002; Kate Taylor, "Irving Goes Bankrupt," *Searchlight*, April 2002.

10. "First Statement of Daniel Davis," High Court of Justice in Bankruptcy, in the Matter

of David John Cawdell Irving (in Bankruptcy) and in the Matter of the Insolvency Act 1986, Between Deborah Lipstadt, Applicant, and Louis M. Brittain, Colin Michael Trevethyn Haig, David John Cawdell Irving, Respondents, No. 257 of 2002.

11. He also accused the Mishcon staff of "arrang[ing] for an anonymous hate-wreath" to be sent to his daughter's funeral and "gloating at her death." David Irving, Lipstadt to Irving: Happy Holidays, and Now Hand Over All Your Possessions, http://www.fpp.co.uk/Legal/Penguin/Lipstadt_demands_all.html (accessed September 15, 2004).

12. Christopher Noxon, "Is the Pope Catholic . . . Enough?" *New York Times Magazine*, March 9, 2003, pp. 50–53, http://www.nytimes.com/2003/03/09/magazine/09GIBSON.html; Peggy Noonan, "Face to Face with Mel Gibson," *Reader's Digest*, March 2004, http://www.readersdigest.co.uk/magazine/melg.htm; "Pain and *Passion*," *Primetime Thursday*, February 17, 2004, http://abcnews.go.com/sections/Primetime/Entertainment/ mel gibson passion 040216-1.html (accessed June 18, 2004).

13. "Palestinian Leader: Number of Jewish Victims in the Holocaust Might Be 'Even Less Than a Million,'" MEMRI Inquiry and Analysis Series, no. 95 (May 30, 2002), pp. 1–5; "Hamas Leader Rantisi: The False Holocaust," Memri Special Dispatch Series, no. 558 (August 27, 2003), p. 1.

14. Ziedan made this statement in conjunction with the library's display of the *Protocols of the Elders of Zion*. After widespread press reports about this exhibit, the library's administration withdrew the *Protocols* from public display and acknowledged that its inclusion showed "bad judgment and insensitivity." In a posting on his own website Ziedan denied the reports that he praised the *Protocols* and condemned it as a "racist, silly, fabricated, book." He did not, however, retract his statement about the gas chambers or the death toll being one million. He defined the Holocaust as having been an action against "Poles, Slavs, Jews, Gypsies, the crippled, and homosexuals" and made a claim that some Nazi soldiers were themselves Jews. "Protocols of the Elders of Zion: Statement by the Director of the Library of Alexandria," "Fourth Statement: Protocols of the Elders of Zion," http://www.ziedan.com/English/zion/ (accessed July 1, 2004).

15. "Saramago 'Turns the Victims into Murderers,' Lau Charges," *Jerusalem Post*, March 27, 2002; "Poet Paulin 'Banned from Harvard,'" BBC News, November 21, 2002, http://news.bbc.co.uk/1/hi/entertainment/arts/2479687.stm (accessed July 1, 2004).

16. Anthony Julius, *Idolizing Pictures: Idolatry, Iconoclasm, and Jewish Art* (London: Thames & Hudson, 2000), p. 62. See also Judith Shulevitz, "Shock Art," *New York Times Book Review*, March 23, 2003, p. 27.

17. *Observer*, March 3, 2002. See also *Sunday Star-Times* (Auckland, New Zealand) March 10, 2002, *Evening Standard* (London), March 28, 2002, *Independent* (London), April 23, 2003, *The Age* (Australia), May 7, 2003.

AFTERWORD

1. See, e.g., "Holocaust Denial," Wikipedia, The Free Encyclopedia, available at en.wikipedia.org/wiki/Holocaust_denial#The_Irving_affair; see also Donald Watt, "History Needs David Irving," *Evening Standard*, April 11, 2000.

2. Norman G. Finkelstein, *The Holocaust Industry* (New York: Verso, 2003), p. 71.

3. Jacob Weisberg, "The Heresies of Pat Buchanan," *New Republic*, October 22, 1990, p. 22.

# INDEX

# About the author

# About the book

# Read on

Insights,
Interviews
& More . . .

# Meet Deborah E. Lipstadt

Jillian Edelstein

DR. DEBORAH E. LIPSTADT is Dorot Professor of Modern Jewish and Holocaust Studies at Emory University in Atlanta, where she directs the Rabbi Donald A. Tam Institute for Jewish Studies. She is the author of *Denying the Holocaust: The Growing Assault on Truth and Memory* and *Beyond Belief: The American Press and the Coming of the Holocaust.*

Professor Lipstadt was a member of the official White House delegation to the sixtieth anniversary of the liberation of Auschwitz (January 26–27, 2005). She served as a historical consultant to the United States Holocaust Memorial Museum, and was subsequently appointed by President Clinton to two consecutive terms on the United States Holocaust Memorial Council. She was a member of the Executive Committee of the Council and chaired the Educational Committee and Academic Committee of the Holocaust Museum. In addition, Professor Lipstadt has been called upon by members of the United States Congress to consult on political responses to Holocaust denial. From

1996 through 1999 she served as a member of the United States State Department Advisory Committee on Religious Freedom Abroad. In this capacity she, together with a small group of leaders and scholars, advised Secretary of State Madeleine Albright on matters of religious persecution abroad.

Professor Lipstadt has taught at the University of Washington and UCLA. In Spring 2006, she was a visiting professor at the Pontifical Gregorian Institute in Rome where she taught a course on Holocaust memoirs. She is frequently called upon by the media to comment on matters of contemporary interest. She is widely quoted in and a regular contributor to a variety of periodicals.

She maintains a Weblog (blog) at www.lipstadt.blogspot.com. ༀ

> " She advised Secretary of State Madeleine Albright on matters of religious persecution abroad. "

# Why I Wrote
## *History on Trial*

THIS BOOK TRIES TO CONVEY THE EXPERIENCE of going from a relatively quiet existence as a professor to being a defendant in a six-year legal battle that garnered worldwide attention. For three months in the winter of 2000, in courtroom 73 of the Royal High Court in London, Judge Charles Gray presided over *Irving v. Penguin and Lipstadt.* I sat quietly listening as David Irving attacked me and my work. He aimed his barbs not only at me, but at Holocaust history and at the Jewish community. Much, if not all, of what he said about me was simply wrong. Yet there was little I could do to challenge it because at the insistence of my attorneys I was neither testifying nor giving press interviews. Though my words had provoked this libel case, I had to depend on others to make my case for me. For someone who has always tried to maintain control over her life this was excruciatingly difficult.

Though keeping quiet was extraordinarily hard, in many other respects I was lucky. I had a stellar legal team. They tracked Irving's sources. At that point, his inventions and distortions could not abide the light of day. His claims collapsed.

I faced another obstacle. I had to raise 1.5 million dollars to pay for my defense. Luckily a group of people, both Jews and non-Jews, stepped forward to assist me. They asked for no public recognition. In fact, many of them thanked me for the opportunity to be part of this effort.

In addition, my university, Emory,

66 Keeping quiet was extraordinarily hard. 99

supported me in an unprecedented fashion, giving me travel funds, reduced teaching loads, and great moral support. Emory even hired someone to teach my courses while I was in London, thereby preserving the students' opportunity to learn about the Holocaust. One of my objectives in writing this book was to inform readers not only about the mendacity of Holocaust deniers, but also about the sort of goodness exemplified by my supporters. This generosity is a major part of the story.

Another significant aspect of this experience was the response of Holocaust survivors. My interactions with them were profoundly powerful. They sat quietly in court while Irving ridiculed them and claimed that they were either liars or psychotic. They kept telling me that I was their "hero." While I appreciate being praised for what I do, I found their adulation unnerving. I felt undeserving of such gratitude from Holocaust survivors.

Only after the trial did I realize that their praise had less to do with what I had done and far more to do with what had *not* been done sixty years earlier, when they so desperately needed help. I was reminded of the verse in Exodus that describes Moses's encounter with an Egyptian taskmaster beating an Israelite slave:

> And Moses looked here and there and he saw that there was no person and killed the Egyptian.

Rabbinic commentators, uncomfortable with the textual suggestion that Moses was checking to ensure no one would see him kill the Egyptian, say he was actually looking for a "person, someone of stature" to do justice. ▶

> " My interactions with Holocaust survivors were profoundly powerful. "

**66** For the Holocaust victim, the callousness of the bystander was almost as painful as the cruelty of the perpetrator. **99**

### Why I Wrote *History on Trial* (continued)

When he realized there was no one to dispense justice he knew he had to act on his own.

During the Holocaust the victims looked "here and there" for help. There were few persons, governments, or institutions, including the Red Cross and the Vatican, willing to respond. It was not necessarily antisemitism which motivated their inaction. Many simply did not care. In the face of evil they were neutral. All that Jews heard was a resounding, if not deafening, silence. For the victim, the callousness of the bystander was almost as painful as the cruelty of the perpetrator.

Now, many decades later and in vastly different circumstances, survivors felt that there was someone to fight for them. This time there was no neutrality. In defending myself against Irving I had pierced the silence that so haunted them. It did not matter that my fight could not, in any way, be compared to the suffering they experienced. It did not matter that I faced no physical threat. It did not matter that my battle could not bring back their loved ones or mitigate their suffering. My fight became symbolic of what had been absent sixty years earlier. In dramatic contrast to the Holocaust, this time they, for they saw themselves as standing by my side, won. ∾

# Answers to Frequently Asked Questions

*Since the publication of* History on Trial *Professor Lipstadt has heard from many readers. Here, she shares her responses to the questions they most often ask her.*

### In what way was history on trial?

Because I was the defendant and the trial was being held in a UK courtroom we had to prove the truth of what I had written about David Irving. We had to demonstrate that his "version" of history as it regards the Holocaust was bogus. And we did precisely this. We also demonstrated that you can't say history means anything you want it to mean. You must maintain a fidelity to the facts. There is a massive cache of documents about the Holocaust in general and the killing process in particular. We know in fairly great precision how the murders and, for that matter, the entire Final Solution were conducted. While various historians may interpret these documents differently, they can't and don't invent things that are not there.

### Besides debunking Irving, what else did the trial accomplish?

This trial was a victory for history and historians. A stellar team of historians did scrupulous research which guaranteed our victory. In essence, this trial was emblematic of the passing of the torch of memory from Holocaust survivors, the youngest of whom are in their seventies, to historians. Poet ▶

66 There is a massive cache of documents about the Holocaust in general and the killing process in particular. 99

**Answers to Frequently Asked Questions**
*(continued)*

Paul Celan asked who will be the witnesses for the witnesses? This trial demonstrated that historians will be those witnesses.

The trial also demonstrated to people who might have thought that there was a semblance of truth to deniers' arguments that they are bunk. We proved to Judge Gray and to four judges from the Court of Appeal that deniers have made up their claims out of whole cloth.

### Why did you fight back?

In Britain the defendant must prove the truth of what she wrote. If I had not defended myself, Irving would have won by default and could have claimed that the Royal High Court of Justice declared his description of the Holocaust to be legitimate.

Remember, this is a man who moved in two worlds. His books were being reviewed in venues such as the *New York Times* and the *Times Literary Supplement.* Privately he was telling audiences at his talks things like: "More people died in Senator Kennedy's car in Chappaquiddick than died in the gas chambers at Auschwitz." He wasn't dangerous because of absurd statements such as this. He was dangerous because he was thought of as a serious historian with a "bit" of a problem about the Holocaust.

### Does David Irving understand that the suit backfired on him?

I have no idea, but it certainly did. If he had not sued me, no one would have known

> 66 In Britain, the defendant must prove the truth of what she wrote. 99

the extent to which he fabricated and misrepresented evidence. Historians had long known that he wasn't telling the truth when he claimed he could exonerate Hitler, prove no one was gassed in Auschwitz, or demonstrate that there was no plan to murder the Jews. However, no one knew how blatant his misrepresentations of history were. Irving may have thought he could get away with mangling history. Once he sued me, his house of cards collapsed.

*Would the trial and its outcome have been different if there had been a jury?*

I don't think so. However, we might have presented the case differently. A jury might not have read the thousands of documents as carefully as Judge Gray did. We would have had to follow the historical narrative in a more orderly fashion and present the experts' findings in greater detail in the courtroom. It probably would have been—I shudder at the thought    a much longer trial.

   The other difference would have been that a jury would have delivered a verdict, but not the 350-page judgment which so stunningly excoriated Irving. The *Observer* described the judgment as "one of the most crushing judgments ever dumped over an English plaintiff."

*What's happened to Holocaust denial since your trial?*

Many Holocaust denial groups have fallen upon hard times. Some have closed up shop. ▶

66 No one knew how blatant his misrepresentations of history were. 99

Irving and (by extension) the deniers' loss was so overwhelming—if not embarrassing—that much of the support for the denial movement melted away. It may eventually resurrect itself, but for the moment it seems to be on the ropes. This is not just my opinion. Bradley R. Smith, a leading Holocaust denier, recently wrote: "Irving's defeat at that trial was the most serious single blow that revisionism has ever received. . . . It was the Lipstadt trial that convinced serious people that, okay, revisionists had taken an interesting run at the Holocaust story, they had failed in full view of the Western world, and there was no reason to worry about Holocaust revisionism any longer." For once I find myself agreeing with a denier.

The arena in which Holocaust denial thrives is the Arab/Muslim world. According to MEMRI, the organization which translates articles in the Arab press, in 2003 a top Hamas activist referred in the organization's weekly to the "myth of the 'gas chambers' " and complained that "David Irving was sued" because of his Holocaust denial (MEMRI, "Special Dispatch—Palestinian/Arab Antisemitism," August 27, 2003). In December 2004 two well-known Holocaust deniers were interviewed by Iran's Mehr News Agency. Robert Faurisson spoke of the "big lie of the alleged Holocaust" and the Australian Holocaust denier Fredrick Toben decried the "Holocaust lie" and called for a "Holocaust exposé" (*New York Sun,* January 24, 2005). And of course, the president of Iran has denied the Holocaust.

66 Many Holocaust denial groups have fallen upon hard times. Some have closed up shop. 99

*Does it bother you that you're unlikely to recoup any of the money you and your supporters spent on your defense?*

In the UK, loser is supposed to pay costs. But it would have been such a costly process that it seemed wiser to abandon the effort. Remember, this trial was not about money and bankrupting Irving. It was about history and defending me against libel charges. Though I would have liked to repay my supporters.

*Do you worry that, as survivors of the Holocaust die off, deniers will successfully attack the history of the Holocaust?*

Holocaust survivors worry about this. I also used to as well. However, now I am more sanguine. Obviously, the person who can say "this is *my* story, this is what happened to *me*" has a unique potency. We shall desperately miss them when they are gone. Nonetheless we won this victory without calling survivors. We relied on documents, material evidence, and testimony given at trials in the immediate postwar period. My victory should reassure survivors that deniers' threats can be addressed by relying on the historical record.

*C-SPAN's* Book TV *wanted to put you on and then follow your appearance with one by David Irving. What happened?*

C-SPAN's *Book TV* wanted to tape a speech I was to give at Harvard. I was looking forward to presenting my book to an audience of bibliophiles. Then I learned that C-SPAN ▶

66 This trial was not about money and bankrupting David Irving. It was about history and defending me against libel charges. 99

intended to "balance" (their word) my presentation with one by Irving. This would have created a debate between us that I have long refused to have. I cannot imagine them "balancing" an appearance by a specialist on African American history with someone who says slavery is a myth.

When I protested, C-SPAN said that they broadcast "all sorts of opinions" (Holocaust denial is an "opinion"?). When I observed that the court declared Irving a liar, a senior C-SPAN producer responded: "We broadcast liars all the time. We put on members of Congress." I said that if they insisted on this "balance" they could not cover my talk. (Obviously, if they wanted to broadcast a talk by Irving at some other time that was their right.)

Frustrated, I was about to hang up when I added—almost as an afterthought—that I assumed that if I did not appear they would not broadcast Irving. "No," the producer said, "we plan to broadcast him in any case." I was too flabbergasted to ask the obvious: "Where's the balance in that?"

Hundreds of historians and social scientists signed a petition circulated by the David Wyman Institute condemning C-SPAN. C-SPAN admitted it received thousands of e-mails and letters, virtually all of them condemning their decision. Articles appeared in dozens of other papers. I even appeared on *The O'Reilly Factor*. People were incredulous, particularly since this is a network that does not have a policy of presenting two sides of an issue. Why did they insist on "balance," particularly when "the other side" had been

66 C-SPAN's *Book TV* wanted to tape a speech I was to give at Harvard. I was looking forward to presenting my book. . . . Then I learned that C-SPAN intended to 'balance' (their word) my presentation with one by Irving. 99

12

judged to be a liar and falsifier of history? Ultimately, I am more disturbed by C-SPAN's stance than by Holocaust deniers.

*In November 2005 Austrian police arrested David Irving on an outstanding 1989 warrant for having given speeches denying the Holocaust. What is your reaction to this?*

While I am generally opposed to outlawing Holocaust denial, I understand that Holocaust denial has a different resonance in Germany and Austria. Before Irving's February 2006 trial, I called on the Austrians to release him. He should not be a martyr on the altar of free speech. After my trial, Irving was left deflated. Many people thought he looked silly. That's why I call the last chapter "The Court Jester." The only court sentence I want for him is obscurity.

*Irving's lawyer says he intends to recant his denial of gas chambers and plead guilty. What's this about?*

In September 2005 Irving was still claiming that gas chambers were a scientific impossibility. Now his lawyer says it was evidence he saw in Moscow archives that convinced him there were gas chambers. What caused this volte-face? Had he even been in Moscow since the trial? If this is based on his 1990s research in Moscow, why did he insist during the trial that gas chambers were a myth? It makes no sense. Irving seems to think he can say whatever he wants and no one will know he is fabricating. ▶

“ People were incredulous, particularly since this is a network that does not have a policy of presenting two sides of an issue. ”

### Answers to Frequently Asked Questions
*(continued)*

*Iranian president Mahmoud Ahmadinejad has denied the Holocaust and wants to convene a conference to "investigate" the Holocaust. What's your reaction?*

Such a conference will surely raise many of the deniers' familiar arguments that we demolished in my trial. Some people have dismissed him as crazy. I say crazy *like a fox*. This enhances his stature in Iran and the Muslim world, as do his calls for Israel's destruction. It does not, of course, say much for his audience if Holocaust denial and destruction of another state wins him support. In contrast to most deniers, he has the potential to cause real damage. He may soon have his finger on the "button." That's not a reassuring thought.

*Has your life changed since the trial?*

I certainly have a "higher" profile and more name recognition. Many people look to me to speak out on the denial of other genocides, such as the Armenian, or on current genocides, such as in Sudan. I try to use my voice as efficaciously as possible. In general, things have returned to normal. I am back doing what I love best—teaching and writing.

> 66 In general, things have returned to normal. I am back doing what I love best—teaching and writing. 99

# Cold

## On the 60th Anniversary of the Liberation of Auschwitz

IN LATE DECEMBER 2004 I received a call from the White House Presidential Personnel Office asking if I would be part of a small American delegation representing the president and the nation at the sixtieth anniversary of the liberation of Auschwitz. The dates fell smack at the beginning of the semester. I am loath to miss classes. Nonetheless, I decided that this merited the absence, and my dean agreed.

The delegation, which was being led by Vice President Dick Cheney, included: Elie Wiesel; United States Representative Tom Lantos and his wife, Annette, both Holocaust survivors; Fred Schwartz, who had spearheaded the rebuilding of a synagogue in the town of Auschwitz; and Feliks Bruks, a Polish American who had been imprisoned by the Nazis in three concentration camps. When I asked the White House official why I had been included, she explained that it was because of my work, especially my legal travails exposing Holocaust deniers.

So that was how I found myself in the distinguished visitors lounge at Andrews Air Force Base in Maryland on Tuesday, January 25. We boarded a Gulfstream jet that seemed like it might have seated forty, but was configured for ten passengers and six crew members. From the outside it looked like a miniature Air Force One, with the words *United States of America* emblazoned on the side. When we landed in a blinding snowstorm in Kraków, a convoy of police cars, limos, ▶

> **❝** We boarded a Gulfstream jet that seemed like it might have seated forty, but was configured for ten passengers and six crew members. From the outside it looked like a miniature Air Force One. **❞**

### Cold (*continued*)

SUVs, and vans moved forward across the tarmac to greet us. The American ambassador to Poland, Victor Ashe, emerged from a car and thanked us for coming. Our luggage was unloaded and placed on a truck that preceded us to the hotel. By the time I entered my room the luggage was waiting for me. It was all very heady and quite unlike my life as a professor.

But these sybaritic pleasures were severely tempered by the reason for our visit. While I sat in the "control room," a hotel suite that had been turned into an office, dealing with my e-mail, behind me State Department officials vigorously debated the most efficient way to get us to Auschwitz-Birkenau for the following day's ceremony. After listening for a while, I turned around and observed that there was something surreal about discussing how to get to the death camp, the largest "cemetery" in the world, punctually. We laughed uncomfortably.

The next day we sat for three long hours in the falling snow listening to orations and participating in the commemoration. After a while the speeches, many by heads of state, began to morph one into another. What could the statesmen say, surrounded by camp survivors, in the shadow, literally, of the gas chambers? I was reminded of Adorno's pronouncement that "writing poetry after Auschwitz is barbaric." It seemed to me that on a day such as this prose fared little better, except for the words of those who had actually experienced the camps.

I tuned out the speakers and began to reflect on those survivors' writings, which were very much with me because I had just finished teaching a course on memoirs of the Holocaust.

66 What could the statesmen say, surrounded by camp survivors, in the shadow, literally, of the gas chambers? 99

16

In *Still Alive,* Ruth Kluger describes watching an SS guard preening on the other side of the barbed wire with a walking stick that had a loaf of bread stuck to the end. He tormented the starving prisoners by dragging the bread in the mud. Watching the bread destroyed in the dirt hit Kluger "like a blow in the diaphragm because it was such a crudely sarcastic expression of undifferentiated hatred."

Primo Levi describes a similar experience in *Survival in Auschwitz.* During his first days at the camp he saw a large icicle hanging outside his window. Driven by thirst he reached out and grabbed it only to have a "large heavy guard prowling outside" brutally snatch it away. "Warum?" Levi asked. The guard replied: "Hier ist kein warum." Here there is no why.

Sitting there in my four layers of clothing, heavy socks, special boots, earmuffs, and hat, and nursing a cup of hot coffee which our minders had kindly provided us, I was thrust back to the final days of the camp. The Germans, unwilling to let 60,000 surviving Jews fall into the hands of the Red Army, forced them to march through the snow toward Germany, where they were put in concentration camps.

In *Speak You Also,* Paul Steinberg recalled that as the march began he knew that "one thing is certain: In the days to come, many will die just when their wildest dreams are about to come true. And that will be the cruelest blow of all." And Steinberg was correct. So many people died that the trek entered history as a "death march."

In the final chapter of his memoir Levi describes in detail the situation at Auschwitz during the days before the arrival of the Red Army. Levi, left behind in Auschwitz's ▶

> 66 Sitting there in my four layers of clothing, heavy socks, special boots, earmuffs, and hat, and nursing a cup of hot coffee I was thrust back to the final days of the camp. 99

so-called hospital, saw the camp decompose. "No more water, or electricity, broken windows and doors slamming in the wind. . . . Ragged, decrepit, skeleton-like patients . . . dragged themselves everywhere on the frozen soil, like an invasion of worms."

Levi attributed his survival during those difficult last days to the friendship and support of a small group of men who were fellow hospital patients. Their only goal, he told Philip Roth years later, was to save "the lives of our sick comrades." On the night of January 26 one of them died. Levi and his friends were too cold and exhausted to bury him. There was nothing to do but go back to sleep and wait for the next day. "The Russians arrived while Charles and I were carrying Sómogyi a little distance outside. He was very light. We overturned the stretcher on the gray snow. Charles took off his beret. I regretted not having a beret."

Sixty years later, as darkness fell over Auschwitz, I turned to one of the members of our delegation and said: "It's really cold. I regret not having worn another layer of clothing." Suddenly Levi's words came cascading back on me. I was embarrassed. And then, without explaining why, I stood up in silent tribute not just to Sómogyi, but to the countless, nameless others who had died there or those (like Elie Wiesel's father) who died soon after the death march. I also stood for people like Levi, who survived but bore the terrible wounds of the place for the rest of their lives.

Despite the sharp wind I took off my hat. After all, I had one. ⌒

*This essay originally appeared in* The Chronicle of Higher Education.

> 66 And then, without explaining why, I stood up in silent tribute not just to Sómogyi, but to the countless, nameless others who had died there. 99

D on't miss the next book by your favorite author. Sign up now for AuthorTracker by visiting www.AuthorTracker.com.

Manufactured by Amazon.ca
Bolton, ON

21495760R00233